FOCUS ON BUSINESS

4th edition

von

Shaunessy Ashdown

Michael Benford

Isobel Williams

Steve Williams

unter Mitarbeit
der Verlagsredaktion

9783464204337 Focus on Busin.4th

Cornelsen

Verfasser/innen: Shaunessy Ashdown, Berlin
Michael Benford, Bochum
Isobel Williams, Berlin
Steve Williams, Corio Bay Media, Melbourne

Berater/innen: Anne Arheiliger, Neuss
Dr. Hans Oestreich, Lemgo

Projektleitung: Andreas Goebel

Außenredaktion: Janan Barksdale, Berlin

Redaktionelle Mitarbeit: Alice Gleeson, Stefanie Heimann, Oliver Busch (Wörterverzeichnisse)

Bildredaktion: Gertha Maly

Umschlaggestaltung: werkstatt für gebrauchsgrafik, Berlin

Layout und technische Umsetzung: Oxana Rödel, Absatz DTP-Service, Teltow

Illustrationen: Oxford Designers & Illustrators

Erhältlich sind auch:

Handreichungen für den Unterricht mit CD-ROM und 2 Audio-CDs	ISBN: 978-3-464-20437-5
Workbook mit Audio-CD und Lösungsschlüssel	ISBN: 978-3-464-20439-9
Webcodes auf www.cornelsen.de/cbb	
Online-Zusatzmaterialien auf www.cornelsen.de/cbb	

www.cornelsen.de

Die Links zu externen Webseiten Dritter, die in diesem Lehrwerk angegeben sind, wurden vor Drucklegung sorgfältig auf ihre Aktualität geprüft. Der Verlag übernimmt keine Gewähr für die Aktualität und den Inhalt dieser Seiten oder solcher, die mit ihnen verlinkt sind.

1. Auflage, 1. Druck 2012

Alle Drucke dieser Auflage sind inhaltlich unverändert und können im Unterricht nebeneinander verwendet werden.

Druck: Stürtz GmbH, Würzburg

ISBN 978-3-464-20433-7

Inhalt gedruckt auf säurefreiem Papier aus nachhaltiger Forstwirtschaft.

VORWORT

Focus on Business 4th edition ist ein Lehrwerk für zweijährige kaufmännische Bildungsgänge, die auf dem mittleren Abschluss aufbauen und zur Fachhochschulreife führen. Das Lehrwerk führt von Stufe B1 des Gemeinsamen europäischen Referenzrahmens zu Stufe B2.

Focus on Business 4th edition besteht aus den folgenden, klar voneinander abgegrenzten Teilen:

Refresher Course

Dieser Teil dient der Wiederholung grammatischer Grundstrukturen und der Einführung in wirtschaftliche Themen wie *Work experience* oder *Business ideas*.

Main Course

In sieben Units werden aktuelle Themen aus der Welt der Wirtschaft behandelt, jeweils anhand zweier Perspektiven (A – *People and business* und B – *Business and society*), die auf die Auftaktseite *Focus* folgen und mit einer stärker handlungsorientierten Seite *Task options* sowie einem *Grammar checkpoint* abgeschlossen werden.

Die Themenauswahl, die zentrale Wirtschaftsthemen wie *Types of business*, *Environment*, *Marketing and advertising*, *Globalization* und viele weitere umfasst, folgt lehrplanbezogenen Kriterien. Der Aufgabenapparat ist klar kompetenzorientiert; die jeweils behandelten Kompetenzen weden in den Aufgabenüberschriften beschrieben. Ein weiterer Aspekt der Aufgaben ist die systematische Prüfungsvorbereitung, sowohl in Form authentischer Prüfungsaufgaben wie auch anhand hinführender Übungen, die die für die Prüfung notwendigen Fertigkeiten aufbauen.

Secretarial Activities

Hier wird die mündliche und schriftliche Kommunikation in kaufmännischen Berufen trainiert. Von Writing *e-mails* über *Telephoning* bis *Making appointments* oder *Welcoming a visitor* werden alle wichtigen Situationen und Kommunikationsformen behandelt und systematisch eingeübt.

Commercial Correspondence

Dieser Teil behandelt alle wichtigen Brieftypen für die Handelskorrespondenz. Anhand umfangreicher Listen englischer Wendungen und Ausdrücke mit Übersetzungen, die sich unmittelbar auf die Praxisaufgaben beziehen, wird systematisch ein Repertoire für die schriftliche Korrespondenz aufgebaut.

In diesem Abschnitt werden auch *Job applications* behandelt, während das *Business glossary* wichtige Materialien zum Nachschlagen wie z. B. die Incoterms© 2010 oder *Terms of payment* enthält.

Der Anhang enthält ergänzende Materialien; neben den *Partner files* sind dies vor allem:

Exam practice: Musterprüfungen zur Vorbereitung der Abschlussprüfung,

Skills: ein anwendungsbezogener Leitfaden zu Lernstrategien, auf den im Verlauf des *Main Course* durchgehend verwiesen wird,

Grammar summary: eine übersichtliche Zusammenfassung der wichtigsten Grammatikstrukturen

sowie umfangreiche Wörterverzeichnisse.

Zur Differenzierung und selbstständigen Weiterarbeit stehen zu jeder Unit des *Main Course* **Webcodes** zur Verfügung, die mit klaren Verweisen gekennzeichnet sind und von den Lernenden auf www.cornelsen.de/cbb abgerufen werden können.

Wir hoffen, dass Ihnen die Arbeit mit **Focus on Business 4th edition** Freude bereitet und das Lehrwerk zu einem gelungenen und erfolgreichen Unterricht beiträgt.

Die Autoren und der Verlag

CONTENTS

Refresher Course

Page	Unit	Title	Grammar
6	A	**Work experience**	Simple present; present progressive
11	B	**Gap year**	Simple past; adverbs of time, place and frequency
16	C	**First day at work**	*Will* future; possessive 's
21	D	**A dispute at work**	*Going to* future; pronouns
26	E	**A business idea**	Modal auxiliaries and their substitutes
31	F	**Where has all the money gone?**	Present perfect

Main Course

Page	Unit	Title and texts	Background briefing	Task options	Grammar checkpoint
36	1	**Getting started in business** > A new venture > The Virgin Group	> Migration in Europe > Three ways to do business	Telephone interview; CV	Present perfect and simple past; articles; *some* and *any*
46	2	**Business cultures** > Culture shock! > Getting the product right		Presentation; role-play	Past perfect and simple past; past perfect progressive
57	3	**Marketing and advertising** > Marketing decisions > A visit to Randelson Advertising	> The AIDA model of advertising	Protest letter; online research	*If*-sentences (types 1, 2 and 3)
68	4	**Welcome to the future** > Masdar: the world's first carbon-neutral city > The future of global shipping	> CO_2 and the environment	Interview; research and presentation	Passive (mixed tenses, questions, instructions with modal verbs)
77	5	**The business of fun and games** > Foreign travel and long-haul flights > When the Games come to town	> Geographic diversity of air travel	Brainstorming; role-play	Reported speech (statements and questions)

Page	Unit	Title and texts	Background briefing	Task options	Grammar checkpoint
86	6	**The changing workplace** > India rising > The outsourcing trend in IT	> Economic development and jobs	Job interviews	Adjectives and adverbs; comparisons
97	7	**In the global marketplace** > Where is it from? > Sweatshops: Who wins and who loses?	> Banana production	Analysis of lyrics; research and presentation	Relative clauses and contact clauses; gerund/infinitive

Secretarial Activities

Page	File	Title
108	A	**Writing e-mails**
114	B	**Telephoning and voicemail**
118	C	**Making appointments**
122	D	**Travel arrangements**
126	E	**Hotel reservations**
131	F	**Welcoming a visitor**

Commercial Correspondence

Page	File	Title
134	1	**The layout of business letters**
140	2	**Enquiries**
147	3	**Offers**
154	4	**Orders and acknowledgements**
165	5	**Payments and reminders**
175	6	**Complaints**
184	7	**Job applications**
193	8	**Business glossary**

Appendix

204	Exam practice
210	Files
220	Skills
236	Grammar summary
252	Basic word list
258	Unit word list
288	A–Z word list
307	Irregular verbs
309	Quellenverzeichnis

Work experience

Luke is 16 and comes from Bristol in the South-West of England. Most weeks Luke writes a new page for his blog. He is doing work experience this week.

http://www.lukes_blogspot.co.uk/blog52

Apple (12) Amazon eBay Yahoo! News (255)

About me | Blogs | Archive | Comments | Contact me

Luke's Blog

Work experience! **Wednesday, 12 November, 8 p.m.**

I'm tired this evening – very tired. Why?

I'm doing work experience this week. I get up at half past five every morning – the bus into town leaves at a quarter past six, so I'm always in a hurry. I don't get home until about six o'clock in the evening. Working life is HARD! Hmm, wait a minute. Maybe you don't live in the UK and don't know about work experience. OK, here's how it works:

In England, students do work experience when they're in year 10 or year 11 (14–16 years old). It's an opportunity to try a job while you're still at school or college. You choose the type of work, write letters and phone employers and maybe go for an interview – just like a real job. The work placement – or experience (it's the same thing) – usually lasts about two weeks.

What about me? I'm working in a big computer store in town. It's good because I'm interested in IT and retail. This week I'm working in the office. Maybe that doesn't sound so interesting, but it is: there are a lot of different jobs to do here. There's the purchasing department – they order the stock; there's the customer service department – they handle customer queries and problems; there's the accounts department – they keep financial information, and so on. It's surprising how many people work 'behind the scenes' in a big store like this: customers who use the store rarely see these people. Everyone's nice to me here and I'm learning a lot. I do a different job every day – that's cool. Today I worked in purchasing, tomorrow I'm in the personnel department. They keep records for all the employees, write job advertisements, things like that.

So what do I actually do at work? Sometimes I work on the computer, updating records and completing form letters. Sometimes I photocopy paperwork or send faxes, answer the phone or make the tea and coffee. In other words, I do a lot of the things a normal employee does.

Do I want to work here when I leave school? I'm not sure yet, to be honest. But that doesn't matter: I'm finding out about the world of work.

That's all for tonight, folks – I'm off to bed!

1 LOOKING AT THE TEXT

A Answer the questions.

1 Why does Luke find working life hard?
2 How do students in England get a work placement?
3 Where is Luke's work placement?
4 Why does Luke say that the office staff work 'behind the scenes'?
5 How are the staff treating Luke?
6 What does Luke like about his work placement?
7 What administrative tasks does Luke do in the office?
8 What is Luke not sure about?

> **Praktikum: work experience/placement**
> Students do **work experience** when they are in year 10. (*nicht zählbar*)
> I'm doing **a work placement** at the moment. (*zählbar*)

Now you

B Write a short comment for Luke's blog (about 100 words). The expressions in the boxes will help you.

1 Tell him about work experience in Germany.

> *In Germany, students do work experience when they are ...*
> *It usually lasts for ...*
> *It is organized by ...*

2 What are the advantages/disadvantages of a work placement, in your opinion?

> *A work placement is useful / not very useful if ...*
> *In my opinion/view, work placements are ... because ...*

2 WORKING WITH WORDS

A Replace the words in *italics* with a word of a similar meaning. The words that you need are in the same order in the text.

1 It's sometimes *difficult* to be nice to customers all day.
2 Work experience is *a chance* to try a job that interests you.
3 English students *normally* organize their own work placements.
4 In a big *shop* like PC World, there are several office staff.
5 *Many* companies take work experience students.
6 The customer service department *deals with* customer complaints.
7 You should phone them if you have a *question* about your purchase.
8 I'm not *certain* that this is the right job for me.

B Find the words or expressions in the text on page 6.

1 A person who pays other people to work for him/her.
2 Business which involves selling goods to the public.
3 Concerning money.
4 A notice in a newspaper or a website.
5 To change (a document etc.) so that it contains the latest information.
6 A type of letter which has gaps to fill in.
7 All types of printed documents.
8 A person who works for a company.

3 LOOKING AT GRAMMAR: THE SIMPLE PRESENT

Aussage		Verneinung			Frage		
I	work	I	don't (do not)	work	do	I	work?
you	work	you	don't (do not)		do	you	
he/she/it	*works*	he/she/it	***doesn't (does not)***		***does***	he/she/it	
we	work	we	don't (do not)		do	we	
you	work	you	don't (do not)		do	you	
they	work	they	don't (do not)		do	they	

Das Verb to be (sein):

Aussage	Verneinung	Frage		
I'm (I am)	I'm not (I am not)	am	I	... ?
you're (you are)	you aren't (you are not)	are	you	
he's, she's, it's (he is, she is, it is)	he (*etc.*) isn't (he (*etc.*) is not)	is	he/she/it	
we're (we are)	we aren't (we are not)	are	we	
you're (you are)	you aren't (you are not)	are	you	
they're (they are)	they aren't (they are not)	are	they	

1 I ***get up*** at half past five every morning.
2 The work placement usually ***lasts*** about two weeks.
3 I ***don't*** usually ***work*** in the office.

Wir benutzen das ***Simple present***, um regelmäßige Ereignisse (1) und andauernde Zustände (2, 3) auszudrücken. Daher kommen die folgenden Zeitadverbien häufig mit dem ***Simple present*** vor (siehe auch die unterstrichenen Ausdrücke in den Beispielsätzen):

always | never | often | rarely | sometimes | occasionally | now and then | generally | normally | regularly | usually | every day/week/month ... | on Mondays/...

⚠ Kurzformen (*doesn't*, *don't* usw.) werden im Gespräch und im informellen Schriftverkehr gebraucht (3). In formellen Schreiben (Geschäftsbriefen usw.) sind Langformen üblich.

A Make sentences in the simple present to explain what these people do in their jobs.

EXAMPLE > Accounts manager – make financial decisions
> *The accounts manager makes financial decisions.*

1 Purchasing manager – order new stock
2 Personnel assistant – update employee records
3 Sales assistants – serve customers
4 Accounts assistant – keep financial records
5 Customer service representatives – handle customer queries
6 Personnel manager – write job advertisements
7 Work experience students – try different jobs
8 Luke – make the tea and coffee
9 Julie – photocopy paperwork and answer the phone
10 Purchasing assistant – complete forms and send faxes

B Luke has some questions to ask Lucy, a sales assistant. Write questions in the simple present.

EXAMPLE > we / have / a coffee break / every morning?
> *Do we have a coffee break every morning?*

1 how long / be / the coffee break ?
2 where / I / put / these keyboards ?
3 how / the cash register / work ?
4 the customers / ask / a lot of questions ?
5 what time / the store / close / this evening ?
6 how many customers / you / serve / each day ?
7 when / you / usually / go / to lunch ?
8 where / you / have / lunch ?
9 you / have / a boyfriend ?
10 what / you / do / on Saturdays ?

C Make these sentences negative.

EXAMPLE > Luke gets home at 4.30 p.m. > *Luke doesn't get home at 4.30 p.m.*

1 Luke's bus leaves at 7 a.m.
2 Mrs Patterson is the personnel manager.
3 You work here on Saturday afternoons.
4 The accounts department keeps employee records.
5 The sales assistants handle customer problems.
6 Luke is a sales assistant.
7 We're work experience students.
8 The store sells mobile phones.
9 Most shops in town are open on Sundays.
10 Work experience lasts three weeks.

4 LOOKING AT GRAMMAR: THE PRESENT PROGRESSIVE

Aussage		Verneinung		Frage		
I'm (I am)	working	I'm not (I am not)	working	am	I	working?
you're (you are)		you aren't (you are not)		are	you	
he's, she's, it's (he is, she is, it is)		he (*etc.*) isn't (he (*etc.*) is not)		is	he/she/it	
we're (we are)		we aren't (we are not)		are	we	
you're (you are)		you aren't (you are not)		are	you	
they're (they are)		they aren't (they are not)		are	they	

> This week I'***m working*** in the office.

Wir benutzen das ***Present progressive*** für vorübergehende, noch nicht abgeschlossene Situationen und Handlungen. Daher kommt das ***Present progressive*** häufig mit den folgenden Zeitadverbien vor:

at present | at the moment | currently | now | today | this week/month/year

⚠ Beachten Sie, dass folgende Verben in der Regel keine ***progressive***-Form haben:

believe | hate | know | like | love | mean | notice | see | seem | think | understand | want | wish

A Put the verbs into the correct form of the present progressive.

EXAMPLE > Ahmed (do) work experience with us this week.
> *Ahmed **is doing** work experience with us this week.*

1 I (work) in the accounts department at the moment.
2 Anna (make) us some coffee – would you like a cup?
3 Everyone (enjoy) the nice weather this week.
4 We (write) letters to employers this afternoon.
5 That's Emma over there – she (handle) a customer query.
6 Jules and Barry (update) customer records today.
7 You (work) with them this week.
8 I (do) a training course this afternoon.
9 Luke (not work) hard at the moment.
10 Julie and Chloe (not enjoy) their work experience this week.

B **Ask Luke questions about his work experience. Use the present progressive.**

EXAMPLE > you / learn / a lot here ? > *Are you learning a lot here?*

1 you / enjoy / your work placement ?
2 you / make / new friends ?
3 the other employees / help / you ?
4 the work / become / boring ?
5 your boss / give / you / lots of feedback ?
6 why / you / work / in a computer store ?
7 you / write / a report about your work experience ?
8 your friends / do / work experience too ?
9 where / they / work ?
10 they / write / blogs too ?

C **Make the sentences negative.**

EXAMPLE > Josh is working in an office. > *Josh isn't working in an office.*

1 Sarah is enjoying her work placement.
2 She's doing lots of interesting tasks.
3 The other staff are being nice to her.
4 She's learning a lot about the world of work.
5 We're looking forward to the weekend.
6 You're working very hard, Luke.
7 I'm using the photocopier at the moment.
8 Barry is updating the accounts right now.
9 The manager is handling a customer query.
10 The sales assistants are selling a lot of computers today.

D **Present progressive or simple present? Choose the correct tense.**

EXAMPLE > The careers advisor generally ***helps*** / *is helping* students to get a work placement.

1 I *look / am looking* for a work placement at the moment.
2 Every year the students in year 10 *do / are doing* work experience.
3 Currently 20 students *work / are working* in different companies around town.
4 Usually they *find / are finding* it very enjoyable.
5 However, this year some students *don't enjoy / aren't enjoying* it much.
6 Sometimes employers *aren't giving / don't give* the students enough help.
7 All the same, you *always learn / are always learning* a lot from a work placement.
8 This week I *go / am going* for an interview with a law firm in the high street.
9 The firm *takes / is taking* several work experience students each year.
10 This year they *don't take / aren't taking* as many students as usual.

5 TRANSLATION

Translate the sentences into English. Use the simple present or the present progressive as appropriate.

1 Stefan versendet gerade ein Fax.
2 Birgit kocht immer Tee und Kaffee für die Mitarbeiter (*staff*).
3 Diese Woche arbeiten sie in der Buchhaltung (*accounts department*).
4 Ben benutzt gerade den Kopierer.
5 Die Praktikanten (*work experience students*) erledigen jeden Tag andere Aufgaben (*different tasks*).
6 Unsere Einkaufsleiterin bestellt (*order*) gewöhnlich die Produkte (*products*).
7 Anna telefoniert jeden Tag mit Kunden.
8 Ab und zu nehme ich Anrufe entgegen (*answer the phone*).
9 Arbeitet gerade jemand an diesem Computer?
10 Freitags gehe ich 30 Minuten früher nach Hause.

Gap year

1 3 **Every year thousands of school-leavers take a year off before they begin a full-time job or a course at college. For most of them, this 'gap year' is a mixture of casual work and holiday.**

http://www.goingplacesmagazine.com/forum

Apple (12) Amazon eBay Yahoo! News (255)

Benvenuto Welcome Willkommen Bienvenue GOING PLACES

It makes me angry when I read all these stories about 'gap years'. You know the sort of thing: 'I worked in California as an au pair,' 'I looked after baby elephants in Thailand,' or 'I helped to build a school in Namibia,' and so on. Youth magazines always have stories like this – it sounds as if everybody does it.

Well, I can't take a gap year, and none of my friends are taking one. The reason? We don't have rich parents to pay for it. We live in the real world, so we need to get a job and earn money when we leave school.

Daniel, Germany

You're wrong, Daniel: you can take a gap year without rich parents. I did!

I travelled around the world last year. My round-the-world ticket wasn't expensive: it cost €1200. I earned the fare and spending money myself. How? I worked as a waitress in a restaurant. It took three months to save enough money for my trip – that left me nine months to see the world.

On my trip I visited Ireland, Canada, Cambodia, Vietnam, India and Turkey. Most of those places are cheap to live in. In Cambodia I got by on €10–15 a day. Ireland and Canada were expensive, of course, but I worked for a month in Canada. I don't have any special skills or training, but I got a job in a sandwich shop in Vancouver. I made sandwiches for $10 per hour. It wasn't much money, but the work was OK and it helped me to make ends meet.

Before my gap year I was quiet and shy. I soon learned to get along with people, and I'm a lot more self-confident now. My English is a lot better too.

Claudine, France

Claudine's right, Daniel. Anyone can afford a gap year. All you need is imagination and a bit of planning.

You don't have to go to exotic, faraway places like Claudine did. I took my gap year right here in the Netherlands. I worked in a youth hostel in Haarlem for two months, then I completed a training course as a windsurfing instructor on the IJsselmeer. After that I got a job teaching kids to windsurf.

A gap year says a lot about you – it shows that you have initiative and determination. It also shows that you aren't scared to try new things. That's why employers and colleges are usually pleased to see a gap year in your CV – it makes you stand out from the crowd.

Tom, Netherlands

I worked as a waiter/waitress.
Ich habe als Kellner/in gearbeitet.

1 LOOKING AT THE TEXT

A Read the web forum, then match the opinions below to the three contributors. Some opinions may match more than one person.

EXAMPLE > 1 *Tom*

1 'A gap year in your own country is just as good as a foreign trip.'
2 'An experience like this can give you new skills.'
3 'Gap years are just for wealthy people.'
4 'Gap years aren't a luxury, they're a good preparation for the world of work.'
5 'I visited lots of countries in my gap year.'
6 'It sounds great, but it isn't realistic.'
7 'It's important to start earning money as soon as you can.'
8 'There are casual jobs for backpackers who need more cash.'
9 'You don't need a lot of money to do one.'
10 'You'll have a better chance of a good job later.'

B Answer these questions about the text.

1 Why does Daniel get angry when he reads youth magazines?
2 According to Daniel, what do you need if you want to take a gap year?
3 What does Daniel intend to do instead of taking a gap year?
4 Why didn't Claudine have a whole year for her 'gap year' trip?
5 What did Claudine do when she needed more money?
6 How has her gap year made Claudine more interesting to a potential employer?
7 What did Tom learn to do during his gap year?
8 Why is a gap year good for your future career, according to Tom?

Now you **C Write your own post for the 'Going places' web forum. What is your opinion? Is a gap year a good idea? Is it just for wealthy students? Give reasons. Write about 100 words.**

2 WORKING WITH WORDS

A Complete the idiomatic expressions. The expressions are in the same order in the text.

1 Luke just doesn't live in the ... ... – his ideas are so unrealistic.
2 If you have a low-paid job, it's difficult to ... ... on what you earn.
3 Many backpackers do casual jobs during their trip to make ... meet.
4 It's important to get ... ... your colleagues.
5 I see from your CV that you do voluntary work for the Red Cross. That ... ... about your character.
6 Applicants who ... ... from the ... are more likely to get the job.

B Complete the sentences with verbs from the box.

afford | completed | costs | earn | get | look | pay | saved | take | tried

1 A round-the-world trip is too expensive – I can't ... it.
2 As an au pair, Mila had to ... after two horrible kids.
3 We've got enough money for our tickets, but how will we ... for food and accommodation?
4 I didn't ... much when I worked as a skiing instructor, but it was fun.
5 Which ... more – a round-the-world ticket or a return flight to Australia?
6 Instead of spending his money, Tobias ... it all for his big trip.
7 Before she started work at the summer camp, Maike ... a course in first aid.
8 I didn't think I would like windsurfing, but when I ... it, I loved it.
9 You won't ... a holiday job unless you show a bit more initiative.
10 Will you ... a gap year before you start your apprenticeship?

3 LOOKING AT GRAMMAR: THE SIMPLE PAST

Aussage		Verneinung			Frage		
I	worked	I	didn't (did not)	work	did	I	work?
you		you				you	
he/she/it		he/she/it				he/she/it	
we		we				we	
you		you				you	
they		they				they	

⚠ Achtung: Unregelmäßige Verben haben eine Sonderform, die man sich merken – auswendig lernen! – muss (siehe Seite 00).

Das Verb *to be* (sein):

Aussage		Verneinung		Frage	
I	was	I	wasn't (was not)	was	I?
you	were	you	weren't (were not)	were	you?
he/she/it	was	he/she/it	wasn't (was not)	was	he/she/it?
we	were	we	weren't (were not)	were	we?
you	were	you	weren't (were not)	were	you?
they	were	they	weren't (were not)	were	they?

1 I ***visited*** Ireland, Canada, Cambodia, India and Turkey last year.
2 When I was on my gap year, I ***got*** a job teaching kids to windsurf.
3 My round-the-world ticket ***wasn't*** expensive.
4 Did you ***find*** your job in the sandwich shop useful?
5 I ***didn't need*** much money when I visited Singapore.

Wir benutzen das ***Simple past***, um abgeschlossene Ereignisse und Zustände in der Vergangenheit zu beschreiben. Daher kommen Zeitangaben wie die folgenden häufig mit dem ***Simple past*** vor:

yesterday | last week/month/year | two/three months ago | in 2001 | When ...

A Complete the sentences with the simple past of the verbs in brackets. Careful: several of the verbs are irregular.

EXAMPLE > Daniel *read* an article about gap years in a magazine. (read)

1 The article ... him angry. (make)
2 He ... to write a post for a web forum called 'Going places'. (decide)
3 Claudine ... to Daniel's post. (reply)
4 She ... with his opinion about gap-year students. (disagree)
5 She ... about her own gap-year experience. (write)
6 She ... around the world without spending a lot of money. (travel)
7 Tom from the Netherlands also ... a reply on the forum. (post)
8 He ... his gap year at home in the Netherlands. (spend)
9 He ... a course in water sports. (do)
10 After that he ... a job as a windsurfing instructor. (get)
11 After reading their replies, Daniel ... his mind about gap years. (change)
12 He even ... to plan his own gap-year trip. (start)

B Ask Claudine and Tom four questions each about their gap years. Use the simple past.

EXAMPLES > *Did you like Cambodia, Claudine?*
> *Why did you take your gap year in the Netherlands, Tom?*

C Callum Campbell from Edinburgh had a lot of plans for his gap-year trip but things didn't go as planned. Write about Callum's trip, adding your own details where necessary.

EXAMPLE > *In January Callum flew to Australia. He visited Aunty Betty in Sydney but he didn't go surfing on Bondi Beach ...*

Gap-year travel plans – Callum Campbell

January
✓ Fly to Australia.
✓ Visit Aunt Betty in Sydney.
✗ Go surfing on Bondi Beach.

February
✓ Drive to Darwin.
✗ Work on a crocodile farm.

March
✓ See the Outback.
✗ Photograph kangaroos.
✗ Ride a camel in Alice Springs.

April
✓ Take the train to Adelaide.
✗ Pick grapes in the Barossa Valley.
✗ Go swimming with dolphins.

4 LOOKING AT GRAMMAR: ADVERBS OF TIME, PLACE AND FREQUENCY

1 I travelled around the world ***last year***.
2 I'm a lot more self-confident ***now***.
3 I got a job ***in a sandwich shop in Vancouver***.
4 ***Before my gap year*** I was quiet and shy.
5 ***In Cambodia*** I only spent €10–15 a day.
6 Youth magazines ***always*** have stories like this.
7 Employers and colleges are ***usually*** pleased to see a gap year on your CV.
8 I ran out of money ***once***.

- Zeitangaben (Wann?) und Ortsangaben (Wo/Wohin?) stehen meistens am Satzende (1–3).
- Zur besonderen Betonung kann die Zeit- bzw. Ortsangabe an erster Stelle stehen (4, 5).
- Häufigkeitsadverbien der unbestimmten Zeit (z. B. *always, usually, generally, often, sometimes, never*) stehen unmittelbar vor dem Hauptverb (6), aber hinter einer Form des Verbs *to be* (7).
- Andere Häufigkeitsangaben (z. B. *annually, daily, once, twice, every day/week/year, on Mondays*) stehen meist am Satzende (8).

A Put the words and phrases in the correct order to make sentences. If there are two correct options, write both.

EXAMPLE > about visiting India / Bill / dreams / often
> *Bill often dreams about visiting India.*

1 all the time / her gap-year plans / Maria / thinks about
2 I / on Saturdays / play tennis / usually
3 a foreign language / is / it / never / to learn / too late
4 as a surfing instructor / in Thailand / Lukas / worked
5 about missing backpackers / are / every year / stories / there
6 is / quite safe / travel in the USA / usually
7 a good idea / always / is / it / to travel with a friend
8 Anna / as an au pair / during her gap year / worked

B Which is the best place for the adverbs / adverbial phrases in italics: A, B or C?

1 Silke A got a job in B marketing C. — *after her gap year*
2 A Students of my parents' generation B took gap years C. — *rarely*
3 It A is B difficult C to take a break from your career. — *usually*
4 A People don't B have a good time C in their gap years. — *always*
5 Brad A worked B as a waiter C. — *in New York*
6 Jonas A looks at B the same job websites C. — *every day*
7 A Most people B spend C more than they intended. — *when they're on holiday*
8 A Do backpackers B travel alone or with friends C? — *generally*

5 TRANSLATION

Translate the sentences into English.

1 Während meines Jahres zwischen Schule und Ausbildung (*gap year*) bin ich nach Australien, Südafrika und Großbritannien gereist.
2 Gewöhnlich arbeiten Schulabgänger (*school-leavers*) einige Monate, um sich einen Auslandsaufenthalt (*trip abroad*) leisten zu können.
3 Es ist immer wichtig, gut mit Kolleginnen und Kollegen (*your co-workers*) auszukommen.
4 Viele Arbeitgeber suchen Leute, die Eigeninitiative und Entschlusskraft haben.
5 In Manchester hat Fabian als Kellner gearbeitet.
6 Die Bezahlung war nicht besonders gut, aber sie hat ihm geholfen, über die Runden zu kommen.
7 Er ist heute viel selbstbewusster und nicht mehr so schüchtern.
8 In Schottland kam Jessica mit £25 am Tag aus.
9 Für ein Jahr Auszeit zwischen Schule und Ausbildung (*gap year*) braucht man viel Taschengeld.
10 Wer ein interessantes Jahr zwischen Schule und Ausbildung im Lebenslauf hat, sticht aus der Menge heraus.

C

First day at work

1 4

On their first day at work, most school-leavers feel a bit nervous. Yet there's really nothing to be nervous about: with good planning, the day should be a positive experience. Gina Schultz has written to a business forum to get some tips for her first day at work.

http://www.business-forum-online.com/qa

Apple (12) ▾ Amazon eBay Yahoo! News (255) ▾

BUSINESS Q & A

First day – help!

I start my new job on Monday – my first 'proper' job after leaving college. I want to make a good impression on my new colleagues. Does anyone have any tips for me? **Gina S.**

1

Congratulations, Gina! Your first day at work is a lot like your first day at school. Do you remember how nervous and excited you felt? There were so many new people to meet, new places to find and new things to learn. The difference is, now you're an adult and you can make plans to help you get through the first day. **Luke G.**

2

Here's my tip, Gina: Every company has its own dress code. Some are formal and conservative, others are more casual. Make sure that you fit in: your first day isn't the time to express your individuality! You should wear clothes that are comfortable but look professional. **Powerdresser**

3

You'll be excited on the night before your first day but try to get a good night's sleep. Get up early and have a good breakfast. With all the meetings and new things to learn, your first day will pass quickly, and you probably won't have time for a proper lunch. It's a good idea to put a few snacks in your bag so you don't run out of energy during the day. **iSnack**

4

First impressions are important. A late arrival on the first day will make the new worker look lazy or disorganized, so make sure that you arrive on time. Find out exactly how long it will take you to get to work. It's a good idea to do a 'trial run' the week before your first day so that you know when to leave home on the 'big day'. Good luck! **Earlybird**

5

You will meet a lot of new people on your first day. In conversation, use people's names* as often as possible: 'Anna, can you help me with this? … Thanks, Anna' and so on. That will help you to remember them. If you aren't sure what your colleagues' names are, ask. That's much better than calling someone by the wrong name! When you get home, write down all the names, job titles and responsibilities of the people you met. Something like this: 'John Smith, Sales Director, runs the sales department' etc. There will be lots of gaps, but you will fill them in by the end of the week. **Marek**

6

Well done, Gina! You will learn a lot of new information in the next few days, and taking notes is a good way to take it all in. If something doesn't make sense, ask. Asking questions won't make you look stupid: it's better to check than to get it wrong. **JedHughes**

7

During your first week, there will be 'slack periods' while you wait for people to give you work or training. Keep busy by using this time to find out more about the company. If you have internet access, use it to look at the company's website – not to update your Facebook page! **BusyBee**

* In English-speaking countries it is common to use first names in the workplace. For addressing people outside your own company, 'Mr/Miss/Mrs/Ms (Smith etc.)' is safer, unless the person uses your first name.

1 LOOKING AT THE TEXT

A Choose the most suitable title for each post to the forum. There are two titles that you do not need.

a Arrive on time
b Be professional
c Dress the part
d Don't be hungry
e Find your way around
f Keep busy
g Plan to succeed
h Remember names
i Take notes

B Choose the best ending for each sentence: a, b or c.

1 Gina wants advice about how to ...
   a get along well with her new colleagues.
   b impress her new boss.
   c learn on the job.
2 Luke G. says that Gina ...
   a will feel nervous on her first day.
   b should grow up.
   c should stay at school.
3 According to Powerdresser, ...
   a Gina should wear formal clothes.
   b it is better to wear similar clothes to your colleagues.
   c it is important to show your individual style.
4 iSnack thinks that Gina ...
   a should forget about lunch.
   b might be too busy for lunch.
   c should bring some snacks for her colleagues.
5 Earlybird advises Gina to ...
   a check her travel time to work.
   b take the bus to work on the first day.
   c find the fastest route to work.
6 Marek thinks that ...
   a it is normal to forget the names of people you have just met.
   b it is easier to remember someone's name if you use it often.
   c you should ask your colleagues to write their names on a list.
7 JedHughes tells Gina to ...
   a write down important information.
   b avoid asking too many questions.
   c concentrate hard so that she does not miss any important information.
8 BusyBee suggests that Gina could use any free time to ...
   a update her social networking page online.
   b chat with her colleagues.
   c research her new firm.

Now you **C Your online friend from Scotland, Lisa McDonald, starts a new course at college next week. She does not know anyone there and is nervous. Give her advice for her first day (in about 100 words).**

2 WORKING WITH WORDS

A Complete the sentences with words of opposite meaning to the underlined ones. The words you need are all in the text.

1 It's a long day: I ... work at 8 a.m. and I don't finish until 6.30 p.m.
2 At first Gina was ... by her new job but she soon became bored.
3 Your clothes are a bit casual for this company, Marc. We have a ... dress code.
4 It's better to get to work too ... than too late, don't you think?
5 Eric is a very hard-working employee: nobody could call him ... .
6 I used to be quite ... in my work, but these days I have an organized work routine.
7 What's that man's name? I always forget it. I just find it difficult to ... for some reason.
8 Don't treat me as if I'm ... – I'm just as clever as you.

B Complete the sentences with the correct prepositions from the box. You need some of them more than once.

by | for | in | on | out | through

1 There's so much work. How can I get ... it all?
2 I'm sure you'll fit ... here – you're just the sort of person we want.
3 I'm afraid we've run ... of time for today, but we'll continue tomorrow.
4 It's important to get to work ... time if you want to create a good impression.
5 Where can I find ... more about the company?
6 I accidentally called my new boss ... the wrong name – I called him Barry instead of Gary.
7 Can you help me to fill ... the gaps in the company organization chart?
8 There's a lot of new information, I'm not sure I've taken it all ... yet.
9 My first day was a bit boring: I had to wait ... people to explain things to me.
10 Jack made a good impression ... the interviewer with his intelligent answers.

3 LOOKING AT GRAMMAR: THE *WILL* FUTURE

Aussage		Verneinung			Frage		
I'll (I will)	work	I	won't (will not)	work	Will	I	work?
you'll (you will)		you				you	
he'll, she'll, it'll (he will, she will, it will)		he/she/it				he/she/it	
we'll (we will)		we				we	
you'll (you will)		you				you	
they'll (they will)		they				they	

1 Your first day *will pass* quickly.
2 You*'ll be* excited on the night before your first day.
3 You *won't have* time for a proper lunch.
4 Gina *will be* 19 in July.
5 I*'ll give* you some tips if you like.

Wir benutzen das *will future*, um zukünftige Situationen und Ereignisse vorherzusagen (1–3) und um Aussagen zu machen über Ereignisse, die mit Sicherheit eintreten werden (4). Wir können damit auch spontane Entscheidungen und Versprechen ausdrücken (5).

A **In many companies, new employees take part in an induction programme, which introduces them to the company. Describe the programme to Gina, using the *will* future.**

EXAMPLE > *On Monday morning the managing director will give a talk.*
> *On Monday afternoon ...*

Induction Programme – Newland Textiles plc

	a.m.	p.m.
Monday	managing director's talk	go on tour of building
Tuesday	meet your colleagues	induction interview (personnel manager)
Wednesday	fill in salary forms for accounts	training session (head of department)
Thursday	start normal work routine	

B **In her induction interview Gina wants to ask some questions. Use her notes to write questions in the *will* future.**

EXAMPLE > *Will I get a company email address?*

company email address?
business card?
first month's salary – when? how much?
computer training?
meet my manager – when?
holiday – how much?

C **Offer to help the new employee. Use *will* and the words in brackets.**

EXAMPLE > I can't find the accounts department. (show)
> *I'll show you the way. / I'll show you where it is.*

1 I can't find the toilet. (take there)
2 I don't know the people in my department. (introduce)
3 I've forgotten how to fill in this salary form. (help)
4 I don't understand this computer programme. (explain)
5 My mouse is broken. (replace)
6 Somebody has taken my pen. (lend)
7 Now I don't have anything to write on. (get a notepad)
8 Oh, no! My computer has crashed! (phone IT support)
9 Now my phone doesn't work. (check it)
10 I'm so unhappy! I want to go home! (make a cup of tea)

4 LOOKING AT GRAMMAR: POSSESSIVE 'S

1 Look at the ***company's*** website.
2 Are you Mr ***Fox's*** secretary?
3 If you aren't sure what your ***colleagues'*** names are, ask.
4 Use ***people's*** names as often as possible.

- Um Zugehörigkeit oder Besitz zu zeigen, hängen wir 's an das Nomen an (1).
- Nach *-s*, *-x* oder *-z* wird 's [ɪz] ausgesprochen (2).
- Bei Nomen im Plural kommt der Apostroph **nach** dem *-s* der Pluralendung (3).
- Bei Nomen mit unregelmäßigem Plural (d. h. ohne *-s*) bildet man die Possessivform mit angehängtem *'s* (4).

⚠ Possessiv *'s* von *'s = has/is* unterscheiden: *Steve's (= is) the new manager. He's (= has) worked in several companies.*

⚠ Nicht vergessen: Apostrophe werden auch gebraucht, um Kurzformen zu bilden: *I'll, don't* usw.

Rewrite the sentences correctly with apostrophes where they are needed.

EXAMPLE > Wheres Mrs Joness office, please?
> *Where's Mrs Jones's office, please?*

1 Its important for a company to train its staff.
2 Youre Mr Mumtazs new assistant, arent you?
3 Whats Emilys surname? – Its Watts: Emily Watts.
4 Hey! Give me that pen back! You cant go round taking peoples pens, you know.
5 The companies employees credit cards were stolen by the thieves.
6 Its often difficult to remember peoples names, dont you think?
7 Thats the bosss parking space; I wouldnt park there if I were you.
8 If you arent sure what your colleagues job titles are, ask them.

5 TRANSLATION

Translate the sentences into English.

1 Am ersten Arbeitstag werden Sie aufgeregt und nervös sein.
2 Sie werden viele neue Infos erhalten.
3 Ich werde Notizen machen, damit ich alles behalte.
4 Sie werden neuen Kolleginnen und Kollegen begegnen.
5 Sie werden keine Zeit haben, um alles aufzuschreiben.
6 Wie lange werde ich für den Weg zur Arbeit (*to get to work*) brauchen?
7 Eine verspätete Ankunft wird keinen guten Eindruck machen.
8 Ich werde dafür sorgen (*make sure*), dass ich rechtzeitig ankomme.
9 Hoffentlich werde ich einen Internetzugang haben.
10 Ihr erster Arbeitstag wird schnell um sein (*pass quickly*).

D

A dispute at work

Dan Griffiths from Cardiff, Wales, works in the sales department of a company which makes office furniture. He is having a difficult time at work because of a colleague. Dan meets his friend Marcus O'Reilly and they discuss Dan's problem.

***das Mobbing* = bullying**
oder harassment
(*nicht*: mobbing)

MARCUS: Hi, Dan! How's it going?

DAN: Oh, hi, Marcus. Not that well, really.

MARCUS: Why's that?

DAN: Oh, work is getting me down a bit. My supervisor is giving me a hard time.

MARCUS: I thought you liked your supervisor.

DAN: That was the old one. She was nice, but she left the company a few months ago. My new supervisor is awful. Mrs Patterson, that's her name. She's making my life a misery. She gives me far too much work, and then, when I can't do it all, she says that I'm lazy and incompetent.

MARCUS: Really? She used those words, did she?

DAN: Yes, that's actually what she said: 'The trouble with you, Dan, is that you're lazy and incompetent.' And she said it in front of the whole office. It was really embarrassing.

MARCUS: What did you say?

DAN: Nothing. I was so shocked, I couldn't think of anything to say. Later, I tried to talk to her about it in private, but she was 'too busy' to see me.

MARCUS: She can't treat you like that, Dan. It isn't fair.

DAN: That isn't the worst of it, though. She made a mistake with a sales order – a big mistake. A customer ordered five office chairs and she dispatched fifty-five by mistake, that's a whole lorry load, from London to Glasgow, 350 miles. The sales manager is going to be furious when he finds out.

MARCUS: Well, that shows that she's the incompetent one, not you.

DAN: Yes, but I entered the order into the computer system. She's blaming me for the whole thing. But it's not my fault, it's hers. I can't prove it, though.

MARCUS: Right. Well that does sound bad. What are you going to do about it? You aren't going to put up with this treatment, are you?

DAN: No, of course not. I'm going to hand in my resignation. But first, I'm going to find another job.

MARCUS: What? You're just going to give up, in other words? You should defend yourself – complain to your supervisor's manager, for instance.

DAN: What's the point? He isn't going to take my side against my supervisor, is he? You know what management are like: they all stick together.

MARCUS: Hmm, I'm not sure about that. Anyway, it isn't a question of taking sides. Companies have an official grievance procedure to deal with problems like yours. This is harrassment, Dan, or to put it another way, she's bullying you.

DAN: Yes, you're probably right. If I make an official complaint, though, it won't help. I know someone who did that, and there was always a 'black mark' against his name after that. He never got the interesting projects, or the extra training. In the end, he left the company.

MARCUS: Well, it's up to you, Dan. She won't stop bullying, though. After you, there will be another victim ...

1 LOOKING AT THE TEXT

A Read the dialogue, then decide which statement best matches the situation.

1 Dan is unhappy because he has a problem at work. He made a big mistake with an order, and his supervisor, Mrs Patterson, is going to fire him.
2 Dan is unhappy because he has a problem at work. He has too much work to do and now his supervisor, Mrs Patterson, is going to leave the company.
3 Dan is unhappy because he has a problem at work. His supervisor, Mrs Patterson, is bullying him. Dan is going to look for another job.

B Decide whether the following statements are true or false. Correct the false ones.

1 Dan's previous supervisor was nicer than Mrs Patterson.
2 Mrs Patterson thinks that Dan is good at his job.
3 She criticized Dan when she spoke to him in her private office.
4 Dan thinks that the mistake with the sales order is his fault.
5 He expects the sales manager to be very angry about it.
6 Dan has found another job and plans to leave the company.
7 Marcus thinks that Dan should tell Mrs Patterson about the problem.
8 He advises Dan to follow the company's official grievance procedure.
9 Dan doesn't think that a formal complaint will help the situation.
10 Marcus thinks that Mrs Patterson will bully someone else if Dan leaves.

Now you

C You are Dan. Decide what you are going to do and why, then tell Marcus (about 80 words).

2 WORKING WITH WORDS

A Complete the advice leaflet with words from the text. The first letter of each missing word has been given to help you.

Workplace h... [1]

This is a situation that many people have to face at some point in their working lives. It may take the form of physical bullying, unwanted sexual interest or just embarrassing comments. The v... [2] often b... [3] himself or herself for the situation. The important thing to remember is that it isn't your f... [4]. Don't just p... u... w... [5] the problem: talk to someone about it.
If necessary, you can make an official c... [6]. Your company should have a grievance p... [7] to deal with problems like yours.
If you need further advice, phone our hotline on 1300 123123.

B Complete the sentences with words from the text.

1 Who took down the ... ? Was it you or Mrs Patterson? (*Kundenauftrag*)
2 Hello, I'd like to ... five of your office chairs, please. (*bestellen*)
3 Certainly. I can ... those by the end of the week for you. (*versenden*)
4 You'll need to speak to the ... about a discount. (*Verkaufsleiter*)
5 I just need to ... your details into our system. (*eingeben*)
6 The workers are getting more and more unhappy with the ... . (*Geschäftsführung*)
7 We need more ... to help us keep up with new technology. (*Fortbildung*)
8 If you have a problem with your work, you should talk to your ... about it. (*Vorgesetzte/r*)
9 I'm going to get a new job before I hand in my ... . (*Kündigung*)
10 A customer has made a ... about me to the manager. (*Beschwerde*)

3 LOOKING AT GRAMMAR: THE *GOING TO* FUTURE

I'm (I am)	going to work	I'm not (I am not)	going to work	am I	going to work?
you're (you are)		you aren't (you are not)		are you	
he's, she's, it's (he is, she is, it is)		he (etc.) isn't (he (etc.) is not)		is he/she/it	
we're (we are)		we aren't (we are not)		are we	
you're (you are)		you aren't (you are not)		are you	
they're (they are)		they aren't (they are not)		are they	

1 I***'m going to find*** another job.
2 We ***aren't going to put up with*** this treatment.
3 The sales manager ***is going to be*** furious about this.

Wir benutzen das ***going to future*** für:
- Pläne und Absichten (1, 2),
- Ereignisse, deren baldiges Eintreten bereits während des Sprechens offensichtlich ist (3).

⚠ Beachten Sie, dass der Gebrauch von *will* und *going to* oft von der Absicht des Sprechers abhängt. Im Zweifelsfall ist es ratsam, das neutralere *will future* zu benutzen.

A Look at the pictures. What is going to happen?

EXAMPLE > 1 *He is going to miss the bus.*

1 miss the bus

2 fall off the table

3 have a headache in the morning

4 be late

5 score a goal

6 rain

B **This is your work diary for tomorrow. Answer the questions in complete sentences.**

08.00	Breakfast meeting with Bruce Harcourt (Nikon UK)
08.30	↓
09.00	↓
09.30	Project meeting with Janice, Barry and Mia
10.00	↓
10.30	↓
11.00	Fax the sales offer to Munich
11.30	
12.00	Lunch with UK sales representatives (until 13.30)
12.30	↓
13.00	↓
13.30	↓
14.00	Take call from Julian Parrish at MicroSystems, Paris
14.30	
15.00	Video conference with Bill (New York) and Amy (San Francisco)
15.30	↓
16.00	↓
16.30	Coffee with Val Berwick
17.00	Check cost accounting with Jessica (Accounts)
17.30	
18.00	

1 Who are you going to have breakfast with?
2 Who is going to be at the project meeting (apart from you)?
3 Where are you going to fax the sales offer to?
4 How long are you going to be at lunch for?
5 Who is going to phone at 2 p.m.?
6 How long is the video conference going to last?
7 Who are you going to have coffee with at 4.30 p.m.?
8 Who is going to check the cost accounting with you?

C **Choose the more suitable reaction: a or b.**

1 'My car won't start.'
a 'I'll give you a lift.'
b 'I'm going to give you a lift.'

2 'What are your plans for the weekend?'
a 'I'll go to a football match.'
b 'I'm going to go to a football match.'

3 'What's tomorrow's date?'
a 'Tomorrow will be the 15th.'
b 'Tomorrow is going to be the 15th.'

4 'Beth's supervisor is giving her a hard time.'
a 'What will she do about it?'
b 'What is she going to do about it?'

5 'It isn't long until the sales conference.'
a 'Will you give a presentation?'
b 'Are you going to give a presentation?'

6 'I'm having problems with this software.'
a 'The IT technician will help you.'
b 'The IT technician is going to help you.'

4 LOOKING AT GRAMMAR: PRONOUNS

Subjekt	Possessivpronomen	Objekt	Reflexivpronomen
I	my	me	myself
you	your	you	yourself
he	his	him	himself
she	her	her	herself
it	its	it	itself
we	our	us	ourselves
you	your	you	yourselves
they	their	them	themselves

> Das Possessivpronomen steht vor einem Nomen: *But it's not **my** fault ...*

> Reflexivpronomen im Singular: *-self*; im Plural: *-selves*

> Im Englischen verwendet man im Rückbezug auf das Subjekt kein Personalpronomen, sondern ein Reflexivpronomen: You should defend ***yourself*** (~~you~~).
I taught ***myself*** (~~me~~) to play the guitar.

> Viele deutsche Reflexivverben sind **keine** Reflexivverben im Englischen, z. B.:

sich fühlen	*to feel*	sich vorstellen	*to imagine*
sich konzentrieren	*to concentrate*	sich treffen	*to meet*
sich beschweren	*to complain*	sich Sorgen machen	*to worry*

Complete the sentence with the correct English word.

EXAMPLE > I need *your* advice about *my* boss. (*euren, meinen*)

1 Excuse ..., is this ... briefcase? (*mich, Ihre*)
2 Can I borrow ... pen? – Sure. Help ... . (*dein, dir*)
3 Lisa has only ... to blame – it's all ... fault. (*sich selbst, ihr*)
4 Is he going to deal with the complaint ... ? (*selbst*)
5 These are ... coffee cups – ... cup is over there. (*unsere, Ihre*)
6 We're looking for Mary and Bill Wilson's place – could you tell ... which is ... house? (*uns, ihr*)
7 The job ... is OK; it's ... supervisor that's the problem. (*selbst, mein*)
8 Sorry, I can't do this for ... . You'll just have to do it ... . (*euch, selbst*)
9 Should I talk to ... ... , or should I ask someone else to do it for ... ? (*ihr, selbst, mich*)
10 I respect people who deal with problems ... , but there are times when you need to ask others for ... help and advice. (*selbst, ihre*)

5 TRANSLATION

Translate the sentences into English. Use the *going to* future where appropriate.

1 Sie müssen sich bei Ihrer Vorgesetzten beschweren, nicht bei mir.
2 Wo treffen wir uns: bei dir (*at your place*) oder in der Stadt?
3 Was habt ihr am Wochenende vor?
4 Mein Vorgesetzter will alles selber machen.
5 Die Chefin (*manager*) wird wütend sein, wenn sie das hört.
6 Sven wird morgen seine Stelle kündigen.
7 Machen Sie sich keine Sorgen über den Irrtum: Es war nicht Ihre Schuld.
8 Ich brauche deine Hilfe nicht: Ich kann auf mich selbst aufpassen (*take care of*).
9 Wenn ich mich beim Chef beschwere, wird es nichts bringen.
10 Das wirst du dir wohl nicht gefallen lassen, oder?

A business idea

1 6

College leavers Amy Walsh and Jessica Roberts from Sydney, Australia, want to start a new business. They send a letter to the 'Job Guru', who writes a column in a local newspaper.

The Job Guru

Dear Job Guru,

My friend Jessica and I want to go into business together. Our business idea is a mobile car detailing service. We are going to call it 'Shine On'.

We are both interested in cars, of course. I love sports cars, but Jessica is more interested in old cars from 1919 to 1930. We often go to car shows and talk to car owners, and they say that we could make quite a lot of money in detailing if we can do a good job.

As well as cleaning the vehicles thoroughly inside and outside, we will use wax and polish to make the cars look as good as new. I have experience in furniture repair and Jessica is a qualified spray painter, so we can offer a complete vehicle restoration service: we can repair torn seats and scratched paint, as well as cleaning the cars.

We already have a second-hand van and a garage that we can use, so we needn't buy much equipment. We can visit customers in our van, so we needn't rent an office, and we can store our equipment and the van in the garage. My brother is going to design a website and print some leaflets for us.

What do you think?

Amy Walsh (19)

Dear Amy

This sounds like a great idea. You know your market, you have the relevant skills and lots of enthusiasm.

However, you must do your 'homework' before you commit yourselves to an idea like this. The same basics apply to any business start-up.

Research the market. You have already done some informal research: you have chatted to car owners at shows. You now need some 'hard figures'. How many customers will you be able to get? How much will you be able to charge? Are there other car detailing services in your area? They might take some of your customers.

Then there are your expenses. You already have a vehicle, and that is a good start, but there are other things you will need to buy. How much money will you really need to get started? What turnover will you have to achieve in order to stay in business?

You should separate your expenses into fixed assets – things like vehicles, computers and other equipment which will last a long time – and regular expenses such as cleaning supplies – polish, wax and soap – and, of course, fuel for your van.

Before you make a decision about the business, you should draw up a business plan. This should include all your expenses as well as the money you expect to earn. Then you should seek advice from a professional – a small-business advisor, for example. He or she will be able to check over the plan and tell you whether you have a good chance of success.

Finally, good luck!

1 LOOKING AT THE TEXT

A Read Amy's letter. Which of these advertisements best describes the service that Amy and Jessica want to offer?

1

Shine On car repairs. We will get your vintage sports car back on the road! Phone: 0407 293 286 (Amy) or 0407 293 287 (Jessica).

2

Shine On car cleaning. We will make your old car look as good as new! Phone: 0407 293 286 (Amy) or 0407 293 287 (Jessica).

3

Shine On chauffeur-driven car hire. Would you like a vintage sports car for your wedding or other special event? Phone: 0407 293 286 (Amy) or 0407 293 287 (Jessica).

B Read the whole text. Complete these sentences about the text in your own words.

1 Amy and Jessica want to start a business that ...
2 They got their idea from ...
3 The cars will look like new because ...
4 If your car has some scratches or a torn seat, ...
5 The garage will be useful for ...
6 They won't have to spend a lot on advertising because ...
7 When you have an idea for a new business, you shouldn't ...
8 Your market research should include ...
9 Fixed assets include ...
10 You'll need to buy cleaning supplies and fuel ...
11 A business plan will help ...
12 To find out whether your business is likely to succeed, ...

Now you **C What kind of business would you start? Write down your business idea in about 60 words.**

2 WORKING WITH WORDS

A Complete the sentences with words from the box. There are more words than you need.

charge | commit | customers | equipment | expenses | fixed asset | offer | regular | rent | research | service | store | turnover

1 A ... is a task that you perform for someone in exchange for money.
2 How much will you ... me for my moped? – €300.
3 I won't sell you the garage, but you can ... it from me for €250 a month.
4 We need to find somewhere to ... the goods before we sell them.
5 How much are you going to ... for your car detailing service? – €30 an hour.
6 Do not forget that there will be ... , because you will have to buy supplies for your business.
7 Your computer is a ... because it will last a long time.
8 The ... is the total value of goods or services sold by a company during a particular period of time.
9 We need tools and machines for our business, and we need somewhere to keep all this ... .
10 The people who buy your products or services are your ... .

B Can you find the English expressions in the text? They all include the word 'business'.

1 ein Unternehmen gründen
2 Geschäftsidee
3 Unternehmensgründung
4 im Geschäft bleiben, den Betrieb aufrechterhalten
5 Geschäftsplan
6 Unternehmensberater/in für Kleinbetriebe

3 LOOKING AT GRAMMAR: MODAL AUXILIARIES AND THEIR SUBSTITUTES

Um zu sagen, was geschehen kann, muss, darf, soll usw., benutzt man ein modales Hilfsverb (z. B. *may*, *can*, *must* usw.) in Verbindung mit einem Hauptverb.
Modale Hilfsverben (nicht jedoch die Ersatzverben) haben bei allen Personen immer die gleiche Form (keine -*s*-Endung also bei *he/she/it*).
Modale Hilfsverben können nur im Präsens gebraucht werden (Ausnahme: *could* = konnte/n, könnte/n). Um andere Zeitformen zu bilden, muss man ein geeignetes Ersatzverb nehmen.

Notwendigkeit:	*must* (müssen)
Ersatzverb:	***have to***
Beispiele:	> We ***had to*** do lots of market research.
	> You ***must*** research the market.
	> You ***will have to*** buy cleaning supplies.

Keine Notwendigkeit:	***need not/needn't*** (nicht brauchen)
Ersatzverb:	***not have to***
Beispiele:	> We ***need not*** rent an office.
	> They ***will not have to*** buy a van.

Verbot:	***must not/mustn't*** (nicht dürfen)
Ersatzverb:	***not be allowed to***
Beispiele:	> Amy ***must not / will not be allowed to*** use her parents' car.

Fähigkeit:	***can/could*** (können, in der Lage sein)
Ersatzverb:	***be able to***
Beispiele:	> Jessica ***could not*** drive a year ago.
	> We ***can*** visit customers in our van.
	> A small-business advisor ***will be able to*** check over the plan.

Möglichkeit:	***may/might/could*** (dürfen/dürften/könnten)
Beispiele:	> They ***may/might/could*** take some of your customers.

Empfehlung:	***should/ought to*** (sollen, sollte/n)
Beispiele:	> You ***should/ought*** to draw up a business plan.

Erlaubnis:	***can/may*** (können/dürfen)
Ersatzverb:	***to be allowed to***
Beispiele:	> ***You can/may*** (formell) borrow my van today, Amy.
	> Do you think we ***will be allowed to*** use Mum's vacuum cleaner?

A Complete the advice about 'Computing for small businesses' with suitable modal verbs. There may be more than one correct answer.

EXAMPLE > You *must* include computer equipment in your business plan. (*Notwendigkeit*)

Computing for small businesses

1 You ... spend a lot of money on a computer system for your business start-up. (*keine Notwendigkeit*)
2 A cheap PC ... handle most of the tasks a small business requires. (*Fähigkeit*)
3 However, you ... make sure that the system is suitable for your needs. (*Empfehlung*)
4 ... it handle the latest accounting software, for example? (*Fähigkeit*)
5 If you or your employees travel a lot, it ... be better to buy laptop computers. (*Möglichkeit*)
6 You ... use illegal copies of expensive software packages like Microsoft Office. (*Verbot*)
7 If they are found on your computer network, your business ... get into a lot of trouble. (*Möglichkeit*)
8 However, there are open-source alternatives that you ... use for a small fee, or without paying any money at all. (*Erlaubnis*)
9 Most importantly, you ... make adequate arrangements to back up your data. (*Notwendigkeit*)
10 Losing all your business records, for example in a fire, ... easily put you out of business. (*Möglichkeit*)

B Amy and Jessica started their car detailing business, and at first it was a big success. However, they soon started to have financial problems.
To find out what happened, rewrite these sentences in the simple past. Use a substitute verb where necessary.

EXAMPLE > Amy and Jessica must get help from a small-business advisor.
> *Amy and Jessica had to get help from a small-business advisor.*

1 They must increase their turnover.
2 They mustn't borrow any more money from their parents.
3 Unfortunately, they cannot charge their customers more. (*Fähigkeit*)
4 They must find more customers.
5 They can make more money by working longer hours. (*Fähigkeit*)
6 They must reduce their expenses.
7 They may use Amy's brother's office equipment. (*Erlaubnis*)
8 Luckily, they need not sell their van.
9 The bank cannot lend them any more money. (*Fähigkeit*)
10 On the other hand, they can have more time to pay their bills. (*Erlaubnis*)

4 LOOKING AT GRAMMAR: COUNTABLE AND UNCOUNTABLE NOUNS

1 We have ***a van*** and ***a garage***.
2 They can detail ***five cars*** a day.
3 I have printed ***200 leaflets***.
4 You will need ***polish***, ***wax*** and ***fuel*** for your van.
5 We need to buy ***50 litres of fuel***, ***20 cans of polish*** and ***15 tubes of wax***.
6 Let me give you ***a piece of advice***: ...
7 A computer is ***an expensive piece of equipment***.

- Nomen mit Pluralform sind **zählbar**. Sie können mit Zahlen und dem unbestimmten Artikel *a/an* gebraucht werden (1–3).
- Nomen ohne Pluralform dagegen sind **nicht zählbar**. Sie können also nicht mit Zahlen und *a/an* gebraucht werden (4).
- Möchten wir ein nicht zählbares Substantiv zählbar machen, dann müssen wir eine geeignete Mengenangabe hinzufügen (5), z. B. litres of fuel, sums of money.
- *Advice, evidence, information, news, research, furniture* und *equipment* sind ebenfalls nicht zählbar. Um diese Nomen zählbar zu machen, benutzen wir *a piece of* ... (6, 7).

⚠ *Goods* (Ware, Waren) wird immer im Plural gebraucht:
delivery of the ***goods*** – Lieferung der **Ware**

Make tables like the ones below. Put the nouns in the box into the correct column. Give the plural form of the countable nouns. Add a suitable quantifier to the uncountable nouns so that you can use them in the plural.

Countable noun	Plural
company	companies
...	...

Uncountable noun	Plural
equipment	pieces of equipment
...	...

~~company~~ | ~~equipment~~ | family | fuel | furniture | homework | industry | information | money | news | person | van | vehicle | woman

5 TRANSLATION

Translate the sentences into English.

1 Die Firma konnte keine neuen Kunden gewinnen (*get*).
2 Wirst du viele (*a lot of*) Hausaufgaben machen müssen?
3 Das ist keine gute Nachricht.
4 Wir sollten jetzt einen Geschäftsplan erstellen.
5 Wie viel Geld brauchen Sie für Ihre Geschäftsidee?
6 Eine Unternehmensgründung muss nicht sehr riskant (*risky*) sein.
7 Die Unternehmensberaterin gab mir ein paar gute Ratschläge.
8 Natürlich dürfen Sie jederzeit bei uns anrufen, wenn Sie Rat brauchen.
9 Diese Garage könnte für Ihre Bedürfnisse (*needs*) zu klein sein.
10 Wir müssen nicht viele Büromöbel kaufen.
11 Wann wird die Ware in Manchester ankommen?
12 Er darf nicht vergessen, dass die Zahlung (*payment*) bald fällig (*due*) ist.

Where has all the money gone?

Alex Judd started an online retail business several months ago. Unfortunately the business has not gone as well as he originally hoped. He emails a friend for advice: Ellen Spokes, who has just finished a course in accountancy. Ellen emails him her advice.

E-MAIL

Dear Ellen

You may remember that I told you about my new business, a vintage clothes store on eBay. You said that you would be happy to give me financial advice. Well, I think I need it now.

I buy second-hand clothes at low prices in local charity shops, at car boot sales and from friends – or friends' parents and grandparents. I mostly buy fashions from the 1960s and 1970s. Then I clean them, repair them and advertise them in my eBay store: 'RetroModo'. The old clothes are quite popular, and some items sell for more money than new clothes.

I have been in business for eight months. I have received lots of orders, and I have been really busy. In fact, the business has boomed. The trouble is, I have not made much profit yet. Lots of money has come in from sales, but I have spent most of it on more stock, so there is very little profit.

I attach some spreadsheets which contain my financial records. Could you take a look at them for me? Maybe you can tell me where I have gone wrong.

Best wishes
Alex

retromodo-income.xls
retromodo-expenses.xls

RetroModo

E-MAIL

Hi Alex

Thanks for your email. It was good to hear from you – I was wondering how you were getting on. I am delighted to help if I can.

I have had a good look at your spreadsheets, and yes, there is a problem.

I think that the problem is your price structure. To put it simply, your prices are too low, and you are paying too much for your stock.

This often happens with businesses that sell second-hand goods. The idea only works as long as the suppliers – in your case, charity shops, car boot sales and friends – do not know what the goods are worth in the wider marketplace. Unfortunately for you, they have realized that, and they have put their prices up.

I can see two solutions to your problem. The first one is to increase your own prices, so that you make more on each sale. Your customers might not be willing to pay more, though. The other solution is to try a new area, e.g. handmade jewellery, or military clothing.

I hope this helps you. Please email me again if you need any more advice.

All the best
Ellen

***Kleidung* = clothes/ clothing**
The old **clothes** are popular. (*plural*)
I sell (a lot of) **clothing** over eBay. (*nicht zählbar*)

1 LOOKING AT THE TEXT

A Read Alex's email. Which of the following statements best describes his problem?

1 Alex isn't earning much money because he can't find enough vintage clothing to sell.
2 Alex isn't earning much money because few people want to buy old clothes at high prices.
3 Alex is earning quite a lot of money but he has to spend most of it on more clothes to sell.

B Read both emails. Decide whether the statements below are true or false. Correct the false ones.

1 Alex gets his second-hand clothes for free.
2 Some people pay more for old clothes than for new ones.
3 Not many people have bought clothes from Alex.
4 Alex's customers haven't paid him yet.
5 He has spent a lot of money on buying more stock.
6 Ellen has created some spreadsheets for Alex's business.
7 Ellen thinks that Alex is selling his clothes for too little money.
8 Ellen has three possible solutions for Alex.
9 Alex's suppliers don't want much money for their goods.
10 Ellen advises Alex to sell different goods in his store.

Now you **C What do you think of Alex's business? Would you buy clothes from it? Why (not)? Have you ever bought or sold goods on eBay? If so, were you happy with the experience? Write about 100 words. The expressions in the box may help you.**

In my view, Alex's business idea is ...
What I like / concerns me about it is this: ...
Personally, I would / would not ...
In the past, I have ...
I occasionally / often ...
In my experience, ...

2 WORKING WITH WORDS

A Complete each sentence with the correct preposition from the box.

at | for | on | to

1 The great thing about eBay is that you can buy good stuff ... low prices.
2 How much do old leather jackets sell ... on eBay?
3 Lucy doesn't spend much money ... new clothes.
4 Hey, Josh! Come over here and take a look ... these trainers!
5 How is Brooke getting ... with her new business start-up?
6 These shoes are expensive, but if you want good quality, you have to pay ... it.
7 As I see it, the solution ... your problem is to charge more for your stock.
8 If you make more money ... each sale, you'll increase your profit.

B Complete the sentences with words from the e-mails. The first letter of each word is given.

1 We sell both new and s... furniture.
2 Do you want more customers? A... your business on our website.
3 Hello, is that the sales department? I'm calling about my o... of 20 boxes of shampoo.
4 Sorry, we don't have that item in s... . You'll have to wait about four weeks.
5 The business failed because it didn't make a p... .
6 These Microsoft Excel s... show how much we've earned and how much we've spent.
7 If you aren't happy with the g... , you can return them within 14 days.
8 We're waiting too long for things to arrive. We need a new s... .
9 I've made another s... ! I've sold ten computers already, and it's only 11 o'clock.
10 All her clothes are h... – she doesn't wear anything that comes from a factory.

3 LOOKING AT GRAMMAR: THE PRESENT PERFECT

Aussage		Verneinung			Frage		
I've (I have)	worked	I	haven't (have not)	worked	have	I	worked?
you've (you have)		you	haven't (have not)		have	you	
he's, she's, it's (he ***has***, she ***has***, it ***has)***		he *(etc.)*	***hasn't (has not)***		has	he/she/it	
we've (we have)		we	haven't (have not)		have	we	
you've (you have)		you	haven't (have not)		have	you	
they've (they have)		they	haven't (have not)		have	they	

1 I ***have been*** in business for eight months. I ***have not made*** much money yet.
2 I ***have had*** a good look at your spreadsheets.
3 Alex has learned a lot since he started his business.
4 He ***has*** just ***sold*** a jacket for €250.

- Wir benutzen das ***Present perfect*** für nicht abgeschlossene Handlungen, die in der Vergangenheit begonnen haben, aber noch andauern bzw. einen Bezug zur Gegenwart haben (1).
- Wir benutzen das ***Present perfect*** auch für Handlungen, die irgendwann geschehen sind. Der Zeitpunkt ist entweder unwichtig oder unbekannt: Im Vordergrund steht die Tatsache, dass etwas geschehen ist und ein Bezug zur Gegenwart besteht (2).
- Wenn das ***Present perfect*** mit *just* steht, bedeutet es „gerade (eben)" (3).
- Folgende Zeitangaben kommen häufig mit dem ***Present perfect*** vor:

already | always | before | ever? | just | never | not yet | recently | since ... | yet?

⚠ Mit *since* (seit) benutzt man das ***Present perfect***, nicht das ***Simple present*** (4).

⚠ Wird der Zeitpunkt genannt, darf das ***Present perfect*** nicht gebraucht werden. Man muss in diesem Fall das ***Simple past*** benutzen (siehe Unit B). Vergleichen Sie:

I have already sent you the money. (unbestimmter Zeitpunkt: ***Present perfect***)
I sent you the money last week. (bestimmter, abgeschlossener Zeitpunkt: ***Simple past***)

A Make sentences in the present perfect. Be careful about irregular verbs!

EXAMPLE > I / buy / a lot of things / on eBay
> *I have bought a lot of things on eBay.*

1 I / never / sell / anything / online
2 Alex / make / more money / recently
3 I / send / you / two emails / since Tuesday
4 we / look at / a lot of websites / this week
5 I / always / be interested in / retro fashions
6 someone / just / order / more goods / from our store
7 Ellen / always / give / Alex / good advice
8 we / earn / €2300 / since we started
9 you / find / a lot of cheap clothes / on eBay ?
10 I / not see / Alex's eBay store yet

B Which of these things have you already done? Which have you not done yet?

EXAMPLE > *I have already opened a bank account.*
> or: *I have not opened a bank account yet.*

1 open a bank account
2 apply for a credit card
3 use PayPal to shop online
4 sell goods on eBay
5 buy books from amazon.de
6 spend €500 on clothes in one day
7 drive a car
8 decide what to do when you leave school
9 do work experience
10 talk to a careers advisor

C Now form questions to find out what your partner has/has not done.

EXAMPLE > 1 *Have you opened a bank account?*

D Only one sentence in each pair is correct. Which one?

1 a Alex always enjoyed shopping on eBay.
b Alex has always enjoyed shopping on eBay.
2 a A year ago he had an idea for an eBay store.
b A year ago he has had an idea for an eBay store.
3 a Unfortunately the store did not make much money yet.
b Unfortunately the store has not made much money yet.
4 a So far his turnover was between €150 and €300 each month.
b So far his turnover has been between €150 and €300 each month.
5 a At first, Alex bought retro clothes very cheaply.
b At first, Alex has bought retro clothes very cheaply.
6 a Since then, the price of the clothes increases.
b Since then, the price of the clothes has increased.
7 a He already thinks about closing his business.
b He has already thought about closing his business.
8 a A few days ago he has asked a friend for advice.
b A few days ago he asked a friend for advice.

E Complete the text with the correct tense (present perfect or simple past) of the verb in brackets.

Mixed experiences with eBay

Liz Ellis is a keen mountain biker. Until recently, she *bought* [1] (buy) most of her gear * new and ... [2] (pay) a lot of money for it. Then a friend ... [3] (introduce) her to eBay.

Since then, Liz ... [4] (use) eBay a lot. She ... [5] (have) both good and bad experiences with it.

A few months ago, she ... [6] (buy) a GPS from an eBay seller for just €20. It ... [7] (be) a very good GPS: Liz ... [8] (see) the same one in the shops later for €200. The GPS ... [9] (arrive) the next day and it ... [10] (work) very well ever since.

Then she ... [11] (order) a bike helmet for €45. The helmet ... [12] (arrive) in the post, but it ... [13] (not be) the same colour as the one in the picture. Liz immediately ... [14] (complain) to the seller but so far she ... [15] (not receive) a reply and the seller ... [16] (not give) her a refund either. A lot of other people ... [17] (have) problems with the same seller and now eBay ... [18] (ban) him.

After that bad experience, Liz ... [19] (not stop) buying goods on eBay, but she ... [20] (learn) an important lesson: not all eBay sellers are honest, so you need to read the information on the website carefully.

* gear = *Ausrüstung*

4 TRANSLATION

Translate the dialogue into English. Think about whether the present perfect or the past simple is needed in each case.

SVEN Lukas, ich habe dein altes Moped letzte Woche bei eBay (*on eBay*) gesehen.

LUKAS Ja, aber niemand wollte es haben.

SVEN Wahrscheinlich war der Mindestpreis (*reserve price*) zu hoch.

LUKAS Vielleicht, aber ich habe es inzwischen an einen Bekannten (*someone I know*) verkauft.

SVEN Wirklich? Wer hat es gekauft?

LUKAS Kevin Schmidt hat mir gestern €150 dafür gegeben.

SVEN €150?? Aber es war schrottreif (*a piece of junk*)!

LUKAS Nein, es war in Ordnung (*OK*). Kevin hat sich wenigstens seitdem nicht beklagt.

SVEN Ist er schon damit gefahren (*ride*)?

LUKAS Ja, klar. Er hat es gleich (*at once*) nach Hause gefahren.

SVEN Wirklich? Ist er heil (*safely*) angekommen?

LUKAS Ja, soviel ich weiß (*as far as I know*). Er hat sich seitdem nicht gemeldet (*be in touch*).

Getting started in business

FOCUS

1 Astrid

2 Tim

3 Fatima

A *I've just finished a full-time commercial course at a vocational training college in Essen. My course included a work placement abroad, so I spent a month in the library of the University of Cumbria in the beautiful village of Ambleside in the North of England, where I stayed in a house with two other girls. Everyone was so nice to me! They took me to see the horse racing in York, and to Scotland as well. I know it's not always as nice as this in a new culture, but I loved it and I want to go back to the UK again very soon!*

B *I moved to England from Germany when I was 18. My English was non-existent and I wanted to learn the language, so I worked at the university bookshop in Manchester. Later I became interested in politics, and in May 1997 I became the *MP for Birmingham Edgbaston. The UK is an extraordinarily open society.*

** member of parliament*

C *I wanted to travel after leaving college, so I registered with the European Voluntary Service (EVS). I didn't just want to go to France, the Netherlands or Belgium because I've already been there, so I chose a project at a youth centre in Slovakia where the local children get help with their homework and learn English and German as well. I also help train the boys' football team, which keeps me fit. The youth centre is in Slovakia but most of the people there speak Hungarian because it's only 8 km from Hungary. Hungarian's very hard but luckily the centre's website is in English.*

1 Read the speech bubbles and follow these steps.

1. Match the speech bubbles with the people above.
2. Make a list of the seven EU countries mentioned in the three descriptions. What is the capital of each country and what language is spoken there?
3. How many countries are there in the European Union? How many more can you name?

2 Which of the three people above is doing something you have done or would like to do? Explain your answer in 60–80 words. Use the expressions below.

I would like to ... (e.g. travel / see new places / get to know new people)
I have ... (e.g. been to Spain / worked in a shop / worked on a farm)
A work placement would make me ... (e.g. speak a foreign language)
I would have the chance to ... (e.g. understand a new culture)
If I study/work in ... (e.g. the UK), I'll be able to ... (e.g. get a better job / work in the USA)

A People and business

BEFORE YOU READ

A **Do you know anyone who has set up a business? Describe what happened in a few sentences.**

B **Would you like to set up your own business? Explain what sort of work you would like to do and why.**

A new venture

1 8

Expatriot Briton describes how he set up a business

Jamie Roberts, Agüimes, Gran Canaria

I was in my early 20s. I'd just qualified as a diving instructor in the UK but found the English Channel too cold, so I booked a week's diving at a school in Gran Canaria. My first dive there was like setting foot in an underwater paradise. I was delightfully happy!

My week's holiday was over in a flash but just as the next group of tourists was arriving, one of the diving instructors fell ill, so the owner of the school asked me to stand in for him. He told me the tourists all spoke English (my Spanish was rudimentary), so I gave it a try and my first job as a diving instructor was a roaring success! Time flew and suddenly I had been a diving instructor for a whole year and even saved some money. Then I met Rosa, a local girl from Las Palmas who was studying to become an English teacher. Her father was a fisherman but the fish had gone further north, so his boat was lying idle. Youth unemployment was high, so there was no future in Gran Canaria for Rosa and her two teenage brothers. She was planning to leave.

Then one day I had an idea. Why not paint up Rosa's father's old fishing boat and open a diving school? As a qualified diving instructor, I had always wanted to be my own boss and Rosa could do the paperwork. We looked at the figures and calculated that with hard work we would make a profit. Her father gave us his boat and in October Rosa applied for a business licence, which they said would take a few weeks. We needed premises, so in January I found an old café near the beach. They wanted three months' deposit but the rent was low so we took it. Rosa's father, brothers and I painted up the boat and converted the café into an office. Rosa and her brother Juan set up a website in English and Spanish, and we advertised in UK diving magazines. The enquiries started pouring in and we desperately needed to open the school in time for the spring diving season, but with no licence we knew we would go bankrupt before we started! The local banks refused to give us a loan because we had no cash flow, so I made a desperate phone call to my parents in Brighton, and they lent me €25,000. At last, two months later, we got the licence and the business took off. Now, 10 years later, we have three Dolphin Diving Schools, Rosa and I are married, her brothers are the best diving instructors in Gran Canaria, but my Spanish is still pretty weak.

(453 words)

1 UNDERSTANDING THE TEXT

A Read the text and then write sentences a–f in your book in the right order.

EXAMPLE: *1 (c) Jamie Roberts became a qualified diving instructor.*

a He met a Spanish girl called Rosa.
b He went diving in Gran Canaria.
c Jamie Roberts became a qualified diving instructor.
d Jamie and Rosa have three diving schools.
e Rosa applied for a business licence.
f They converted an old café into their business premises.

B Complete the sentences with information from the text.

1 Jamie Roberts learned how to dive in ...
2 He loved diving in ...
3 When one of the Spanish diving instructors fell ill ...
4 Rosa was planning to leave Gran Canaria because ...
5 Jamie and Rosa used an old café as ...
6 People read about Jamie and Rosa's diving school ...
7 In January Jamie and Rosa were afraid that ...
8 Rosa's brothers are now ...

2 VOCABULARY CHECK: SETTING UP A BUSINESS

Find words in the text to match the definitions.

1 a firm or company
2 the person to whom something belongs
3 the problem of not having a job
4 numbers
5 a document which gives you permission to do something, e.g. drive a car
6 the building or land which a company uses to do its work
7 a sum of money that must be paid before you can rent something
8 home page
9 to lose so much money that you cannot run a business (*two words*)
10 money lent by a bank

3 WORKING WITH FACTS AND FIGURES

A With a partner make lists of all the languages and and different national backgrounds in your class, and/or at your college. How many different languages and backgrounds have you got on your list?

B Make a bar chart or a pie chart to show how many different national backgrounds there are in your class and then present it to the class. Begin like this:
In this class ...% of the students are from ....

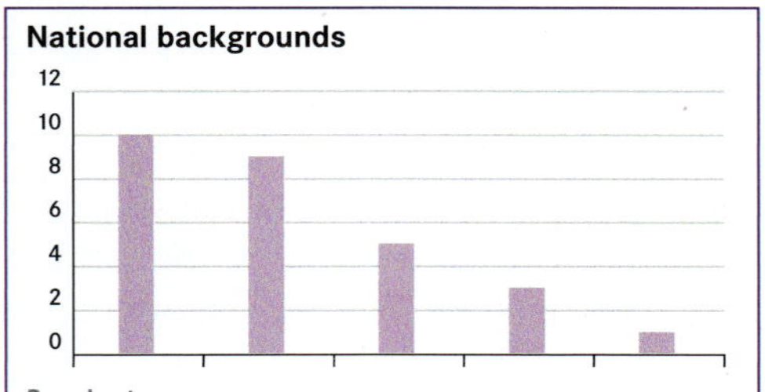

Bar chart

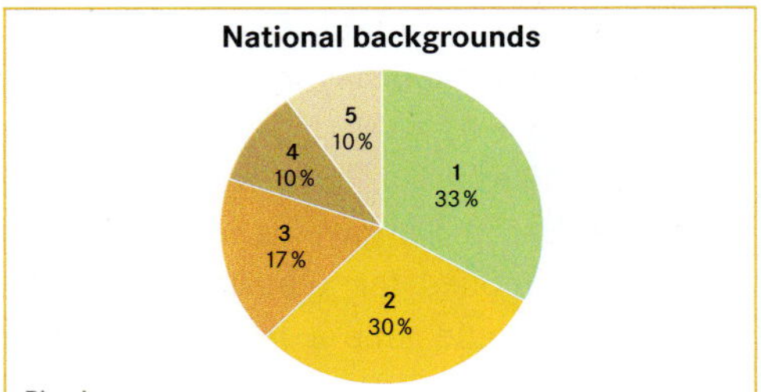

Pie chart

C **Study the diagram in the background briefing box below and make a list of the following:**

a) the countries of emigration b) the countries of immigration

BACKGROUND BRIEFING Migration in Europe

EU citizens are free to work and live in any member state, and since the beginning of the twenty-first century many people have moved to another country to find work and have settled down there. Some countries have become countries of immigration and others countries of emigration. In general there has been a move from east to west.

In addition, in some countries the population is shrinking and in others it is growing. By 2050 the population of some countries will have shrunk by more than a third.

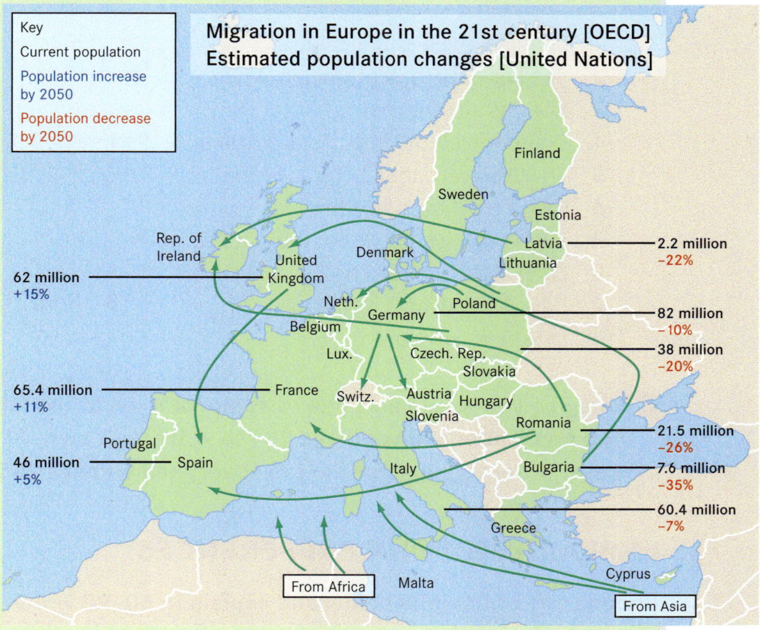

D **Write at least five sentences about migration between European countries. Use the expressions in the language box.**

a large number of ...	*currently*
to emigrate to	*at the moment*
to immigrate to	*in the future*
to settle down in	*in 30/40 years' time*
to move to	*to rise by ...% to ...*
by the year 2050 (+ future perfect)	*to fall by ...% to ...*
since ... (+ present perfect)	

E **Calculate what the population of the countries listed in the diagram will be in 2050 and then write at least five sentences about population changes in Europe. Use the expressions in the language box.**

F **Follow these steps to give a short presentation.**

1 With a partner make a list of the advantages and disadvantages of an open labour market. Think of things like foreign languages, different cultures, the types of jobs available and wage levels.

2 Read the section on presentations in the Skills files on page 231 and plan your presentation.

3 Give a short presentation to the class.

> Skills, p. 231

1 9

4 LISTENING: FIRST DAY AT WORK

A **Janina Witt has just got a job at the Monkbar Hotel in York. Turn to page 210 and read the e-mail which Janina has received from the hotel. Make a list of the questions you would ask Debbie Wharton at your first meeting. Then listen to the dialogue and make a note of the questions Janina asks. Are they the same as yours?**

B **Read the sentences below and listen to the dialogue again to complete them.**

1 Janina arrived at the hotel ...
2 She has already sent Debbie Wharton ...
3 She has already met ...
4 Debbie listed the important points to be discussed in her ...
5 The fire evacuation point is in the ...
6 If you want to open a fire exit, you just ...
7 Janina will be able to eat her ... and ... at the hotel.
8 Early shift is from ... to ...
9 Day shift is from ... to ...
10 Late shift is from ... to ...

C **Imagine you would also like to apply for a job at the Monkbar Hotel in York. Use the Job Applications file on page 184 to write your own CV and cover letter to apply for the job advertised on page 185.**

> Commercial Correspondence, p. 184

5 EXPLAINING YOUR PREFERENCES

Choose one of the jobs below and explain in 60–80 words why you would or would not like to do it. Use the language box to write your answer.

> a volunteer in a foreign country
> a work placement student in a foreign country
> a café owner in Tenerife or Mallorca
> a waiter/waitress
> a hotel maid / room attendant
> an office worker
> a factory worker
> a member of parliament

Introduction
Working as a ... would be ... (e.g. exciting/interesting/hard work)
The job of a ... is ...
If you work in a ..., you have to ... (e.g. clock in and out / do shift work)
When you're on holiday, you only ... (e.g. see the hotel)
Own experience
I work in ... (e.g. a shop) at the weekends / two evenings a week / in the holidays
I once worked ... (e.g. in a shop/café/restaurant / on a farm)
I have never worked but my mother/father ... (e.g. works in a factory)
Opinion
I think / I believe / In my opinion, ...
I would/wouldn't like to ... (e.g. be an office worker)
I like to work with ...
I think working in ... would be ...
I don't like ... (+ -ing)
It is important to ... (e.g. be my own boss / see how other people live / earn money)

> Webcode: FOBU1A01

B Business and society

BEFORE YOU READ

Why do people take risks to open their own business? Look at the pictures above and explain what some people want and what can go wrong.

1 10

The Virgin Group

In 2010, Richard Branson, the famous inventor of the Virgin brand, was worth £2.6 bn and his empire included approx. 200 companies all over the world. In an interview in 2007 he said his first business venture had been at the age of nine when he planted some Christmas trees on a piece of land near his home in London. His plan was to sell them at 18 and move to the Indonesian island of Bali with the profits. Technically speaking, he was a sole trader because he did not intend to share the profits with anybody, he was his own boss and he had unlimited liability, meaning he bore all the risk. Rabbits ate his Christmas trees and he lost everything. Statistics show that 80% of all small businesses fail like Richard Branson's, but this did not stop him.

In 1970, he started again as a sole trader selling records by mail order and made a profit. In 1972, believing that the major record labels were not giving young people what they wanted, he set up Virgin Records Limited, which was a very different sort of company. He signed up unknown bands such as the Sex Pistols and Boy George. These rock and pop singers were more of a risk, so the company was a private limited company. The word limited (Ltd) in a company's name means its liability (financial responsibility) is limited, and the people who have put money into the company can only lose their investment and no more. (In contrast, sole traders have unlimited liability. If, for example, an electrician who is a sole trader makes a mistake working on a house and it burns down, he must pay for all the damage, even if it means he has to sell his personal property, e.g. his house, his car etc.) Richard Branson, therefore, had little to fear when there was fighting at the Sex Pistols' concerts because he could only lose the money he had put into his company.

Richard Branson added more and more private limited companies to the Virgin Group including an airline, Virgin Atlantic. In 1985 he needed a large amount of cash to fund his airline and other business activities so he formed a public limited company called The Virgin Group plc and sold shares in this company on the stock exchange. By selling shares to the public he was able to get the cash he needed to buy new planes for his airline, but he did not like his new role as the chairman of a public limited company because he had to tell the shareholders what he was doing and also show a profit. He was no longer free to do what he wanted, so in 1987 he bought back all the shares for £200 million and made his company into a private limited company again. (476 words)

1 UNDERSTANDING THE TEXT

A Match the sentence halves.

1 Richard Branson started to do business
2 He wanted all the profit
3 He ran the risk
4 His first business venture
5 Richard Branson's next company was
6 If you invest in a private limited company
7 If you are a sole trader
8 A public limited company gets a lot of money

a a private limited company.
b when he was only nine years old.
c from the stock exchange.
d you can only lose the money you have invested.
e you can lose all your personal property.
f of losing everything.
g for himself.
h failed.

B Answer the questions on the text in your own words.

> Skills, p. 226

1 What did Richard Branson want to do with the profit from the Christmas trees?
2 Why did Richard Branson not move to Bali at the age of 18?
3 Why was Richard Branson prepared to risk money on new, unknown bands like Boy George?
4 Why did he form a public limited company for his Virgin Atlantic airline?
5 Why did he buy Virgin Atlantic back again with his own money?

2 VOCABULARY CHECK: DESCRIBING A COMPANY

Find suitable words in the second and third paragraphs of the text to fill in the gaps.

A lot of people buy books by … … [1] these days. The biggest company is Amazon, which was … … [2] in the USA in 1994. Amazon is a company with limited … [3], so investors can only … [4] the money they have invested in it. They have no … [5] for any mistakes the company makes. A big company like Amazon is a … [6] limited company because this type of company needs a large … [7] of capital to finance its activities. Someone who invests in a plc is called a … [8]. The head of a plc is the … [9]. Once a year he or she has to explain why the company has made a … [10] or a loss.

BACKGROUND BRIEFING Three ways to do business

Sole trader
- The company belongs to the sole trader.
- The sole trader takes decisions alone.
- He gets all the profit.
- He could lose everything.

UK: Private limited company (Ltd)*
US: Limited liability company (LLC)
- The company belongs to a closed circle of members.
- The members decide what is best for the company.
- The members share the profits.
- The members can only lose the money they have invested.

UK: Public limited company (plc)
US: Corporation (Corp./Inc.)
- The company belongs to the shareholders, who are members of the public.
- The directors decide what is best for the company and the shareholders.
- The shareholders share the profits.
- The shareholders can only lose the money they paid for the shares.

* In South Africa, Australia and New Zealand: Proprietary limited company (Pty Ltd)

3 CHOOSING THE TYPE OF COMPANY TO SET UP

A Study the background briefing box and then complete the sentences with answer a, b or c.

1 The person who bears most risk is ...
   a a member of a private limited company.
   b a sole trader.
   c a shareholder in a public limited company.

2 A private limited company is owned by ...
   a the members.
   b the public.
   c a sole trader.

3 A sole trader has ... to make decisions.
   a little freedom
   b the least freedom
   c the most freedom

4 A shareholder in a plc ...
   a bears all the risk.
   b gets all the profit.
   c gets some of the profit.

5 Members of the public ...
   a can buy shares in a private limited company.
   b can buy shares in a public limited company.
   c can buy a sole trader's business.

6 Bankruptcy is a serious risk for ...
   a a sole trader.
   b a director of a public limited company.
   c a member of a private limited company.

B Match the companies in the box with the speakers.

East-West Fashions | Solar Power | Trekking and Mountaineering

1 John

My politics are green. I'm not rich but I have invested my extra money in a company which I hope will generate environmentally friendly energy. If the company does well, I'll get a share of the profits in a few years' time!

I worked for a big bank in the City of London for about 10 years and, as my hobby is travelling to distant places, I saved hard and set up a travel agency for trips to Africa and Asia with some close friends. We each invested £50,000 and so far the business has done well. If the worst came to the worst, I'd lose the money I invested but not everything I own!

2 Jill

3 Joanne

I opened a fashion boutique and imported clothes from India. For six months it was great and I made a lot of money for myself, but then the fashion changed and I suddenly had hundreds of dresses that nobody wanted. I couldn't pay the rent and then they cut off the phone. I went bankrupt.

C Decide what type of business each company above is: a sole trader, a private limited company or a public limited company. Explain your answer in a few sentences. Begin like this:

I think / In my opinion ... is a ... (e.g. public limited company) / is owned by a ... (e.g. a sole trader) because ...

> Webcode: FOBU1B01

C Task options

A You decide to get a job in the UK after leaving school, so you first look at www.rausvonzuhaus.de. This takes you to the following link. Study the web page and complete the statements below.

Live-in Jobs for Backpackers in the UK!

FREE SERVICE!

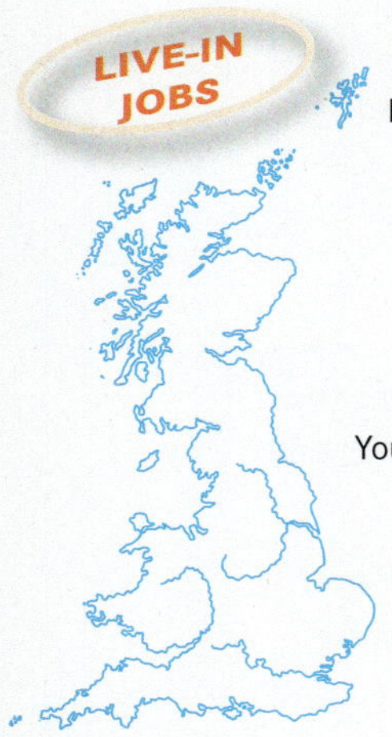

Are you a backpacker about to travel to the UK on a working holiday? There is an easy and free way to organise a live-in hotel job – waiting, bar, reception and housekeeping – all over Scotland, England & Wales.

Free Live in Job Service! Why Pay?

Sally Cooper has been finding travellers & backpackers seasonal and summer employment across the UK since 1996. All jobs last between 3–6 months and come with room and meals. Summer jobs for singles, couples and groups.

The service is free. Sally simply gives you a list of jobs when you ring. You can ring her every day for an update until you get work. Backpack your way to a job UK. Sally also offers hotel employment in chefing and supervisory positions ... visit www.hotel-jobs.co.uk

Or if you are looking for a London Pub Job visit londonpubjobs.co.uk

100s of new jobs each week!

For Information contact Sally Cooper at
sally.cooper@btinternet.com
Phone ***0044 1763 76222*** *Fax* ***0044 1763 727981***

FAQs

Q Should I call or e-mail Sally before I travel?
You can telephone or e-mail from your home country but it is far better to telephone on arrival in the UK.

Q Is it easy to find a job at a hotel?
Very easy! There's always enough work!

Q What clothes do I need for hotel work?
Smart dark trousers (no jeans!) or skirt (not too short!!), a white shirt and reasonable shoes.

Q Will I have an interview?
In most cases you will have a telephone interview. Sometimes they want you to bring your CV along to a face-to-face interview.

1 A backpacker is ...
  a a rucksack.
  b a big rucksack.
  c a person with a big rucksack.

2 Housekeeping means ...
  a cleaning hotel rooms and making beds.
  b cleaning a private house.
  c keeping your room clean.

3 Seasonal employment means ...
  a a permanent job.
  b a job for a few months.
  c a summer job only.

4 Sally Cooper prefers it if you ...
  a phone her before you arrive in the UK.
  b e-mail her before you arrive in the UK.
  c phone her after you arrive in the UK.

5 For hotel work you need ...
  a new flip-flops.
  b stiletto heels.
  c good flat shoes.

6 Interviews are ...
  a usually face-to-face.
  b usually over the phone.
  c always face-to-face.

B With a partner prepare answers to the following questions and then role-play a telephone interview with each other. Take it in turns to play both roles.

1 What sort of person are you? (e.g. team player, flexible, reliable, helpful, sociable)
2 What are your hobbies? (e.g. sport, board games, dancing, music, theatre, reading)
3 What are you strengths and weaknesses? (e.g. very active, need excitement, stay out late)
4 What are your plans for the future? (e.g. get a job, study, travel more, get married, have a family)
5 Would you like to ask us any questions? (e.g. working hours, accommodation, type of hotel guests, pay, meals included with the job?)

C Use the example on page 187 to write your own CV.

> Commercial Correspondence, p. 187

D Grammar checkpoint

1 PRESENT PERFECT AND SIMPLE PAST

> Grammar Summary, pp. 237–238

Put the verb in brackets into the present perfect, present perfect progressive or simple past.

JIM Hi, Ann. Hi, Leo. *Have you seen*[1] (you/see) Julie? She ...[2] (leave) her mobile phone in my car and ...[3] (it/ring) all morning.

ANN I ...[4] (speak) to her yesterday, but she ...[5] (not tell) me her plans for today. What about you, Leo? ...[6] (you/speak) to Julie lately?

LEO No. I ...[7] (see) her in the library but she ...[8] (be) at the computer so I ...[9] (not disturb) her.

ANN She was probably checking websites for job offers. Last week ...[10] (she/go) for an interview and ...[11] (she/wait) for an answer ever since. The company ...[12] (not contact) her yet, though.

JIM Oh. I'd better find her right now. Perhaps someone from the company ...[13] (try) to call her.

LEO That would be great. I hope they ...[14] (decide) to give her the job.

2 ARTICLES

> Grammar Summary, pp. 250–251

Complete the instructions for a hotel trainee. Add *a/an, the* or – (for no article).

1 We want ...[1] guests to feel at home in ...[2] hotel. Always remember to greet ...[3] people with ...[4] pleasant smile.
2 We prefer ...[1] guests to pay by ...[2] credit card. If ...[3] guest would like to pay with ...[4] cash, make sure you write ...[5] receipt.
3 You will not have to work at ...[1] night but you will always have to work ...[2] weekends. One weekend you will do ...[3] early shift, ...[4] following weekend you will work on ...[5] day shift.
4 During ...[1] week, we have mainly ...[2] business guests but at ...[3] weekends we often have ...[4] guests who have booked ... [5] bus tour to ...[6] city. We get ...[7] most bus tours in ...[8] spring.
5 We have ...[1] customers who book ...[2] accommodation when they have tickets for ...[3] concert or ...[4] exhibition. It's often difficult to get ...[5] seat at ...[6] Opera House so if you can get ...[7] opera ticket for a guest, they usually give you ...[8] extra tip.
6 Sometimes ...[1] guest causes ...[2] trouble, but ...[3] most of them are pleasant. If ...[4] somebody has ...[5] complaint, call ...[6] supervisor on ...[7] house phone. Never forget that ...[8] customer is always right.

3 *SOME* AND *ANY*

> Grammar Summary, p. 250

Complete the conversation with *some/any, somebody/anybody, something/anything, somewhere/anywhere*.

A Hi. I haven't seen you for ages. Have you been doing ...[1] interesting lately?
B Didn't ...[2] tell you? I was doing my work placement.
A Oh, right. I think ...[3] mentioned it last week. Did you go ...[4] exciting?
B Yes. I went to Ireland. I wanted to go ...[5] I'd never been before.
A That sounds good. Did you make ...[6] new friends?
B Yes. I got to know ...[7] new people.
A Was there ...[8] especially interesting?
B Well, there was ...[9] interesting. He's called Liam.
A OK. Tell me ...[10] about him.
B He owns a boat and he takes out ...[11] who would like to do ...[12] fishing.
A So he doesn't really do ...[13] all day except sail out to sea and catch fish? That sounds like ...[14] I would like to do. ...[15] people have a very easy life, lazing about all day on a boat.
B Oh, it's not such an easy life. If he doesn't work, he doesn't earn ...[16] money. It's his first business venture and he had to borrow ...[17] money from the bank to get started.

Business cultures

FOCUS

1 Label pictures 1–8 with captions a–j. Two captions are not needed.

- a arriving punctually
- b bowing
- c exchanging business cards
- d greeting
- e shaking hands
- f queuing at a bus stop
- g tea with milk
- h hamburgers and hot dogs
- i light breakfast
- j big cooked breakfast

2 Guess the answers to the questions below using the countries listed in the box and the photos above. There is sometimes more than one answer.

China | Germany | India | Japan | the UK | the USA

In which country or countries ...

1. do people drink tea with milk?
2. do people eat a lot of 'fast food' like hamburgers and hot dogs?
3. does a man shake a woman's hand before he shakes a man's?
4. do people sometimes eat large cooked breakfasts?
5. should you give a business partner your business card with both hands?
6. do people queue at a bus stop?
7. do you press your hands against each other to greet someone?
8. do people bow to greet each other?

3 Can you think of any more cultural differences? Make a list and explain and/or demonstrate them to the class.

A People and business

BEFORE YOU READ

A **Make a list of all the foreign countries you have been to. What languages did you speak there?**

B **Describe any differences you noticed, e.g. food, drink, shopping, bars, restaurants, (un)friendliness, helpfulness, politeness, local customs, etc.**

http://www.

Business Blogs

STORIES, ADVICE AND THE INTERNET'S BEST BUSINESS BLOGS

TOPIC OF THE MONTH | BLOGS | ARTICLES | INTERVIEWS | TIPS FOR BLOGGERS

This month's topic: culture shock!

Have you got an interesting story to tell about doing business abroad? If so, share it with others on **Business Blogs**. Meanwhile read about some of the culture shocks people got when they went to distant places or did business with people from other cultures and at first had no idea what was happening.

1 India

When I arrived in Chennai I tried to take a bus but there was a little problem – there were no bus stops and no bus timetables! There were wonderful old buses crowded with people everywhere, and everybody except me knew where they were going. When I got on the bus, the people were all talking to each other and everyone was very friendly to me. The bus stopped whenever and wherever the passengers wanted. **Leon Keller, Swiss businessman**

2 Switzerland

Where I come from there is no strict division between work and leisure time. When you go to work, you are with your friends. It's like a big family and you don't clock in or out. I got a shock when I started working at the bank in Zürich because at one minute to five the office was full but at one minute past it was empty! **Swati Gupta, India**

3 India

One day while I was talking to an Indian colleague at work, someone called him on his mobile. He answered the call and started a new conversation. I said, 'Hey, what's going on?' but he just carried on talking to me while talking to the other guy at the same time. Then he started writing an e-mail which had something to do with what he was saying on his mobile. Then his landline rang and he answered it with his free hand. Nobody found this strange.
Doug Fletcher, UK

4 Japan

I called our Japanese supplier in Tokyo and asked the export sales director to deliver the goods within six weeks instead of ten. He said, 'Let's talk about that later.' The first time he said this I waited a few hours and called him again. He gave me the same answer. The next day I called him again and he said, 'Tomorrow's a good time to talk about that.' That was three months ago and the delivery time is still ten weeks. **Ron Jones, USA**

5 China

We were invited out to a meal by our Chinese hosts. My company's managing director, as the guest of honour, sat furthest from the door with the Chinese director and the other important managers at the top table. We all sat in order of importance, so I sat closest to the door. My company's managing director proposed a toast and we all raised our glasses in strict order starting with the top table and working down to mine. We all drank at the same time and then our managing director said, 'Shall we eat?' and ate first. That was the sign for us to start eating, too. **Silke Koch, Germany**

(437 words)

1 UNDERSTANDING THE TEXT

Read the text and answer the questions.

1 **India** What differences can you see between the Indian busses and public transport in the West?
2 **Switzerland** Describe how the Indians and the Swiss see leisure time and time at work.
3 **India** Describe how you would feel if someone did this to you in the West. Why would you feel this way?
4 **Japan** Explain what the Japanese supplier did not want to say. Can you think of any reasons for this?
5 **China** Explain why Silke Koch sat closest to the door and not at the top table. What might her job be at the company?

2 VOCABULARY CHECK: THE BUSINESS BLOG

Find words in the business blog to match the definitions.

1 a list of bus times
2 someone who travels on a bus
3 free time
4 to put your card into a machine to show you have arrived for work (*two words*)
5 another word for a man
6 telephone (not a mobile)
7 a company which sells you the goods you want
8 two or three (*two words*)
9 the most important person invited to an event (*three words*)
10 drinking to wish someone happiness or success

3 DESCRIBING YOUR IDEAL COMPANY

What sort of employee are you and what would be your ideal company to work for? Follow the steps below to find out.

1 Answer the questionnaire on the following page.
2 Compare your results with those of other class members.
3 With a partner prepare a short presentation called 'Our ideal company'. Use the phrases below.

At our ideal company ...
... everyone would ... (e.g. have flexible working hours, clock in and out).
... (e.g. friendliness / punctuality / efficiency / good results) would be very important.
... it would be important to ... (e.g. eat together / go home early / do overtime).
At the end of the day we would ... (e.g. go straight home, meet socially, organize social events).
We would always/never ... (e.g. disagree with my boss, criticize people publicly, do what my boss said).
Meetings would be ... (e.g. a chance to chat, as short as possible, open-ended).

QUESTIONNAIRE

What sort of employee are you?

Time

1 Is punctuality at work ...
- a very important?
- b important?
- c unimportant?

2 Is punctuality in your private life ...
- a very important?
- b important?
- c unimportant?

Overtime

3 If your boss suddenly asked you to stay at work late to finish an important order, would you ...
- a say no and go home at the usual time?
- b stay for a short time only?
- c change your plans and stay for as long as necessary?

Meals

4 Do you think it's best to have ...
- a a short lunch break, sometimes on your own?
- b a fixed lunch break for everyone at the same time?
- c a long, flexible lunch break with colleagues?

Work and pleasure

5 Should your work and private life be ...
- a strictly separate?
- b mostly separate?
- c combined?

Meetings

6 Should meetings be ...
- a as short as possible?
- b a way of getting new information?
- c a chance to chat with colleagues?

Decision-making

7 Should big decisions be taken by ...
- a the boss?
- b experts?
- c everyone concerned?

8 Is it important to do what ...
- a the boss thinks is right?
- b you think is right?
- c the group thinks is right?

Conflict

9 If people at work talk too much during team meetings, do you ...
- a complain to your boss?
- b speak to them publicly at the next meeting?
- c speak to them privately?

Feedback

10 Should your boss give you feedback ...
- a if your work is bad?
- b if your work is good?
- c on a regular basis?

Score

Give yourself three points for every 'a', one point for every 'b' and no points for every 'c'. Use the table in file 14 on page 215 to find out what sort of employee you are.

4 LISTENING: A COMPANY PRESENTATION

Skills, pp. 223 + 228

1 12

A Listen to the presentation on Google. Make notes on the following points:

1. What is Google?
2. When was it founded?
3. How much of its income comes from advertising?
4. How much money did it get from selling its shares in 2004?
5. Why is Google a good place to work?
6. What do some people dislike about Google?

B Use your notes to write about 100 words on Google.
Begin like this: *Google is the world's most popular ...*

5 PRESENTING A COMPANY

Skills, p. 231

Some very large companies in Europe and America either have an extremely informal atmosphere like Google or are very formal like the Chinese company described in the Business Blog. With a partner, choose a global player (e.g. a software giant, a major car manufacturer, a major internet or energy provider), do some research and give a short presentation to the class. Use the language boxes below to help you. Before you start, read the section on presentations on page 231.

Introductions
Hi / Good morning/afternoon/evening. My name's ... (first and surname, *e.g. Silke Meier*).
This is my colleague ... (first and surname).
Presentation
Background
- *The company was founded in ...* (date) *... by* (person/company).
- *The managing director / chief executive officer (CEO) / president is ...*
- *It has ... employees in ...* (locations).
- *Last year its turnover was ... (e.g. €8,000,000) and its profit margin was ... (e.g. 10%).*

Location
- *It's located in ... / Its headquarters are in ... / Its head office is in ... / The parent company is located in ...*
- *It has a subsidiary in ... / It has a factory in ... / It has agents in ...*

Products
- *Its ... (products) are made of ... (materials, e.g. pure wool / wood / steel / plastic).*
- *It's famous for ...* (goods/services).
- *Its products include ...* (goods/services).

Markets
- *It sells/exports its products/services to ... (e.g. customers all over the world).*
- *The goods are bought by ...* (customer) *in ...* (place).

Thanks
Thanks for listening. / Thanks for coming to this presentation.
Questions
If you have any questions, I'll/we'll be happy to answer them.

Webcode: FOBU2A01

B Business and society

BEFORE YOU READ

A **Make a list of as many household appliances as you can think of.**

B **Choose two or three of them and explain what extra work you would have to do if they broke down. Begin like this:** *If the washing machine broke down, I/we would have to ...*

Getting the product right

1 In 1899, when the Miele company was founded, it made machines for farmers to separate cream from milk and make cheese. It then used the same technology to wash clothes and, unwittingly, started a social revolution. At the beginning of the 20th century washing the clothes was a back-breaking and time-consuming job usually performed by women. It often took several days because everything was done by hand and the water used was heated on an open fire. Miele set itself the goal of improving its products year by year and in March 2009, the Vatican newspaper *l'Osservatore Romano* wrote that 'the washing machine did more to liberate women in the 20th century than the pill or the right to work'.

Yesterday ...

2 After its success with washing machines, Miele diversified its range of products, even manufacturing cars and bicycles for a short time, but soon returned to its core business of making the labour-saving devices for which it is known today. Like Marks and Spencer in the UK, Miele was one of the first companies in Germany to introduce medical insurance, a pension scheme and housing for its employees. It believed that contented employees would be loyal to the company and make high-quality goods. Its slogans 'Forever better' and 'Miele – a decision for life' show that the company's goal is to make the best appliances on the market, with a life expectancy of 20 years or more.

3 As a limited partnership, the Miele & Cie. KG is owned by 60 or so shareholders who belong to the families of the two founders, Carl Miele and Reinhard Zinkann. As the Miele company is not publicly owned, it is not under pressure to 'increase shareholder value', i.e. to show a profit every quarter. It is therefore able to plan for longer periods of time than publicly owned companies, which are often forced to borrow capital to buy up competitors and expand production in order to show a profit. Miele only uses the capital it has earned to buy new production facilities and, unlike many other manufacturing companies, it has minimized outsourcing to low-wage countries. It even has its own electronics plant in Gütersloh to develop the electronic controls for its appliances. Although most of its production facilities are no further than a day's trip from its headquarters in Gütersloh, almost two thirds of the company's sales come from exports. (396 words)

and today

1 UNDERSTANDING THE TEXT

A Match headings a–e with paragraphs 1–3 of the text. Two of the headings are not needed.

a First-rate products and conditions
b New products every year
c Machines do the heavy work
d Minimizing costs
e Long-term planning

B Answer the following questions. Look on page 226 for help with answering questions.

> Skills, p. 226

1 When was the Miele company founded?
2 What did farmers do with the first Miele machines?
3 Why was washing clothes back-breaking work in 1900?
4 What products other than washing machines did Miele make?
5 What did Miele do to help its workers?
6 How long does Miele expect its products to last?
7 Who is Miele owned by?
8 Can members of the general public buy shares in Miele? Give reasons for your answer.
9 What country do most Miele employees work in?
10 Where does Miele sell most of its products?

2 VOCABULARY CHECK: DESCRIBING A COMPANY

A Copy and complete the chart on word families based on words in paragraph 2. Use a dictionary if necessary.

Word families		
Verb	*Noun*	*Adjective*
to produce	*production or product*	*productive*
…1	*success*	…2
to manufacture	…3	–
to introduce	…4	…5
to employ	…6	…7
–	…8	*loyal*
…9	*decision*	…10
…11	*expectancy*	…12

B Rewrite each sentence from the text so that it contains the words in capitals and has the same meaning.

EXAMPLE Washing the clothes was time-consuming. LONG
> *It took a long time to wash the clothes. / Washing the clothes took a long time.*

1 Miele started a social revolution. CHANGED
2 Miele diversified its range of products. DIFFERENT
3 Miele is able to plan for longer periods of time than publicly owned companies. SHORTER
4 The company's goal is to make products with a life expectancy of 20 years. LAST
5 Miele has minimized outsourcing. GERMANY
6 Most of its production facilities are no further than a day's trip from Gütersloh. CLOSE

3 DEALING WITH A BUSINESS PARTNER'S REQUEST

You work in the customer services department at Miele in Gütersloh and deal with the North American market. Today you receive the following e-mail from a household appliance dealer in the USA.

E-MAIL

From: "Al Winters, Winters Household Appliances" <al.winter@linkallusa.com>
Subject: Adapter for hot and cold water connection for Miele washing machines
Cc:
Attachment(s):

Ladies and Gentlemen:

Here in Tallahassee, Florida, most of my customers only have a cold water supply for their washing machines but, according to the installation guide (see excerpt below), your washing machines need to be connected to both the hot and cold water supplies with a Y-adapter.

Water connection

If the machine is being connected only to a cold water supply, both the hot and cold water intake hoses must be attached to the cold water valve through the use of a Y-adapter (available at a hardware store). Both hoses must be connected to a water source or the machine will not function properly.

Unfortunately, Y-adapters are often out of stock at our local hardware stores, which means the customer has to wait, or buys a washing machine from a different manufacturer.

For this reason I suggest that you make a small change to the design of the washing machines supplied to this market or include a Y-adapter with each machine.

I look forward to your reply with interest.

Sincerely,

Al Winters

Proprietor
Winters Household Appliances

A Complete the following sentences with information from the e-mail.

1 The dealer's shop is in ...
2 The owner of the shop is ...
3 Most of the local people connect their washing machines ...
4 A Y-adapter is needed because ...
5 The local hardware stores ...
6 If customers are not prepared to wait for an adapter, they ...
7 Al Winters suggests changing the design or ...

B Refer to the section on complaints on page 175 to write a reply using the following details.

Commercial Correspondence, p. 175

Situation

Sie (eigener Name) haben sich nach einem zuverlässigen Lieferanten für das Passstück für den Heiß- und Kaltwasserzulaufschlauch erkundigt und empfehlen dem amerikanischen Händler die Firma Green's Household Accessories, 10299 Southside Boulevard, Jacksonville, FL 32256, Tel.: (904) 538-0750, die einen guten Ruf auf diesem Gebiet hat.

Aufgabe

Verfassen Sie eine E-Mail mit heutigem Datum an die amerikanische Firma unter Berücksichtigung folgender Punkte:

- angemessene Anrede und Verabschiedung
- Dank für E-Mail mit gestrigem Datum
- Verständnis für Schwierigkeiten
- kurzfristige Konstruktionsänderung für nordamerikanischen Markt leider nicht möglich
- zuverlässiger örtlicher Lieferant ist ermittelt und kontaktiert worden
- Angabe der Adresse
- Lieferung per FedEx innerhalb von 24 Stunden
- Hoffnung, dass Kunde mit dieser Lösung einverstanden ist
- Signaturschlusszeile angeben: Miele & Cie. KG, Güttersloh, Registriergericht Gütersloh, HRA 3268

4 CALLING THE CUSTOMER BACK

The day after replying to Al Winters' e-mail you receive another e-mail from him.

E-MAIL

Ladies and Gentlemen:
I sent you an e-mail on an urgent matter two days ago and have still not received a reply. Please call me today at 01 (850) 874-4091.

Sincerely,
Al Winters

A Prepare yourself for your telephone conversation with Al Winters by making notes on what you wish to say. To structure your notes use:

- the telephone phrases on page 116.
- expressions from the section on complaints on page 178.

Group your ideas under the following headings:

Introduction / Apology / Explanation / Solution / Delivery / Polite ending

B With a partner take turns to play the roles of Al Winters and the employee in Customer Services at Miele.

Use the role card for Al Winters in file 25 on page 219.
The employee's telephone no. is 00 49 5241 221 88-287.

1 14

C Listen to the recording of the telephone conversation between Al Winters and the employee in Customer Services at Miele and take notes on the differences between what you hear and your own version of the role-play. Then do the role-play again using the notes you have taken.

Webcode: FOBU2B01

C Task options

A Match the jobs with the pictures 1–6.

building contractor | business person | car mechanic | cashier | factory worker | hairdresser

1 15 **B Copy and complete the table below by listening to the three people interviewed on the street. Which of the jobs above have been left out?**

	Type of company	Size of company	Number of employees	Products	Markets
1	...	...	...	...	...
2	...	...	...	...	...
3	...	...	...	...	...

C Use the notes you have taken to describe a local company where a friend or a member of your family works. Choose one of the two options below: a presentation or an interview.

> Skills, pp. 231 + 233

1 Use the headings in the table above and the section on presentations on page 231 to give a short presentation on the company.

2 Work with a partner. Using the phrases you have just heard in the interviews, take turns to role-play short interviews about the companies you have chosen.

D Grammar checkpoint

1 PAST PERFECT

> Grammar Summary, p. 238

Link each pair of sentences using the expression in brackets. Use the underlined words first, put one clause in the past perfect and add a comma where necessary.

1 Miele invented the washing machine in 1899. Washing clothes was a hard and tiring job. (before)
Before Miele invented the washing machine in 1899, washing clothes had been a hard and tiring job.
2 Women became liberated. Labour-saving devices began to appear on the market. (once)
3 They increased production. Miele saw there was a demand for washing machines. (soon after)
4 Miele and other firms started to provide health insurance for their workers. Some companies did not offer social packages. (until)
5 The company invested in new facilities. They earned the money to pay for them. (before)
6 The company cut down on outsourcing. The owners agreed that they should keep as much of their production as possible in Germany. (as soon as)

2 PAST PERFECT OR SIMPLE PAST

> Grammar Summary, pp. 237–238

Complete the text using the past perfect or the simple past form of the verb in brackets.

This month's topic: culture shock!
Write your comment here:
I …[1] (start up) my company in 2010. Last month, I …[2] (begin) discussions with the manager of a Russian oil concern. He …[3] (contact) me a few weeks earlier after he …[4] (see) my website. Four days ago I …[5] (fly) to Moscow to have talks. Until then, we …[6] (never meet) face to face. We …[7] (always discuss) everything by e-mail.
Before I …[8] (decide) to do business with him, I …[9] (read) about Russian managers in a business blog. According to the blog, Russians … [10] (be) hard business partners. I …[11] (go into) the meeting ready for anything.
But, by the time we …[12] (get) to the end of the meeting, all my fears about hard Russians …[13] (disappear). I …[14] (find out) later that my new business partner …[15] (study) at an American university. Perhaps that …[16] (make) him such an easy-going business partner.

3 PAST PERFECT, PAST PERFECT PROGRESSIVE OR SIMPLE PAST

> Grammar Summary, pp. 237–239

The owner of a company is describing how she got started in business. Complete the sentences using the correct form of the verbs in brackets.

1 I *had been thinking*[1] (think) about starting my own business for a long time but I …[2] (never take) the first steps.
2 One morning, on the way to work, I …[1] (meet) Mary. I …[2] (work) for her in her export company once. I …[3] (be) her sales director. I …[4] (not see) her for ages.
3 Mary …[1] (not look well). She …[2] (suffer from) a serious illness for some months.
4 Because she …[1] (be) ill, she …[2] (not look after) her business properly. Her company …[3] (lose) money while she …[4] (be) in hospital.
5 I …[1] (decide) to buy the company from her. Once she …[2] (sell) the business, she …[3] (begin) to get better.
6 After she …[1] (recover), Mary …[2] (join) me as a partner.
7 Our company …[1] (go) public last year. We …[2] (do) excellent business before we …[3] (take) this step.
8 Our profit margin …[1] (climb) steadily from the day I …[2] (take over) the business. Last year our turnover …[3] (be) €10 m.

3 Marketing and advertising

Main Course

FOCUS

1 **Which logos do you recognize? Have you ever bought any of these brands? Why/why not? What brands are popular at your school?**

1 16 **2** **Copy the table below and complete it by listening to three friends talk about brands.**

good quality | good value for money | positive feelings | influence of advertising | impress other people | show you have good taste / show that you are cool/special | show that you care about the environment / your appearance

	Nicolas	Bryan	Khanh
Brand(s) he/she likes	...	...	...
Reason(s) for buying brand(s)	...	...	...

3 **Follow these steps to discuss brand awareness.**

1 Work with a partner and interview each other. For which of the products below is the brand important to you? For which products is the brand unimportant?

bicycles | computers | drinks | glasses | fast-food restaurants | furniture | jeans | shoes | stereo systems | travel businesses

Do you look at the brand when you buy ... ?
What about ... ?
I always / don't ever look at the brand when I buy ...
I look for [brand] when I buy ...
I don't care about brands.

2 Now do a class survey. Find out how many care about the brand for each of the items on the list.

3 Work with a partner. Use the phrases below to compare your results to the survey results in file 6 on page 212.

For	*jeans, cars, shoes,*	*60%* *13 out of 20*		*of*	*the people surveyed* *our class* *our group* *them* *us*	*thought the brand was important.*
		the brand was	*more* *less* *as*	*important for*		*than* *as* — *it was for ...*

A People and business

BEFORE YOU READ

Ice Duchess Frozen Foods Ltd makes products which are sold in grocery stores. Employees from four different departments are pictured here. Match each department with the description of its responsibilities.

a Responsible for investigation, innovation and improvement of products and processes
b Responsible for creating new products
c Responsible for organizing the work in the factory and producing the goods efficiently and on time
d Responsible for finding out which products may be interesting to customers. Also responsible for the strategy for promoting, selling and distributing the products. This includes setting prices and planning product launches.

Product Development (PD)

Martin Green

Marketing

Diana Fortnoy

Research and Development (R & D)

Sujata Mishra

Production

Vojta Stivek

Marketing decisions

E-MAIL

To:	Diana Fortnoy <d.fortnoy@ice-duchess.co.uk> , Sujata Mishra <s.mishra@ice-duchess.co.uk>, Vojta Stivek <v.stivek@ice-duchess.co.uk>
From:	Martin Green <ma.green@ice-duchess.co.uk>
Subject:	'Shaped Pizza' meeting on Monday
Attachments:	ShapedPizza_ProductBrief.docx ShapedPizza_Packaging.jpg

Dear Shaped Pizzas team
I've got great news! We've got permission from the Managing Director to develop a new line of novelty pizzas in different shapes. I'm really excited about this, and also excited about developing it with such a great team.

I've scheduled our first team meeting for Monday from 9 a.m. to 11 a.m. According to your online schedules, you are all free then so everybody has to come. No excuses!

Attached is the product brief for the shaped pizza line. Please familiarize yourself with it before the meeting. The target group is defined but, as you can see, there are still some decisions we will have to make at the meeting.

Diana, before the meeting, we need you to carry out some market research. Could you please determine the size of the market? I know we will sell all over the UK, but will this product also be marketed abroad? Also, what share of the market are we trying to get? And what about the size of the pizzas? And the price? This product was originally conceived for teens. Do we want to stay with this concept, or do we want to try to market to a wider group?

You can see under the *USPs that we want these pizzas to have unusual shapes, but we have to consider practical aspects, like how they will be shipped and displayed in the supermarkets. Have a look at the Packaging Designer's idea, which I've attached as a jpg. Would something like that be possible? Vojta, what do you think? Can anybody think of any other good, clear USPs?

Sujata, could you please test what shapes are possible from a food-preparation standpoint?
See you on Monday!

Best wishes
Martin

* USP = Unique Selling Point or Unique Selling Proposition

ShapedPizza_ProductBrief.docx

Product brief

Product: Shaped pizzas
Name: Crazy Shapes
USPs:
- **fun shapes:** heart ? shamrock ? star ?
  other shapes ?
- **other USPs** ?

Target group / Market:
- **Sex:** both sexes, but females more than males
- **Age:** 14–19
- **Income:** high
- **Education:** secondary school (parents: higher education)
- **Shopping habits:** large supermarkets evenings and weekends

Market: UK (Ireland ? Europe ? Americas ?)
Size of market: ?
Market share: ?
Size: 600–700 g
Packaging: plastic wrap with sticker label
Price: ?

1 UNDERSTANDING THE TEXT

Read the e-mail and the product brief and answer the questions.

1 What is the purpose of the meeting on Monday?
2 Why did Martin Green leave question marks on the product brief?
3 What do Diana Fortnoy, Sujata Mishra and Vojta Stivek have to do before the meeting? Use the phrases below to summarize their 'to do' lists.

Diana/Sujata/Vojta has to ...	*read ...*	*determine / figure out ...*
They all have to ...	*carry out ...*	*decide (on) ...*
	find out ...	*think of / come up with ...*

1 17

2 LISTENING: A PRODUCT DEVELOPMENT TEAM MEETING

First look at the product brief and copy the lines with question marks onto a piece of paper or your computer. Then listen to three excerpts from the PD team meeting. What information can you add to the product brief?

3 VOCABULARY CHECK: MARKETING

A The same word is missing in all of the sentences below. What is it?

1 The size of the ... for this product is about 1.6 million.
2 The ... share we are trying to get is 25%.
3 We are going to ... this product in the UK and Europe.
4 If you want to ... to teenagers, you have to know what they like and where they shop.
5 When we develop a product, we carry out ... research.

B Connect the words and expressions in A and B to make phrases used to talk about marketing.

1

A		B
	unique ... *a line of ...* *to develop ...*	*... products* *... selling points* *... a product*

2

A		B
	packaging ... *to set ...* *to plan ...*	*... a product launch* *... a product's price* *... design*

4 CONFIRMING THE RESULTS OF A MEETING

Write a post-meeting e-mail from Martin Green to the rest of the team. Write at least 100 words and include the points below. Use the information on writing e-mails on pages 110–112 to help you.

> Secretarial activities, pp. 110–112

> Congratulate everyone on a productive meeting.
> Tell them you are attaching the new, updated product brief. Ask them to check it for mistakes.
> Inform them of the date of the next meeting in about three weeks, and the date of the product launch in about three months.

5 WRITING A PRODUCT BRIEF

You are going to create a product brief for one of the following products.

a car with the name Zippy | a line of paper products | glow-in-the-dark wallpaper | a home security service | light-up clothing to wear at nightclubs | an unusual-looking electric bicycle | a high-energy snack

Before you write the brief, work with a partner to choose a product and make a mind map around it. Use the tips on making mind maps in the skills file on page 225 to help you.

> Skills, p. 225

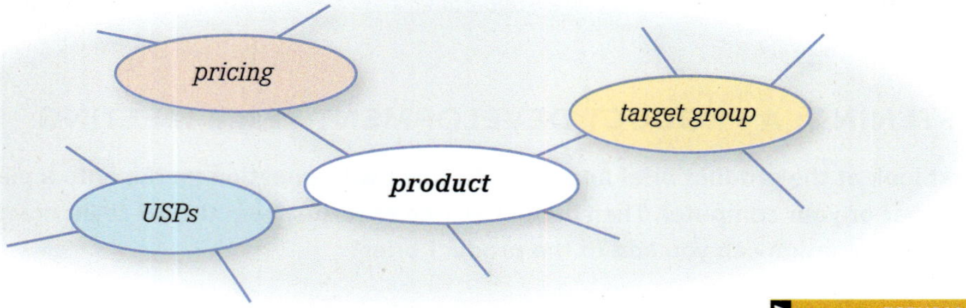

> Webcode: FOBU3A01

B Business and society

BEFORE YOU READ

A **Tell your partner about an advertisement you have seen recently. Say what type of advertisement it was, where you saw it and why you remember it.**

billboard | brochure | full-page ad in a newspaper/magazine | pop-up internet ad | poster | leaflet | small classified ad | TV/radio commercial

clever | disgusting | funny | glamorous | shocking | silly | strange

B **Which of the following jobs do people in an advertising agency do?**

buy advertising space in magazines | create advertisements | deal with customers | make clothes to appeal to different target groups | watch trends | write advertising copy | make decisions about which media to advertise a product in | repair electronic devices

1 18

A visit to Randelson Advertising

The loft offices of Randelson Advertising in Manhattan are decorated to inspire creativity. Hundreds of clever print advertisements and colourful works of art are on display.

Larry Niemann, 36, hangs up his telephone, smiles broadly and calls out the name of a major department store. His colleagues in the **Account Services** Department know what this means: Niemann has won the agency a chance at developing an ad campaign for the store. As the account executive, Niemann is the one who will have the contact with the customer as well as coordinate the work between the departments. His next steps will be to meet with the customer and to write a brief for the other departments, describing what the customer needs. 'I enjoy building relationships with customers,' he says. 'I'm a people person.'

You could say that everyone at Randelson Advertising is a 'people person'. They have to be. Only the account services department has daily contact with customers, but everyone here (with the possible exception of computer programmers) works very closely with other colleagues in teams. This is typical of advertising agencies.

Perhaps less typical is the ad campaign idea currently brewing in the **Creative** Department. The proposed television commercial is based on the AIDA model and features two beautiful mermaids looking longingly at a very fat fisherman. They pull him under- ▶

Creative Director Randelson and part of her team

water, seductively remove his jeans ... and swim away, leaving him in his underwear.

The last shot is of the mermaids, each of them wearing one leg of the fisherman's jeans. The slogan: 'Perfect jeans are no myth.' The idea is unusual, but the customer did not call Randelson to get an unoriginal campaign. They want an interesting and effective ad that makes an impact. 'I'm going to present this idea to the customer tomorrow,' says Creative Director Sophie Randelson, 40, with a twinkle in her eye. 'I think it's brilliant, and I hope they'll think so, too. I don't think the **Production** Department is looking forward to shooting underwater, though.' Randelson founded the agency seven years ago.

The people who work in ad agencies do about two dozen different jobs. Some of these jobs – e.g. graphic artist, buyer or copy editor – also exist in other types of companies but, in advertising, there is something everyone has in common: the goals of advertising effectiveness and customer satisfaction.

The **Strategy** Department is a whirlwind of activity, but Strategist Eva Duda, 27, sits concentrated among the chaos. She is researching the facts needed for creating an advertisement for a fitness centre, and strategizing the best messages and methods to use to reach the health-conscious target audience. Along with account services and creative, her department is considered to be one of the three pillars of the modern advertising agency.

In Randelson's **Media** Department, the buyers purchase ad space in magazines, newspapers, TV shows, cable channels and internet sites, and try to understand the audience for each of these media.

Randelson also has its own **Interactive** Department, where they create the digital components of an advertising campaign, including websites, banner ads and interactive applications. Designer Raul Cornejo, 32, says he loves his job because 'You never stop learning. This year, I'm creating Flash animation, but next year I may have to learn a completely new programming language, if the industry changes.'

Change is the only thing which is constant in the world of advertising. If Randelson is lucky, it will be the one setting the trends in advertising instead of following them. (577 words)

1 UNDERSTANDING THE TEXT

A Read the text, concentrating on the different departments of an advertising agency. In which department would you hear each of the following statements?

1 *The best way to advertise to these customers is with print ads in shopping malls.*

2 *I'd like your channel to run our commercial during the 10 o'clock news.*

3 *Thank you for enquiring about our agency. What product would you like to advertise?*

4 *When the visitor clicks on the customer's logo, he'll be sent to this web page.*

5 *Come on, you guys! Life is too short for boring adverts! We need some fresh ideas!*

6 *Are the models dressed yet? OK, let's start shooting this commercial!*

B **The diagram below shows Randelson Advertising's three 'pillars' as described in the text and various jobs that people do in the different departments. Copy the diagram and complete it with the names of the departments.**

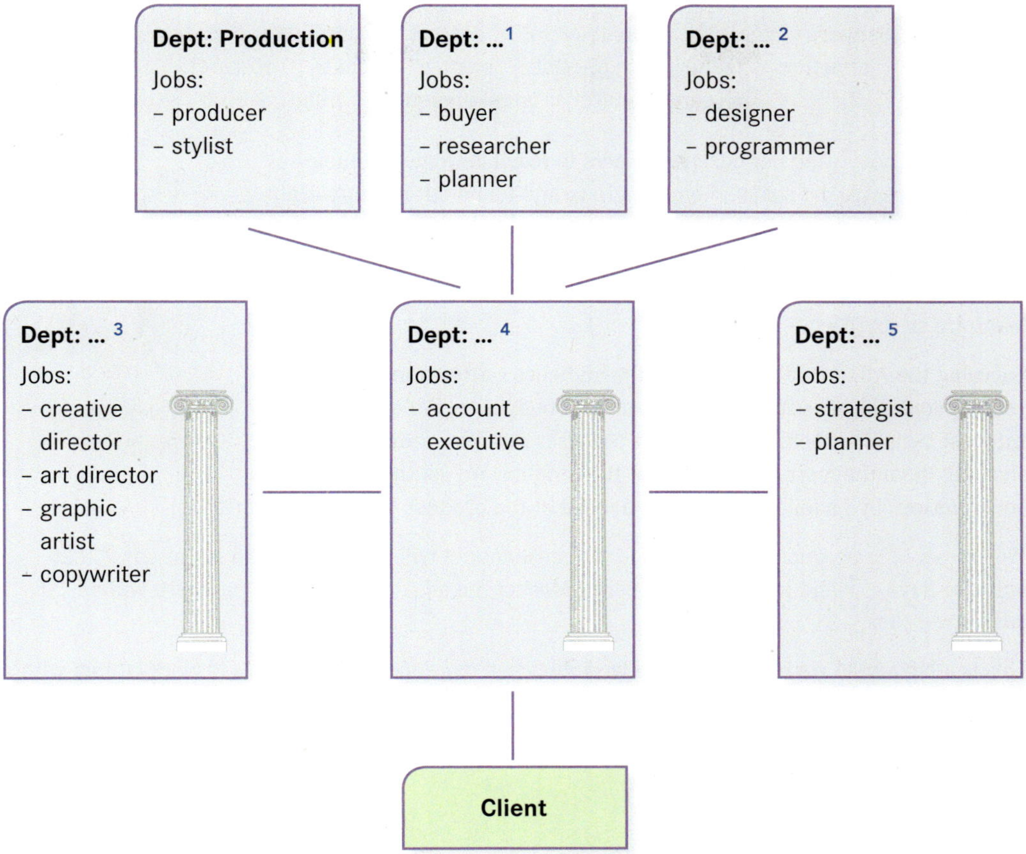

2 UNDERSTANDING HOW AN ADVERTISING AGENCY WORKS

How do the departments in an advertising agency work toward the goal of advertising effectiveness? Follow these steps to write a text.

1 First make notes in your exercise books about each department's responsibilities. You do not have to limit yourself to tasks mentioned explicitly in the text; try to 'read between the lines' and think about the jobs people do in each department.

Account services:	*get relevant information from customers; ...*
Creative:	...
Strategy:	...
Media:	...
Production:	...
Interactive:	...

2 Use your notes to write a text of about 100 words. Describe each department and say which department you think is most important, and why.

> Skills, p. 228

3 VOCABULARY CHECK: ADVERTISING

Complete Sophie Randelson's statement about her jeans advert with words from the box. There is one word you do not need.

banner | campaign | commercial | contact | coordinate | create | effective | featuring | present | print | purchase | research | slogan | space | target audience | trend

Randelson: The ...[1] that our customer wants to reach is women in their early twenties. We did some ...[2] on this group and found out two important facts: first, these women have a hard time finding the 'perfect' jeans; second, mythology and magic are very 'in' right now for this group, and we wanted to follow this ...[3]. That's how our copywriter came up with the ...[4] 'Perfect jeans are no myth'.

Sophie Randelson, 40, Creative Director

So, using the AIDA model, we attract the audience's **attention** by ...[5] other young people: lovely young ladies, a comical young man. We arouse their **interest** by telling them a story which promises sex. We ...[6] **desire** by showing them the mermaids' desire for the product. We get the consumer to act (= **action**) by giving them the brand name of the product. This is ...[7] advertising!

We are not only producing this TV ...[8] for the customer; it will be one part of a larger ad ...[9] that will also have ...[10] and internet components. Most of the ad ...[11] that we will purchase will be ...[12] ads on websites.

This is a big job, so we have to ...[13] the work between our departments. I have to work closely with the account executive, who has the direct ...[14] with the customer. She will be there when I ...[15] our ideas to the customer. It's important to build relationships in this business.

1 19 **Listen to check your answers.**

BACKGROUND BRIEFING The AIDA model of advertising

Attention People will decide in the first few seconds if they want to listen to you or not, so you have to really get their attention. A good way to do this is by surprising them, or by asking an engaging question such as 'Have you ever ...?' or 'Can you see ...?'

Interest Once you have their attention, you have to arouse their interest. One way to do this is by demonstrating advantages and benefits of the product. It is best if you can get them actively involved, and leave them wanting more.

Desire The next step is to create a desire in them for the product. You can do this by showing them that it will solve some of their problems or by showing them how much other people want and approve of the product.

Action Now, encourage action by giving them the brand name of the product. You want them to buy your product or at least to get more information. You should make this as easy for them to do as possible.

4 ANALYZING AN ADVERTISEMENT

Study the background briefing box and then choose one of the advertisements below. Identify how the advertisement you've chosen uses the four principles of AIDA.

1 A mobile billboard

1 20 **2 A radio commercial**

3 An online advert

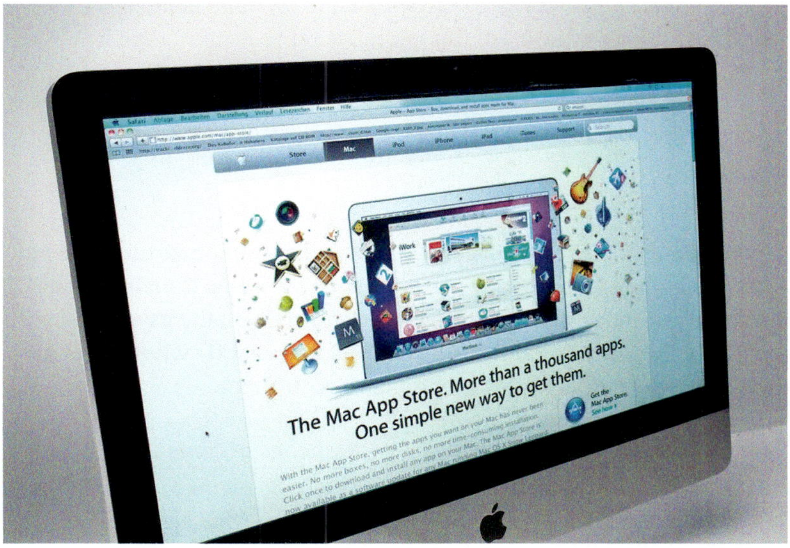

> Webcode: FOBU3B01

C Task options

A **Have you ever been disappointed with a product or service? What did you do about it? Tell your partner about the experience.**

B **Read this protest letter and tell your partner what happened to Florian Sander when he shopped at MyTunes.in.**

Dear Sir or Madam

Complaint about MyTunes.in one-device policy

I am writing to express my disapproval of MyTunes.in policy of selling music downloads which are only playable on one device. I have already written an e-mail to you but have received no reply.

As consumers of music, we have always been able to play CDs on as many CD players as we choose, and the same principle should hold for music downloads.

What makes MyTunes.in's policy even worse is that the consumers are not informed about it before they make their purchase. If the customers knew that they would only be able to play their purchase on one device, they would have the chance to download it to their MP3 players or to whichever device they use most. As for me, I downloaded my purchase onto my desktop computer, which I rarely use to listen to music.

I would like to buy items from MyTunes.in in the future, but I will not do so again until this unfair policy is corrected. I like MyTunes.in products, and the prices are very good, but this is a matter of principle for me.

Yours sincerely

Florian Sander
Florian Sander

C **Do some online research. Find at least two organizations a consumer can turn to when he or she wants to complain about a company's products or services. Consider complaints about international purchases people often make from Germany as well as purchases within Germany. For each organization you find, say exactly what types of complaints they handle, and how you can file a complaint with them.**

organization	*types of complaints*	*means of filing*
example organization	*e.g. international e-commerce*	*e.g. via online form, letter or telephone hotline*

D Grammar checkpoint

1 *IF*-SENTENCES TYPE 1

> Grammar Summary, p. 244

The *Focus* advertising agency is meeting with a client who is launching a computer aimed at young teenagers. The words below were said at the meeting. Turn them into full sentences, using *if*-sentences type 1. Add a comma where necessary.

1 we / design a cool advertising poster / everybody / pay attention
If we design a cool advertising poster, everybody will pay attention.
2 we / place advertisements in teenage magazines / we / reach our target group
3 you / have a competition / you / get people's interest
4 your customers / be happy / you / add a free computer game to the package
5 you / launch the product in November / parents / buy it for Christmas
6 you / show that the computer is good value for money / parents / be happy to buy it
7 we / think up a good slogan / people remember the product
8 we / focus on the USPs in the TV commercials / we / grab our target audience

2 *IF*-SENTENCES TYPE 2

> Grammar Summary, p. 244

After the meeting, the creative designer at *Focus* is unhappy and writes an e-mail to her colleagues. Complete her e-mail with the correct forms of the verbs.

E-MAIL

I'd just like to say that I wasn't very happy with the results of this morning's meeting. If we *had*[1] (have) more time, I *would ask*[2] (ask) for a second meeting but this e-mail will have to do.
Before we go ahead with the campaign, it …[3] (be) super if you …[4] (think about) the following points:
- We are dealing with a company that no one knows. If the client …[5] (be) a brand name, we …[6] (build up) our reputation.
- The client is unwilling to invest money. If he …[7] (give) us a bigger budget, we …[8] (hire) a big star for our campaign.
- He is also unwilling to take a risk. If he …[9] (allow) us more creative freedom, we …[10] (be able to produce) an interesting advertising campaign.

If my feelings about the brief …[11] (be) more positive, I …[12] (be) happy to go ahead with the campaign but I don't believe in the client and I don't believe in the product. If I …[13] (do), I …[14] (not recommend) turning down this project.
…[15] (it be) so bad for us if we …[16] (not take on) this client?

3 *IF*-SENTENCES TYPE 3

> Grammar Summary, p. 244

Use the words to write about a meeting which went wrong from the start.

Begin like this: *If Rob hadn't woken up late, he would have …*

1 not wake up late / catch the early bus

2 not miss the bus / get to the meeting on time

3 pack his bag carefully the night before / not forget his notes

4 have his notes with him / know what to say

5 be more professional / win the contract for his firm

6 get the contract / his boss / not fire him.

Welcome to the future

FOCUS

1 Sort the following energy sources into two categories: fossil fuels and renewable energy.

2 How much do you know about energy production? Work with a partner to answer the questions.

1 At the moment the most important energy source is oil. What are the problems with oil? Use the prompts below or think of your own ideas.

damage | pollute | release carbon | run out someday | conflict between nations

2 How has energy production changed in the last 20 years? Use phrases from the box.

produce more and more / less and less ...
become more and more / less and less expensive/popular/...
there are more and more / fewer and fewer ...

A People and business

BEFORE YOU READ

A **Name some ways that cities can damage the environment.**

B **Copy this table into your exercise book, then sort the words and phrases below into the three categories. Compare your list with a partner or with the class.**

buildings with reduced energy requirements | carbon emissions | cycling and walking | emissions from cars | energy conservation | solar/photovoltaic power | renewable energy | fossil fuel consumption | sustainable lifestyle | biofuels | waste production | wind turbines

environmentally friendly	*harmful to the environment*	*not sure*
...	...	...

1 21

Masdar: The world's first carbon-neutral city

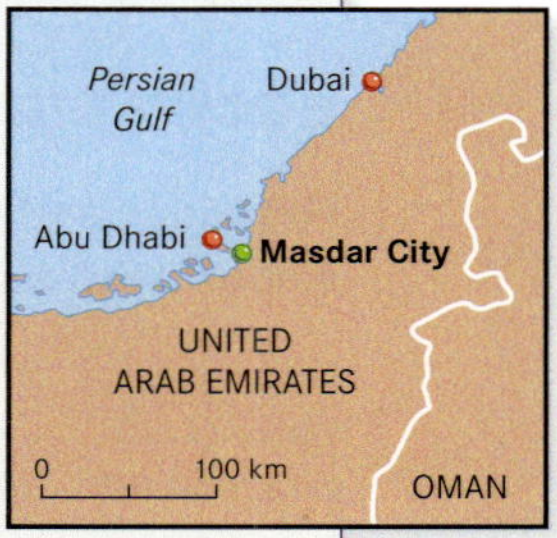

In April 2006, The United Arab Emirates decided to create Masdar, a city covering 640 hectares. The compact, high-density city is being designed to run entirely on renewable energy. It will be a world model of energy conservation with zero carbon emissions and zero waste. Compared to average urban levels, fossil fuel consumption will be reduced by 75%, water demand by 300% and waste production by 400%.

The city's 50,000 residents will live on streets modelled on traditional Middle Eastern architecture, but draped with fabrics that convert sunlight into electricity. Canals will run alongside the streets, some of which will be only 10 feet wide, to protect pedestrians from the heat, which averages over 40°C in the shade during the summer.

The construction materials used will considerably reduce energy requirements. The relationship of one building to the next will provide shade. Solar collectors will be on roofs throughout the city.

Masdar will be completely free of cars and their emissions. Cycling and walking will be the most common means of travel. A fully automated, electric Personal Rapid Transit System will provide a flexible and comfortable alternative to private cars.

Masdar project

Palm and mangrove plantations will create a green belt around the city to provide raw material for biofuels, a new industry that, say developers, may one day supplement oil and gas revenues. The tiny emirate is the fifth largest exporter of oil in the world, but it is envisaged that Masdar City will not need a drop. Sultan Al Jaber, the chief executive of Masdar, says, 'Years ago in the Middle East we lived a very sustainable lifestyle. We are bringing that back by creating a compact city where people don't need to use a car.'

There will be fields of solar concentrating mirrors in the desert, and wind turbines will catch breezes from the Gulf.

Masdar headquarters (model)

A solar-powered desalination plant will provide drinking water. Wastewater will be purified and recycled back to the city. In the process, it will be used to grow tree plantations, contributing to the city's biofuels strategy.
The first stage of development will set the tone for the entire project: the construction of a state-of-the-art photovoltaic power plant that will deliver the energy required to build the entire city!
One day, all cities will be built like this, but for those of us living in other parts of the world, we might have to wait a while. (400 words)

Adapted from 'Masdar Plans World's First Green City', sustainablebusiness.com

1 VOCABULARY CHECK: ENERGY AND THE ENVIRONMENT

Make sentences about Masdar with words and phrases from the pre-reading task on page 69. When possible, change the word's role in the sentence, e.g. change a noun to a verb.

EXAMPLE
energy conservation: The architecture of Masdar's buildings will *conserve energy*.

2 COMPARING AND CONTRASTING

First copy and complete the table below with information from the article. Then write a short text of approximately 100 words comparing Masdar with cities of today.

	Masdar
carbon emissions	...
waste	...
fossil fuel consumption	...
water demand	...

3 WRITING A COMMENT

Comment on the author's statement that, in the future, all cities will be built like Masdar. Give reasons for your answer.

> Skills, p. 227

4 RESEARCHING ENVIRONMENTAL ISSUES

Do one of the following research projects and present your findings to the class.

1 What eco-friendly policies has your town/country introduced to make life 'greener'? Research these and make a list. Then describe a 'green' policy which does not yet exist where you live but which you would like to see introduced.
2 Research Dubai, the largest city of the United Arab Emirates. Make a list of environmental problems associated with this city as well as similarities to Masdar City.
3 If you research online, you will quickly find many cities in the world which are known for being environmentally friendly. Choose one of these cities and tell the class about its 'green' qualities, the measures it has taken to be environmentally friendly, its eco-friendly infrastructure, etc.

> Skills, pp. 224 + 231

> Webcode: FOBU4A01

B Business and society

BEFORE YOU READ

Look at the pictures of the ships in this article. What unusual features do they have?

1 22

The future of global shipping

Shipping is considered a very inexpensive way to transport goods. Moving a shipping container can cost as little as €375 - about two cents per kilogram. 90% of the world's cargo, or about 2.4 trillion kilograms each year, travels this way. That's about the same as moving every person in the world six times. As international trade grows, so does the use of ships to carry goods around the earth. What are the environmental concerns and what is being done to address them? This article features the work of two innovative maritime companies.

SkySails

The shipping industry produces more carbon dioxide than the rail and aviation industries combined. The problem of shipping's greenhouse gas emissions is being tackled by the company SkySails GmbH. When a ship using this company's technology leaves port, it looks like any other diesel-powered vessel. Once the ship reaches the open sea, however, it reveals its weapon in the fight against climate change: a kite.

The SkySails system is already in use today. The International Maritime Organisation estimates that up to 100 million tons of carbon emissions can be eliminated worldwide every year with this technology. It can cut fuel consumption in half on good days and save an average of 10-15% in fuel each year. SkySails kites can be installed on a wide variety of ships, but they cannot fully replace the vessels' conventional engines.

The Orcelle

The shipping company Wallenius Wilhelmsen Logistics has designed a 'zero-emission' ship which, if it were ever built, would be remarkably environmentally friendly. It is called the 'Orcelle', the French word for the critically endangered Irrawaddy dolphin. With its dolphin-like fins, the Orcelle will harness wave energy, and it will use its three large, rigid sails covered in solar panels to collect wind and solar energy. The energy the ship collects can be used immediately or combined with hydrogen and stored in the ship's fuel cells. The only two by-products the fuel cells would produce would be heat and water vapour.

The design of the Orcelle's hull would make the use of ballast water unnecessary. When a large conventional ship is emptied of cargo, it needs to be balanced by the intake of a huge amount of sea water. This 'ballast water' is then emptied at the next port when the ship is filled with cargo. Through the intake and discharge of ballast water, biological materials, including plants, animals, viruses and bacteria are moved around the oceans, and this can cause extensive ecological damage to the marine environment. With the Orcelle, there would be no harmful emissions into the sea.

The innovative design of the Orcelle does not mean that capacity is sacrificed. Designed to transport cars, the ship will be able to carry 50% more vehicles than today's modern roll-on roll-off vessels.

Unfortunately, the Orcelle is not intended to be built as such, but the designs may serve as inspiration for the development of future ships, and similar vessels may be sailing the seas as soon as 2025. (502 words)

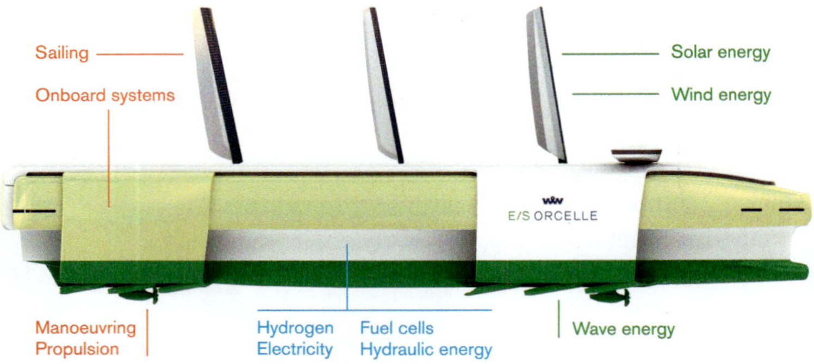

1 UNDERSTANDING THE TEXT

A Answer the questions on the text.

1 What reason does the text give for the popularity of shipping by sea?
2 What environmental hazards of conventional shipping does the text focus on?
3 What are the advantages of each ship in terms of monetary and environmental cost?
4 Does the article mention any disadvantages of either of the ships?

B What do these numbers from the text signify? Use the phrases below in your answers.

1 375
2 90
3 2.4 trillion
4 100 million
5 10–15
6 50

the percentage/cost/number of ...
the weight that ...
the increase/decrease in ...

2 DISCUSSING ENVIRONMENTAL TECHNOLOGIES

A Which company, SkySails or Wallenius Wilhelmsen, do you think has made a bigger contribution to the shipping industry and to preserving the environment? Tell your partner the reasons for your choice.

B As a class, make a list of technologies which claim to be environmentally friendly. Then, with a partner, give each one a grade: 1 (most 'green') – 5 (least 'green'). Discuss your results with your classmates.

Skills, p. 233

3 VOCABULARY CHECK: GLOBAL SHIPPING

Translate the underlined words and phrases.

EXAMPLE

Ninety per cent of the world's cargo, or about 2.4 trillion kilograms each year, travels this way.
Neunzig Prozent des Welthandels beziehungsweise circa 2.4 Billionen Kilogramm Fracht werden so pro Jahr transportiert.

1 Moving a shipping container can cost as little as €375.
Ein Versandcontainer kann für ... 375 € transportiert werden.

2 That's about the same as moving every person in the world six times.
Das ist ..., als wenn man jeden Menschen auf der Welt ... transportieren würde.

3 The problem of shipping's greenhouse gas emissions is being tackled by the company.
Das Problem von Treibhausgas-Emissionen durch Schiffsverkehr wird von der Firma ... .

4 The IMO estimates that up to 100 million tons of carbon emissions can be eliminated.
Die IMO schätzt, dass ... 100 Millionen Tonnen Kohlenstoff-Abgase eliminiert werden können.

5 The only two by-products the fuel cells will produce will be heat and water vapour.
... Nebenprodukte, die Brennstoffzellen dann produzieren, sind Hitze und Wasserdampf.

6 Similar vessels may be sailing the seas as soon as 2025.
Ähnliche Seefahrzeuge könnten ... 2025 auf den Meeren fahren.

4 SUMMARIZING A TEXT

A Which of the following most accurately summarizes the text?

1 When a ship with SkySails leaves port, it looks like any other, but then, when it is out at sea, it flies a huge kite which pulls it along the water. The Orcelle's uniqueness can always be seen. It is named after a dolphin and rather looks like one, with large 'fins' on top. The fins are really sails with solar panels in them.

2 A shipping container can be moved with relative ease from a ship to a train to a lorry. The container's versatility makes it ideal for shipping cargo internationally, and so this is how the vast majority of the world's cargo is shipped. SkySails technology will help move containers even more cheaply, and the Orcelle will do the same for cars.

3 The vast majority of the world's cargo is transported by sea. This is very cheap, but the ships are damaging the environment. SkySails and the Orcelle are examples of new technologies which have been developed to tackle this problem.

B Write a full summary of the text based on the best short summary above. Write about 150 words.

> Skills, p. 228

BACKGROUND BRIEFING CO_2 and the environment

Experts are increasingly unified in the opinion that climate change is, at least partly, man-made. The main cause appears to be greenhouse gases, especially carbon dioxide (CO_2), that we are releasing into the atmosphere. Experts believe global warming, if it is not controlled, will lead to changing weather patterns, rising seal levels and an increased frequency of natural disasters, among other things. If global warming continues as predicted, it will eventually have a significant effect on human health and well-being. Heatwaves will claim the lives of the sick and the elderly. Water shortage will increasingly become a source of international conflict. Farmland will dry up, causing food shortages. Coastal land will disappear, forcing people to resettle.

It is important to remember that carbon dioxide emissions are only one measure of environmental damage. Shipping, for example, also pollutes our rivers and oceans.

Global CO_2 emissions

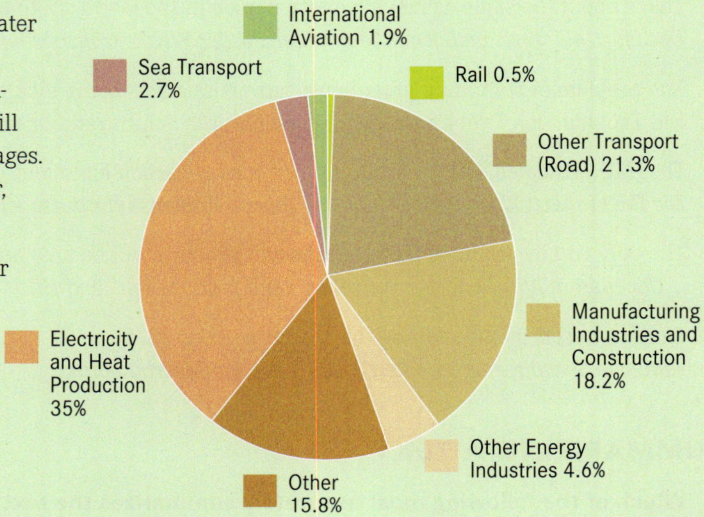

5 DISCUSSING ENVIRONMENTAL ISSUES

A Read the text and study the pie chart in the background briefing box, then do the following tasks.

1. According to the text 'The future of global shipping' (pages 71–72), 90% of the world's cargo is transported by sea. But according to the chart above, sea transport accounts for only 9.8% of CO_2 emissions caused by transport (four categories). What does this suggest about the environmental friendliness of sea transport?
2. Comment on the statement 'Technologies like SkySails and those planned for the Orcelle would make a significant impact on CO_2 if they were implemented on a large scale.' Write 100 words and include the following:
   - > arguments for and against this suggestion
   - > your opinion, supported by facts and/or statistics
   - > a conclusion in which you briefly repeat your thesis
   - > a suggestion on how to lower global CO_2 emissions

> Skills, p. 227

B Answer the following questions with a partner or in a group.

1. Do you think climate change is a real concern for your generation? Why/Why not?
2. What can people like you do to influence the level of CO_2 emissions? Look at the pie chart for ideas. What *can't* 'ordinary' people do about the problem?
3. What groups or organizations do you think should be responsible for finding solutions?

> Webcode: FOBU4B01

C Task options

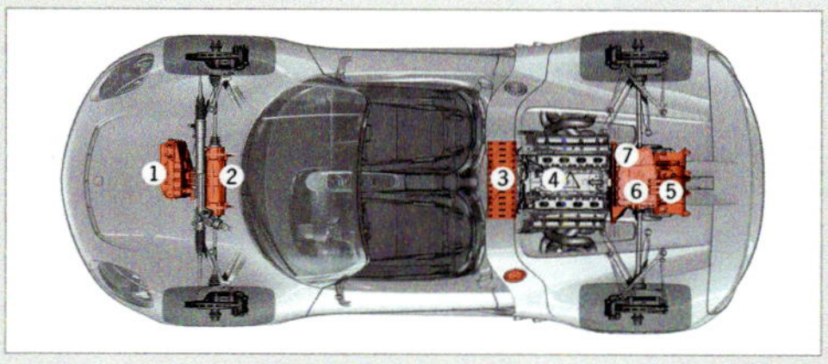

1 Power electronics
2 Electric drive
3 Lithium ion battery
4 V8 high RPM engine
5 Porsche Doppelkupplungsgetriebe (PDK) (= dual clutch transmission)
6 Electric motor
7 Power electronics

1 23

A In this interview, race car driver Orlando Ricci describes one of his favourite cars: the Porsche 918 Spyder. Listen and correct the six mistakes in the technical highlights below.

Technical highlights

1 Same chassis as the Carrera GT
2 0–62km/h in 32 sec
3 Top speed: 189 mph
4 Hybrid engine
5 One electric motor, two petrol motors
6 Better V8 petrol engine than the Porsche RS Spyder
7 Four driving modes: E Drive, Hybrid, Sport Hybrid, Rocket Hybrid
8 E-Boost push-to-pass feature for overtaking other cars
9 Mileage: 33 mpg

B What advantages (e.g. speed) are discussed in the interview? Are there any drawbacks to this car? Listen again, if necessary.

C Choose the correct words to complete these sentences from the interview. Then translate the words in the context of the sentence.

EXAMPLE
Let me ***give*** / *say* you some of the technical details. *sagen*

1 ... there is racing *technique* / *technology* in the car.
2 It's *still* / *even* faster than the Carrera GT.
3 What's different *about* / *with* it is that it's a hybrid car.
4 The front wheels are powered *from* / *by* an electric engine, ...
5 ... petrol engine is the same *like* / *as* the V8 engine in the Porsche RS Spyder race car.
6 *It gives* / *There are* four driving modes.
7 The car is *capable* / *able* of going 16 miles in this mode, ...
8 ... electric power and petrol power *are* / *is* both used in a way which maximizes fuel efficiency.
9 That's *about* / *safely* 33 kilometres per litre of petrol.
10 You *mustn't* / *don't have to* sacrifice looks for environmental friendliness.

D Research a modern technological development and present it to the class, using the structure below.

> Skills, p. 231

1 The present situation: which technology is in use today and why
2 The problems with the current situation
3 The new technology that is supposed to solve the problem
4 Advantages and disadvantages of the new technology

Here are some areas to consider when choosing a technology to present.

agriculture | communication | computers | energy | medicine | transportation

D Grammar checkpoint

1 PASSIVE: MIXED TENSES

Grammar Summary, p. 243

Read this article about eco-friendly policies in London. Put the underlined sections into the passive, using *by* where necessary. Be careful with the word order.

Start like this: *The local authorities in London were warned by environmentalists about the city's carbon emissions.*

In the early years of the 21st century, environmentalists warned the local authorities in London about the city's carbon emissions[1]. In 2007, the Lord Mayor of London, Ken Livingstone, introduced the city's Climate Action Plan[2]. At the time, Livingstone promised some changes[3]. 'The city will cut CO_2 emissions by 60%[4] within the next 20 years,' he explained. 'We hope that local companies will supply at least 25% of the city's power[5].'

Over the years, the London authorities have put parts of the plan into action[6]. The city council offers incentives to residents who improve the energy efficiency of their homes[7]. The Chamber of Commerce continually reminds companies to invest in green technology[8].

Talking today, an environmentalist said, 'You will always find someone who complains about extra costs but the main thing is that we are not wasting valuable resources[9]. Apart from that, with clean air and warmer homes, people are feeling the benefits of the Climate Action Plan[10].'

2 PASSIVE QUESTIONS

Grammar Summary, p. 243

A You were listening to a programme about the future of global shipping when reception on your solar-powered radio began to fade. Your friend heard the programme on a conventional radio. Ask him the questions below. Use the passive form and *by* where necessary.

1 What amount of cargo do container ships transport?
What amount of cargo is transported by container ship?
2 On what type of ship can they install the kites?
3 What do the fins of the Orcelle do?
4 How does the ship collect solar energy?
5 What two by-products do the fuel cells on the ship produce?
6 What does ballast water do to the environment?
7 How many cars will the Orcelle carry?
8 Are they going to build the Orcelle soon?

B Find the answers to the questions in the text on pages 71–72. Write the answers using the passive form.

3 PASSIVE INSTRUCTIONS WITH MODAL VERBS

Grammar Summary, p. 243

Put these instructions into the passive. Be careful with the word order.

1 In case of fire, you must not use the lift.
In case of fire, the lift must not be used.
2 You need to check oil and water levels every week.
3 You may take up to five kilos on board as hand luggage.
4 Everyone must wear names tags at all times in this building.
5 You must wash your hands before you handle food.
6 You may borrow books for up to three weeks. After that, you have to pay a fine.
7 We may ask you to return the credit card to the bank.
8 You should not write down your password.

5

Main Course

The business of fun and games

FOCUS

1 **Cornwall and Mallorca are two regions which rely heavily on tourism. Look at the photos. What effects do you think tourism might have on these two places?**

County Cornwall, England

Island of Mallorca, Spain

2 2

2 **Listen to two people talk about the positive and negative effects of tourism on their home. Who mentions which of the effects below?**

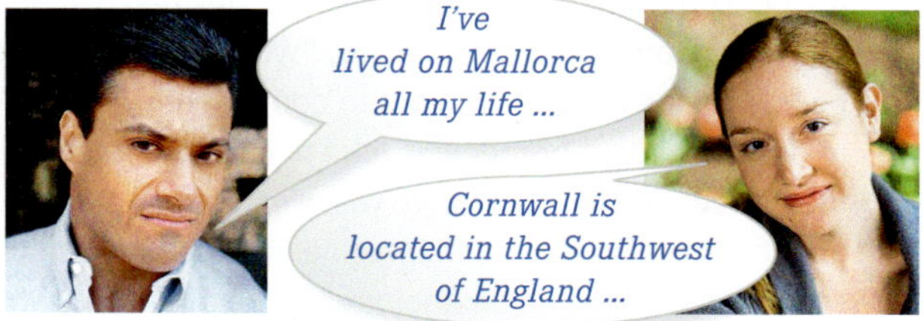

Positive	*Negative*	
creation of jobs	*air pollution*	*lack of green spaces*
economic prosperity	*congestion (too many cars)*	*overpriced pubs and restaurants*
improved infrastructure	*crowding (too many people)*	*seasonal parking charges*
more interesting life for the natives	*destruction of native culture*	*too much rubbish*
opportunities for job training	*lack of affordable housing*	*water shortages*

3 **With a partner, make a list of four other places where tourism is very important. Then rank them in the following ways, and give reasons for your rankings.**

> From 'most dependent on tourism' to 'least dependent on tourism'
> From 'best place to live year-round' to 'worst place to live year-round'

A People and business

BEFORE YOU READ

Look at the background briefing box on page 74. What does the pie chart say about the impact of air transport on the environment?

2 3

www.tellusyourviews.co.uk

Work	Leisure	Environment	Technology	Media

Foreign travel and long-haul flights:
What do YOU think?

Come on, England!! Why should we stay at home just because some eco-warriors want to protect the fish or something? When I go on holiday, I want to see as much as I can before partying through the night to some club tunes with other party animals. If loads of people spend their money there, who can complain? That's more jobs for everyone! I just want to come back with a fantastic tan. Let's face it: my impact on the environment is really small compared to a big company, say, and I don't really care much about what anyone else thinks – sun, sand, sex and saaaangria for me please, waiter! footy4eva

---

Modern-day tourism certainly is bad news for the environment. We simply can't go on living like this! Whether it is Brazilian rainforests, Spanish water supplies or the polar ice caps, nature is simply not able to replace these resources at the same rate as we are removing them. Why not spend your holiday at home? There are plenty of things to see and, whilst you may not get a tan, you won't be damaging the environment nearly as much and you'll also be helping your local community by spending money in your own country. save_the_whales

---

I own a restaurant in a ski-resort area of the Rocky Mountains. On an emotional level, it breaks my heart that global warming will one day make skiing impossible here. If I acted according to my environmental conscience, I would have to close down my business because I rely on people taking long-haul flights to come here to ski. Obviously, this is not an option I am willing to consider. On a practical level, I find myself in a catch 22: I need tourists to fly here, but their effect on climate change will eventually destroy the skiing industry my whole town depends on. The only solution I can imagine is more environmentally friendly transportation. I hope scientists create this technology before all the snow melts. snowchefjim

---

I spent my gap year working in an orphanage in Ecuador. Now I attend a university in the Netherlands, where I study Spanish and Business Studies. Whilst I feel guilty each time I step onto a plane, spending time in Spanish-speaking countries is an integral part of my course, and with regular cheap flights available from Holland to Spain, it's easy to suppress my conscience. Obviously, when I'm in a country, I integrate myself into the community much more than your average tourist and I always use public transport to get around if I can, but that doesn't negate the effects of plane travel. I do feel bad about it but I don't really see a way of resolving this conflict between language study and environmental friendliness.

lucyjbrown99

(466 words)

1 UNDERSTANDING THE TEXT

Summarize the viewpoints expressed in the four forum posts. Use the phrases below and the 'language for writing' on the cover flap at the back of the book to help you.

... is strongly in favour of ...	*... wishes he/she could ...*
... has reservations about ...	*... thinks that the consequences are ...*
... fiercely objects to ...	*... has a bad conscience because ...*
... does not care about ...	

> Skills, p. 228

2 WRITING A FORUM POST

Choose one of the following tasks.

1 A German friend of yours has heard you talking about this forum and wishes to write her own post but is unable to speak any English. Use her notes to write a text for her.

> *fahre gern in Urlaub*
> *möchte andere Länder, Leute und Kulturen sehen, ihnen aber nicht schaden*
> *bin Mitglied einer Umweltorganisation um die Schäden wieder gutzumachen*
> *es gibt aber auch viele andere Dinge, die wir machen können ohne zu fliegen*

2 Write to one of the people in the forum telling them ...
> what you think of their ideas.
> what you think they should consider and why.
> what you think about mass tourism and why.

BACKGROUND BRIEFING Geographic diversity of air travel

Today, the global airline industry consists of over 2000 airlines operating more than 23,000 aircraft, providing service to over 3700 airports.

While the number of trips (regardless of the length of stay) increased by about 31% between 1998 and 2005, the number of short trips (one to three overnight stays) has increased by 47%.

The number of Chinese air travellers rose from 16 million in 1990 to nearly 85.9 million in 2002 and to 160 million in 2006.

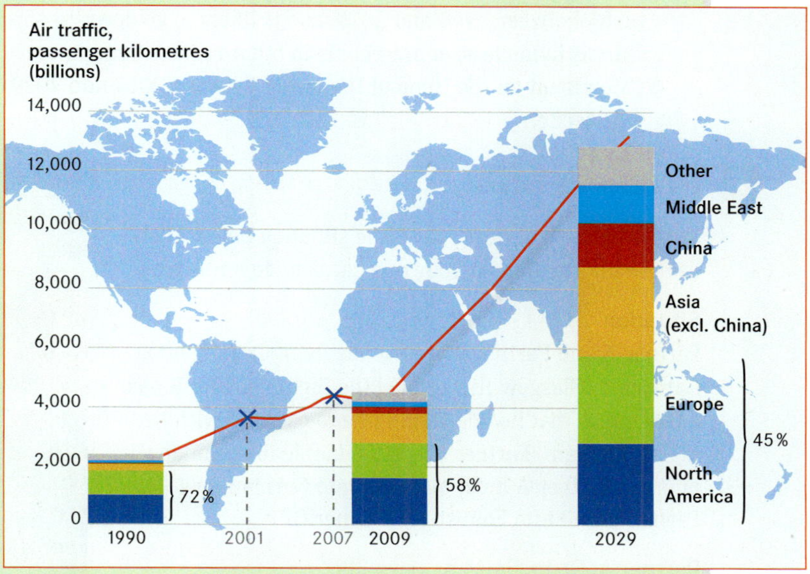

3 ANALYSING A DIAGRAM

> Skills, p. 232

A Study the background briefing box on the previous page, then use the table below to describe the diagram.

Between 1990 and 2009	*the (overall) traffic level* *the amount of air traffic* *China's share of all flights* *Europe's dominance in air travel* *the difference between Western and Asian countries*		*increased/decreased …* *rose/fell …* *remained constant.* *levelled out.* *doubled/tripled.* *grew smaller/larger.*	*dramatically.* *unexpectedly.* *sharply.* *markedly.* *gently.* *slightly.*
Today		*is*	*increasing/decreasing …* *rising/falling …* *levelling out.*	
			remains constant.	
In the future		*will* *is predicted to* *is expected to* *should*	*increase/decrease …* *rise/fall/grow …* *double/triple.* *level out.*	

B Answer the following questions with a partner.

1 Which of the following events do the two blue crosses on the diagram refer to? Explain what effect the events had on air traffic and why?

- > the introduction of the euro currency
- > terrorist attacks
- > the financial crisis
- > World Cup football tournaments

2 Why did the European and North American proportion of air travel decrease from 72% to 58% between 1990 and 2009, and is likely to go down to 45% in 2029? Are people in these areas flying less, or are people in other regions flying more?

3 Comment on the trend of the graph between 2009 and 2029. Do you agree with the projection?

4 INTERPRETING

Work in groups of three. Read the situation below, then use the information on your role cards to do a role-play.

Situation

Partner A and Partner B are friends flying from London Gatwick to Glasgow Airport. On the flight, Partner B has a few issues that he/she would like to clear up with the flight attendant (Partner C), but is unable to speak any English. Partner A must interpret into German for Partner B and into English for Partner C.

Partner A: Go to file 24 on page 219.
Partner B: Go to file 13 on page 214.
Partner C: Go to file 5 on page 212.

> Webcode: FOBU5A01

B Business and society

BEFORE YOU READ

A Have you ever seen a major sporting event such as a championship football game or a national swimming competition? Tell your partner about it.

I attended a/an	*local*	*football*	*game*	*at a stadium.*
I saw a/an	*regional*	*rugby*	*match*	*at a field.*
	national	*athletics*	*event*	*at a tennis court.*
	international	*tennis*	*tournament*	*at a pool.*
	Olympic	*swimming*	*competition*	*at a racetrack.*
		auto racing		*at an arena.*
		ski jumping		*at a ski slope.*
				on television.

B Guess whether the following statements are true or false. Then find the answers in the text and correct the false statements.

1 The Olympics and the FIFA World Cup always make a huge profit for the host cities.
2 The Olympic Games boost tourism to host cities.
3 Large sporting events create permanent jobs and benefit the local economy.
4 Sport stadiums built for the Olympics and the World Cup are used by many people long after the championships are over.

2 4

When the Games come to town

How sports championships really affect local tourism

by David Lambert

I am aware that I am in the minority. I am one of the few people I know who is anti-Olympics and anti-FIFA World Cup. I feel a bit sad when I say this, because I used to love these championships. I even spent years working on the organizing committee when my own country hosted one. I thought that the event would attract tourists to our country and magically boost our economy. But it was this experience that showed me that the obscene costs to the taxpayers make these prestigious events a liability rather than an asset.

These events are all about competition, but the most important competition is the need to make a profit. In a travelling sports event like the Olympics or the World Cup, the organizers must convince the hosts that the event will be good for their city, and they usually underestimate the costs. The Mayor of Montreal told his citizens in 1976 that the Olympics 'can no more have a deficit than a man can have a baby'. Unfortunately, history defied this mayor's personal law of nature and Montreal ended up with a debt of €1.1 billion, which took 30 years to pay off. The 2004 Summer Olympics in Athens was originally estimated at €1 bn.

The 2004 Athens Olympics cost the country more than €10 bn.

The actual cost turned out to be a whopping $10.6 bn, and this increased the budget deficit of the entire country.

The argument that championships will boost tourism for their hosts is probably a myth. Many of the people who visit a city during championships would have gone anyway, but they time their trips to coincide with the Games. This may explain why tourism usually falls - yes, falls - after the Olympics leave town. Greece's visitor numbers stayed below their pre-Games level for two years.

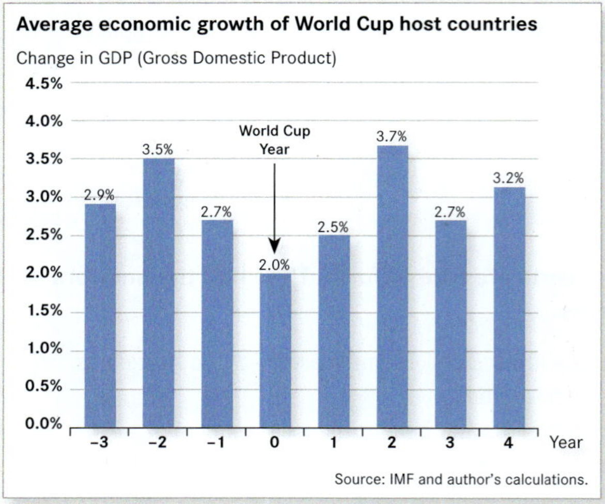

Business owners who have expected fans to buy things from them while they are in town are often disappointed. The visitors usually only spend their money in small areas of the city. Retailers in both Atlanta and Vancouver who were outside of the district where events were held actually reported a fall in business during the Olympics. The championships are supposed to bring 'employment opportunities', but these are not permanent positions; they are very temporary jobs in which people generally do not gain any employable skills.

Believe it or not, there has never been a single study of a large sporting event that has found evidence of significant economic benefits. History shows that host countries are more likely to see lower economic growth in the year of a World Cup than they are to see higher growth, and economic recovery in the years after the games is insignificant (see bar chart).

When a city hosts a major sporting event, millions are spent on building new stadiums or improving existing ones. Once the championships are over, these money pits often go unused, and maintaining them is expensive. The homes of 4,707 Beijing residents were demolished so that the Olympic Bird's Nest Stadium could be built, but it has hardly been used since the Games, and costs €69 m a year to maintain. Both Barcelona and Atlanta are home to entire ghost towns of former Olympic Villages. World Cup host South Africa built a new stadium which seats 65,000, but typical attendance at a football game there is only 5,000, and as I write, London has just built a 12,000-seat handball arena for 2012, but most Brits do not even know this sport exists. Who is going to fill these seats when the Games are over? The money spent on hiring construction workers and purchasing materials from local suppliers is generally thought to benefit the local economy, but this money would be better spent on building other things, like hospitals or schools.

Advocates of championships, unable to support their economic arguments with figures, inevitably site 'intangible benefits' of hosting championships: the 'feel-good factor' of the event, for example. Does bankruptcy feel good?

(651 words)

Many people lost their homes to make way for the Beijing Bird's Nest, here under construction in 2007.

1 UNDERSTANDING THE TEXT

Complete the following sentences from the author's point of view.

1 The author used to love championship sports until ...
2 Organizers claim that cities will profit from hosting games, however ...
3 Championships only seem to boost tourism because ...
4 Historically, the GDP of host countries has ...
5 Huge venues are built for championship games, and the tickets are sold out for the championships, but afterwards ...

2 VOCABULARY CHECK: OPPOSITES

A Match the words 1–10 with their opposites in the box.

1 host
2 low
3 liability
4 benefit
5 debt/deficit
6 rise
7 permanent
8 build
9 local
10 underestimate

asset | demolish | fall | overestimate | visitor | global | hurt | profit | high | temporary

B Translate the sentences into English. Use words from the previous exercise for the words in *italics*.

1 Jenny hat Souvenirs vor dem Stadion verkauft und € 125 *Gewinn* gemacht.
2 Ich habe für meinen Urlaub nicht genug gespart und hatte € 200 *Schulden* als ich nach Hause kam.
3 Die Stadt hat ein altes Industriegebäude *abgerissen*, um Platz für ein neues Stadion zu schaffen.
4 Man sollte nie *unterschätzen*, wie sehr eine Sportveranstaltung die Moral heben kann.
5 Die positive Wirkung, die der Sieg in der FIFA Weltmeisterschaft auf das Land hatte, war nur *vorübergehend*.
6 Würden Sie sagen, dass dieser Spieler ein Gewinn oder eine *Belastung* für seine Mannschaft ist?
7 Tourismus *nützt* vielen *lokalen* Wirtschaftszweigen.

3 MIND MAP: SPORT INDUSTRY

A Make a mind map around the term 'sport industry' that includes ways money is earned and spent. Use information from the text and your own idea.

> Skills, pp. 225 + 229

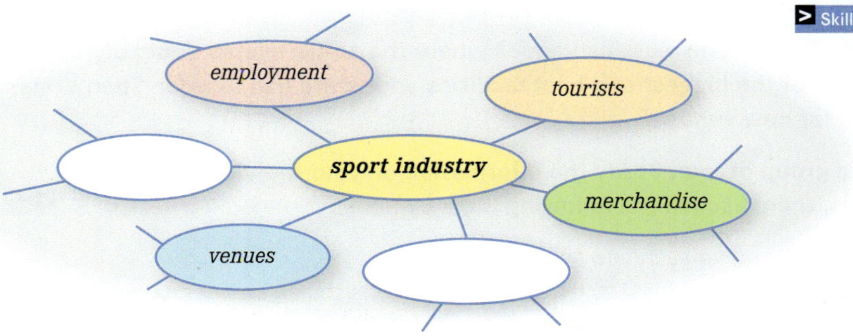

B Write a text of about 100 words on the pros and cons of hosting major sporting events. Conclude by suggesting how these events could be made more beneficial (or less damaging) to local economies.

> Webcode: FOBU5B01

C Task options

pan-european games

A Read the situation.

Your state (*Bundesland*) is going to host the first ever Pan-European Games, a sports event similar to the Olympics, except on a much smaller scale. Roughly 1,000 athletes from all over Europe will compete, and fans will come from all over the world to watch them. The Games will be held in the summer in five years' time, and will feature these events:

Athletics (running, jumping, throwing, etc.)

Basketball and wheelchair basketball

Swimming (racing, diving, synchronized swimming, water polo)

Gymnastics (floor exercise, parallel bars, pommel horse, etc.)

Football

Your state must build at least one new venue, because €200 m from the EU has been 'earmarked' for this purpose. That means that the money can only be spent on a new venue, and if a venue is not built, your state will lose this money.

The new venue is the only thing paid for with EU money. The rest of the event will have to be paid for by taxpayers in the state.

B As a class, brainstorm existing venues where the above events could be held. Try to think of the biggest and best facilities your state has to offer. Then brainstorm locations for new venues.

C Work in a group of four. Study the information on your individual role cards, then discuss the following:

> Skills, p. 233

- the best location for each new sports venue
- whether any other building or infrastructure projects should be undertaken and, if so, which?
- how taxpayers should pay for the Games

Partner A: Go to file 2 on page 211.
Partner B: Go to file 17 on page 216.
Partner C: Go to file 11 on page 214.
Partner D: Go to file 9 on page 213.

D Grammar checkpoint

1 REPORTED SPEECH – STATEMENTS

> Grammar Summary, p. 241

A friend would like to know what people said during a TV programme about tourists and the effects of tourism on their town. Use the words in brackets to start your sentences. Remember to change pronouns, time and place when necessary.

1 "Tourism helps the local economy but it also creates a lot of problems. Everyone knows that it's destroying the environment." (A local man said ... / He added ...)
A local man said that tourism helped the local economy but it also created a lot of problems. He added that everyone knew that it was destroying the environment.

2 "I've turned my home into a guest house and I offer bed and breakfast. I don't have a big pension so the extra income is useful." (A pensioner said ... / She explained ...)

3 "Congestion and pollution have been making people's lives a misery for years. As soon as the tourists arrive next year, I'm going away on holiday." (A woman said ... / She went on to say ...)

4 "We are looking at ideas which will attract more tourists to the area. One thing that has been suggested is a leisure park." (A member of the town council explained ... / He mentioned ...)

5 "It's pretty dead here in winter. I don't care what the old people think, we need the tourists because they bring a bit of life to the place." (A teenager said ... / He argued ...)

6 "This was a lovely place when I first came here twenty years ago because it was obvious then that the villagers had worked hard to make it attractive to tourists. It's sad to see that so much has changed in the last few years and it's beginning to look like every other holiday resort on the planet." (A visitor told the reporter ... / She complained ...)

2 REPORTED SPEECH – QUESTIONS

> Grammar Summary, p. 243

An immigration officer is interviewing a man who has just got off a plane at Chicago O'Hare Airport. Report the immigrations officer's questions.

1 "Are you entering the country for business or for pleasure?"
The immigration officer asked the man ...
The immigration officer asked the man if he was entering the country for business or for pleasure.

2 "Do you have a valid entry visa?"
He enquired ...

3 "Can I see your passport, please?"
The immigration officer asked ...

4 "Where are you staying in Chicago?"
He wanted to know ...

5 "How long do you plan to stay?"
He asked ...

6 "Are you carrying any weapons, drugs or illegal substances?"
He was interested to know ...

6 The changing workplace

FOCUS

1 **Name some 'developing' countries. On what continents are the poorest, least developed economies concentrated?**

2 **Look at the map and the pie charts and answer the following questions.**

1. Which economic sectors are dominant in poorer countries, and which sector is dominant in wealthier countries?
2. How would this map look different if the data was from 100 years ago? Which colour would Germany be: green, orange or blue?

Distribution of GDP by economic sector

The map below shows the dominant economic sector in each country.

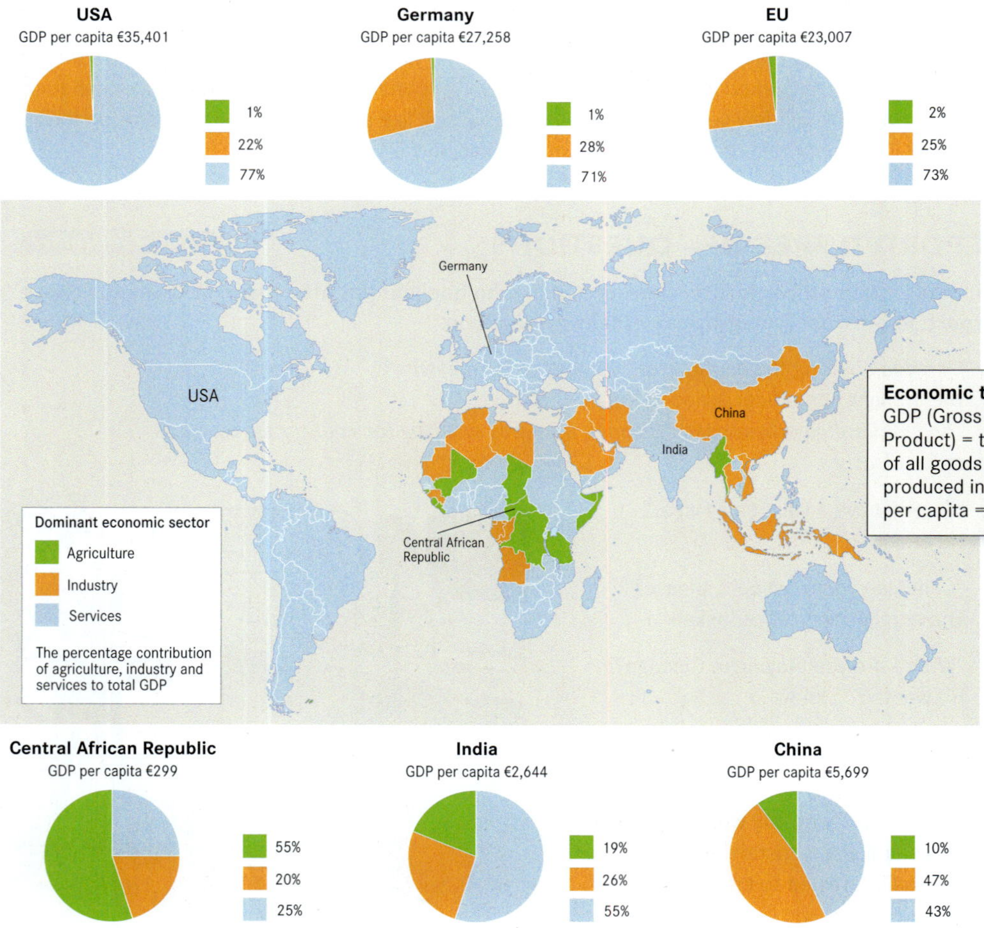

Economic terms
GDP (Gross Domestic Product) = the total value of all goods and services produced in one year.
per capita = per person

A People and business

BEFORE YOU READ

Look at the following table and describe what has happened to the GDP per capita and how each sector of the Indian economy has changed. Skills, p. 232

India GDP distribution by sector				
	Agriculture	**Industry**	**Service**	**GDP per capita**
2010	19%	26%	55%	€ 730
2000	24%	27%	49%	€ 412
1990	33%	27%	40%	€ 290
1980	38%	24%	38%	€ 202
1950	58%	15%	27%	no data

India rising

by Arjun Sharma

For many years, people around the world associated only three things with India: food, spirituality and, unfortunately, poverty. When India gained independence from Britain in 1947, it was indeed a very poor country whose economy was based primarily on agriculture.

A lot has changed since 1947. During the second half of the last century, we slowly became an industrialized nation. Many Indians left their farms in the countryside to work in urban factories producing textiles and other export goods. Many of these factories were built by foreign companies – most notably from the UK – which closed down their manufacturing operations at home and moved them here. In India, the migration of jobs from agriculture to industry is still continuing, but today most of the new jobs are being created in the service sector, which is growing rapidly. In 1991, our government undertook economic reforms that encouraged foreign investment and outsourcing contracts, with great success. Nowadays, people associate more modern images with India, including pills, computers and friendly voices on the telephone.

Pharmaceutical companies

After the economic reforms of 1991, one of the industries that took off was the manufacture of pharmaceuticals. At first, India became known for making cheap, substandard copies of Western drugs and selling them to developing countries. But more recently India has been gaining respect in this industry, as well as in other manufacturing industries. The manufacturing of goods requiring high-skill production and very low prices has become one of India's specialities.

Software companies

India is home to a huge number of software companies, both native and foreign. All together, these companies produce around €50 bn revenue each year. That's only about 6% of our GDP, but the influence it has had on the economy and our role in the world marketplace is enormous.

Call centres

People in wealthy English-speaking countries are always calling us on the telephone. They may think that they're speaking to someone at the bank down the street, but their call really goes all the way to a call centre in Mumbai or Bangalore, which the bank has hired to take customer calls. Britain's busiest telephone number, the information hotline for the National Rail, has now outsourced half of its 50 million calls per year to India.

Indian call centres are just one well-known example of global outsourcing. India gets by far the most outsourcing contracts of any country in the world: contracts for IT services and also back-office services such as human resources, finance and accounting.Our laws which encourage off-shore investing are just one reason for this. Another reason is that there are a lot of well-educated people here, and a trained brain in India is just as good as a trained brain in the West, but the Indian brain comes much cheaper.

This does not mean that India is now all smiles and lotus blossoms. We still have a lot of people living in poverty. The people in the countryside have seen little benefit from our economic growth. Foreign factories have taken away – and continue to take away – a lot of agricultural land. Many rural families have lost their young people to the economic opportunities of the big cities. However, these same families are surviving from money that their children – employed in factories and offices – send back home. This growth has become a basis for optimism in India. While other countries suffered recession in the late 2000s, India's economy has kept growing, and it is projected to keep growing very rapidly.

(580 words)

1 UNDERSTANDING THE TEXT

A **Make lists of the positive and negative effects of Indian economic growth.**

Positive	*Negative*
Image of poverty being replaced by other images	*Manufacture and sale of substandard drugs*
...	...

B **How does the text confirm the statistics in the pre-reading task? Find passages in the text that confirm the following:**

- the rise of the industrial sector
- the rise of the GDP per capita
- the rise of the service sector

2 6

2 LISTENING: ANOTHER VIEWPOINT

A **Listen to Priya Namakkal talk about her experience with outsourcing, and answer the questions.**

The work is mind-numbing, but the pay is excellent.

Name: Priya Namakkal
Age: 23
Lives: Bangalore, India
Job: Data Entry Clerk

1 Why did Priya move to Bangalore?
2 What does she like about her job? What doesn't she like about it?
3 Who are her clients?
4 How has outsourcing changed young people's lives in Bangalore?
5 How has it changed the city of Bangalore?
6 What is Priya's opinion of outsourcing in general?

B **Listen again. What information in the text 'India rising' does Priya confirm? Take notes.**

EXAMPLE
got job in service sector/IT
...

New shopping mall in Bangalore

C **Priya Namakkal's story is very typical. Do you think people like her are 'winners' from economic development, or are there no winners?**

3 ANALYSING A DIAGRAM

A **Look at the diagram in the background briefing box. What trends does it show?**

B **Complete the text in the background briefing box with the words and numbers below.**

2 | 30 | demand | early stages | growth | highly | include | labour intensive | less | manufacturing industry | outsources | material goods | replaces | society

BACKGROUND BRIEFING Economic development and jobs

In the ...[1] of economic development, food production is very ...[2], so many people work in the agricultural sector. As a ...[3] becomes industrialized, technology does more and more work for the people. It ...[4] most of the agricultural workers and, later, some of the industrial workers, too. Another reason why jobs in these sectors disappear is that the developing country ...[5] more and more agricultural and industrial production to ...[6] developed countries. A reason for the ...[7] of the service sector is that, as the per capita income (income per person) rises, the ...[8] for services also rises.

Essen, Germany in 1864

Service-sector jobs are jobs which do not contribute to the production of ...[9]. These jobs ...[10] medics, teachers, bankers and police officers, just to name a few examples.

Germany is somewhat exceptional because it is a ...[11] developed economy which has maintained a large ...[12]. Today, about ...[13]% of Germans work in agriculture, but approximately ...[14]% still work in industry.

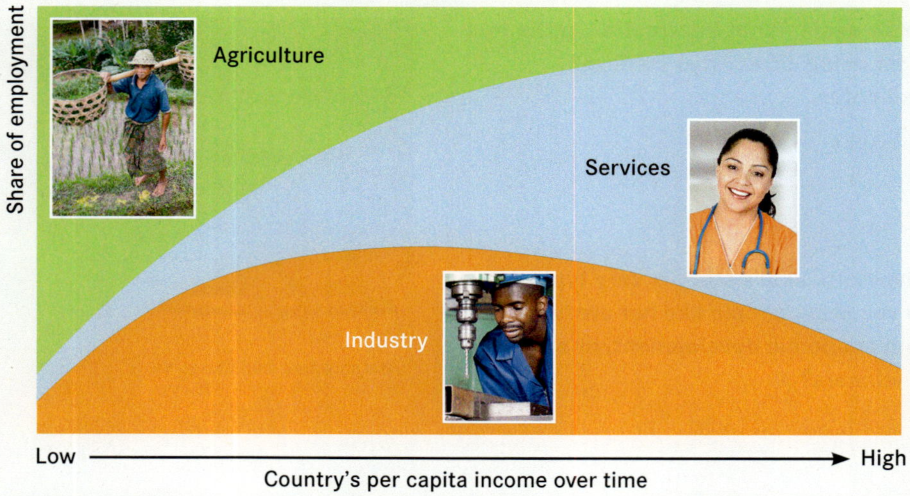

Webcode: FOBU6A01

B Business and society

BEFORE YOU READ

Look at the pie charts below. What reason for Germany's outsourcing of IT staff do they show?

Hourly wages of IT Workers

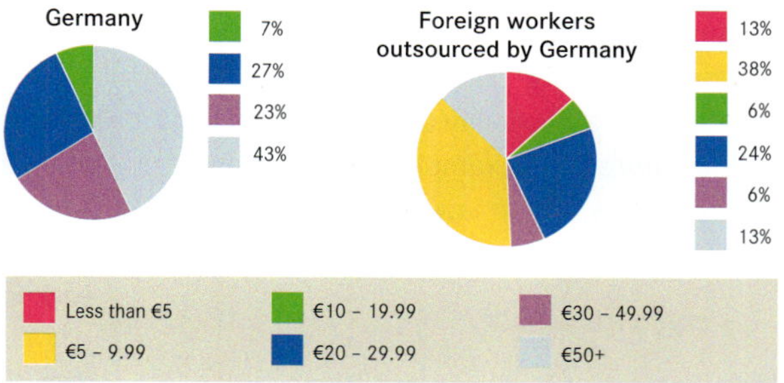

2 7

The outsourcing trend in IT

The competition between the internal IT department and the external provider

Companies which just a few years ago had huge IT departments are laying off staff and hiring other companies to meet their technology needs. This practice has become so popular that the value of IT outsourcing contracts in Western Europe in 2011 was estimated at €228 bn, with a yearly increase of about 5%. The reason for the popularity of outsourcing is that external IT providers have shown that they can adapt to companies' changing technology needs, and that they can do so at competitive prices.

One area in which internal IT departments are quickly losing this competition is the public sector, where budgets are getting smaller. The City Council of Cropping, England, for example, wants to have all of its IT services outsourced by 2017. British Telecom will run the communications, Fujitsu will run the infrastructure from Japan, and Tata will run the application management from India. 'This means,' says the Council's Chief Information Officer (CIO) Priya Waldorf, 48, 'that I need completely new skills on my internal IT staff.'

New career field: geek meets suit

Internal IT departments will still exist in some form. They will keep some of their highly skilled technical people who will decide the best strategy for the company's technology. And they will also hire new people who can deal with the changing needs of the department. Cornelia Neff, 27, is one of these people. She was hired by Waldorf earlier this year to manage the relationships between the Council's IT department and its external IT providers. 'I'm part geek, part suit,' Neff says, referring to her valuable mix of computer and business skills.

The business skills needed by today's internal IT departments go way beyond those of a typical programmer. Nowadays internal IT staff

Cornelia Neff: 'part geek, part suit'

have to know project management, supplier management and contract management. They have to be able to talk to, listen to and understand the needs of their company's IT users. And they have to use these skills to choose the best outsourcing contracts and get the most out of the relationships with their providers.

Neff studies a new outsourcing contract on her computer screen. 'I have to be very careful how I write this,' she says anxiously. 'I have to predict what flexibility the Council will need in the future. For example, the government might pass a minor law, and that could increase the data storage we need.'

Rise of the freelancer

Rick Forrest, 32, sits in his home office in Edinburgh, designing the new Web platform for the Council's public calendar of events. He has never spoken with Neff or anyone who works in Cropping. In fact, he has not been hired by the Council. He is working for one of the Council's external IT providers.

As a freelance worker, you might say Forrest is at the bottom of the outsourcing food chain – outsourced by the outsourced. When his former employer laid him off six years ago (and outsourced *his* job), he 'thought the world was going to end'. There are some drawbacks to working freelance: he has to pay his own health insurance and save money for his retirement by himself. But there are also some big advantages to freelancing: he can make his own work schedule and he does not have to worry about getting fired.

What about finding customers? 'That was difficult at the beginning,' says Forrest, 'but over the years I've developed a base of clients that like my work. I haven't had to look for work in a long time.' (560 words)

Freelancer Rick Forrest in his home office

1 UNDERSTANDING THE TEXT

A Answer the following questions about the text.

1. Why are companies reducing the size of their IT departments? What are some of the consequences?
2. Why is an IT project manager probably more valuable to a modern internal IT department than a typical programmer?
3. What are freelancers? How are they different from employees?

B Match the quotation with the speaker.

Priya Waldorf
Cornelia Neff
Rick Forrest

1 *It's my job to get our overseas suppliers to fulfil the needs of our customers. That can be difficult to coordinate.*

2 *I have no boss, so I can take a day off whenever I want, as long as my clients are taken care of.*

3 *We're looking to hire someone who has some IT experience but who can also manage our suppliers overseas.*

2 VISUALIZING THE PROCESS OF OUTSOURCING

A Complete the text with the words in the box.

budget | company | freelancer | skills | staff | suppliers

The outsourcing trend does not exist only in IT or in the public sector, it is happening in many industries. The first thing that usually happens is that a ...[1] gets reduced. Then, the company lays off ...[2] and outsources work areas. Finally, the company hires a smaller number of people to manage the ...[3]. When a worker gets laid off, he or she sometimes goes to work for an external supplier, or he becomes a ...[4]. If a worker learns supplier management ...[5], he or she sometimes keeps the full-time job at the ...[6].

B Copy the cause-and-effect diagram into your exercise book or onto your computer and complete it with the underlined phrases from the text above. Two answers have been done for you.

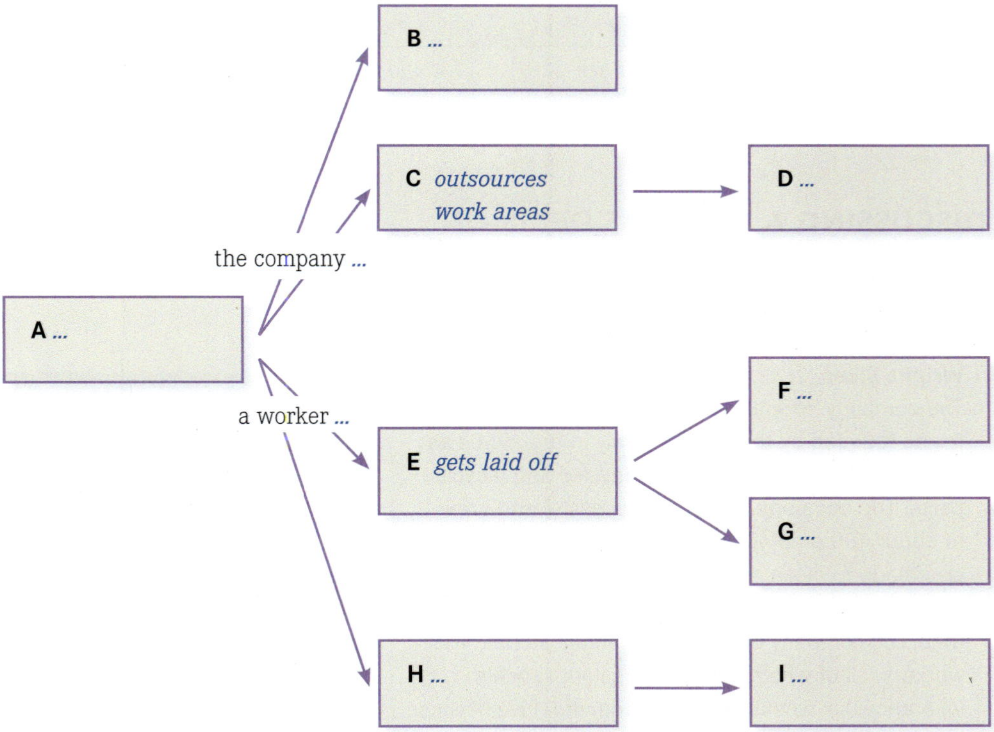

3 RESEARCHING ONLINE

Do some online research. Find three examples of companies that have outsourced jobs, either domestically or internationally. Make notes as in the example.

EXAMPLE

Company: British National Rail
Job: telephone hotline worker
Outsourced to: Comtech in India

> Skills, p. 224

4 WRITING A COMMENT

Comment on whether working as a company employee or as a freelancer would be better for you personally. Include a brief summary of the text 'The outsourcing trend in IT'. Before you start writing, sort the following aspects into one of the four columns of the table.

> Skills, p. 227

dealing with company politics
freedom to work for whomever I want
setting my own hours
more structure and routine
more personal responsibility
having to motivate myself every day
working every day with the same colleagues
a boss checking my work
health insurance provided by the employer
being my own boss

working in a company		*working freelance*	
I would like ...	*I wouldn't like ...*	*I would like ...*	*I wouldn't like ...*
...	...	...	...

5 DISCUSSING A BUSINESS DECISION

A **Read the text about Wright Bikes. How is the company's story similar to other stories you have read about in this unit?**

Wright Bikes

The company Wright Bikes has a long history. It was founded by the Wright family in the 1950s as a manufacturer of high-quality bicycles and bicycle parts. The company was very successful and grew to about 100 employees. Then, in 1975, the decision was made to close down the local factory and have the products made more cheaply in Taiwan. Since then, the company employs only about 30 full-time workers, all of whom get decent salaries, health insurance, six weeks' paid vacation, etc. Five of these full-timers make up the customer service department. It is their job to deal with customers via telephone and e-mail. Now an urgent need to cut costs makes it very tempting to 'let them go' (= sack them) and hire service providers in other, poorer countries to replace them.

B **You are the business managers at Wright Bikes. Form groups of three to discuss what your company should do.**

Partner A: Go to file 18 on page 216.
Partner B: Go to file 12 on page 214.
Partner C: Go to file 10 on page 213.

> Skills, p. 233

> Webcode: FOBU6B01

C Task options

A Read the tips for job interviews below. Then work with a partner to come up with at least two more tips.

Tips for job interviews

Even if you plan to start your own business someday, chances are you will want to work for someone else for a while first, and you will have to interview for the job.

1 Think about why you want the job and be able to put this into words. At first, you may only have a strong feeling that you want it, and this is a great sign and may be enough for you, but your employer will want to hear you talk about your interests and desires in connection with the position. This is also true for any written correspondence you have with potential employers.
2 Even if dress is normally casual at the employer's, you should still dress up. Wear a suit, if you have one. Everyone will know it is just for the interview and they will appreciate your effort. No one will worry that you will come to work every day overdressed.

3 If the position you are applying for is in another city, your interview may well take place via webcam, and you will need to prepare. Choose a tidy, professional-looking background to sit in front of. Make sure everything technical is working at your end. Test the sound, the picture, the lighting in the room, etc. with a friend before the employer calls you.
4 If the job you are applying for is, well, not particularly attractive, nobody will expect you to say it is what you want to do for the rest of your life. For example, if it is a job passing out flyers, you do not have to say 'It's always been my dream to stand on a street corner and distribute information!' Nevertheless, you will have to say why you want this particular job. Say something like 'I enjoy contact with people and I want to practise approaching strangers.' You will also have to give the impression that you plan to do the job for a while and not quit after just one day.

5 Be nice to *everybody*, even the people who seem 'unimportant'.

B With a partner, follow these steps to brainstorm what to say in an interview.

1 Make a list of jobs that people your age (or a little bit older) do.
2 Then pick three jobs and come up with good, realistic answers for the question 'Why do you want this job?'. Refer to tips 1 and 4 in the text, and the file on job applications starting on page 184.
3 Finally, give another group your answers to this question and let them guess which jobs they relate to.

C Role-play a job interview with your partner. Ask each other the following questions.

Interviewer	Interviewee
Why do you want this job?	What training would I receive?
What relevant experience do you have?	Who would I be working with?
When could you start?	What are the most challenging parts of the job?

D Grammar checkpoint

1 ADJECTIVES AND ADVERBS

> Grammar Summary, p. 246

Add the words in brackets to the sentences. Put the adjectives into the adverb form when necessary.

1 ~~enormous~~ | ~~important~~ | rapid | ~~underdeveloped~~ | wealthy

After independence in 1947, India was one of the world's *underdeveloped*[1] countries. In the 90s, however, the government introduced *important*[2] reforms which boosted the economy *enormously*[3]. Though working people in India today are not ...[4] compared to those in the West, the economy is growing ...[5].

2 cheap | excellent | good | high-quality | Indian

The country is ...[1] known for the manufacture of ...[2] goods which can be bought ...[3]. All over the world, ...[4] software companies have an ...[5] reputation.

3 fluent | foreign | high | main

Apart from manufacturing, ...[1] entrepreneurs wishing to outsource services often choose India. Two of the ...[2] attractions are the ...[3] number of educated people and the fact that so many people speak English ...[4].

4 economic | great | regular | slow | young

On the downside, rural communities have not benefited ...[1] from India's ...[2] expansion. Farmland has been turned over to factories and ...[3] people are moving to the cities to find work. It is hoped that conditions in the countryside will ...[4] improve as people who have found work in the cities send money home ...[5] .

5 global | optimistic | steady

Despite ...[1] downturns, the economy continues to rise ...[2] and India can look to the future ... [3].

2 COMPARISON OF ADJECTIVES AND ADVERBS

> Grammar Summary, p. 247

Put the words in brackets into the correct form of the comparative or superlative.

Working at the call centre is not the *most exciting*[1] (*exciting*) job I've ever had but it's much ...[2] (*good*) than any of the other jobs I've done. The work is not ...[3] (*hard*) as the work I did before. I have to be ...[4] (*patient*), though. Some callers are ...[5] (*difficult*) than others. They expect an answer to their problem ...[6] (*quick*) as possible. The ...[7] (*bad*) caller I had spoke ...[8] (*fast*) than anyone I had ever spoken to in my life. When I asked him to speak ...[9] (*slow*), he said he would report me to my boss. He said I should be ...[10] (*polite*). Most of the callers are ...[11] (*friendly*) than he was. The ...[12] (*nice*) caller I ever had said I was the ...[13] (*helpful*) person he had spoken to at a call centre. I think the day that he called was one of my ...[14] (*good*) days at work.

In the global marketplace

FOCUS

1 **This smartphone is advertised as 'Made in America', but is it? Use the information below to describe where the product was made.**

Start like this: *The software was designed and developed in the USA, but the integrated circuit ...*

1 Software designed and developed in 

2 Integrated circuit for video processor made in 

3 Display produced in 

4 Touch control modules designed by a company in and manufactured in their factory in 

5 Bluetooth module created by a firm in the ; manufacture outsourced to 

6 Minerals for semi-conductors mined in  at mines owned by a company based in 

7 Assembled in 

Key to the flags > file 7, p. 212

2 **Talk in groups about your favourite possessions. How much do you know about where the things you own were made?**

A People and business

BEFORE YOU READ

Match the words to the pictures.

cotton | fabric | factory | garment | hanger | label | rack | sewing machine

THE HUFFINGTON POST

THE INTERNET NEWSPAPER: NEWS BLOGS VIDEO COMMUNITY

FRONT PAGE | POLITICS | BUSINESS | ENTERTAINMENT | TECH | MEDIA | LIFE&STYLE | CULTURE | COMEDY | HEALTHY LIVING | WOMEN | LOCAL | MORE

Where is it from?

Craig and Marc Kielburger

"Nice T-shirt," I heard someone say. "Where's it from?"

The fashionista offered a store's name.

The question lingered.

Where is it from? Not just this shirt. Any shirt. Look at your own label. Where is it from? And who is it from?

In the beginning, there was a child.

He is in a cotton field in Uzbekistan, the second-largest cotton exporter in the world. He is working not because he wants to, but because he has to.

Cotton makes up 60 percent of his country's export earnings, so everyone is expected to contribute, even children. In 2000, UNICEF estimated 22.6 percent of kids aged 5 to 14 were harvesting the cotton. Some were given plastic water bottles filled with pesticide to spray on the crop.

The most fortunate child gets 3 cents for every kilogram picked – a kilogram worth $1.15 on the world market.

The Uzbek government maintains that no child labor exists in their country. Still, come September, rather than heading to school, the children diligently pick the cotton, pack it up and ship it off.

You see, most countries that grow cotton do not have their own textile industries. So, the raw material for the shirt travels to a manufacturer in China.

There, in massive factories the size of multiple football fields, machines transform the cotton into T-shirt fabric. Laborers are paid cheap wages here and produce the cloth at discounted prices before passing it on to a woman in Bangladesh.

There, cotton textile manufacturing is king. About 4000 garment factories fill the capital of Dhaka and employ 2.5 million people, mostly women.

The woman making our specific T-shirt arrives at work at 5 a.m. and spends 13 hours at her sewing machine. She is surrounded by younger workers, some under the legal working age of 13.

The woman makes about $25 monthly - the minimum wage - barely enough to afford food and her squalid living conditions.

Still, she works without complaint. Her fear is conditions getting better, because then the company might leave Bangladesh for a place with more employer-friendly laws. If that happens, she would face unemployment, hunger and potentially prostitution to keep her family alive.

So, she finishes the T-shirt and passes it on for its journey across the Pacific. In the hands of dockworkers, the shirt is loaded onto a ship and sent to North America.

In the back of a truck, someone drives it across the country to a shopping mall. It is unloaded and placed on a rack by a teenager.

That teen likely gets minimum wage. Currently, the U.S. federal minimum wage is $7.25.

From there, the item is bought - one of about 1.4 billion cotton T-shirts sold annually in North America. It is pulled over your head. It is thrown in the wash. It begs the question, "Where's it from?"

The short answer would be the store in the mall. But the short answer neither tells us the whole story nor makes us informed consumers.

T-shirts do not just magically appear on hangers. Chances are, they have crossed more borders than you.

(510 words)

The Huffington Post, 6 February 2009,
www.huffingtonpost.com

1 UNDERSTANDING THE TEXT

A Copy and complete the flowchart showing the story of the T-shirt in the article. Then use the flow chart to explain the supply chain to your partner.

EXAMPLE

A child in Uzbekistan picks the cotton. Then the cotton is shipped to ... where ...

Where:	Uzbekistan		...[2]		...[4]			...[8]		
Who:	*a child* [1]		labourers		a woman	...[6]		driver	...[10]	consumers
What:	picks the cotton		...[3]		...[5]	...[7]		...[9]	...[11]	...[12]

B Who from the story might have made these statements?

1 'Why do I only get three cents per kilogram for this crop when it's worth $1.15? Someone is really stuffing their pockets here!'

2 'I hope our government doesn't make any new laws to protect us workers. If they do, my factory's customers will take their business elsewhere, and I will lose my job.'

3 'My pay is the lowest in the country, but since I'm in a developed country and not a developing country, it's not really very low.'

4 'Wow, this T-shirt only costs $6! I suppose some workers might have been exploited, but I'm going to buy it anyway. If I pay more at a different store, the big corporations will pocket the money; their workers won't see any of it.'

2 DISCUSSING GLOBALIZATION

Do you agree with what the consumer in the previous exercise says? Tell your partner why or why not. Use the following phrases.

I agree / I don't agree, because ...
That consumer is right/wrong, because ...
The consumer is partly right.
I agree somewhat.
I strongly disagree.
I think/believe/feel that ...

3 VOCABULARY CHECK: GLOBAL ECONOMY

A Find the following phrases in the people's statements in exercise 1B.

1 verdient sich eine goldene Nase
2 ihre Geschäftsaktivitäten anderswohin verlagern
3 Entwicklungsland
4 einige Arbeiter wurden vielleicht ausgebeutet
5 die Großkonzerne
6 sich das Geld in die eigene Tasche stecken

B Match each word to its definition.

1 afford	a a person or company that produces goods in large quantities
2 conditions	b a person, company or country that sells goods abroad
3 crop	c a large quantity of a farmed plant
4 discounted price	d a reduced charge
5 earnings	e the lowest wage that an employer is allowed to pay by law
6 exporter	f basic ingredient that is used to make a product
7 manufacturer	g not having a job
8 minimum wage	h to have enough money to be able to buy or do something
9 raw material	i the circumstances in which people work or live
10 unemployment	j the amount of money that has been made

4 WRITING A COMMENT

Assess the attitude of your society or of your schoolmates towards consumption. Write 80–100 words and include the following:

- whether or not you think that others are concerned about issues like workers' rights or the environment when they buy products
- arguments and facts to support your opinion
- a consideration of the counter-argument
- a suggestion on how awareness of ethical consumption issues could be improved
- a conclusion in which you briefly repeat your thesis

> Skills, p. 227

5 TALKING ABOUT FAIRTRADE

A Which ethical food label do you know? When you go shopping, how often do you buy foods that carry such labels?

SOIL ASSOCIATION ORGANIC · FAIRTRADE® · RAINFOREST ALLIANCE CERTIFIED · ASSURED FOOD STANDARDS

B Complete the text from the Fairtrade website with the words from the box.

development | health and safety | in advance | long-term | producers | prohibited | salaries | sustainable | union | vote

Fairtrade International (FLO)
http://www.fairtrade.net/
Apple (26) Amazon eBay Yahoo! News (1,448)
English (EN) | Sitemap | Text Size A A A | Search

FAIRTRADE INTERNATIONAL
About us | About Fairtrade | Standards | Products | Producers | Resources | News

The FAIRTRADE Certification Mark is a registered trademark of Fairtrade Labelling Organizations International (FLO). It certifies that products meet the following social, economic and environmental standards set by Fairtrade.

- The majority of the members must be small …[1] who run their farm mainly by using their own and their family's labour. All members have a voice and …[2] in the decision-making process of the organization.
- Forced labour and child labour is …[3].
- Workers have the right to join an independent …[4] to collectively negotiate their working conditions.
- Working conditions are equitable for all workers. …[5] must be equal or higher than the regional average or than the minimum wage in effect. …[6] measures must be established in order to avoid work-related injuries.

Companies trading Fairtrade products must:

- Pay a price to producers that aims to cover the costs of …[7] production: the Fairtrade Minimum Price.
- Pay an additional sum that producers can invest in …[8]: the Fairtrade Premium.
- Partially pay …[9], when producers ask for it.
- Sign contracts that allow for …[10] planning and sustainable production practices.

www.fairtrade.net

C With a partner discuss the benefits of Fairtrade standards to producers, traders, workers and consumers. What, if any, are the drawbacks?

> Webcode: FOBU7A01

B Business and society

BEFORE YOU READ

Many of the clothes and shoes we buy in the West have been produced in so-called sweatshops. What do you know about sweatshops? What are the benefits to the manufacturers? What are the benefits for consumers? What are the consequences for the people who work in the sweatshops?

www.tellusyourviews.co.uk

Work | Leisure | Environment | Technology | Media

Sweatshops: Who wins and who loses?

What do YOU think?

Do we really want to do sport in shoes that have been made by slaves working 24/7 in unhealthy conditions? We all want to save money and everyone likes to find a bargain but I'd rather pay more for my running shoes than know that some poor kid in a faraway country is being exploited. Sweatshop workers often do not earn enough money to buy the products that they make.

Ethical Ed

I don't agree with Ethical Ed. Even though wages and working conditions look poor compared to the standards of developed nations, the money is better and the jobs themselves are actually improvements over what the people worked at before. The other thing that gets forgotten is that the multinationals who use sweatshops are helping the local economy.

Think About It

It's naive to argue that multinationals help the economies of poor countries. The truth is that many of the multinationals who use sweatshops do not pay taxes in the foreign country, so they don't contribute anything to the host country's tax revenue. Apart from that, many of these sweatshops do not care about ecological standards. They pollute the water supplies and the air with the chemicals they use in production.

Critical Consumer

Come on, it's not just the multinationals who win. The workers benefit, as they can earn a wage, allowing them to feed their families. Consumers benefit as they can get high quality shoes and other garments at a lower cost than stuff that is made in Europe. I earn a very low wage and I could not afford to buy clothes for my kids if there were no sweatshops.

SingleMum

When I started here I was 14 years old. I was glad to find work. Yes, we work long hours and the work is hard, and we also get paid less than workers in the West. But we're all well off by Thai standards and, more importantly, we have work that is dignified. We don't have to work on the streets.

MaiThai

MaiThai is lucky. She's not one of the 200 million slave labourers in the world who have been robbed of their childhood. In my job, I've seen nine-year-old coal miners, eight-year-old prostitutes, and children who work 18 hour shifts 7 days a week in sweatshops in the most awful conditions. A whole range of goods produced by child labourers is sold in the west, including textiles, carpets and toys. Why do we turn a blind eye to this exploitation of children? When we buy products made by children, we are supporting slavery.

Campaigner

www.anti-slaverysociety.com

(428 words)

1 UNDERSTANDING THE TEXT

The editor of the forum cut the final sentence from each of the statements. Match the sentences below to the posts.

a Everybody benefits from sweatshops.
b I get a feeling of self-respect from the work I do.
c Multinational companies should operate according to international labour agreements and environmental laws.
d Some workers are paid only 24 cents for each pair of $50 shoes they produce.
e What is the cost of these goods? For us, they are cheap; for the child who has made them, the price is his life.
f Making shoes is a much better option than subsistence farming, picking over rubbish tips or prostitution.

2 VOCABULARY CHECK: MANUFACTURING ABROAD

Rewrite the sentences below replacing the expressions in *italics* with synonyms from the text. The synonymous expressions are in the same order in the text. You may have to change the sentence structure.

1 The sweatshop workers are *treated in a bad way so that someone else can benefit.*
2 If you buy cheap clothes, you might *boost the supply of money in a particular region.*
3 Some of the factories do not follow the *rules for protecting the environment.*
4 My father works for *very little money* so he doesn't have the money to buy us expensive clothes.
5 Some sweatshop workers *earn enough money to live compared to other people in their country.*
6 The goods are cheap, but *we are ignoring* the fact that they are made by slaves.

3 WRITING A FORUM POST

Choose one of the following tasks.

1 A German friend of yours wishes to join the discussion on the forum but is unable to speak any English. Use his notes to write his post in English.

> *Ich habe nicht viel Geld.*
> *Ich kaufe deswegen lieber weniger Markenware und eher billige Klamotten.*
> *Aber kann es sein, dass die Sweatshop-Arbeiter dann noch schädlicheren Tätigkeiten nachgehen müssen, um ihren Lebensunterhalt zu bestreiten?*

2 Write to one of the people in the forum telling them ...

> what you think about their post.
> what you think about cheap sports garments and why.

> Webcode: FOBU7B01

C Task options

2 10

A Listen to the song, then work with a partner and study the lyrics. Find references to the conditions of banana plantation workers at the time the song was sung.

The Banana Boat Song, a calypso which became popular in the 1950s, was based on a folk song which plantation workers sang as they loaded bunches of bananas into boats for transport abroad. The words of the song are written and sung in the local dialect.

Jamican-American singer Harry Belafonte in 1957

Banana Boat Song

Day, me say day-ay-ay-o
Daylight come and me wan' go home
Day, me say day, me say day, me say day
Daylight come and me wan' go home

Work all night on a drink of rum
Daylight come and me wan' go home
Stack banana till de morning come
Daylight come and me wan' go home

Come, Mister tally man, tally me banana
Daylight come and me wan' go home
Come, Mister tally man, tally me banana
Daylight come and me wan' go home

Lift six foot, seven foot, eight foot bunch
Daylight come and me wan' go home
Six foot, seven foot, eight foot bunch
Daylight come and me wan' go home

Day, me say day-ay-ay-o
Daylight come and me wan' go home
Day, me say day, me say day, me say day
Daylight come and me wan' go home

A beautiful bunch of ripe banana
Daylight come and me wan' go home
Hide the deadly black tarantula
Daylight come and me wan' go home

Jamaican plantation in the 1950s

Calypso: a style of Afro-Caribbean music which originated in Trinidad and Tobago. The roots of calypso lie in the arrival of enslaved Africans. As they were not allowed to speak with each other, the slaves communicated through song. After the abolition of slavery in 1865, workers continued to work on plantations – and they continued to sing. In the 1950s, Harry Belafonte, an American singer with Jamaican roots, achieved worldwide success with his album, Calypso, which was the first album to sell over one million copies. The words of old calypsos give us an insight into social and/or political conditions in the years they were recorded. Today, calypsos are sung at carnival time and continue to provide satirical comments on current affairs.

Mister tally man: the overseer who counts (or 'tallies') the numbers and weights of the bunches of bananas the worker brings to the ship

Tarantula: a poisonous spider that lives in bunches of bananas

B **Read the background briefing text about banana production. In groups, talk about the conditions of banana plantation workers today and in the 1950s. What, if anything, has changed since the song was written? Make notes.**

BACKGROUND BRIEFING **Banana production**

Bananas are one of the most commonly eaten foods in the world. The trees grow wild in many tropical countries where people pick the fruit and use the leaves as plates and for wrapping food for cooking on open fires. The first commercial plantations which were used to produce bananas for export were set up by Portuguese colonists in the Atlantic Islands, Brazil and western Africa in the 15th and 16th centuries.

Plantation workers in Costa Rica

In the 1870s, modern transportation networks of steamships and railroads started to make it easier for producers to distribute bananas. Soon, companies like today's multinationals Chiquita Brands International and Dole began to ship bananas all over the world.

Whereas bananas used to be very expensive, today a carton of bananas weighing 18.4 kilos sells for about 18 dollars in an international market. Plantation workers earn between 5 and 15 dollars a day depending on the weather conditions and on the density of the crop. A banana plant grows to between 6 and 7.5 metres in height. A bunch of bananas can weigh from 30 to 50 kilos.

Workers in the processing area

The average banana plantation worker starts work at 5 a.m. and works until 6 p.m. with a 30 minute lunch break. Employees could take more breaks but it would cost them too much.

Until the 1980s, extremely toxic chemicals were used to kill pests and weeds. The chemicals were sprayed onto the plants – and the workers – from planes above the plantations. Today, ethical groups try to make sure that plantation owners apply standards which protect the environment and the workers.

C **Choose another product and research the conditions under which it is produced, then present your findings to the class. Make your presentation as interesting as possible by using pictures, a song or an excerpt from a film.** Skills, p. 231

D Grammar checkpoint

1 RELATIVE CLAUSES AND CONTACT CLAUSES

> Grammar Summary, p. 248

Complete the text with relative pronouns. Which relative pronouns in the text can be omitted (*weggelassen*)?

Fair Trade versus Food Miles

When you're shopping, are you one of these people *who/that*[1] looks for the Fairtrade logo? Buying goods ...[2] carry an ethical food label reassures us that we're supporting poor workers, most ...[3] live in faraway countries. It's nice to know that we're helping.

But, stop! Before you put that packet of organic beans into your trolley, how do you deal with the food miles – the distance ...[4] the food has travelled before it gets to the supermarket? Is it a good idea to choose food ...[5] has been brought to Europe on a plane ...[6] emitted tons of CO_2 into the atmosphere? And that's not the end of the journey. After the plane landed, the goods were loaded into refrigerated trucks ...[7] spewed out fumes as they travelled along the motorways to the supermarket. Apart from the pollution ...[8] is destroying the atmosphere, long-distance transportation of food means extra packaging, ...[9] uses up resources.

Aidan Young, ...[10] organization 'Buy Local' campaigns for regional products, says: 'Why do we import food ...[11] we could easily grow ourselves?' It's a question ...[12] everyone ...[13] is concerned about the problems ...[14] are caused by pollution should ask themselves.

2 GERUND/INFINITIVE

> Grammar Summary, p. 245

Complete the sentences with the correct form of the verb in brackets.

1 Julie avoids *wearing* (*wear*) clothes that are made in sweatshops.

2 Can you imagine ... (work) 18 hours a day in a noisy, dirty factory?

3 John has decided ... (*look for*) T-shirts made from ethically-grown cotton.

4 The factory owner gave up ... (*employ*) underage workers last year.

5 I don't enjoy ... (*shop*) at the supermarket. I prefer ... (*shop*) at the local market.

6 The supermarket has stopped ... (*sell*) Fairtrade coffee. People can't afford ... (*buy*) it.

7 She asked me ... (*make sure*) the beans were local but I forgot ... (*check*) the label.

8 I don't remember ... (*see*) strawberries in the shops at Christmas when I was a child. I refuse ... (*buy*) them.

Secretarial activities

Page	File	Title
108	A	Writing e-mails
114	B	Telephoning and voicemail
118	C	Making appointments
122	D	Travel arrangements
126	E	Hotel reservations
131	F	Welcoming a visitor

Commercial correspondence

Page	File	Title
134	1	The layout of business letters
140	2	Enquiries
147	3	Offers
154	4	Orders and acknowledgements
165	5	Payments and reminders
175	6	Complaints
184	7	Job applications
193	8	Business glossary

Writing e-mails

Meet Top Act Event Management

Top Act Event Management GmbH in Düsseldorf has the task of organizing a three-day sales conference in Düsseldorf for Cherry Solutions Incorporated, a major American software developer. Representatives from all over Europe are coming to Germany to take part in the conference. Nina Wittstock, Top Act's chief executive officer, plans to invite a celebrity speaker.

1 Read Nina's e-mail to a famous rock star and complete the sentences.

To:	"Rob Heldof" <call_me_rob@boomrats.com>
Subject:	"Get the world online" conference in Düsseldorf, Germany, 01–04 May 20..
Cc:	"Bill Hampton, President" <bill.hampton@cherry-sol.com>
Attachment(s):	Programme Düsseldorf Conference.pdf

Dear Rob

I hope you had a good trip back home to Ireland after speaking at the World Aids Day meeting in South Africa last month. Many thanks for finding the time to talk about coming to Düsseldorf to be a guest speaker at Cherry Solutions' annual convention in May.

The theme this year is 'Get the world online' and I know how passionately you support Internet access for poor countries and the 'One laptop per child' charity. Our brochure on this year's programme is attached for your information.

Please let us know when you would be available and what your fee would be. All travel and hotel expenses will, of course, be paid by Cherry Solutions Incorporated.

I very much look forward to welcoming you to Düsseldorf in May.

Best wishes

Nina
Chief Executive Officer
Top Act Event Management

Top Act Event Management GmbH, Düsseldorf, Registergericht Düsseldorf, HRB 4920,
Geschäftsführerin: Nina Wittstock

1 Rob Heldof is a celebrity from ...
2 Last month he was in ...
3 Nina wants Rob to speak in ...
4 The conference is about ...
5 Cherry Solutions Incorporated will pay Rob's ...

2 **Rob forwards Nina's e-mail to Zoe Kline, his personal assistant. Say if the statements under this e-mail are true or false. Correct the false statements.**

To:	"Zoe" <zoe.kline@boomrats.com>
Subject:	Re: "Get the world online" conference in Düsseldorf, Germany, 01–04 May 20..
Cc:	
Attachment(s):	Programme Düsseldorf Conference.pdf

Hi Zoe

I've just got this e-mail from Top Act.

Tell them Thursday 01 May's OK. 8 pm is a good time and I'll be with Lily, so we'll need a double room in a hotel nearby but just for one night because we're off to Rio the next day.

Can they pick us up at the airport about 2 hours before? I'll make the usual speech and I don't want a fee for this but they'll have to pay my expenses and donate €50,000 to OLPC. Could you make that clear to them?

If there are any problems, just give me a ring.

Atb

Rob

1 Rob wrote to Top Act.

2 Rob is flying to Brazil alone.

3 Rob will get €5,000 for speaking at the conference.

4 Rob wants Zoe to call him if there is a problem.

3 **Read Zoe's e-mail to Nina and finish the sentences on the next page with the right answers.**

To:	"Nina Wittstock, Top Act Event Management GmbH" <nina.wittstock@top-act.de>
Subject:	Re: "Get the world online" conference in Düsseldorf, Germany, 01–04 May 20..
Cc:	"Rob Heldof" <call_me_rob@boomrats.com>
Attachment(s):	OLPC_mission_statement.pdf

Dear Ms Wittstock

Rob is currently touring with his band and has asked me to reply to your kind invitation on his behalf.

He will be delighted to speak at the convention and suggests 8 pm on 01 May. His speech will be entitled 'Mission or Market?' and will deal with the Third World project 'One laptop per child' http://laptop.org/en/vision/index.shtml. OLPC's mission statement is attached to this mail.

Rob will be with his partner (Lily Boyd) and would like to be picked up at Dusseldorf Airport and taken to the venue about two hours before his speech. As regards accommodation, he will require a double room for one night in a comfortable hotel not too far away. I would also point out that he is a vegetarian.

Apart from payment of expenses, Rob charges no fee for such appearances but requires the company in question to make a donation of €50,000 to 'One laptop per child'.

Please confirm that you agree to these terms. I will then let you have details of Rob's flight times and any other information required.

Best regards

Zoe Kline
Personal Assistant to Rob Heldof

1 Zoe Kline
   a works for Nina Wittstock.
   b works for Rob Heldof.
   c is Rob's girlfriend.

2 Rob
   a is too busy to reply to Nina's e-mail personally.
   b doesn't want to reply to Nina's e-mail.
   c doesn't want to speak at the conference.

3 Rob's hotel room should be
   a at Düsseldorf Airport.
   b about two hours away from Düsseldorf Airport.
   c near the venue.

4 Rob wants to give poor children
   a money.
   b vegetarian food.
   c laptops.

How to write e-mails

More than 90% of businesses use e-mail because it is quick, convenient and cheap. Here are some important things to remember before you hit 'send'.

To:	
Subject:	
Cc:	
Attachment(s):	

Salutation
Body
Complimentary close

Subject (Betreff):
This is the same as for a business letter. Begin with a capital letter and keep it short.

Cc: 'carbon copy' (Kopie)

Writing the e-mail
Most mistakes are made here: *E-mails are not always informal.* Like business letters they can be formal or informal but unlike business letters they can be sent to thousands of recipients by mistake.

Salutation / Complimentary close
If you do not know your business partner, use one of the polite forms below. If the relationship becomes more friendly, your business partner will start using informal forms and you should then do the same. Let your business partner take the initiative.

	Salutation	Complimentary close
Polite	Dear Ms Brown Dear Mrs Brown Dear Miss Brown Dear Mr Brown Dear Dr Brown	Regards Best regards Best wishes Yours sincerely
Friendly	Good morning James Dear Kim Dear Kim and Jim	Regards Best regards Best wishes
Informal	Hello Kim Hi Kim Kim	All the best (Atb) Best Cheers Must rush

Body of the e-mail
Tips for better communication:
> Start the e-mail with a capital letter.
> Never use text message short forms (CUL8R, etc.).

- Write in paragraphs separated by a free line.
- If you write back in the spaces between the lines of the original e-mail and/or in a different colour,
  - do not use red
  - do not underline words
  - do not write in **bold letters**
  - do not write in CAPITALS
  - do not use exclamation marks!

  because it sounds as if you are angry or think the reader is stupid.
- Most e-mails are read on-screen, so keep yours as short as possible.

Points of style

Use short forms to be friendly (I've, we'll, he'd etc.) and long forms to be more formal.

Finishing the e-mail

If you know your business partner well, it is enough to sign off with your first name. If you do not, add your position and the name of your company under it.

Useful phrases

Starting an e-mail	**Einleitung**
How are things? I hope you're well. I hope you had a good trip to ... I am writing to ... (ask for information on ... / book a room for ... / confirm that ...).	Wie läuft's? / Wie geht's? Hoffentlich geht es dir/Ihnen gut. Hoffentlich hattest du / hatten Sie eine gute Reise nach ... Ich schreibe ... (mit der Bitte um Informationen über ... / um ein Zimmer für ... zu reservieren / um zu bestätigen, dass ...).
Answering or forwarding an e-mail	**Eine E-Mail beantworten oder weiterleiten**
I was delighted to receive your mail ... Many thanks for your mail ... (about / inviting me to ...). I've just got ... (your e-mail / an e-mail from ... / a phone call from ...).	Ich habe mich sehr über deine/Ihre E-Mail ... gefreut. Vielen Dank für deine/Ihre E-Mail (über ... / mit einer Einladung zu ...). Eben habe ...(ich deine/Ihre E-Mail / eine E-Mail von ... / einen Anruf von ...) erhalten.
Getting to the point	**Auf den Punkt kommen**
I'd/We'd/They'd like to know ... (if/what/..., e.g. if you'll be arriving after midnight). I'm pleased/delighted to accept ... (your invitation / your offer). My plane/train arrives at ...	Ich/Wir/Sie möchte(n) wissen, (ob/was/..., z. B. ob Sie nach Mitternacht eintreffen werden). (Sehr) gerne nehme ich (deine/Ihre Einladung / dein/Ihr Angebot) an. Mein Flugzeug landet um ... / Mein Zug kommt um ... an.
Request	**Anfrage**
Please let me have some information on ... Could you tell me if/what/... ? Could someone ... (e.g. pick me/us up at the airport)? Would you send us ..., please?	Bitte schicken Sie mir Informationen zu ... Würden Sie mir bitte mitteilen, ob/was/... ? Könnte jemand ... (z. B. mich/uns am Flughafen abholen)? Würden Sie uns bitte ... schicken?

Giving information	Auskunft erteilen
Please refer to the attachment for ... (e.g. the timetable for the visit). Click the link for more details / directions to ... (e.g. the hotel).	... (z. B. das Programm für Ihren Besuch) kann der Anlage entnommen werden. Klicke / Klicken Sie auf den Link, um weitere Einzelheiten / eine Wegbeschreibung ... (z. B. zum Hotel) zu erhalten.
Closing sentence	**Schlusssatz**
Many thanks for your assistance ... Looking forward to ... I/We look forward to ... (meeting you / your friends). Please let me know what your plans are.	Vielen Dank für deine/Ihre Hilfe. Ich freue mich auf ... Ich/Wir freuen uns darauf, (dich / Sie / deine/ Ihre Freunde kennen zu lernen). Lass mich bitte / Bitte lassen Sie mich wissen, was du für Pläne hast / Sie für Pläne haben.

4 Use the useful phrases to write an e-mail.

Situation

Sie sind Helena Sawicki, Nina Wittstocks Assistentin. Sie haben inzwischen mehrere E-Mails mit Robs Personalassistentin, Zoe Kline, ausgetauscht. Heute ruft das Steigenberger Park-Hotel in Düsseldorf an und möchte wissen, ob Rob und Lily nach 23:00 Uhr eine vegetarische Mahlzeit im Hotelrestaurant einnehmen möchten, denn die Küche schließt normalerweise um diese Zeit, würde aber extra für Rob geöffnet bleiben. Der Chefkoch schlägt Spargel (*asparagus*) vor, ist aber selbstverständlich bereit, Robs Wünschen zu entsprechen.

Aufgabe

Sie sind Helena Sawicki. Schreiben Sie eine freundliche E-Mail folgenden Inhalts an Zoe Kline.

> Bezug auf telefonische Anfrage des Steigenberger Park-Hotels in Düsseldorf
> Bitte um Mitteilung, ob Rob und Lily planen, nach der Tagung im Hotel zu essen
> Der Chefkoch schlägt Spargel vor (*the chef suggests ...*), wird aber natürlich das kochen, was Rob möchte.
> Das Hotel bittet um eine kurze Mitteilung, sollten Rob und Lily nach 23:00 Uhr essen wollen.
> Angemessene Verabschiedung

5 Use the useful phrases to write an e-mail.

Situation

Nach der Tagung in Düsseldorf erhält Nina Wittstock folgende Einladung von Rob Heldof nach Irland. Nina ist begeistert und schreibt sofort an Rob zurück.

To:	"Nina Wittstock" <Nina.wittstock@top-act.de>
Subject:	Weekend break in Ireland? 06–08 August 20..
Cc:	"Zoe" <zoe.kline@boomrats.com>
Attachment(s):	Directions to Barrywood Castle.pdf

Hi Nina

Dusseldorf was great fun and I think OLPC is going to get some more donations now. Thanks for your support!

I'm writing to invite you to spend a weekend at my place in the beautiful Irish countryside near Cork. Some good friends of mine are coming and they would very much like to meet you. Bring a friend if you like – the more the merrier!

Click on the link for directions to my house. You can't miss it!

http://www.panoramio.com/photo/25335149

Must rush

Rob

Aufgabe

Als Nina Wittstock schreiben Sie Ihre Antwort an Rob mit Kopie an Helena Sawicki unter Berücksichtigung folgender Punkte:

- Informelle Anrede
- Sie nehmen die Einladung dankend an.
- Sie möchten Ihren Lebensgefährten Barry Black mitbringen.
- Kann man Sie am Flughafen abholen?
- Ankunft 15:15 Uhr am 06.08.20.. am Cork International Airport
- Sie freuen sich darauf, seine Freunde kennen zu lernen.
- Angemessene Verabschiedung

B

Secretarial Activities

Telephoning and voicemail

Nina Wittstock is the chief executive officer of Top Act Event Management in Düsseldorf. Today she is trying to contact a celebrity speaker for an event in Düsseldorf.

2 11

1 Use words from the box to complete the dialogue and then listen to the recording to check your answers.

calling | hold | message | number | speak to | this is | unavailable | urgent

VOICE: Thank you for calling Rob Heldof's press office. If you wish to contact his fan club, press 1. If you wish to leave a ... [1], press 2. If you wish to make a donation to a Rob Heldof charity, press 3. For all other calls, please press zero and ... [2] the line.
NINA: I hate these automatic systems! Come on! This is important.
ZOE: Good afternoon and thank you for calling Rob Heldof's press office. How can I help?
NINA: Hello, ... [3] Nina Wittstock from Top Act Event Management in Germany. I'd like to ... ... [4] Rob about the conference in May.
ZOE: Well, I'm very sorry, Ms Wittstock, but Rob is ... [5] at the moment. He's actually at his castle in Ireland and it's quite hard to reach him there.
NINA: I see. Well it's very ... [6].
ZOE: Can I take a message?
NINA: No thanks. I'll try him on his mobile.
ZOE: Well, I wish you good luck! Have you got his ... [7]?
NINA: Yes, I've got it, thanks.
ZOE: Good. Please let me know if there's anything else I can do for you.
NINA: OK, I will.
ZOE: Thanks for ... [8]. Goodbye, Ms Wittstock.
NINA: Bye.

2 12

2 Now Nina calls Rob on his mobile. Listen to the dialogue and fill in the missing words.

ROB: Hello?
NINA: Hello Rob. It's Nina ... [1]! How are you?
ROB: Fine thanks, and you?
NINA: Fine. Is this a ... [2] time to call you, Rob?
ROB: It's fine. I'm out in the countryside taking a ... .
NINA: Sorry, I didn't quite ... [3] that.
ROB: I'm taking a walk in the countryside.
NINA: Oh I see! You're taking a walk in the countryside. That sounds great! Anyway, I just wanted to ... [4] that everything was all right for the conference.
ROB: I'm sorry but I didn't quite catch that, Nina. You're ... [5] up.
NINA: This must be a bad ... [6].
ROB: OK, it's a bit better now. Go ... [7].

NINA: As I was saying, I just wanted to check that everything was all right for the conference.

ROB: This is no good, Nina! I'm ... [8] I can't hear you! Call ... on the landline. Did you ... [9] that?

NINA: Call who?

ROB: Zoe! Call Zoe on the landline. OK?

NINA: Well, actually, I've just called Zoe and ...

ROB: That's right! Call Zoe!

NINA: OK! ... [10] do that.

ROB: Nice talking to you, Nina! Bye.

NINA: Bye.

3 Find two expressions in the dialogues for each of the following headings.

You answer the phone → You say who you are → You say why you're calling → You offer to help the other person → You finish the phone call

4 Match the meanings on the left with the expressions from the dialogues on the right.

1 wait
2 Hurry up!
3 not able to come to the phone
4 I can't hear every word clearly
5 very important
6 Are you free to talk?
7 I didn't hear what you said
8 I understand
9 Please do what you wanted to do
10 Did you hear what I said?

a urgent
b Did you get that?
c I didn't catch that
d Go ahead
e unavailable
f hold the line
g I see
h You're breaking up
i Come on!
j Is this a good time to call you?

2 13

5 Nina tells her PA, Helena Sawicki, to phone for her. Helena gets Zoe's voicemail and leaves a message. Listen to the recording and complete the sentences below.

1 Helena phones ...
2 If she wants to be contacted she must ...
3 Helena's number is ...
4 Nina's number is ...

2 14

6 Helena gets an interesting phone call. Listen to the recording and choose the correct statements.

1 Helena speaks to
 a Rob Heldof.
 b Zoe Kline.
 c Nina Wittstock.

2 Rob wants
 a to contact the other speakers.
 b to contact the other guests.
 c the names of the other speakers.

Saying telephone numbers

0 is 'oh' or 'zero'.
00 is 'double oh' or 'zero, zero'.

Say each number separately:
0172 is 'oh-one-seven-two' or 'zero-one-seven-two'.
+ 49 is 'plus four-nine'.

3 Helena
   a will e-mail the information needed.
   b cannot e-mail the information needed.
   c has e-mailed the information needed.

4 Rob Heldof is coming to the conference in Düsseldorf
   a alone.
   b with Lily.
   c without Lily.

5 He will be flying to Germany
   a from the UK.
   b from Los Angeles.
   c from Ireland.

6 Before the conference in Düsseldorf, Top Act
   a will pick Rob up at the airport.
   b will pick Rob up at his hotel.
   c won't pick Rob up.

Spelling words on the phone

D is capital 'd' or upper-case 'd'.
d is small 'd' or lower-case 'd'.
Use the spelling alphabet to spell difficult word like 'Xavier':
That's capital 'x' for X-ray, 'a' for alpha, 'v' for Victor, 'i' for India, 'e' for echo and 'r' for Romeo.

The spelling alphabet

A	Alpha	N	November
B	Bravo	O	Oscar
C	Charlie	P	Papa
D	Delta	Q	Quebec
E	Echo	R	Romeo
F	Foxtrot	S	Sierra
G	Golf	T	Tango
H	Hotel	U	Uniform
I	India	V	Victor
J	Juliet	W	Whisky
K	Kilo	X	X-ray
L	Lima	Y	Yankee
M	Mike	Z	Zulu

Useful phrases

Answering the phone

Top Act Limited. Good morning. How can I help?
What can I do for you?
Hello?
Speaking.

Saying who you are

It's Nina Wittstock from ...
It's Nina calling.

Saying why you're calling

Can I speak to ..., please? / Am I speaking to ...?
I'd like to speak to ... about ...
I just wanted to (check that ...).
I'd like to know ... (if/what/...).
I'm just calling to ask you ... (if/what/about/...).
Could you tell me ... (if/what/...)

Reacting to what you hear

I see. (*anything*)
That's great/marvellous! (*good thing*)
Oh dear! (*bad thing*)
Oh really! (*surprise*)

Apologizing

I'm (very) sorry but ...
I'm afraid I can't ...

Poor connection

I'm sorry but you're breaking up.
This must be a bad connection.
Did you get that?

Person is not available

... is unavailable at the moment.
... is out of the office.

Promising action

I'll ... / I'll do that.
We'll get back to you as soon as possible.

Offering help

Can I take a message?
Is there anything else I can help you with?
Please let me know if there's anything else I can do for you.

Finishing the call

Thanks for calling.
Nice talking to you.
Talk to you soon.
Bye.
Goodbye,
Have a nice day.

7 With a partner use the table of useful phrases to write or act out the following dialogue.

A Helena Sawicki (PA to Nina Wittstock at Top Act Event Management)	B Lily Boyd (Rob Heldof's partner)
1 Answer the phone.	
	2 Say who you are and ask to speak to Nina Wittstock.
3 Apologize and explain that Ms Wittstock isn't available at the moment.	
	4 Tell her it's urgent.
5 Offer to take a message.	
	6 Tell her you'd like to know why you haven't received a plane ticket for the Düsseldorf conference.
7 Promise to pass on the message and get back to her.	
	8 Finish the call.
9 Thank her for calling and wish her a nice day.	

8 With a partner use the table of useful phrases to act out the following dialogue.

Partner A

You are DJ 60 Cent, a famous American rapper. Today you get a call from Top Act Event Management in Düsseldorf on your mobile phone. Follow the steps below to play your role. (Partner B has steps 2, 4, 6 and 8.)

1 Answer your mobile phone.
3 Say you're the person she wants and ask what you can do for her.
5 Say you have received it and will sign and send it back.
7 Finish the call.

Partner B

Go to file 16 on page 215.

9 Follow the instructions to leave a voicemail message.

Sie sind Nina Wittstock. Top Act Event Management hat den amerikanischen Rapper DJ 60 Cent für einen Auftritt in Düsseldorf engagiert. Er hat gebeten, dass man ihm telefonisch mitteilt, um wie viel Uhr sein Auftritt ist. Da er nicht ans Telefon geht, hinterlassen Sie ihm eine Nachricht folgenden Inhalts.

> Sie geben Ihren Namen, den Ihrer Firma und Ihre Handy-Nr. (+49 176 ...) an.
> Er wollte wissen, wann er am Samstagabend dran ist (*when you're on*).
> Er ist nach *Ethnoscream* dran um ca. 23 Uhr.
> Er möge Sie wissen lassen, wenn Sie sonst noch etwas für ihn tun können.
> Sie wünschen ihm einen schönen Tag.

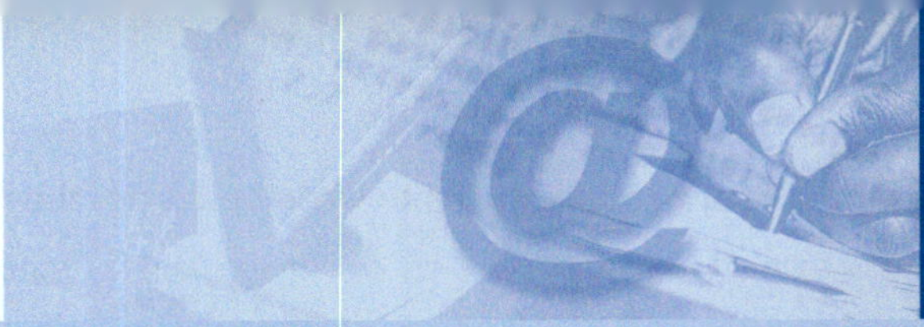

C

Secretarial Activities

Making appointments

Helena Sawicki works for Top Act Event Management. She is personal assistant to Nina Wittstock, the company's chief executive officer (CEO). Top Act has the task of organizing a three-day international sales conference in Düsseldorf for Cherry Solutions Incorporated, a major American software developer. Bob Heldof, a famous rock star, is to speak at the meeting. Today Helena phones Zoe, Rob's personal assistant, to make an appointment for a press conference when he arrives in Düsseldorf.

2 15

1 Use the diaries on the following page to select the correct words in the telephone dialogue below. Then listen to the recording to check your answers.

ZOE: Good morning and thank you for calling Rob Heldof's press office. How can I help?

HELENA: Hello, it's Helena Sawicki in Germany. Is that Zoe?

ZOE: Yes, it is. Nice to talk to you again, Helena.

HELENA: Nice to talk to you too, Zoe. I'm just calling to ask you about holding a press conference with Rob Heldof when he comes here in May. Nina Wittstock wants one either before or after his speech on Thursday *afternoon / evening* [1] and she'd also like him to go on a breakfast *TV / radio* [2] show the next day.

ZOE: Oh right. Just let me look at his diary. I have it here on my phone. OK, go ahead.

HELENA: When does Rob arrive in Düsseldorf on the first?

ZOE: He arrives in the *morning / afternoon* [3] but he'll have jet lag.

HELENA: Oh I see. How about a press conference at six o'clock in the afternoon *after / before* [4] his speech?

ZOE: He's going *shopping / sightseeing* [5] with Katie in the afternoon. That'll take about three hours at least. What about 11 o'clock after the conference?

HELENA: I'm afraid that won't work out because he's having a *meeting / a meal* [6] then. How about Friday morning at about 10 a.m.?

ZOE: I'm not sure. He wants to buy some new sunglasses for Rio. And then his flight is at *12.00 / 1.30* [7].

HELENA: I see. OK. Let's look at Thursday again. What about after his *dinner / speech* [8] at about 9.30 p.m.?

ZOE: Yes, he's free then but let's make it ten o'clock to give him a bit more time.

HELENA: Great!

ZOE: I'll check with him and get back to you.

HELENA: That's marvellous. Oh, and please ask him if he wants to go on the breakfast show on *Thursday / Friday* [9] morning.

ZOE: What time would that be?

HELENA: It starts at 6.30 a.m. but how about *eight / nine* [10] o'clock?

ZOE: Mmm, I'm not sure. I'll ask him and get back to you as soon as possible. Talk to you soon. Bye.

HELENA: Bye.

Terminkalender Nina Wittstock

Mai 20..	Mai 20..
Donnerstag 01	Freitag 02
09:00	07:00 Chat, chat, chat breakfast TV (bis 09:00 Uhr) + Rob um 08:00?
10:00	08:00
11:00	09:00 Pressekonferenz mit Rob?
12:00	10:00 Pressekonferenz mit Rob?
13:00	11:00 Frühstück Peter Raffay
14:00	12:00
15:00	13:00
16:00	14:00
17:00	15:00 Tennis
18:00 Pressekonferenz mit Rob?	16:00
19:00 Pressekonferenz mit Rob?	17:00
20:00 Vortrag Rob H.	18:00
21:00 Pressekonferenz mit Rob?	19:00
22:00 Pressekonferenz mit Rob?	20:00
23:00 Ethnoscream	
23:30 Restaurant Steigenberger Park-Hotel	21:00 Boxkampf ESPRIT Arena Düsseldorf
00:00	00:00 Empfang VIP Lounge

Rob Heldof's diary on Zoe Kline's smartphone

Thursday	01/05/20... ▶
Time	**Appointments**
09:00 am	9.05 am Arrive DUS
10:00 am	
11:00 am	
12:00 am	
01:00 pm	
02:00 pm	
03:00 pm	
04:00 pm	Shopping with Katie
05:00 pm	Shopping with Katie
06:00 pm	Shopping with Katie
07:00 pm	Shopping with Katie
08:00 pm	Speech
09:00 pm	
10:00 pm	
11:00 pm	Dinner at hotel
00:00 pm	restaurant
Priority	**To do**
High	**Read through speech for DUS**
Low	**Check weather in DUS**
	Don't forget
Jet lag!!!	

Friday	02/05/20... ▶
Time	**Appointments**
07:00 am	
08:00 am	
09:00 am	
10:00 am	Buy sunglasses!
11:00 pm	
12:00 pm	
01:00 pm	1.30 pm DUS Fly to Rio (21 hrs!!!)
02:00 pm	
03:00 pm	
04:00 pm	
05:00 pm	
06:00 pm	
07:00 pm	
08:00 pm	
09:00 pm	
10:00 pm	
Priority	**To do**
High	**Buy sunglasses**
Low	**Check weather in Rio**
	Don't forget

2 16

2 Nina Wittstock phones Rob Heldof at the airport. Listen to the phone call and then say if the following statements are true or false. Correct the false statements.

1 Rob arrives at Düsseldorf Airport in the afternoon.
2 Rob's girlfriend isn't with him.
3 Rob's girlfriend is ill.
4 Rob is ill.
5 Rob is free this afternoon.
6 Nina wants to have the press conference earlier.
7 Nina wants to have the press conference at 8 p.m.
8 The conference will be in a TV studio.
9 Britt Elsner will e-mail Rob later.
10 Nina is tired and wants to get some sleep now.

Useful phrases

Suggesting a meeting

I'd like to make an appointment at ... (*time*) on ... (*day*).
What about ... (e.g. having lunch, meeting at the airport)?
Would you/he/she be able to (e.g. talk on our show tomorrow)?
Would it be possible to meet ... (e.g. while you're/he's/she's here / in town)?

Suggesting a time

How about ... (e.g. meeting at 2 p.m.)? It'll take about ... (e.g. three hours)
How about ... (e.g. 9.30) at ... (e.g. the hotel reception / the airport)?
Would you/he/she be available ... (e.g. tomorrow morning at seven)?
Do you / Does he/she have time to meet later today / tomorrow?

Checking availability

Just let me look at my/his/her diary.
What time would that be?
I'm not sure. I'll check. / I'll get back to you.

Declining

I'm afraid that won't work out because ... (e.g. he's having a meal / he's going shopping).
That time's bad for me/him/her, I'm afraid.
How about 9.30 instead?

Accepting

Yes, I'm/he's/she's free then.
I've/He's/ She's got nothing/something on this afternoon / that day / then.
Let's make it ... (e.g. 2.15 p.m.). That will give me/him/her a bit more time.

Finishing the conversation

Great! Thank you very much.
That's marvellous!
I really appreciate it.
I/We look forward to seeing you/him/her then.

3 With a partner, role-play this situation.

Partner A
You are Britt Elsner and you have a TV chat show from 5.30–9.00 a.m. on Friday morning. At 4 p.m. on Thursday afternoon you phone Rob Heldof and arrange an appointment with him to talk on your show. You would like him to come on first at 7.25 a.m. before three other guests. They are Mr Smarty, the famous German rapper; Natasha Merck, the famous German model; and a Catholic priest from Düsseldorf called Father Hubert. You want Rob to be on your show for at least half an hour, so the latest time is 8.30 a.m. The topic is giving money to charity.

Partner B
Go to file 15 on page 215.

4 With a partner, role-play this situation.

Partner A
You are Father Hubert. You have just been on a TV chat show together with Rob Heldof. It's 10.30 a.m. after the show. You phone Rob to ask him to autograph a T-shirt that you want to auction for charity (suggest a charity, e.g. SOS Kinderdorf).

Suggest meeting him

- at his hotel in Düsseldorf
- somewhere in Düsseldorf city centre (e.g. at [Calvin Klein] boutique with designer sunglasses)
- at Düsseldorf Airport this afternoon.

Partner B
Go to file 19 on page 216.

5 With a partner, role-play this situation.

Partner A
You are Natasha Merck, the famous German model. A week after the TV talk show where you met Rob Heldof, you are in Rio de Janeiro on a photo shoot for a famous fashion designer.

You are modelling summer fashions. You have Rob's business card and this morning you phone him on his mobile to arrange to meet. You want to talk about a boycott of real fur in fur coats (you know Rob is a vegetarian). Suggest the Copacabana Palace Hotel at 3 p.m. or the Passeio Público (public garden) at 6 p.m. today.

Partner B
Go to file 3 on page 211.

Travel arrangements

Rob Heldof, the famous rock star, has invited Nina Wittstock, the chief executive officer of Top Act Event Management in Düsseldorf, to spend the weekend at his castle near Cork in Ireland. It's Sunday evening and Nina needs some help with a last-minute booking, so she phones Zoe, Rob Heldof's PA. Zoe is staying a few minutes away in the gatehouse.

2 17 **1 Read or listen to the dialogue and then complete Zoe's notes.**

ZOE: Hello?

NINA: Hi, Zoe, It's Nina. I hope it's not too late.

ZOE: It's only ten o'clock! Rob calls me at all hours! How can I help?

NINA: I've just seen a text I got from Germany. I have to get to a lunch invitation in London tomorrow but I'm not sure about flight times. I tried to phone Germany but couldn't get through. Reception at this castle is very poor, so I tried your number and it worked!

ZOE: That's great. Just give me the details, so I can make a note of them.

NINA: I'm invited to the Savoy Grill in Central London for lunch at one o'clock tomorrow. It's a surprise invitation from Bill Hampton, the President of Cherry Solutions Incorporated. Rob spoke at their conference in Düsseldorf last month.

ZOE: Oh yes, I remember it very well indeed! It was a great conference. Right, I'll just check the flights from Cork to London for you. Just let me go online here on my laptop ... (*Speaking to herself*) ... Cork ... to ... London ... Here we are. Any particular airport in London?

NINA: I really don't know. How many are there?

ZOE: There are five – Heathrow, Gatwick, Stansted, Luton and London City Airport – but I can see here that there are no flights from Cork to Luton Airport and also none to London City Airport, which is a shame because it's very central. Anyway, I can see there are a couple of flights landing at London in the morning.

NINA: That's great! How can I book one? Can I do it online?

ZOE: Yes, that's no problem at all. I think the problem might be getting from the airport to central London in time.

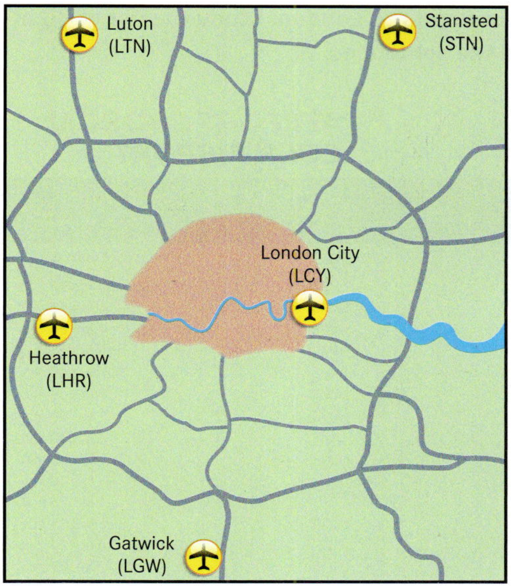

NINA: Oh I see! What about the Underground? Isn't it direct?

ZOE: Unfortunately not. You'll have to change if you take the Tube. It runs from Heathrow but not from Gatwick, Stansted or Luton.

NINA: The Tube?

ZOE: Oh sorry! That's what we call the London Underground.

NINA: Oh, I see.

ZOE: You could always take a taxi or a minicab to the restaurant. There's a fast coach or train service from the other airports, too.

NINA: Oh dear! It sounds very complicated!

ZOE: I'm afraid so. Look, why don't I drive over now and then we can use the desktop computer in Rob's study to go online and book everything?

NINA: That's a marvellous idea, Zoe!

ZOE: OK. I'll be with you in five minutes. Bye.

NINA: Bye.

Check transport links for Nina Wittstock!

Nina

Invited to ... 1 at the Savoy ... 2 in Central ... 3 at ... 4 o'clock tomorrow.

Invitation from ... ... 5, President of ... 6 Solutions Incorporated.

N. can fly from Cork to ... 7, ... 8 or ... 9 Airport.

No flights to Luton Airport or ... ... 10 Airport.

Tube link from ... 11 Airport to central London.

Can go from other airports to central London by ... 12, ... 13, fast ... 14 or ... 15.

2 **This is the information that Zoe gets about flights to London. Study the list of flight times from Cork to London and complete the sentences.**

Home | Departure | Arrival

AERFORT CHORCAÍ
CORK AIRPORT

London, United Kingdom

Carrier	Departs	Arrives	Via	Duration
EI/BA	ORK 6:10	LGW 11:55	AMS	5 hrs 45 min
EI/KL	ORK 6:10	LGR 10:50	AMS	4 hrs 40 min
EI/BA	ORK 6:10	LGR 11:00	AMS	4 hrs 50 min
EI/BA	ORK 6:10	LGR 12:05	AMS	5 hrs 55 min
EI/KL	ORK 6:10	LGR 13:50	AMS	7 hrs 40 min
EI/LH	ORK 6:10	LGR 14:15	AMS	8 hrs 05 min
EI/BD	ORK 6:10	LGR 14:15	AMS	8 hrs 05 min
KL	ORK 6:10	LGR 10:50	AMS	4 hrs 40 min
KL	ORK 6:10	LGR 13:50	AMS	7 hrs 40 min
EI	ORK 7:30	LGR 9:00		1 hrs 30 min
FR	ORK 8:10	STN 9:25		1 hrs 15 min
EI/AF	ORK 10:50	LHR 16:25	CDG	5 hrs 35 min
EI/BA	ORK 10:50	LHR 17:25	CDG	6 hrs 35 min
EI/AF	ORK 10:50	LHR 18:15	CDG	7 hrs 25 min
EI/BA	ORK 10:50	LHR 18:25	CDG	7 hrs 35 min
EI/AF	ORK 10:50	LHR 19:20	CDG	8 hrs 30 min
EI/BA	ORK 10:50	LHR 19:35	CDG	8 hrs 45 min
EI	ORK 11:50	LHR 13:05		1 hrs 15 min
FR	ORK 12:55	LGW 14:20		1 hrs 25 min
EI	ORK 16:00	LHR 17:15		1 hrs 15 min
EI	ORK 20:00	LHR 21:15		1 hrs 15 min
FR	ORK 21:45	STM 23:05		1 hrs 20 min

17.06.20... Show ✓ Nonstop Flights ✓ Direct Flights ✓ Connecting Flights

Notes: *ORK = Cork, AMS = Amsterdam, CDG = Charles de Gaulle (Paris)*

1 Carrier means
   a someone who carries your luggage.
   b a shopping bag.
   c an airline.

2 Duration means
   a how much earlier you have to arrive at the airport.
   b how long the trip will take.
   c the time difference between Cork and London.

3 There are flights from Cork to
   a three airports near London.
   b two airports near London.
   c one airport near London.

4 Most of the flights to London are
   a direct flights.
   b via the Netherlands.
   c via France.

5 The earliest arrival time in London is
   a 6.10 a.m.
   b 9.00 a.m.
   c 10.50 a.m.

6 The shortest flights are
   a only to London Heathrow (LHR).
   b to London Heathrow or London Gatwick (LGW).
   c to London Heathrow or London Stansted (STD).

3 Use the information in the journey planner and the words in brackets to complete the sentences. Use *if*-sentences type 1 (*if* + present, *will/won't* + infinitive).

At 9.30 a.m. on Monday morning Nina uses her netbook to go online at Heathrow Airport. She wants to see if it would be a good idea to go to the restaurant by public transport.

1 If Nina (leave) Heathrow airport at 09.52, she (arrive) at Charing Cross Underground Station at …
2 She (have to) leave at … or … if she (not want) to walk much.
3 Her journey (take) the least time if she (leave) at …
4 If she (want) to leave before 10 a.m., she (have to) walk from a bus stop to an …
5 If she (leave) Heathrow Airport at … or … she (arrive) at Charing Cross Station at 11.25.

Journey Planner

Choose your route/s from the options below

Journey Summary

Departing: Monday 17 June 20.. at: 10:00
From: London Heathrow Airport; Harrow Road / London Road
To: Charing Cross Unterground Station

Route	Depart	Arrive	Duration	Interchanges
1	09:52	11:16	**01:24**	
2	09:57	11:19	**01:22**	
3	10:01	11:19	**01:18**	
4	10:02	11:25	**01:23**	
5	10:04	11:25	**01:21**	
6	10:16	11:40	**01:24**	

earliest | earlier | later | latest

2 18

4 Nina checks her mobile and finds a text from Zoe. Listen to the telephone conversation between Nina and the minicab company and make a note of:

- the name of the company
- the fare for a one-way trip to central London
- how long the trip will take
- where Nina is now
- how long Nina will have to wait for the minicab to arrive
- what other information she gives the minicab company

Hotel reservations

Nina Wittstock, the chief executive officer of Top Act Event Management in Düsseldorf is invited by Rob Heldof to see him play unplugged at the Edinburgh Festival in August. He will be there with his band for a week. She asks Helena Sawicki, her personal assistant, to book her a room.

1 **Look at Helena's online enquiry and complete the sentences on the opposite page.**

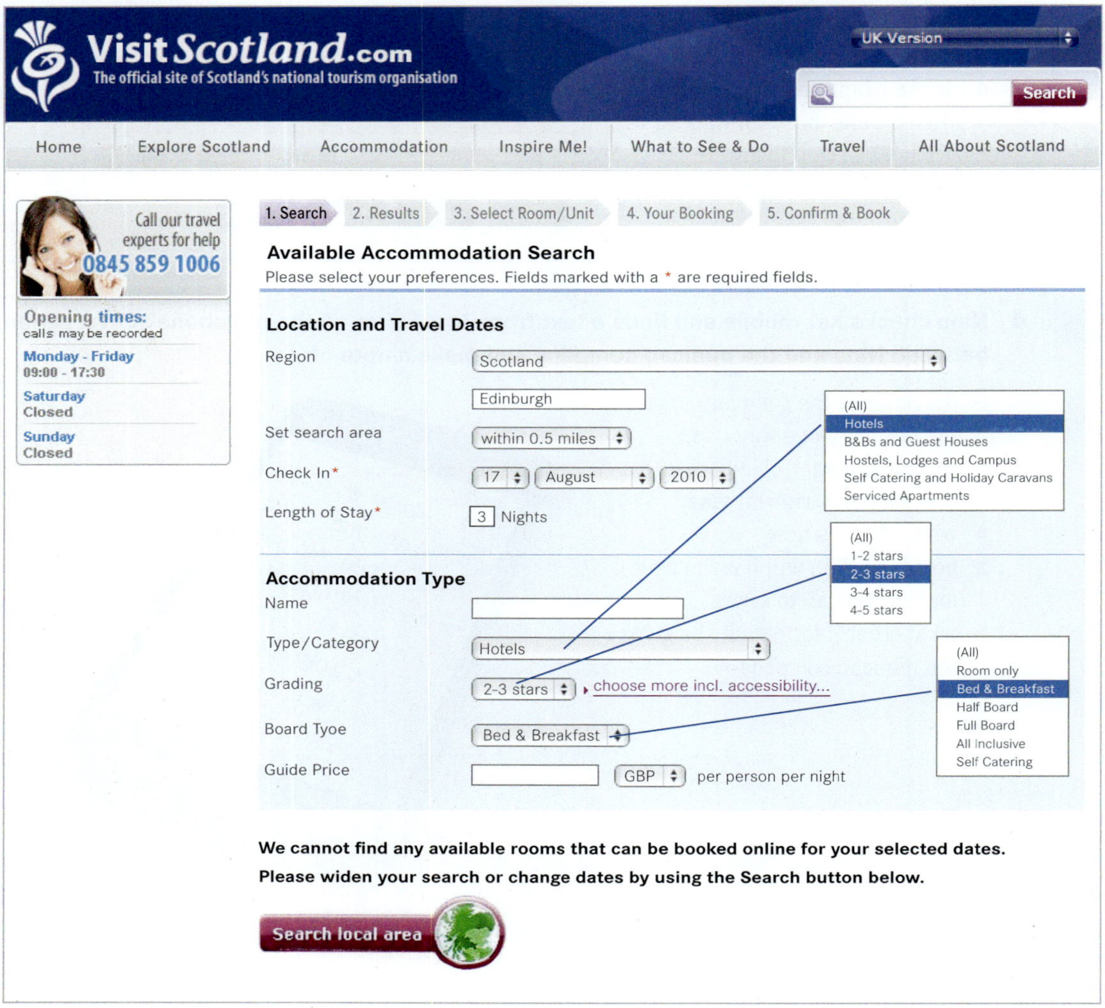

1 The Edinburgh Festival is in
   a England.
   b Scotland.
   c Wales.

2 Helena wants to book a
   a self-catering apartment.
   b guest house.
   c hotel.

3 Helena wants to find a room
   a within five miles of Edinburgh.
   b within a mile of Edinburgh.
   c within half a mile of Edinburgh.

4 Nina Wittstock wants to have
   a breakfast at the hotel.
   b all her meals at the hotel.
   c breakfast and an evening meal at the hotel.

5 The website shows prices in
   a dollars.
   b pounds.
   c euros.

6 The message at the bottom means that for the dates Helena wants
   a there are no free hotel rooms in Edinburgh.
   b there are no free rooms in Edinburgh.
   c there are no self-catering apartments in Edinburgh.

Booking accommodation

Meals

B&B means bed and breakfast.
Half board means breakfast and an evening meal.
Full board means three meals a day.
All inclusive normally means that there are no extra charges, e.g. for drinks, snacks or entertainment.
Self-catering means you cook your own meals.

Breakfast

A *continental breakfast* is usually only coffee and bread rolls with butter and jam.
(Note: *jam* = Marmelade. English *marmalade* is *Orangenmarmelade*.)
A *full English breakfast* is a large breakfast, usually with cereal (e.g. cornflakes, porridge, muesli), cooked bacon and eggs, toast, and tea or coffee.

Rooms

Single rooms can have a normal size bed, a *queen-size* (large bed) or a *king-size* (very large) bed.
Double rooms can have a *double bed* (one big bed) or *twin beds* (two single beds).
A *family room* sleeps three or four people.
An *en suite* bathroom or *en suite facilities* means that the room has a bathroom connected to it (with a shower and/or bath tub (*Badewanne*).
A *serviced apartment* means that you have a fully furnished flat with a cleaner.

Facilities/Amenities

Car park / bar / restaurant / wellness centre / spa / sauna / swimming pool / gym (*Fitnessraum*) / wifi, wireless internet (*WLAN*)
Sometimes there is a charge (*Gebühr*) or a surcharge (*Aufpreis*) for a service.
A *guest house* has fewer facilities than a hotel and many only offer bed and breakfast.

Payment

The price (or *rate*) for a room is usually per person per night.
Payment is normally by *credit card*.
If you book through an agency, there can be a *booking fee*.
Sometimes a deposit (*Anzahlung*) must be paid to secure the room.

2 19 **2 Helena phones the hotline to book a room for Nina Wittstock. Read or listen to the dialogue and match the sentence halves.**

VOICE: Welcome to Visit Scotland dot com. All of our agents are currently busy. Your call is important to us. Please hold. Alternatively, you can press zero and leave a voice message. (*Music*)

AGENT: Good afternoon. You're through to David. How may I help?

HELENA: Hello, I'd like to book a hotel room in Edinburgh for three nights beginning Saturday 17 August, but the website says there's nothing left.

AGENT: Well, that's because the weekend you want is the start of the International Festival, so everything is booked up. Could you come a day or so later?

HELENA: Yes, that would be possible.

AGENT: Well, as from Monday 19 August we've got a self-catering apartment at £165 a night.

HELENA: Well, actually the room is for my boss and she doesn't want self-catering. Perhaps there's something a little farther away from the city centre and she can hire a car.

AGENT: I certainly wouldn't hire a car in Edinburgh! There's an excellent bus service 24 hours a day. It's very cheap and you can get an all-day bus ticket for three pounds. A car would be more trouble than it's worth!

HELENA: I see. Well, as I said, my boss prefers a hotel. Have you not got anything at all?

AGENT: Just let me have another look. Well, I've got a four-star *guest house* here, which has just come in. They've got a room with bed and breakfast at £130 a night but it's from Tuesday 20 August. How about that?

HELENA: How far is it from the centre?

AGENT: It's a mile and a quarter, so it's about 20 minutes on foot. It's called Clifford House.

HELENA: That would be fine! We'll take it.

AGENT: Good. There'll be a booking fee of £4 and a 10% deposit to pay to secure the room.

HELENA: That's fine.

AGENT: Could I have the name of the person booking the room and a credit card number and e-mail address, please? Then we'll e-mail you a confirmation number and details of the guest house.

HELENA: Yes, it's for Nina Wittstock. That's N-I-N-A and then W-I-double T-S-T-O-C-K.

1	Helena waits	**a**	he finds a guest house.
2	The rooms are all booked up because	**b**	not too far from the city centre.
3	David first offers her	**c**	than the self-catering apartment.
4	David thinks it would be a bad idea	**d**	an e-mail with a confirmation number.
5	David doesn't find a hotel but	**e**	and speaks to David.
6	The guest house is cheaper	**f**	of 10%.
7	The guest house is	**g**	to hire a car.
8	There is a deposit	**h**	a self-catering apartment.
9	Helena pays	**i**	of the International Festival.
10	The booking agency will send	**j**	by credit card.

Useful phrases

Hotel / Booking Agent	Caller
Greeting the caller	**Saying what you need**
Park Hotel, good morning. How may I help? Welcome to ... (*name of hotel* / *booking agency*). You're through to ... (*first name of agent*).	Hello / Good morning, I'd like to book a ... (single/double/twin room) from ... to ..., please. It's for ... night(s) beginning ... (date of arrival). It's just for me / one person. It's for two/three etc. people.
Offering a room	**Accepting**
I can offer you a ... (*type of room*, e.g. single, double room) for that date / those dates. We've (only) got a ... for that date / those dates.	I'll take it. / We'll take it. That's great! / That's fine.
Offering alternatives	**Leaving the booking open**
I'm afraid we're booked up for those dates. How about ... (e.g. a day later / a self-catering apartment / a guest house)? Could you come ... (e.g. a day/week) later?	Thanks for the information. I'll get back to you. / I'll let you know. **Rejecting** Well, if that's all you've got, I'll leave it.
Finishing the call	
Thanks for calling. Bye. We look forward to seeing you ... (e.g. in May). I'm sorry we couldn't help you, sir/madam. Please try again in a few days. There might be a cancellation.	Thanks very much. Bye. Have you got nothing at all for those dates? Could you let me know if there's a cancellation? Could you recommend another hotel / guest house?
Follow-up questions	
Could you just spell your name for me, please? Could I have ... (e.g. your name / e-mail address / credit card number), please? Would you just let me have the security number on the back (of your credit card), please?	How far is it from ... (e.g. the city centre)? What facilities has it got? / Has it got a ... (e.g. car park, restaurant, bar, spa, wifi [*WLAN*])? Can I book a conference room for ... (*number*) people for ... (*number*) day(s)?

3 With a partner write or act out the following telephone booking.

Partner A

You are Michael/Michaela Lorenz (m.lorenz@oekopur.com). Make a telephone booking at Hotel Vanadisvägen in Stockholm. Include the following details:

Dates:	3rd–6th of next month
Rooms:	4 single rooms
Meals:	Half board – charge?
Conference room:	For 4 people for the 4th and 5th – charge?
Internet:	Needed
Payment:	Visa
Questions:	Shower or bathtub? Other facilities?

Partner B

Look at file 8 on page 213.

★★★
Hotel Vanadisvägen

Luntmakargatan 22
11351 Stockholm
Sweden
Tel. +46 08 162294

Facilities
TV in all rooms
Wifi
All rooms en suite
Underfloor heating
Sauna
Conference rooms

B&B from €100 per person per night
Check out our special mid-week offers!

4 With a partner write and act out the following telephone booking.

Partner A

You are Helena Sawicki at Top Act Event Management in Düsseldorf (Helena.sawicki@top-act.de). You are flying to Sydney with Nina Wittstock, the chief executive officer of your company, next month. You plan to stay for a week to meet some Australian dancers. Make a telephone enquiry to both Australian hotels and then promise to phone them back later if you wish to book. Include the following details and questions:

Dates:	15th–22nd of next month
Rooms:	2 single rooms
Meals:	Half board – charge?
Conference room:	For 20 people for the 21st – charge?
Internet:	Would be helpful
Payment:	MasterCard
Questions:	Gym? Sauna? Swimming pool?

Partner B

Look at file 20 on page 217.

★★★

Travelwise Hotel Sydney

1199 Wentworth Avenue
Sydney 2000
Australia
Call +612 8372 8223
Single rooms from AUD 200 per night (B&B)

Location

Very central
On all bus and train lines
Near Sydney Airport

Facilities

All rooms en suite
Minibar
Air conditioning
Flat-screen TV
Wireless internet (surcharge)
Microwave
Refrigerator
Restaurant
Conference rooms available

★★

Fair Deal Hotel Sydney

222 Goulburn Street
Sydney 2000
Australia
Call +612 221 4567
Single rooms from AUD 100 per night (breakfast not included)
Backpackers welcome!
Special weekend rates!

Location

Centrally located
Near railway station
Near Sydney Airport

Facilities

Some rooms en suite
Minibar
Refrigerator
Satellite TV
Conference rooms available

Welcoming a visitor

Helena Sawicki is personal assistant to Nina Wittstock, the chief executive officer of Top Act Event Management GmbH in Düsseldorf. Today Helena gets a visitor from Ireland.

1 Read the e-mails and complete the sentences below.

1 Zoe Kline is on her way to ...
2 She's late because ...
3 Zoe works for ...
4 Helena has not met Zoe ...
5 Zoe's plane finally lands in Düsseldorf at ...

Hi Helena 13:10

My flight's delayed due to bad weather, so I won't be in Dueseldorf before about 5 o'clock. Can we put the meeting back an hour?

Sorry about the change in plan.

Atb

Zoe Kline
Personal Assistant to Rob Heldof

Hi Zoe 14:12

No problem! Come when you can. I'm here all day.

Looking forward to meeting you personally at last.

Best wishes

Helena

Hi Helena 16:25

Just landed! Should be there in about an hour.

Must rush

Zoe Kline
Personal Assistant to Rob Heldof

Hi Zoe 16:29

Great! See you soon.

Best

Helena

2 20

2 Guess which words are missing in the dialogue and then listen to the recording to check your answers.

HELENA: Hello, you must be Zoe Kline! I'm Helena Sawicki. ... [1] to Düsseldorf! It's so nice to ... [2] you at last!

ZOE: Hello Helena. It's nice to meet you, too. I'm so ... [3] I'm late. I hope I haven't ... [4] your plans for this afternoon!

HELENA: Not at all. Did you have a good ... [5]?

ZOE: Apart from the delay it was fine.

HELENA: Good. Now, can I get you ... [6] before the meeting – tea, coffee, mineral water?

ZOE: I'd ... [7] a cup of coffee!

HELENA: Black or white? Sugar?

ZOE: Black, no sugar, please.

HELENA: Here ... ... [8].

ZOE: Thanks.

HELENA: Now here's the ... [9] for the meeting. We've made a few changes but nothing big. And here's the ... [10] for the next two days.

ZOE: Thanks.

HELENA: Now just let me give you my ... ... [11], in case you need to phone me on my mobile.

ZOE: Thanks. And here's ... [12].

Meeting and greeting

First meeting

> Introduce yourself clearly using your first name and surname and the name of your company if appropriate.
> Use 'Nice to meet you' or 'Pleased to meet you' to greet your guest. Your guest will usually use the same expression as you.
> Shake hands.
> Break the ice with a polite question (see below for examples).
> If the visitor is clearly older and/or more important than you, use his/her surname (e.g. Can I take your coat, Mrs Baker?). Otherwise use first names.
> Have your business card ready to give to the visitor.

Meeting your visitor again a short time later

> Don't shake hands again. You only do this after a long break.
> Listen carefully to see if your visitor is using first names now (e.g. Hi, Nina) and or is still formal (Good morning, Mrs Wittstock) and do the same.
> Make some small talk before getting down to business (see below for examples).

Useful phrases

Host	**Guest**
Speaking to someone for the first time (e.g. in reception, at an airport)	
Hello, is it ... (*name*, e.g. Ms Brown) from ... (*company*, e.g. Global Solutions)? / You must be ... (e.g. Emma Brown) from ... (*company*) / Emma Brown from Global Solutions.	Yes, that's right.
Introductions	
Hello, Ms Brown. I'm ... (*first name*, e.g. Tom) ... (*surname*, e.g. Schmidt) from ... (*company*, e.g. Top Act Event Management). This is my colleague, Silke Rademacher. She's in ... (*department*, e.g. Marketing).	
Nice to meet you. Pleased to meet you.	Nice to meet you (too). Pleased to meet you (too).
Making the visitor feel at home / Small talk	
Welcome to ... (e.g. Germany / Düsseldorf / Top Act Event Management). Did you have a good trip/flight/journey?	Yes, it was fine thanks. / It was a bit bumpy. / There was some turbulence./ We were half an hour late.
Is your hotel all right?	Yes, it's fine. Very comfortable / convenient / easy to find / near the centre.
Can I get you something to drink? / Can I get you anything – tea, coffee or mineral water? / Would you like tea, coffee or mineral water?	Yes, please. / A cup of coffee, please. / I'd love a cup of tea. No, thanks very much.* I ate on the plane/ on the way here.
Is this your first visit to ... (e.g. Essen)?	Yes, it is actually. / No, it isn't actually. I've been here once / twice / a few times before.**

Giving information	
We've booked you in at ... (*name of hotel*, e.g. the Park Hotel). Here's a card with the details.	Oh, thanks. / Great!
Here's a copy of ... (e.g. the agenda of the meeting / the programme for today).	Thanks a lot.
Here's a folder with everything you need.	Thanks for that.
Here's my business card, in case you need to contact me.	Thanks. Here's mine.

* Never just answer with the word 'no'! Native speakers of English find this very impolite.
** Here the host could say 'I see'. This is almost always a good answer.

3 With a partner, use the useful phrases to practise introductions.

Partner A: Use the business cards on this page.
Partner B: Use the business cards in file 22 on page 218.

Role A (with Jonathan Sykes)

Soyang
Europe GmbH
www.soyang.webwasher-dev.de

SOYANG
EUROPE GMBH

Dr. Alexander Mieberg
Managing Director

Soyang Europe GmbH
Hammer Landstraße 1a
41460 Neuss
Germany

Tel.: +49 (2131) 51…
Mobil: +49 (160) 96…
Fax: +49 (2131) 51…
E-Mail: koch@soyang.eu

Role B (with Amanda Lakely)

BRIX Mode GmbH

Sevda Yildiz
Einkaufsleiterin / Purchasing Director

Feldstraße 42
33609 Bielefeld
Germany

Tel.: +49 521 4827764-32
Mobil: +49 179 2049512
Sevda.yildiz@brixmode.de

4 Now make small talk with your partner.

Partner A: Use the business cards above and the background information below.
Partner B: Use the background information in file 22 on page 218.

Role A
You are Dr. Alexander Mieberg.
- You introduce yourself to your visitor.
- You ask about the flight.
- You offer your visitor something to drink.
- You ask about the hotel in Neuss (Holiday Inn).
- You exchange business cards.

Role B
You are Sevda Yildiz.
- You introduce yourself to your visitor.
- You ask about the flight.
- You offer your visitor something to drink.
- You tell your visitor that you have booked her a hotel in Düsseldorf (Parkhotel).
- You give her a card with the address of the hotel.
- You exchange business cards.

The layout of business letters

Me2 Mode GmbH 1
Oststr. 44 • 40211 Düsseldorf
Germany

Tel. +49 211 5922876
Fax +49 211 5922870
Email info@Me2-mode.de
www.Me2-mode.de

•
LM/TK 2
05 July 2012 3
•
URGENT 4
•
High End Fashion Ltd 5
99 High Street
NEWCASTLE
NE3 9LM
GROSSBRITANNIEN
•
Attn. Miss Ryan, Import Section 6
•
Dear Miss Ryan 7
•
Complimentary tickets 8
•
As arranged we enclose two tickets for the Body Culture Fashion Show in Düsseldorf next month and look forward to meeting you at our stand. 9
•
Yours sincerely 10
Me2 Mode GmbH

 11
•
•
Linda Meier (Mrs)
Managing Director
•
•
Encs 12
•
Me2Mode GmbH, Oststr. 44, 40211 Düsseldorf, Registergericht Düsseldorf, HRB 4421
Geschäftsführerin: Linda Meier

1 Letterhead
2 Reference
3 Date
4 Special marking
5 Inside address
6 Attention line
7 Salutation
8 Subject line
9 Body of the letter
10 Complimentary close
11 Signature
12 Enclosure (Enc), Enclosures (Encs)

Leave a free line for each dot (•).

Business letter layout

There is no standard layout for a business letter in the English-speaking world, so a typical block form layout used in Europe is shown here. After the letterhead all the sentences are left aligned (*linksbündig*).

1 Letterhead
There are no fixed rules for the letterhead but it should include the sender's name, postal address, telephone and fax numbers, email address and website address. It often has the company's logo.

2 Reference
Linda Meier (LM) signed the letter and Tina Knopf (TK) typed it. Some companies have different reference systems (e.g. Ref. L/M 07.1000).

3 Date
An all-figure date can be misunderstood. In American English 05/07/09 (or 05-07-09) means May 07, 2009 but in British English it means 05 July 2009. For this reason the month should always be written out and the year should be a four-figure number. The usual order in which a date is written in business letters and forms is: day (in figures) – month (as a word) – year (in figures). The example in this letter is pronounced 'the fifth of July two thousand and twelve' (or 'twenty twelve').

4 Special marking
These include URGENT, CONFIDENTIAL, PRIVATE AND CONFIDENTIAL, PERSONAL, AIR MAIL, REGISTERED, RECORDED DELIVERY. This line can be seen over the address in a window envelope.

URGENT

High End Fashions Ltd
99 High Street
NEWCASTLE
NE3 9LM
GROSSBRITANNIEN

For the attention of Miss Ryan, Import Section

American usage
The US Postal Services (USPS) wishes addresses to be written in capital letters with no punctuation:

MS CHARLIZE DANIELS
MARKETING DIRECTOR
DOWNTOWN MOTORS
450 NORTH MAIN STREET
THIENSVILLE WI 53092
USA

5 Inside address

This is the recipient's address. Always include the country because the same city names can be found in different countries. When writing to a UK address write the town or city in capital letters and the postcode on a separate line under it.

6 Attention (Attn:)

The attention line is under the inside address and close enough to it to be seen in a window envelope. If there is an attention line, the letter may be opened by the company's post department and given to the person named. However, if the inside address starts with someone's name, as in the example below, it may only be opened by that person or their secretary:

Miss Ryan
Import Section
High End Fashion Ltd
99 High Street
NEWCASTLE
NE3 9LM
GROSSBRITANNIEN

7 / 10 Salutation / Complimentary close

In most cases the salutation and complimentary close can be written **without** punctuation and they are linked as shown in the table below. In general, it is always better to write to a named person than a company but if this is not possible, start the letter 'Dear Sir or Madam' and use 'Yours faithfully' as the complimentary close.

Salutation	Complimentary close	Formality	Notes
Dear Mrs Brown	Yours sincerely	Formal	The most commonly used form
Dear Sir or Madam	Yours faithfully	Formal	Only used if the name is unknown
Dear Kim Dear Kim and Jim Jim	Regards Best regards Best wishes Yours	Friendly	Used in business if the writers know each other

8 Subject line

This is written in bold letters or underlined.

9 Body of the letter

The first word always starts with a capital letter. The paragraphs are separated by an empty line.

10 Complimentary close

The name of the sender's company is written under the complimentary close.

11 Signature

Signatures are often hard to read, so write the signatory's name and position under the signature. As there is no real English equivalent to *Sachbearbeiter/-in*, it is best to name the department where the signatory works (e.g. Sales Department for *Verkaufssachbearbeiter*). Women can add their preferred title in brackets after their name if they wish:

Louise Johnson (Miss)	single, younger woman or girl
Louise Johnson (Mrs)	married woman
Louise Johnson (Ms)	single or married women

12 Enclosure

It is sometimes enough just to write Enc or Encs but if necessary, details of the enclosure(s) can be listed like this:

Enc: Ticket or Encs: Tickets

Practice

1 Re-write these German dates in the form *dd* (in figures) – *mm* (as a word) – *yyyy* (in figures) then read them out to your partner.

1 07.05.69
2 12.04.71
3 20.06.00
4 30.09.08
5 21.03.89
6 31.12.09
7 01.01.10
8 05.11.07
9 03.10.90
10 24.02.49
11 04.07.03
12 28.08.12

1 first	**15** fifteenth
2 second	**16** sixteenth
3 third	**17** seventeenth
4 fourth	**18** eighteenth
5 fifth	**19** nineteenth
6 sixth	**20** twentieth (pronounced *twen – tee – eth*)
7 seventh	**21** twenty-first
8 eighth	**22** twenty-second
9 ninth	...
10 tenth	...
11 eleventh	**30** thirtieth (pronounced *thir – tee – eth*)
12 twelfth	**31** thirty-first
13 thirteenth	
14 fourteenth	

2 Find the right complimentary close for these salutations.

1 Dear Ronnie
2 Jim
3 Dear Ms Bush
4 Dear Tina and Tom
5 Dear Sir or Madam

3 The parts of this letter have got mixed up. Write out the letter again in the right order.

Joanne Campbell
Marketing Director
Impact Model Agency
300 Regent Street
LONDON
W1B 3HH
ENGLAND

Encs

Loretta Martin

The enclosed photos are marvellous but I want you to see for yourself and get back to me in time for the press conference on Monday. Talk to you soon.

17 January 20..

Tango Werbefotografie GmbH, Fischerstr. 24, 42369 Neuss
Registergericht Wuppertal, HRB 4867
Geschäftsführer: Sven Harkort

Loretta Martin (Miss)

PERSONAL

Fashion Department

LM/NK

Tango
Werbefotografie
Fischerstr. 24
42369 Wuppertal
Germany

Tango Werbefotografie

Best wishes

Dear Joanne

Photo shoot in Jamaica

4 Use the following information to show the correct layout of a business letter.

Marvin Raschke, who works in the export sales section of Teutoburger Wurstwaren, Bahnhofstr. 1, 49186 Bad Iburg, Germany, dictates a letter to his secretary, Linus Schremp. The letter is to Continental Foods Ltd at 44 Commercial Road, Lancaster LA1 7JJ, England. Herr Raschke wants Mr Rodney Brown in the Imports Department to receive the letter, which is about sales material. The body of the letter is: 'We are pleased to enclose the sales material requested and look forward to hearing from you soon'. He encloses a catalogue with the letter. The date is 09/08/20.. .

Sausages

5 Use the following information to show the correct layout of a business letter.

Mrs Tamara Sawitzki, the chief accountant at Leder Hartmann, Emscherallee 99, 44369 Dortmund, Germany, dictates a letter to her secretary, Raphael Hermanns. The letter is confidential and addressed to Mr Olli-Pekka Mäkinen, the purchasing director of Rimtek Trading Oy, Lempääläkuja 5, 3840 Tampere, Finland. It is about invoice no. 44A for €12,500 dated 01/09/20.. . A copy of the invoice is enclosed. The body of the letter is: 'We would point out that the above-mentioned invoice is now one week overdue and look forward to receiving payment in the next few days.' The date is 11/10/20.. .

Leather goods

6 Use the following information to show the correct layout of a business letter.

Margot Herlitzer, the purchasing director at Fair Fragrance Parfümerie, Ludwigstr. 98, 45239 Essen, Germany, dictates a letter to her secretary, Jessica Degen. The letter is to Ms Charlize Novak, the export sales director at Natural Beauty Products, 4000 East Ocean Boulevard, Long Beach, CA 90803, USA. Frau Herlitzer is writing to Ms Novak about the advertising campaign for Body Flower perfume. The body of the letter is: 'Please find enclosed some photocopies of customers' reactions to the new product. I look forward to your comments with interest.' She encloses the photocopies with the letter. The date is 03/05/20.. .

Perfume

2 Enquiries

1 Sevda Yildiz is the purchasing director of Brix Mode in Bielefeld. Last month she attended the Igedo fashion fair in Düsseldorf, where she talked to Amanda Lakely of Fair Trade Fashions. She now uses the address on Amanda's business card to write an enquiry. Read her letter and match the sentence halves.

A letter of enquiry

BRIX Mode GmbH
Feldstraße 42 • 33609 Bielefeld • Germany
Tel +49 521 4827764   Fax +49 521 4824760   info@brixmode.de

SY/GJ
13 October 20..

Ms Amanda Lakely
Sales Director
Fair Trade Fashions
85 Prices Park
GATESHEAD
NE1 9NF
GROSSBRITANNIEN

Dear Ms Lakely

Enquiry about fashion wear and accessories

I was most impressed by the T-shirts you showed me on your stand at the Igedo fashion fair last month and would now like more information about your company's products.

We are a rapidly growing importer and wholesaler of young people's fashions and accessories with excellent business contacts all over Germany and beyond. At present we are particularly interested in importing good quality, stylish Fair Trade clothing at reasonable prices.

Please let us have your latest catalogue and export price list, including all discounts granted. Details of your terms of delivery and payment and your delivery periods would also be appreciated.

We look forward to hearing from you soon.

Yours sincerely
Brix Mode

S. Yildiz

Sevda Yildiz (Ms)
Purchasing Director

Fair Trade Fashions
Amanda Lakely
Sales Director
85 Princes Park, GATESHEAD NE1 9NF, England
Tel.: +44 191 4982686
Fax: +44 191 4982680
amanda.lakely@fair-trade-fashion.co.uk

Brix Mode GmbH • Bielefeld, Registergericht Bielefeld, HRB 82071, Geschäftsführerin: Karla Wenz

Fair Trade T-shirt

Igedo fashion fair, Düsseldorf

1	Sevda Yildiz is the	a	clothes and accessories for young people.
2	Amanda Lakely is the	b	at the Igedo fashion fair.
3	Brix Mode is	c	catalogue and a price list.
4	Fair Trade Fashions is	d	it will take to deliver the goods.
5	Sevda met Amanda	e	Purchasing Director of Brix Mode.
6	Amanda showed Sevda	f	in Bielefeld.
7	Sevda's company imports	g	some T-shirts.
8	Sevda would like Amanda to send her a	h	in Gateshead, England.
9	Sevda needs to know how long	i	is Karla Wenz.
10	The Managing Director of Brix Mode	j	Sales Director of Fair Trade Fashions.

2 Match the German translations below with points 1–6 in the box.

Beschreibung Ihrer Gesellschaft | Grund für Ihre Anfrage | Angemessene Verabschiedung | Ihr Bedarf | Liefer- und Zahlungsbedingungen | Lieferung | Muster / Probe(n) | Preisangebot | Preisliste | Quelle der Anschrift | Rabatte | Referenzen | Verkaufsmaterial | Vertreterbesuch

Structure of an enquiry

An enquiry covers some or all of the following points:

1 Source of address
2 Description of your company
3 Reason for your enquiry
4 Your requirements:
- quotation
- sales material
- price list
- discounts
- samples
- terms of delivery and payment
- delivery
- representative's visit

5 References
6 Suitable ending

3 Look at the letter to Amanda Lakely and in your exercise book make a note of as many of the points listed under 'Structure of an enquiry' as possible.

EXAMPLE
1 Source of address: *stand at the Igedo fashion fair in Düsseldorf / business card*

4 Find words in the letter to replace the words in italics.

1 *Please tell me more* about your products.
2 My company is *importing more and more young people's clothes all the time.*
3 We have customers both in Germany and *in other countries.*
4 We are only prepared to buy clothing *if it doesn't cost too much.*
5 Please give us details of *any reductions in price you are prepared to make.*
6 We would also like to know *how long it will take to deliver the goods.*

5 **Sevda Yildiz now contacts a Chinese supplier and requests an online quotation for T-shirts. Read the contact form and say if the statements are true or false. Correct the false statements.**

An enquiry by e-mail (using a contact form)

To:	632 Trading Company China
Recipient:	Ms Chen Yu Lan
***Subject:**	Enquiry about fashion wear
***Content:**	Dear Ms Chen Yu Lan We note from your company's website that you sell a wide range of stylish fashion wear. Our company is a major German wholesaler of adults' and children's clothing with many long-standing customers all over Europe. As there is considerable demand for T-shirts at the moment, we would welcome a quotation for the following articles: 1000 men's T-shirts in black, dark blue and grey in S, M, L, Xl and XXL 1000 ladies' T-shirts in white, black and pink in XS, S, M, L and XL Please also let us know if you are able to provide samples. Delivery would need to be made within 6 weeks DDP our premises. References are available on request. We look forward to your early reply with interest. Yours sincerely Sevda Yildiz
***Your company:**	Brix Mode, Bielefeld, Germany
***Your name:**	Mr. Mrs. Miss Ms. (selected: Ms.) Sevda Yildiz
***Your email:**	sevda.yildiz@brixmode.de (Please make sure your email address is correct, otherwise the recipient will not be able to reply.)
***Telephone number:**	+49 521 4827764
***Fax number:**	+49 521 4827760
Your country/region:	Germany
Your homepage:	www.brixmode.de
	Send

1 Sevda wrote a letter to the Chinese company.
2 The Chinese company sells a lot of different types of clothes.
3 Brix Mode only sells its products in Germany.
4 A lot of people are buying T-shirts at present.
5 Sevda doesn't need to know how much the T-shirts will cost.
6 Sevda would like the Chinese company to send her one or two T-shirts.
7 Brix Mode wants the goods to be delivered in six to seven weeks.
8 Brix Mode wants the price of the goods to cover door-to-door transport from China to Germany.

6 Use words from the e-mail to complete the following enquiry to an Indian clothes supplier.

E-MAIL

Dear Mr Narendra

Having studied your company's ... [1], we ... [2] that you are a ... [3] wholesaler of ... [4] and children's clothes. As there is great ... [5] for stylish T-shirts at the ... [6], please send us a ... [7] for 1,000 Panther tops in S, M, L, Xl and XXL. Can you send us some ... [8], so we can see the goods before ordering them? ... [9] would need to be made ... [10] 8 weeks DDP our ... [11] in Germany.

We look forward to your ... [12] with interest.

Yours sincerely
Peter Lorenz
Purchasing Department

Useful phrases

Source of address	**Quelle der Anschrift**
I was most impressed by the ... (*product[s]*) you showed me on your stand at the ... (*name of trade fair/exhibition*).	Ich war von den ... (*Produkten*), die Sie mir auf Ihrem Stand auf der ... (*Name der Handelsmesse/Ausstellung*) zeigten, höchst beeindruckt.
We have seen your company's advertisement in the current edition of ... (*name of publication*) and are most interested in your products.	Wir haben Ihre Anzeige in der aktuellen Ausgabe von ... (*Name der Veröffentlichung*) gesehen und interessieren uns sehr für Ihre Produkte.
We note from your company's website that you sell a wide range of ... (*product*).	Wir entnehmen der Homepage Ihres Unternehmens, dass Sie eine breites Sortiment von ... (*Produkt*) anbieten.
You have been recommended to us by... (*name of the person/company*), who tells us that you have brought out ... (e.g. a new line of costume jewellery).	Sie wurden uns von ... (*Name der Person/Firma*) empfohlen, der/die uns mitgeteilt hat, dass Sie ... (z. B. eine neue Produktlinie im Bereich Modeschmuck) auf den Markt gebracht haben.
Description of your company	**Beschreibung Ihres Unternehmens**
We are a rapidly growing/leading importer and wholesaler of ... (*goods/services*) with excellent business contacts all over ... (*place*) and beyond.	Wir sind ein schnell wachsender/führender Importeur und Großhändler für ... (*Waren/Dienstleistungen*) mit hervorragenden Geschäftskontakten in ganz ... (*Ort*) und darüber hinaus.
Our company is a major/well-established [German] wholesaler of ... (*goods/services*, e.g. camping equipment) both at home and abroad.	Unsere Firma ist ein bedeutender/etablierter [deutscher] Großhändler von (*Waren/Dienstleistungen*, z. B. Campingausrüstung) im In- und Ausland.

We have many long-standing customers all over Europe.	Wir haben viele langjährige Kunden in ganz Europa.
Reason for your enquiry	**Grund für Ihre Anfrage**
At present we are particularly interested in ... (*goods/services*, e.g. environmentally friendly technology) at reasonable prices, as goods of this nature are in great demand at present.	Gegenwärtig gilt unser besonderes Interesse, ... (*Waren/Dienstleistungen*, z. B. umweltfreundlicher Technik) zu angemessenen Preisen, da eine große Nachfrage nach Waren dieser Art zurzeit besteht.
As we are extending our range at present, we are particularly interested in ... (*product*).	Da wir gegenwärtig unser Sortiment erweitern, sind wir besonders an ... (*Produkt*) interessiert.
Your requirements:	**Ihr Bedarf:**
quotation Please send us a favourable quotation for these items / for ... (*product*). We would welcome a quotation for ...	**(Preis)angebot** Bitte schicken Sie uns ein günstiges (Preis) angebot für diese Artikel / für ... (*Produkt*). Wir hätten gerne ein (Preis)angebot für ...
sales material We would therefore/also be grateful if you would let us have a comprehensive catalogue on your entire range. Please let us have your latest catalogue ...	**Verkaufsmaterial** Wir wären Ihnen deshalb/auch dankbar, wenn Sie uns einen umfassenden Katalog über Ihre gesamte Produktpalette schicken würden. Bitte lassen Sie uns Ihren aktuellen Katalog /... zukommen.
current price list ... and export price list	**aktuelle Preisliste** ... und Exportpreisliste
discounts ... including all discounts granted	**Rabatte** ... einschl. aller gewährten Rabatte
samples Please also let us know if you are able to provide samples.	**Muster/Proben** Bitte teilen Sie uns auch mit, ob Sie Muster/ Proben zur Verfügung stellen können.
terms of delivery and payment ... including details of your terms of delivery and payment. Details of your terms of delivery and payment would also be appreciated. Delivery would need to be made DDP (*destination*) our premises. We would require delivery ... (e.g. within 6 weeks / by the end of the month).	**Liefer- und Zahlungsbedingen** ... einschl. Einzelheiten über Ihre Liefer- und Zahlungbedingen. Einzelheiten über Ihre Liefer- und Zahlungsbedingen würden wir ebenfalls begrüßen. Die Lieferung müsste DDP unsere Geschäftsräume erfolgen. Die Lieferung hätten wir gerne... (z. B. innerhalb 6 Wochen / bis Ende des Monats).
representative's visit We would be grateful if a representative could call on us.	**Vertreterbesuch** Wir wären dankbar, wenn uns ein/e Außendienstmitarbeiter/in besuchen könnte.
References	**Referenzen**
References are available on request.	Referenzen sind auf Wunsch erhältlich.
Suitable ending	**Angemessene Verabschiedung**
If your products meet our requirements, we will be in a position to place a substantial order. We look forward to hearing from you soon / in the near future. We look forward to your early reply with interest.	Wenn Ihre Produkte unseren Anforderungen entsprechen, werden wir in der Lage sein, einen größeren Auftrag zu erteilen. Wir freuen uns, bald / in Kürze von Ihnen zu hören. Wir sehen Ihrer baldigen Antwort mit Interesse entgegen.

7 Use the useful phrases to write a letter/fax/e-mail enquiry based on the following details.

Situation

Sie (eigener Name) sind Einkaufsleiter/-in bei der FreiLuft Rhein GmbH, Richthofenstr. 100, 53117 Bonn, Fax-Nr. 0049 228 422390, E-Mail: vorname.nachname@flr.de. Ihre Firma ist ein gut eingeführter Großhändler von Campingzubehör im In- und Ausland. In der aktuellen Ausgabe der Zeitschrift *Campers' World* lesen Sie eine Anzeige über umweltfreundliche Campingausrüstung, die zurzeit sehr gefragt ist. Der Inserent ist die Firma Apex Leisure Ltd, 62 Commercial Road, Nottingham NO4 3FL, England, Fax-Nr. 0044 115 910635, E-Mail: emma@apex-leisure.co.uk.

Camping equipment

Aufgabe

Verfassen Sie mit heutigem Datum eine Anfrage an die englische Firma unter Berücksichtigung folgender Punkte:

- Ihr Ansprechpartner ist Ms Emma Wade, Exportleiterin.
- Bezug auf Anzeige
- Beschreibung Ihrer Firma
- Ihr besonderes Interesse gilt umweltfreundlicher Technik zu vernünftigen Preisen.
- Bitte um Zusendung eines aktuellen Katalogs und der Exportpreisliste
- Bitte um Angabe von Liefer- und Zahlungsbedingungen einschl. aller Rabatte
- Aussicht auf regelmäßige Aufträge, wenn die Ware Ihren Kunden zusagt
- Angemessene Verabschiedung

8 Use the useful phrases to write a letter/fax/e-mail enquiry based on the following details.

Situation

Sie (eigener Name) sind Sachbearbeiter/-in im Einkauf bei Bijou Bianca Modische Accessoires GmbH, Bahrenfelder Chaussee 1, 22761 Hamburg, Fax-Nr. 0049 40 533422, E-Mail: vorname.nachname@bbma.de. Ihre Firma ist ein führender Importeur und Großhändler von Modeschmuck in Deutschland mit vielen langjährigen Kunden. Sie ist gegenwärtig dabei, ihr Sortiment zu erweitern und erfährt von von einer Geschäftspartnerin, Ms Brenda Parker, dass die Firma Daisy Bijoux Ltd, 35 Nightingale Park Road, Manchester M50 3BB, England, Fax-Nr. 0044 161 4882219, E-Mail: aisha.iqbal@daisy-bijou.co.uk, eine attraktive neue Serie von Modeschmuck auf den Markt gebracht hat, insbesondere „Daisy"-Ohrringe und -Armreifen.

Daisy bracelets

Aufgabe

Verfassen Sie mit heutigem Datum eine Anfrage an die englische Firma unter Berücksichtigung folgender Punkte:

- Ihr Ansprechpartner ist Ms Aisha Iqbal, Exportleiterin.
- Bezug auf Empfehlung
- Beschreibung Ihrer Firma
- Grund für Ihre Anfrage
- Sie sind an der neuen Serie von „Daisy"-Ohrringen und -Armreifen besonders interessiert.
- Bitte um Zusendung eines günstigen Preisangebots unter Angabe von Liefer- und Zahlungsbedingungen einschl. aller Rabatte
- Sie möchten auch einen umfassenden Katalog über die gesamte Produktpalette der Firma.
- Aussicht auf einen größeren Auftrag, wenn die Ware Ihren Anforderungen entspricht
- Angemessene Verabschiedung

2 21 **9 Sevda Yildiz visits the stand of a Swedish fashion company called Patrik K at the Igedo fashion fair in Düsseldorf and talks to the head designer about T-shirts. Listen to the dialogue and choose the right answers to complete the sentences.**

1 Sevda first talks to
- a Patrik K.
- b Stig Magnusson.
- c Stig's assistant.

2 Sevda and Stig
- a have met once before.
- b have met many times before.
- c have never met before.

3 Sevda
- a has just seen Patrik K's new designs.
- b wants to see Patrik K's new designs.
- c doesn't like Patrik K's new designs.

4 Sevda's company is interested in placing
- a a small order with Patrik K.
- b a large order with Patrik K.
- c an extremely large order with Patrik K.

5 Stig can give Sevda more information about
- a styles.
- b prices.
- c transport.

6 Patrik K's clothes are made
- a in South America.
- b eastern Europe.
- c Africa and Asia.

7 Sweatshop labour means people work
- a in bad conditions for very little pay.
- b in good conditions for very little pay.
- c in good conditions for good pay.

8 Patrik K can deliver
- a in about one to two months.
- b in about three to four months.
- c in about five to six months.

9 Sevda likes
- a the first T-shirt Stig shows her.
- b the second T-shirt Stig shows her.
- c both the T-shirts Stig shows her.

10 In the next few days
- a Patrik K's representative will call Sevda.
- b Sevda will call Patrik K's representative.
- c Stig will call Sevda.

10 Listen again and summarize the dialogue with the help of these words.

~~Sevda Yildiz~~ → ~~Patrik K stand~~ → ~~Body Look~~ → Stig Magnusson → head designer → T-shirts → styles and fabrics → sales reps → terms and conditions → clothes → hand-picked organic cotton → Egypt and India → sweatshop labour → Sevda → two designs → delivery → three months → exchange → business cards → representative → next few days

Begin like this: *Sevda Yildiz of Brix mode in Bielefeld went to Patrik K's stand at the Body Look fashion show in Düsseldorf. She talked ...*

11 Schreiben Sie ein Memo auf Deutsch von Sevda Yildiz an Frau Hanna Schmidt, Leiterin Herstellung, in dem sie über ihr Gespräch mit Stig Magnusson auf der Igedo berichtet. Benutzen Sie den Vordruck auf Seite 217 (File 21).

12 Schreiben Sie eine Aktennotiz über Sevdas Gespräch mit Stig Magnusson auf Deutsch. Benutzen Sie folgenden Vordruck.

Für	Frau Silke Meyer, Leiterin Marketing Frau Hanna Schmidt, Leiterin Herstellung Herrn Reinhard Müller, Leiter Außendienst	
Verfasst von		am 10. August 20..
Gesprächspartner		
Betrifft		
Schreiben Sie den Text der Aktennotiz hier.		

Offers

2 22 **1 Sevda Yildiz is the Purchasing Director of Brix Mode in Bielefeld. Last month she went to the Igedo fashion fair in Düsseldorf and today she gets a phone call from the one of the companies she visited there. Listen to or read the dialogue and complete the sentences below.**

A telephone quotation

SEVDA Guten Morgen, Brix Mode. Sie sprechen mit Sevda Yildiz. Was kann ich für Sie tun?

PEHR Hello. Do you speak English?

SEVDA Yes, I do. How can I help?

PEHR My name's Pehr Lindquist from Patrik K in Sweden. I'd like to speak to Sevda Yildiz, please.

SEVDA Speaking. Thanks for calling Mr – er ...?

PEHR Lindquist, but please call me Pehr.

SEVDA OK, Pehr, and please call me Sevda.

PEHR Nice to meet you, Sevda. Stig Magnusson asked me to ring you. I'm responsible for exports to Germany and the UK.

SEVDA Thanks for calling! Yes, I liked what Stig showed me at the Igedo Fashion Fair in Düsseldorf. I've also looked at your online catalogue and I think you may have the lines we're looking for.

PEHR Excellent! Was that T-shirts?

SEVDA Yes, that's right.

PEHR What quantities were you thinking of?

SEVDA It would be a trial order, so we'd need a hundred men's and a hundred ladies' in different sizes.

PEHR That's fine. And how about delivery?

SEVDA We'd like them delivered to our premises here, please.

PEHR We can do that for you. No problem. We've got them in stock now, so delivery would take less than a week.

SEVDA Good. How much would they cost?

PEHR I think we could let you have them for €6 each.

SEVDA Six euros ...? Well, we were thinking of about €3 actually.

PEHR We could offer you that price if you ordered a thousand, Sevda! ... All right, as Germany's a good market, I'll go down to €5 but that's the best I can do.

SEVDA And that would include transport and insurance?

PEHR Yes, that would be included, but to an airport nearby. What's the nearest airport to you?

SEVDA Dortmund. It's about 120 km away.

PEHR In that case we could fly the goods to Dortmund and you could pick them up there. Would that be OK?

SEVDA All right, we'll pick them up ourselves but only if you make it 4€, not 5.

PEHR Four euros if you pick them up yourselves? You're a good business woman, Sevda! OK, we'll do it but don't tell anyone!

SEVDA I won't, Pehr! Could you let me have all this in writing please?

PEHR Yes, certainly. I'll send you an e-mail with all the details.

SEVDA Good. I'll get back to you when I've got the e-mail.

PEHR OK, bye for now.

SEVDA Bye.

1 Sevda is phoned by a company in ...
2 The caller is responsible for ...
3 The caller knows that Sevda's company is interested in ...
4 The caller's company can deliver the goods to ...
5 Delivery would not take long because ...
6 The caller first quotes a price of ...
7 He finally quotes a price of ...
8 The caller promises to send Sevda ...

2 **Schreiben Sie ein kurzes Memo auf Deutsch über dieses Telefongespräch. Das Memo ist von Sevda Yildiz an Frau Silke Meyer, Leiterin Marketing.** Suchen Sie zuerst die Stichwörter auf Englisch aus (*z. B. Pehr Linquist, responsible for exports usw.*) und fertigen Sie anhand dieser Ihr Memo an. Benutzen Sie den Vordruck auf Seite 217 (File 21).

3 **Pehr Lindquist sends the following offer to Sevda. Read the e-mail and match the sentence halves.**

An offer by email

E-MAIL

To:	"Sevda Yildiz" <Sevda.yildiz@brixmode.de>
Date:	29 October 20..
Subject:	Quotation for T-shirts
Attachments:	Patrik K collection.pdf, Patrik K price list.pdf

Dear Sevda

As agreed in our pleasant telephone conversation of this morning, I'm pleased to let you have details of our offer in writing and enclose our current illustrated catalogue and price list for your information.

We are a major distributor of fashion wear with an excellent reputation throughout Europe, and will be pleased to supply you with 100 ladies' and 100 men's T-shirts at €4 each. Delivery will be made CIP Dortmund airport within 7 days after receipt of order.

Our terms of payment for an initial order are CWO or, with favourable references, 10 days 3%, 30 days net. If regular orders are placed with our company, open account terms may be granted.

We look forward to receiving your order.

Pehr Lindquist
Export Sales Director

> CIP stands for 'carriage and insurance paid to ...'.
> It is one of the 11 Incoterms (international commercial terms). See page 193 for more details.
> CWO stands for 'cash with order'.
> It is a term of payment. See page 198 for more details.

1 We were very pleased
2 Our company has
3 We enclose our
4 Delivery would be made
5 As you are a new customer, our
6 If you can give us favourable references,
7 Open account terms may be granted
8 We look forward to

a terms of payment would be cash with order.
b we will grant you 10 days + 3%, 30 days net.
c processing your order.
d company's latest catalogue and price list.
e if regular orders are placed with our company.
f to receive your enquiry.
g CIP German airport.
h an excellent reputation throughout Europe.

4 Match the German translations with points 1–8 in the box below.

Anlage(n) | Beschreibung Ihrer Firma / Waren / Dienstleistungen | Bezug auf Anfrage | Angemessene Verabschiedung | Geschäftsbedingungen und Rabatte | Lieferung | Preis | Verkaufsmaterial

5 Look at the e-mail from Pehr Lindquist and in your exercise book make a note of as many of the points listed under the heading 'Structure of an offer' as possible.

6 Use points 1–8 to re-arrange the following letter in a suitable order.

Structure of an offer

An offer covers some or all of the following points:

1 Reference to an enquiry
2 Description of your company / goods / services
3 Sales material
4 Price
5 Terms and discounts
6 Delivery
7 Suitable ending
8 * Enclosure(s) / Attachment(s)

* Letters have enclosures and e-mails have attachments.

A As regards the goods requested, we are pleased to submit the following quotation:
'Highlight' lipstick at €2.50 per unit
'Dazzle' lip gloss at €3.00 per unit

B We feel sure that a trial order will convince you of the quality of our products and look forward to doing business with you.

C Many thanks for the above-mentioned enquiry about 'Highlight' lipsticks and 'Dazzle' lip gloss.

D Our company manufactures a wide range of high-quality products and already has many satisfied customers throughout Western Europe.

E Our terms of payment for an initial order are CWO.

F To download our latest comprehensive catalogue and export price list, please visit our website at www.newlook.co.uk.

G Delivery is made within approx. 30 days after receipt of order.

7 **In the meantime an Indian supplier contacts Brix Mode with an offer. Read the offer and complete the sentences.**

An offer

J.P. Designs Incorporated

44 Mandir Marg
NEW DELHI 110 001
INDIA

SM/AK
25 October 20..

Ms Sevda Yildiz
Purchasing Director
Brix Mode GmbH
Feldstraße 42
33609 Bielefeld
Germany

Dear Ms Yildiz

Your enquiry dated 14 October 20.. about fashion tops

We were delighted to receive your enquiry about our fashion wear and feel sure we can supply you with all the goods you need. Our company manufactures a wide range of high-quality products and already has many satisfied customers throughout Western Europe and North America.

To download our latest comprehensive catalogue and export price list, please visit our website at www.jpdesigns.in.

As regards the goods requested, we are pleased to submit the following quotation:

100 'Iona' ladies' fashion tops, article no. LFD 322, in XS, S, M, L and XL at US$1.50 per unit
100 'Ranjit' men's fashion tops, article no. MFT49, in S, M, L, XL and XXL at US$1.00 per unit

Our prices are quoted FOB Mumbai or Calcutta and delivery is made within approx. 30 days after receipt of order while stocks last. Our usual terms of payment are letter of credit or CWO by PayPal or Western Union bank transfer. Regular customers may be granted preferential terms.

We feel sure that a trial order will convince you of the quality of our products and look forward to doing business with you.

Yours sincerely
J.P. Designs Incorporated

Sunil Mittal
Export Sales Director

The Incoterm FOB stands for 'free on board ...'. See page 194 for more details.

1 The Indian company manufactures ...
2 Many of its customers are in ...
3 Customers can download sales material from ...
4 J.P. Designs Incorporated makes Sevda an offer for ...
5 FOB is a term of ...
6 Delivery will take ...
7 If Sevda wants to pay over the Internet, she can use ...
8 Sunil Mittal wants Sevda to test the quality of his goods by placing a ...

8 **Copy the table below into your exercise book or computer and fill it in to compare the Swedish and Indian offers.**

Name of supplier	*Patrik K, Sweden*	*J.P. Designs Incorporated, India*
Products	...	...
Terms of delivery	...	...
Prices	...	...
Delivery period	...	...
Terms of payment	...	...

Which of the two offers is better? Use the expressions in the language box to explain your opinion in at least 30 words.

I think ... *In my opinion ...* *The Swedish/Indian offer* *... is better / isn't so good* *... is more/less attractive*	*because ...* *... not exactly what is needed* *... only delivers to (e.g. an Indian port)* *... more/less expensive*	*... (much) cheaper/higher/ lower* *... longer/shorter* *Although ...* *I would take the ... offer*

Useful phrases

Reference to enquiry	**Bezug auf Anfrage**
As agreed in our pleasant telephone conversation of this morning / of today, ...	Wie heute (Morgen) in unserem netten Telefonat vereinbart, ...
We were delighted to receive your enquiry dated ... about our ... (e.g. fashion wear).	Wir waren sehr erfreut, Ihre Anfrage vom ... über unser(e) ... (z. B. Modebekleidung) zu erhalten.
I am pleased let you have details of our offer in writing.	Es freut mich, Ihnen ein schriftliches Angebot zukommen zu lassen.
Many thanks for the above-mentioned enquiry / your enquiry dated ...	Wir danken für die oben genannte Anfrage / Ihre Anfrage vom ...
... and feel sure we can supply you with all the goods you need.	... und sind sicher, dass wir Ihnen die Waren liefern können, die Sie benötigen.
Description of your company/goods/ services	**Beschreibung Ihrer Firma/Waren/ Dienstleistungen**
We are a major distributor of ... (e.g. fashion wear, GPS devices) ...	Wir sind ein bedeutender Großhändler für ... (z. B. Modebekleidung, GPS-Geräte) ...
... with an excellent reputation throughout Europe.	... mit einem hervorragenden Ruf in ganz Europa.
Our company manufactures a wide range of high-quality products ...	Unsere Firma stellt eine breite Palette hochwertiger Produkten her ...
... and already has many satisfied customers throughout ... (e.g. Western Europe and North America).	... und hat bereits viele zufriedene Kunden überall in ... (z. B. Westeuropa und Nordamerika).
Sales material	**Verkaufsmaterial**
We enclose our current catalogue and price list for your information.	Wir fügen unseren aktuellen Katalog und die Preisliste zu Ihrer Information bei.

To download our latest comprehensive catalogue and export price list, please visit our website at www.jpdesigns.in.	Um unseren aktuellen Gesamtkatalog und die Exportpreisliste zu downloaden, besuchen Sie bitte unsere Homepage unter www.jpdesigns.in.
Samples are available on request.	Muster sind auf Wunsch erhältlich.
Price	**Preis**
As regards the goods requested, we are pleased to submit the following quotation:	Was die gewünschten Waren betrifft, freuen wir uns, Ihnen folgendes Angebot zu unterbreiten:
... and will be pleased to supply you with 100 ladies' and 100 men's T-shirts at €4 each ...	... und liefern Ihnen gerne 100 Damen- und 100 Herren-T-shirts zu je 4€ ...
... at US$10 per unit.	... zu 10US$ pro Stück.
Terms and discounts	**Geschäftsbedingungen und Rabatte**
Our prices are quoted FOB Calcutta.	Unsere Preise verstehen sich FOB Kalkutta.
Delivery will be made ...	Die Lieferung erfolgt ...
CIP Frankfurt Airport	CIP Flughafen Frankfurt
DDP your (*buyer's*) premises	DDP Ihre Geschäftsräume
Wholesalers are granted a trade discount of ... %.	Großhändlern wird ein Handelsrabatt von ...% eingeräumt.
A quantity discount of ...% is granted on orders for 10 or more ... (e.g. machines, items).	Bei Abnahme von 10 oder mehr ... (z. B. Geräten, Artikeln) wird ein Mengenrabatt von ...% gewährt.
Our terms of payment for an initial order are CWO.	Unsere Zahlungsbedingungen für einen Erstauftrag sind Kasse bei Auftragserteilung.
Our usual terms of payment are letter of credit or CWO by PayPal or Western Union bank transfer ...	Unsere üblichen Zahlungsbedingungen sind per Akkreditiv oder Kasse bei Auftragserteilung per Überweisung durch PayPal oder Western Union ...
... or, with favourable references, 10 days 3%, 30 days net.	... oder bei günstigen Referenzen, 2% Skonto bei Zahlung innerhalb von 10 Tagen, netto bei Zahlung innerhalb von 30 Tagen.
Regular customers may be granted preferential terms.	Stammkunden können bevorzugte Zahlungsbedingungen gewährt werden.
If regular orders are placed with our company, open account terms may be granted.	Wenn unserer Firma regelmäßige Aufträge erteilt werden, kann ein offenes Zahlungziel gewährt werden.
Delivery	**Lieferung**
Delivery is made within approx. 30 days after receipt of order ...	Die Lieferung erfolgt innerhalb ca. 30 Tagen nach Auftragseingang ...
... while stocks last.	... solange der Vorrat reicht.
Suitable ending	**Angemessene Verabschiedung**
We hope our offer is to your liking.	Wir hoffen, dass unser Angebot Ihnen zusagt.
We look forward to receiving your order.	Wir freuen uns, Ihren Auftrag zu erhalten.
We feel sure that a trial order will convince you of the quality of our products and look forward to doing business with you.	Wir sind sicher, dass ein Probeauftrag Sie von der Qualität unserer Produkte überzeugen wird und freuen uns, mit Ihnen eine Geschäftsbeziehung aufzunehmen.
Enclosure(s)	**Anlage(n)**
Catalogue Price list	Katalog Preisliste

9 **Use the useful phrases to write an enquiry based on the following details.**

Situation

Sie (eigener Name) sind Sachbearbeiter/-in in der Verkaufsabteilung der Firma World Navigator GmbH (Querstraße 20, 44866 Bochum, Fax-Nr. 0049 234 9786053, E-Mail: info@worldnavigator.de). Ihre Firma ist ein bedeutender Großhändler für GPS-Geräte mit einem ausgezeichneten Ruf in ganz Europa. Aus Irland erhalten Sie eine Anfrage von Whitefriar Trekking Ltd (31 Wicklow Street, Dublin 8, Irland, Fax-Nr. 00353 1 874 9827, E-Mail: aileen.oreilly@whitefriar.ie).

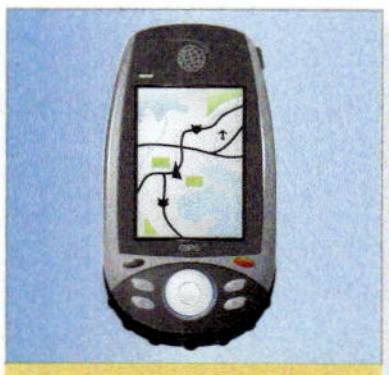
Handheld GPS device

Aufgabe

Verfassen Sie mit heutigem Datum ein Angebot an die irische Firma unter Berücksichtigung folgender Punkte:

> Ihr Ansprechpartner ist Mrs Aileen O' Reilly, Einkaufsleiterin
> Bedanken für Anfrage von vor fünf Tagen
> Beschreibung Ihrer Firma
> Hinweis auf Ihre Homepage unter www.worldnavigator.de mit downloadbarem Gesamtkatalog und Exportpreisliste
> Sie unterbreiten folgendes Angebot:
  - GPS-Gerät vom Typ „eTreck" mit Touchscreen, Artikel-Nr. eT49 zum Preis von 250 € pro Stück
  - GPS-Handgerät vom Typ „Xpedition", Artikel-Nr. XP1 zum Preis von 100 € pro Stück
> Mengenrabatt von 10 % bei Abnahme von 10 oder mehr Geräten
> Lieferung DDP Geschäftsräume des irischen Kunden innerhalb 14 Tagen nach Auftragseingang
> Angemessene Verabschiedung

10 **Use the useful phrases to write an enquiry based on the following details.**

Situation

Sie (eigener Name) sind Sachbearbeiter/-in in der Verkaufsabteilung der Firma Dadias Sportbekleidung GmbH, (Dadias Str. 37, 91074 Herzogenaurach, Fax-Nr. 0049 9132 8740, E-Mail: info@dadias.de). Ihre Gesellschaft stellt eine breite Palette von hochwertigen Artikeln her und hat bereits viele zufriedene Kunden überall in Westeuropa. Sie erhalten eine Anfrage von der Handelskette Sand and Sun Sports in Dubai (P.O. Box 259288, Dubai, Vereinigte Arabische Emirate), Fax-Nr. 00 971 4 3577701, E-Mail: sandsun@eim.ae. Das emiratische Unternehmen interessiert sich für Fußballhemden.

Football shirt

Aufgabe

Verfassen Sie mit heutigem Datum ein Angebot an die emiratische Firma unter Berücksichtigung folgender Punkte:

> Sie schreiben zu Hd. Ms July Dickinson in der Einkaufsabteilung.
> Bedanken für Anfrage nach Fußballhemden von vor 7 Tagen
> Beschreibung Ihrer Firma
> Sie fügen einen aktuellen Katalog mit Preisliste bei.
> Muster sind auf Wunsch erhältlich.
> Alle Preise verstehen sich CIP Flughafen Dubai.
> Großhandelsrabatt von 20 %
> Zahlungsbedingungen bei Erstauftrag sind Kasse bei Auftragserteilung (CWO)
> Lieferung erfolgt innerhalb ca. 30 Tagen nach Auftragseingang
> Angemessene Verabschiedung

Orders and acknowledgements

1 Soyang Europe imports rolls of material for advertising banners. Study the following order and complete the sentences below.

An order

Hammer Landstraße 1a • 41460 Neuss • Germany

SOYANG EUROPE GMBH

JD/TT
04 July 20..

TAYA Canvas Company Limited
110 Huaning Road
200245 SHANGHAI
CHINA

Attn. Mr Andy Zhao, Export Sales Director

Dear Mr Zhao

Order no. BK42 for banner material

Many thanks for your offer dated 28 June 20.. .

We now wish to place an order for the following goods:

Quantity	Description	Article No.	Unit Price ($)	Total ($)
10 rolls	Frontlit banner material	FL136	50.00	500.00
20 rolls	Backlit banner material	BL284	40.00	800.00
			Total price	**1,300.00**

Delivery: FOB Shanghai within 30 days after receipt of order
Packing: Container
Payment: 30% in advance, 70% after completion by transfer to your a/c at the Bank of China

Transport and insurance of the goods from Shanghai to Neuss via the Port of Rotterdam will be arranged by us.

We look forward to receiving your confirmation of order and advice of dispatch in the near future.

Yours sincerely
Soyang Europe GmbH

J. Dahlmann

Julia Dahlmann
Import Department

> The Incoterm FOB stands for 'free on board ...'.
> See page 193 for more details.
> a/c = account

Soyang Europe GmbH Neuss, Registergericht Neuss, HRB 14446, Geschäftsführer: Dr. Christian Koch

1 The TAYA Canvas Company is in ...
2 Julia Dahlmann works in ...
3 Andy Zhao sent Julia Dahlmann an offer on ...
4 All the prices are in ...
5 10 rolls of FL136 cost ...
6 One roll of BL284 costs ...
7 The TAYA Canvas Company has a bank account at ...
8 The goods will be sent in a ...
9 The goods will be sent to Europe by ship to ...
10 The Chinese company will soon send ...

Port of Shanghai

2 Match the German translations with points 1–8 in the box below.

Angaben über die bestellten Waren / Dienstleistungen | Angemessene Verabschiedung | Anlage(n) | Bestätigung / Versandanzeige | Bezug auf Angebot | Internationale Handelsklausel | Liefertermin/-zeit | Lieferung | Preise und Rabatte | Verpackung | Versand | Versicherung | Zahlung

Structure of an offer

An order covers some or all of the following points:

1 Reference to offer
2 Details of goods/services ordered
3 Price(s) and discount(s)
4 Delivery
  > Incoterm
  > delivery date/period
  > transport
  > packing
  > insurance
5 Payment
6 Acknowledgement / Advice of dispatch
7 Suitable ending
8 Enclosure(s)/Attachments

3 Look at the letter to the TAYA Canvas Company and in your exercise book make a note of as many of the points listed under 'Structure of an order' as possible.

4 Study the following order and say if the statements are true or false. Correct the false statements. Look up any new words in the word list at the back of the book.

Quantity	Description	Article No.	List Price	Total
100	HQ printer	HQ3000	€60.00	€6,000.00
250	Quickchip laptop	QC99	€100.00	€25,000.00
			– 30% trade discount	– €9,300.00
			Subtotal	€21,700.00
			+ 19% VAT*	€4,123.00
			Total price	**€25,823.00**
Delivery:	CIF Rotterdam by 30 June 20..			
Packing:	Sturdy cartons			
Payment:	2% 10 days, 30 days net after receipt of invoice			
				*Value added tax = *Mehrwertsteuer*

1 One printer normally costs €60.
2 There is a discount of 19%.
3 The final price of the goods is €21,700.
4 The goods will be delivered to the Netherlands.

5 The seller will pay for transport of the goods from Rotterdam to the buyer's premises.
6 The buyer wants the goods on or after 30 June 20.. .
7 The buyer will get a 10% discount if he pays within two days.
8 The buyer has 30 days to pay after he has received the invoice.
9 The printers and laptops will be packed in lightweight boxes.

5 When writing prices in English, follow the instructions to the right. Study the examples in the two orders on pages 154 and 155, and then write out the following prices in figures.

1 a hundred dollars
2 five thousand dollars
3 ten pounds and fifty pence
4 twenty thousand pounds and seventy-five cents
5 eighty-two dollars and sixty-seven cents
6 thirty pence
7 nine euros and ninety-nine cents
8 a million euros

Writing prices

2 23

6 TT Autobeschriftung GmbH imports materials from China. Listen to the telephone conversation between Markus Schimanski and Susan Wang and complete the sentences below.

1 The Chinese company specializes in
  a DDP film and tape.
  b PVC film and tape.
  c QVC film and tape.

2 The Chinese company can supply tape in
  a any colour.
  b three colours.
  c four colours.

3 *Go faster* tape
  a makes cars go faster.
  b makes racing cars go faster.
  c makes cars look like racing cars.

4 The Chinese company has a special offer for
  a film and tape.
  b film only.
  c tape only.

5 The final price of the film and tape is
  a $10 per roll for the film and $8.50 for the tape.
  b $9 per roll for the film and $7.50 for the tape.
  c $9 per roll for the film and $8.50 for the tape.

6 The German firm will qualify for the special FOB price if it orders at least
  a 100 rolls of film and tape.
  b 75 rolls of film and tape.
  c 50 rolls of film and tape.

7 The German firm will qualify for the special CIF price if it orders at least
  a 100 rolls of film and tape.
  b 75 rolls of film and tape.
  c 50 rolls of film and tape.

8 Delivery will take about
  a four weeks after receipt of order.
  b three weeks after receipt of order.
  c two weeks after receipt of order.

9 The terms of payment are
  a 50% with order and 50% on completion.
  b 70% with order and 30% on completion.
  c 30% with order and 70% on completion.

Structuring an order or acknowledgement

If you are writing about ***two or more items***, use a table with headings (see exercises 1 and 4) to make your order easy to understand. Use headings such as Quantity / Description / Catalogue No. [number] / Article No. / Colour / Size / Unit Price / List Price / Total. Under the table use the headings Subtotal / Discount / Trade discount / Quantity discount / Cash discount / 19% VAT [value added tax] / Total, as necessary.
Use extra headings *under* the table to give more information, e.g. Delivery / Payment / Packing / Insurance / Transport.
If you are only writing about ***one item***, just use headings, e.g.

Article:	eTreck GPS device
Catalogue no.:	GPS3000
Quantity:	10
List price:	€250.00
Quantity discount:	10%
VAT:	19%
Total price:	€2,677.50
Terms of delivery:	DDP (*destination*) our premises within 10 days after receipt of order
Packing:	Sturdy cartons
Terms of payment:	CWO

Useful phrases

Reference to offer	**Bezug auf Angebot**
Many thanks for your offer dated ...	Vielen Dank für Ihr Angebot vom ...
Having seen your offer on the internet and spoken to you on the telephone, ...	Nachdem wir Ihr Angebot im Internet gesehen und mit Ihnen gesprochen haben, ...
We have seen your offer for ... on the Internet.	Wir haben Ihr Angebot über ... im Internet gesehen.
Details of goods/services ordered	**Einzelheiten über bestellte Waren/ Dienstleistungen**
We now wish to place an order / a trial order for the following goods: ...	Wir möchten einen Auftrag / Probeauftrag über folgende Waren erteilen: ...
[*Headings*] Quantity / Description / Size / Catalogue No.	[*Überschriften*] Menge / Beschreibung / Größe / Katalog-Nr.
Price(s) and discount(s)	**Preis(e) und Rabatt(e)**
[*Headings*] Unit Price / List Price / Catalogue Price / Total	[*Überschriften*] Stückpreis / Listenpreis / Katalogpreis / Gesamt
Subtotal / Total price	Zwischensumme / Gesamtpreis
19% VAT [value added tax]	19% USt [Umsatzsteuer / Mehrwertsteuer]
Delivery	**Lieferung**
Incoterm FOB Shanghai / CIF Rotterdam / DDP (*destination*) our premises	**Incoterm (siehe Seite 193)** frei an Bord (FOB) Shanghai / Kosten, Versicherung Fracht (CIF) Rotterdam / geliefert verzollt zu unseren Geschäftsräumen (DIP ...)
delivery date/period ... within 10 days after receipt of order ... by 30 June 20..	**Liefertermin/-zeit** ... innerhalb 10 Tagen nach Auftragserhalt ... bis zum 30. Juni 20..

transport Transport and insurance of the goods from ... to ... via ... ... will be arranged by us/you.	**Versand** Versand und Versicherung der Ware von ... nach ... über ... wird von uns/Ihnen übernommen.
packing container in sturdy cartons	**Verpackung** Container in robusten Kartons
insurance Insurance will be arranged by us/you.	**Versicherung** die Versicherung wird von uns/Ihnen übernommen
Payment	**Zahlung**
30% in advance, 70% after completion	30% im Voraus, 70% bei Fertigstellung
by transfer to our a/c at ... (*name of bank*)	per Überweisung auf unser Konto bei ... (*Geldinstitut*)
by bank transfer	per Banküberweisung
2% 10 days, 30 days net after receipt of invoice	2% Skonto bei Zahlung innerhalb von 10 Tagen, netto bei Zahlung innerhalb von 30 Tagen nach Rechnungserhalt
Acknowledgement / advice of dispatch	**Auftragsbestätigung / Versandanzeige**
We look forward to receiving your advice of dispatch.	Wir freuen uns auf den Erhalt Ihrer Versandanzeige.
Please send us your confirmation of order and advice of dispatch in the near future.	Bitte schicken Sie uns Ihre Auftragsbestätigung und Versandanzeige in den nächsten Tagen zu.
Suitable ending	**Angemessene Verabschiedung**
We trust the goods will arrive punctually and in good condition ...	Wir vertrauen darauf, dass die Ware pünktlich und in gutem Zustand ankommt ...
... and will place further/regular orders if they sell well.	... und werden weitere/regelmäßige Aufträge erteilen, wenn sie sich gut verkauft.
Enclosure(s)	**Anlage(n)**
order form	Bestellformular

7 Use the useful phrases to write a letter/fax/e-mail order based on the following details.

Situation

Sie (eigener Name) sind Einkaufsleiter/-in bei der Firma TT Autobeschriftung GmbH (Tempelstr 99, 47918 Tönisvorst, Fax-Nr. 0049 2151 450277, E-Mail: vorname.nachname@tt-auto.de). Ihre Firma vertreibt selbstklebende Autobeschriftungsfolien (*film*) und Zierstreifen (*tape*) und bezieht das Material dafür aus China. Sie haben ein Angebot der chinesischen Firma Guangzhou Materials im Internet gesehen (Guangzhou Materials Ltd, Unit 2099, Panyu District, 511450 Guangzhou, China, Fax-Nr. 0086 20 8332 9126, E-Mail: john.wang@guangzhou.com) und die Firma anschließend angerufen.

Tape

Aufgabe

Erteilen Sie der chinesischen Firma einen Probeauftrag mit heutigem Datum unter Berücksichtigung folgender Punkte:

- Ihr Ansprechpartner ist Ms Susan Wang, Verkaufsabteilung.
- Bezug auf Angebot im Internet und Telefongespräch
- Sie bestellen mit Auftrags-Nr. VF247 je 100 Rollen *Go faster tape*, 0,08 mm × 1,07 m zu 7,50 $ pro Rolle, Katalog-Nr. VF8107 und *Self-adhesive film*, 0,10 mm × 1,27 m zu 9,00 $ pro Rolle, Katalog-Nr. SAF10127.

- Lieferung im Container CIF Rotterdam innerhalb von 30 Tagen nach Auftragserhalt
- Zahlungsbedingungen: 30 % im Voraus, 70 % bei Fertigstellung per Banküberweisung
- Bitte um Auftragsbestätigung und Versandanzeige
- Hoffnung auf pünktliche Lieferung der Ware in gutem Zustand
- Aussicht auf weitere Aufträge, wenn die Ware sich gut verkauft
- Angemessene Verabschiedung

8 Use the useful phrases to write a letter/fax/e-mail order based on the following details.

Situation

Sie sind Sevda Yildiz, Einkaufsleiterin bei der Firma Brix Mode GmbH in Bielefeld (Feldstr. 42, 33609 Bielefeld, Fax-Nr. 0049 521 285561, E-Mail: Sevda.yildiz@brixmode.de). Ihre Firma ist ein führender Importeur und Großhändler für junge Mode.

Aufgabe

Verfassen Sie mit heutigem Datum eine Bestellung an die schwedische Firma Patrik K (Björnbo 53, 11825 Stockholm, Schweden, Fax-Nr. 0046 8 609 4988, E-Mail: pehr.lindquist@patrikk.com) unter Berücksichtigung folgender Punkte:

- Ihr Ansprechpartner ist Mr Pehr Lindquist, Exportleiter.
- Bezug auf Angebot vom ... (vor ca. einer Woche)
- Mit Auftrags-Nr. TS826 bestellen Sie 1.000 Damen-Seidenschals (*lady's silk scarf / ladies' silk scarves*) vom Typ „Sunrise", Stückpreis 10,- €, Artikel-Nr. HB49.
- Fordern Sie einen Mengenrabatt von 3 %.
- Errechnen Sie den Endpreis.
- Lieferung CIP Flughafen Düsseldorf innerhalb von 7 Tagen nach Auftragserhalt
- Zahlung: per Banküberweisung, 2 % Skonto bei Zahlung innerhalb von 10 Tagen, netto bei Zahlung innerhalb von 30 Tagen
- Bitte um Auftragsbestätigung
- Hoffen, dass die Ware pünktlich und wohlbehalten ankommt
- Aussicht auf regelmäßige Aufträge, wenn sie sich gut verkauft
- Angemessene Verabschiedung

Lady's silk scarf

Transport

Note: 'To ship' means to transport. The word does not only refer to transport by ship.

- Heavy and/or bulky goods (e.g. coal, oil, machines) are usually shipped by rail or ship.
- Light loads or perishable goods (e.g. fresh flowers from Africa) are normally shipped by air.
- The motorway networks of industrialized countries make it possible to ship goods door-to-door by road.
- Multimodal transport is used for goods in containers, because they can be easily loaded onto trains, lorries, ships and planes.
- The Incoterms (see page 193) define the buyer and seller's responsibilities when goods are shipped.

by rail

by road

by ship

by air

9 **Study the Chinese company's reply to the letter from Soyang GmbH and answer the questions on the opposite page.**

Acknowledgement by e-mail

E-MAIL

To:	julia.dahlmann@soyang.de
Subject:	Your order no. BK42 dated 04 July 20.. for banner material
Attachments:	SuperFlat.pdf

Dear Ms Dahlmann

Many thanks for the above-mentioned order. We are pleased to confirm the details as listed below:

Quantity	Article	Size	Article No.	List Price	Total
10 rolls	Frontlit banner material	5m wide	FL136	$50.00	$500.00
20 rolls	Backlit banner material	4m wide	BL284	$40.00	$800.00
				Total price	**$1,300.00**

As agreed, the goods will be packed in a container and delivered FOB Shanghai by 15 August 20.. at the latest. We note that you will arrange for transport and insurance of the goods from the Port of Shanghai to the Port of Rotterdam and then to your premises in Neuss, Germany.

Payment of 30% of the total amount is now due. Please therefore transfer $390 to our account at the Bank of China. We expect to complete your order in approx. 20 days' time and will inform you as soon as the goods are ready. Payment of the remaining 70% will then be due. As soon as the total amount has been received, the goods will be transported to the Port of Shanghai for shipment and we will send you our advice of dispatch.

We would also like to take this opportunity to draw your attention to our new SuperFlat display material. It is suitable for high resolution posters and is supplied in 50m x 3.20m rolls. A pdf file on the new product is enclosed for your information.

If you have any queries about your order or wish to receive a quotation for our new SuperFlat display material, please do not hesitate to contact us.

Thank you for placing your order with the TAYA Canvas Company.

Yours sincerely

Andy Zhou
Export Sales Director

1 How will the goods be transported from Shanghai to Rotterdam?
2 What does FOB stand for?
3 Where is the German buyer's firm located?
4 What are the terms of payment?
5 Who will pay for transport of the goods from Shanghai to Germany?
6 Why has the Chinese company enclosed a pdf file with its acknowledgement?

10 Match the German translations with points 1–9 in the box below.

Ablehnung des Auftrags | Angebot von Ersatzware | Angemessene Verabschiedung | Anlage(n) | Auftragsbestätigung | Bezug auf Auftrag | Bezug auf neue Produkte / Dienstleistungen | Bitte um Bestätigung | Datum und Art der Lieferung | Liefer- und Zahlungsbedingungen | Preise und Rabatte | Versandanzeige

Structure of an acknowledgement

An acknowledgement covers some or all of the following points:

1 Reference to offer
2 Confirmation of order or
  > offer of substitutes
  > rejection of order
3 Price(s) and discount(s)
4 Terms of delivery and payment
5 Date and mode of delivery
  > advice of dispatch
6 Request for confirmation
7 Reference to new product(s)/services
8 Suitable ending
9 Enclosure(s)/Attachments

11 Look at the e-mail to Soyang GmbH and in your exercise book make a note of as many of the points listed under 'structure of an acknowledgement' as possible.

EXAMPLE
1 Reference to offer: *offer dated 28 June 20..*

Useful phrases

Reference to order	**Bezug auf Auftrag**
Many thanks for the above-mentioned order.	Vielen Dank für den oben erwähnten Auftrag.
Confirmation of order	**Auftragsbestätigung**
We are pleased to confirm the details as listed below:	Wir bestätigen gern die Einzelheiten wie folgt:
offer of substitutes Unfortunately, the article you require is currently out of stock. Might we therefore suggest supplying ... (*substitute*) instead? Please refer to the enclosed brochure/document for more details. The list price of this article is ... . Under the circumstances we are prepared to offer it at ... (*price/Incoterm*) Alternatively, we can supply it at ... (*price/Incoterm*).	**Angebot von Ersatzware** Leider ist der von Ihnen benötigte Artikel nicht vorrätig. Dürfen wir deshalb stattdessen ... (*Ersatz*) vorschlagen? Weitere Einzelheiten können der beigefügten Broschüre/Datei entnommen werden. Der Preis dieses Artikels beträgt ... . Unter den Umständen sind wir bereit, ihn zum Preis von ... (*Preis/Incoterm*) anzubieten. Als Alternative können wir ihn zum Preis von ... (*Preis/Incoterm*) anbieten.

rejection of order We are unfortunately unable to fill/execute/ complete your order.	**Ablehnung des Auftrags** Leider können wir Ihren Auftrag nicht ausführen.
Price(s) and discount(s)	**Preise(e) und Rabatt(e)**
[*Headings*] Unit Price / List Price / Catalogue Price	[*Überschriften*] Stückpreis/Listenpreis/ Katalogpreis
[*Headings*] Total / Sub-total / Total Price	[*Überschriften*] Gesamt / Zwischensumme / Gesamtpreis
quantity discount	Mengenrabatt
Terms of delivery and payment	**Liefer- und Zahlungsbedingungen**
As agreed, the goods will be delivered FOB Shanghai.	Wie vereinbart wird die Ware FOB Shanghai geliefert.
Payment of 30% of the invoice / total amount is now due.	30 % des Rechnungsbetrags/ Gesamtbetrags sind jetzt fällig.
Please therefore transfer $390 to our account at the Bank of China.	Bitte überweisen Sie deshalb 390 $ auf unser Konto bei der Bank of China.
Payment of the remaining 70% will then be due.	Die verbleibenden 70 % des Rechnungsbetrags werden dann fällig sein.
Our terms of payment for an initial order are ... (e.g. CWO [cash with order]).	Unsere Zahlungsbedingungen für einen Erstauftrag lauten ... (z. B. Kasse bei Auftragserteilung (CWO)).
Date and mode of delivery	**Datum und Art der Lieferung**
The goods will be delivered by ... (*date*, e.g. 15 August 20..) at the latest.	Die Ware wird bis spätestens ... (*Datum*, z. B. 15. August 20..) geliefert.
We expect to complete your order in approx. 20 days' time and will inform you as soon as the goods are ready.	Wir rechnen mit der Erledigung Ihres Auftrages in ca. 20 Tagen und werden Sie benachrichtigen, sobald die Ware fertig ist.
The goods will be packed in a container.	Die Ware wird in einen Container verpackt.
We note that you will arrange for transport and insurance of the goods from ... to your premises.	Wir nehmen zur Kenntnis, dass Sie Versand und Versicherung der Ware von ... bis zu Ihren Geschäftsräumen übernehmen werden.
Delivery will be made within approx. 30 days after receipt of order / by the end of the month.	Die Lieferung erfolgt innerhalb ca. 30 Tagen nach Auftragserhalt / bis Ende des Monats.
advice of dispatch As soon as the total invoice amount has been received, ... the goods will be transported to the Port of ... (*city*) for shipment. ... we will send you our advice of dispatch.	**Versandanzeige** Sobald der volle Rechnungsbetrag eingegangen ist, ... wird die Ware zum Hafen ... (*Stadt*) zur Verladung transportiert. ... werden wir Ihnen die Versandanzeige zuschicken.
Request for confirmation	**Bitte um Bestätigung**
Please let us know which offer you prefer.	Bitte lassen Sie uns wissen, welches Angebot Sie bevorzugen.
Reference to new product(s)/services	**Bezug auf neue(s) Produkt(e)/ Dienstleistungen**
We would also like to take this opportunity to draw your attention to ...	Bei dieser Gelegenheit möchten wir Ihre Aufmerksamkeit auch auf ... lenken.

... which is currently on offer.	... das derzeit im Angebot ist.
A pdf file/document / A brochure on the new product is enclosed for your information.	Zu Ihrer Information ist eine pdf-Datei/ Broschüre beigefügt.
Suitable ending	**Angemessene Verabschiedung**
If you have any questions/queries about your order / the (new) product ...	Sollten Sie weitere Fragen/Rückfragen zu Ihrem Auftrag / zum (neuen) Produkt haben, ...
If you or wish to receive a quotation for our new ... (product), ...	Wenn Sie ein Angebot über unser neues ... (Produkt) erhalten möchten, ...
... (please) do not hesitate to contact us / to get in touch with us.	... (bitte) zögern Sie nicht, sich mit uns in Verbindung zu setzen.
Thank you for placing your order with ... (*name of company*).	Vielen Dank für Ihren Auftrag.
Enclosure(s)	**Anlage(n)**
<file name> / Catalogue / Brochure	<Dateiname> / Katalog / Broschüre

12 Use the useful phrases to write a letter/fax/e-mail acknowledgement based on the following details.

Situation

Sie (eigener Name) arbeiten in der Exportabteilung bei der Firma Brix Mode GmbH in Bielefeld (Feldstr. 42, 33609 Bielefeld, Fax-Nr. 0049 521 285561, E-Mail: vorname.nachname@brixmode.de). Ihre Firma erhält von der englischen Firma High End Fashion eine Bestellung über 20 Damen-Seidenschals (*lady's silk scarf / ladies' silk scarves*) vom Typ „Sunrise", Artikel-Nr. HB49, Stückpreis 40 GBP.

Aufgabe

Verfassen Sie mit heutigem Datum eine Auftragsbestätigung an die englische Firma (High End Fashion Ltd, 99 High Street, Newcastle NE3 9LM, England, Fax-Nr. 0044 191 407877, E-Mail: jill.ryan@highend.co.uk) unter Berücksichtigung folgender Punkte:

- Ihr Ansprechpartner ist Ms Jill Ryan, Importsachbearbeiterin.
- Bezug auf Bestellung Nr. 42BK von High End Fashion über Damen-Seidenschals vom ... (*vor ca. 5 Tagen*)
- Darstellung der einzelnen Positionen der Bestellung (Artikel, Menge usw.)
- Mengenrabatt von 5% wird gewährt.
- Errechnen Sie den Endpreis.
- Lieferung CIP Flughafen Newcastle bis ... (*Datum in 10 Tagen angeben*)
- Zahlung: Kasse bei Auftragserteilung per Banküberweisung
- Versandanzeige wird nach Erhalt des Rechnungsbetrags verschickt
- Bezug auf neues Produkt und beigefügte Broschüre / Datei: Damen-Strickjacke (*lady's cardigan*) „Flair"
- Bitte um Mitteilung, falls weitere Informationen über Bestellung oder Angebot über neues Produkt erwünscht
- Angemessene Verabschiedung

Lady's cardigan

13 **Use the useful phrases to write a letter/fax/e-mail acknowledgement based on the following details.**

Situation

Sie (eigener Name) sind Sachbearbeiter/-in in der Verkaufsabteilung der Firma Dadias Sportbekleidung GmbH, (Dadias Str. 37, 91074 Herzogenaurach, Fax-Nr. 0049 9132 8740, E-Mail: vorname.nachname@dadias.de). Ihre Gesellschaft erhält von der Handelskette Sand and Sun Sports in Dubai (P.O. Box 259288, Dubai, Vereinigte Arabische Emirate), Fax-Nr. 00 971 4 3577701, E-Mail: sandsun@eim.ae) einen Erstauftrag über 1.000 Fußballhemden vom Typ „TopShot 2000“ zum Stückpreis von 15,00 €.

Aufgabe

Verfassen Sie mit heutigem Datum ein Schreiben an die emiratische Firma unter Berücksichtigung folgender Punkte:

- Sie schreiben zu Hd. Ms July Dickinson in der Einkaufsabteilung.
- Bedanken für Auftrag über Fußballhemden von vor 7 Tagen
- Ware leider nicht vorrätig
- Vorschlag: Fußballhemd „Kicker 49“, Listenpreis 17,50 €
- Broschüre/Datei ist beigefügt.
- Ihr Angebot: 15,00 € pro Stück bei Lieferung FOB Hamburg oder 17,50 € pro Stück bei Lieferung CIP Flughafen Dubai
- Zahlungsbedingungen Kasse bei Auftragserteilung (CWO)
- Lieferung erfolgt innerhalb ca. 30 Tagen nach Auftragseingang.
- Bitte um Mitteilung, welches Angebot angenommen wird
- Weitere Informationen können jederzeit zur Verfügung gestellt werden.
- Angemessene Verabschiedung

5 Payments and reminders

1 **Fair Trade Fashions in the UK requests payment from Brix Mode in Bielefeld for a consignment of goods. Read the letter and choose the right answers to complete the sentences.**

A request for payment

Fair Trade Fashions

85 Princes Park
GATESHEAD
NE1 9NF
GREAT BRITAIN

JM/TT
10 December 20..

Brix Mode
Feldstraße 42
33609 Bielefeld
GERMANY

Attn. Ms Sevda Yildiz, Purchasing Director

Dear Ms Yildiz

Your order no. FWA 4226 dated 05 December 20.. for fashion wear and accessories

The above-mentioned goods are now ready for dispatch and our invoice for £10,500.00 is enclosed for payment. Please remit the invoice amount to our company's account at NatWest Bank plc in Gateshead:

IBAN:	GB38NWBK57002167984202
BIC:	NWBKGB2LXXX

The goods will be shipped as soon as payment has been received.

For your information we are also enclosing a brochure on our company's latest collection, 'Spring Surprises'. Should you require further information, please do not hesitate to contact us.

Thank you for choosing to place your order with Fair Trade Fashions.

Yours sincerely
Fair Trade Fashions

Joanne Miles

Joanne Miles
Accounts Section

Enc

1 Sevda Yildiz
  a works in Germany.
  b works in England.
  c works in Turkey.

2 Joanne Miles
  a now has to pay £10,500.00.
  b has not yet received £10,500.00.
  c has just spent £10,500.00.

3 Brix Mode has
  a received the goods.
  b paid for the goods.
  c ordered the goods.

4 The German company
  a ordered the goods on 10 December.
  b ordered the goods on 05 December.
  c received the goods on 05 December.

5 The goods are
  a on their way.
  b waiting to be sent.
  c already with the buyer.

6 The brochure is about
  a new fashion wear.
  b the fashion wear ordered.
  c all the company's products.

2 Match the German translations with points 1–5 in the box below.

Weitere Informationen | Anlage(n) | Bezug auf Rechnung für Waren oder Dienstleistungen | Angemessene Verabschiedung | Zahlung

Structure of a request for payment

A request for payment covers some or all of the following points:

1 Reference to invoice for goods or services
2 Payment
3 Further information
4 Suitable ending
5 Enclosure(s)

3 Look at the letter from Fair Trade Fashions and in your exercise book make a note of as many of the points listed under the heading 'Structure of a request for payment' as possible.

4 Use words in the letter from Fair Trade Fashions to fill in the gaps.

I work in the ...[1] department of my company, which means we buy goods. We normally get an e-mail when the goods are ready for ...[2] and sometimes we have to pay the ...[3] before the supplier will ...[4] the goods. If this happens, we ...[5] the amount to the supplier's bank ...[6]. We need two things for this – the supplier's ...[7], which is a very long number and also his ...[8], to make sure the money goes to the right bank.

5 Study the commercial invoice on the opposite page and then answer the following questions.

1 What is the name of (a) the buyer and (b) the seller?
2 How do we know that the goods will be transported by ship?
3 How much of the invoice amount must the buyer pay first?
4 What must the buyer do before the goods can be shipped?
5 What currency is the invoice in?

A commercial invoice

达亚帆布（上海）有限公司

TA YA CANVAS (SHANGHAI) COMPANY LIMITED

上海市闵行经济技术开发区华宁路 110 号 邮编 ：200245

NO. 110, HUANING ROAD, MINHANG ECONOMIC & TECHNOLOGICAL DEVELOPING ZONE, SHANGHAI, P.R. CHINA. P.C.: 200245

TEL: (86-21) 6463 2409 FAX: (86-21) 6463 2157

COMMERCIAL INVOICE

Invoice No. TYSH910
21 March 20..

To:
Soyang Europe GmbH
Osterather Str. 6, 41460 Neuss,
Registergericht Neuss HRB 14446
Tel: +49 2131 512 888 1
Fax: +49 2131 512 888 2

Quantity	Width	Length	Description	Area (m^2)	Unit Price (USD)	Total (USD)
55 rolls	3.20 m	50 m	Matte white banner material, 450 g	8,800	1.51	13,288.00
20 rolls	1.37 m	50 m	Matte white banner material, 510 g	1,370	1.61	2,205.70
					Total	15,493.70

Fifteen thousand four hundred and ninety-three United States dollars and seventy cents only

Terms of payment: 30% deposit, 70% balance to be paid before shipment
Delivery: FCB Shanghai, 4 weeks after receipt of deposit
Packing: Seaworthy container
Name of bank: Bank of China (Shanghai) Ltd
Account number: 031-355-8-313199-4
Swift code (BIC): BKCHSHHH

6 **Write out the following prices in words.**

1 USD 250.50
2 USD 1,000,000.00
3 GBP 99.32
4 GBP 475.36
5 CAD 1,263.47
6 CAD 519.33
7 EUR 637.78
8 EUR 6.51
9 JPY 17,943
10 JPY 25,000

	Infobox		
	Currency	**Abbreviation**	**Symbol**
	United States dollar(s)	USD	$
	euro(s)	EUR	€
	Japanese yen (-)	JPY	¥
	pound(s) sterling	GBP	£
	Australian dollar(s)	AUD	$
	Swiss franc(s)	CHF	Fr
	Canadian dollar(s)	CAD	$
	Hong Kong dollar(s)	HKD	$
	New Zealand dollar(s)	NZD	$

Useful phrases

Reference to invoice for goods or services	**Bezugnahme auf Rechnung für Waren oder Dienstleistungen**
The above-mentioned goods are now ready for dispatch.	Die oben genannten Waren sind jetzt versandbereit.
The goods were dispatched ... (e.g. yesterday).	Die Ware wurde ... (z. B. gestern) versandt.
Payment	**Zahlung**
Our invoice for £5,750.00 is enclosed for payment.	Unsere Rechnung über 5.750,00 £ ist beigefügt.
Please remit the invoice amount to our company's account at NatWest Bank plc in ...	Bitte überweisen Sie den Rechnungsbetrag auf unser Firmenkonto bei der NatWest Bank plc in ...
The goods as per your order no. 1226-D dated 24 March ... are now ready for dispatch.	Die gemäß Ihrem Auftrag Nr. 1226-D vom 24. März ... gelieferten Waren sind jetzt versandbereit.
If payment is made within 10 days, you may deduct a cash discount of 3% from the invoice amount.	Wenn die Zahlung innerhalb von 10 Tagen erfolgt, können Sie 3 % Skonto vom Rechnungsbetrag abziehen.
The goods will be shipped as soon as payment has been received.	Die Waren werden geschickt, sobald die Zahlung eingegangen ist.
Further information	**Weitere Informationen**
For your information, we are also enclosing a brochure and an export price list on our company's latest collection ...	Zu Ihrer Information fügen wir ebenfalls eine Broschüre und eine Exportpreisliste über unsere neueste Mode-Kollektion ... bei.
... which is on offer for the next 30 days.	... das für die nächsten 30 Tage im Angebot ist.
Suitable ending	**Angemessene Verabschiedung**
Please do not hesitate to contact us should you require further information.	Sollten Sie weitere Informationen benötigen, zögern Sie bitte nicht, mit uns in Verbindung zu treten.
We look forward to receiving further orders from your company.	Wir freuen uns, weitere Aufträge von Ihrer Firma zu erhalten.
Thank you for choosing to place your order with Fair Trade Fashions.	Vielen Dank, dass Sie sich entschlossen haben, Ihren Auftrag Fair Trade Fashions zu erteilen.
Enclosure(s)	**Anlage(n)**
Invoice/Brochure/Catalogue/Price list	Rechnung/Broschüre/Katalog/Preisliste

7 Use the useful phrases to write a letter/fax/e-mail about payment based on the following details.

Skiing equipment

Situation

Sie (eigener Name) arbeiten in der Exportabteilung der Firma Sportbedarf Reimann GmbH in Köln (Aachener Str. 220, 50933 Köln, Fax-Nr. 0049 221 2337944, E-Mail: export@sbr.de). Vor einem Monat hat Ihre Firma einen Auftrag über Skiausrüstung (*skiing equipment*) von der schottischen Firma Winter Gear Ltd (222 Grampian Road, Aviemore PH22 1RH, UK, Fax-Nr. 0044 1479 817714, E-Mail: purchasing@wintergear.org) erhalten.

Aufgabe

Verfassen Sie ein Schreiben (Brief, Fax oder E-Mail) an die schottische Firma unter Berücksichtigung folgender Einzelheiten:

- Ansprechpartner: Ms Sheena Murray, Einkaufsleiterin
- Bezug auf Auftrag Nr. SE9756
- Rechnung über 5.875,00 € ist beigefügt.
- Ware wurde gestern versandt.
- Bitte um Überweisung des Rechnungsbetrags auf Ihr Firmenkonto bei der Deutschen Bank in Köln (BIC: DEUTDEDK353, IBAN: DE21700519957229735567)
- 3 % Skonto bei Zahlung innerhalb von 10 Tagen
- Broschüre über Ihre neuesten Skier, die für die nächsten 14 Tage im Angebot sind, liegt bei.
- Weitere Informationen jederzeit erhältlich
- Angemessene Verabschiedung

8 Use the useful phrases to write a letter/fax/e-mail about payment based on the following details.

Situation

(Fortsetzung von Aufgabe 12 *Acknowledgements* auf Seite 163)
Sie (eigener Name) arbeiten in der Exportabteilung der Firma Brix Mode GmbH in Bielefeld. Die englische Firma High End Fashion Ltd hat bei Ihnen Damen-Seidenschals bestellt, und die Ware ist nun versandbereit.

Aufgabe

Verfassen Sie mit heutigem Datum ein Schreiben an High End Fashion Ltd. Berücksichtigen Sie folgende Punkte:

- Ihr Ansprechpartner ist Ms Jill Ryan, Importsachbearbeiterin.
- Bedanken für E-Mail von heute
- Bezug auf Bestellung Nr. 42BK vom ... (vor ca. 7 Tagen) über Damen-Seidenschals
- Die Ware ist versandbereit.
- Ihre Rechnung über 760,00 britische Pfund ist beigefügt.
- Bitte um Überweisung des Rechnungsbetrags auf Ihr Firmenkonto bei der Commerzbank in Bielefeld (BIC: COBADEFF480, IBAN: DE60480400350002588291
- Die Ware wird sofort nach Zahlungseingang verschickt.
- Angemessene Verabschiedung

2 24 **9 Soyang GmbH in Neuss has sold a consignment of banner material to a regular customer called Rimtek Trading in Tampere, Finland. The terms of payment were 10 days 2%, 30 days net after receipt of the goods. Payment is now five days overdue, so Jana König in the accounts department phones Mr Olli-Pekka Mäkinen, the purchasing director of the Finnish company.**

Listen to or read the dialogue and say if the statements are true or false. Correct the false statements.

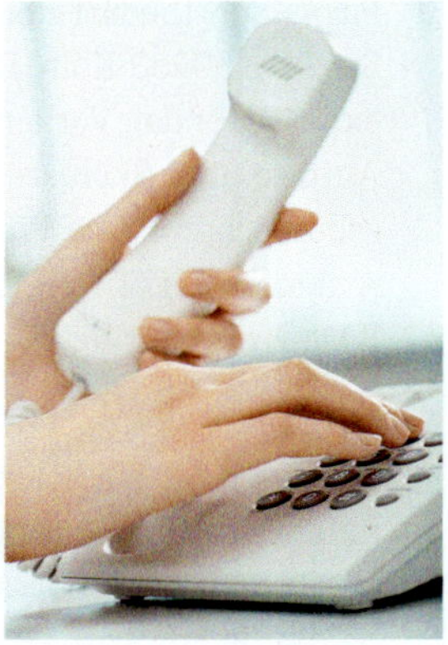

A telephone reminder

OLLI-PEKKA: Rimteck Trading, Mäkinen.
JANA: Hello, it's Jana König from Soyang in Germany.
OLLI-PEKKA: Hello, Ms König. How can I help you?
JANA: Well, I'm just calling to ask you about payment for the consignment of banner material we sent you five weeks ago. It's now five days overdue.
OLLI-PEKKA: Oh, I see! Could I have the order number, please?
JANA: Yes, the number is BM4024.
OLLI-PEKKA: Just a moment ... Right, I have it here in front of me. The material was delivered to the wrong address. It went to our other warehouse 50 km from here, so when it finally arrived at our new premises it was a week late.
JANA: Oh, I see! So are you saying that your company has now moved to a new location altogether?
OLLI-PEKKA: Well, almost. We still have the old warehouse but next week we're going to close it completely and only have the new one where we are now.
JANA: Thanks for the explanation. I understand what happened now.
OLLI-PEKKA: We sent all our suppliers an e-mail with the new address but perhaps it got overlooked. People get so many e-mails these days. Anyway, as payment was agreed 30 days after receipt of the goods, your invoice will be paid the day after tomorrow.
JANA: I see. Well, we didn't get your e-mail, Mr Mäkinen, so will you send it to us again, please?
OLLI-PEKKA: Yes, certainly. Could I have your e-mail address?
JANA: Yes, it's jana.koenig@soyang.eu.
OLLI-PEKKA: Thanks. I'll send you the e-mail again now. One moment ... erm ... OK.
JANA: OK, thanks.
OLLI-PEKKA: Anything else I can do for you, Ms König?
JANA: No, thanks very much and thanks for your e-mail. It's just arrived.
OLLI-PEKKA: You're welcome. Thanks for calling. Bye.
JANA: Bye.

1 Olli-Pekka calls Jana.
2 The Finnish company has not yet paid for the goods.
3 The wrong material was delivered.
4 The new warehouse is 50 km from the old one.
5 The old warehouse is now closed.
6 The Finnish company forgot to tell Soyang about the new address.
7 The Finnish company will pay for the goods in two days' time.
8 Jana still has not got the new address.

Terms of payment and reminders

The terms of payment for new or unreliable customers are usually payment in advance, CWO (cash with order) or letter of credit (*Akkreditiv*), because in each case the seller can be sure of being paid.

Regular and/or trusted customers are given better terms pf payment, e.g.
- open account terms
- 10 days 2%, 30 days net
- 30/60/90 days net
- 1/3 with order, 1/3 on delivery, 1/3 within 30 days after delivery

In most cases, a reminder is therefore sent to a regular and/or trusted customer. The first reminder is a polite reference to the unpaid invoice and a request to pay soon. The second reminder is more forceful. It asks for an explanation and is an urgent request for payment. The third reminder (or final demand) sets a deadline and describes the consequences of non-payment. It is normally addressed to a senior executive and marked 'Confidential'.

10 Read the three reminders and do the following tasks.

1 Write down how much time the customer is given to pay in each reminder.
2 Find the words in the first reminder which make it polite.
3 Explain what will happen if the customer still does not pay after the final demand.

First reminder

26 June 20..

Attn. Ms Margery Ingram, Export Sales Director

Dear Ms Ingram

Invoice no. BT9854 for £8,525.75 dated 18 May 20..

It has most probably escaped your notice that payment of the above-mentioned invoice was due on 18 June 20.. .
We look forward to receiving the sum in question in the next few days.

Yours sincerely

Second reminder

02 July 20..

Dear Ms Ingram

Invoice no. BT9854 for £8,525.75 dated 18 May 20..

We are sorry to note that the above-mentioned invoice is still overdue despite our letter dated 26 June 20.. .

We would very much welcome an explanation of why payment has not been made but, whatever the case may be, we would urgently request you to pay without delay. If payment has already been made, please disregard this letter.

Yours sincerely

Final demand

09 July 20..

CONFIDENTIAL

Dear Ms Ingram

Invoice no. BT9854 for £8,525.75 dated 18 May 20..

We refer to our two previous letters, dated 26 June and 02 July, about the above-mentioned invoice, which is still overdue.

As we have received neither an explanation nor a remittance, we are setting you a final deadline for payment of 7 days. If payment is not made by 16 July 20.., we will stop all further deliveries and take the necessary steps to recover the sum owing.

Prompt payment is all that is needed to settle this matter.

Yours sincerely

11 Study the three reminders and match the sentences halves.

1	Payment of the invoice was due on	a	16 July.
2	The first reminder was written on	b	explanation.
3	The date of the invoice is	c	confidential.
4	The customer has not given an	d	remittance.
5	The special marking is the word	e	deliveries.
6	The final deadline is	f	18 June.
7	Another word for a sum of money is	g	26 June.
8	If the customer doesn't pay the supplier will stop all	h	18 May.

12 Match the German translations with points 1–7 in the box below.

Angemessene Verabschiedung | Anlage(n) | Bezug auf frühere Mahnung(en) | Bezug auf überfällige Rechnung | Bitte um eine Erklärung | Bitte um Zahlung einschließlich Fristsetzung | Folgen bei Nichtzahlung

13 Look at the three reminders and in your exercise book make a note of as many of the points listed under the heading 'Structure of a reminder' as possible.

Structure of a reminder

A reminder covers some or all of the following points:

1. Reference to overdue invoice/ account
2. Reference to previous reminder(s)
3. Request for explanation
4. Request for payment including deadline
5. Consequences of non-payment
6. Suitable ending
7. Enclosure(s)

Useful phrases

Reference to overdue invoice/account	Bezug auf überfällige Rechnung
We are sorry to note that our invoice for ... / the above-mentioned invoice is now ... days/ weeks overdue ...	Wir bedauern festzustellen, dass unsere Rechnung über ... / die oben genannte Rechnung nun ... Tage/Wochen überfällig ist.
... despite out letter dated ... / our telephone call on ... the invoice is now 10 days overdue.	... trotz unseres Schreibens vom ... / Telefonats am ... , ist die Rechnung nunmehr 10 Tage überfällig.
We wish to point out that our sales agreement provides for payment within 30 days at the latest.	Wir möchten darauf hinweisen, dass unsere Verkaufsvereinbarung eine Zahlung innerhalb von spätestens 30 Tagen vorsieht.
Reference to previous reminder(s)	**Bezug auf frühere Mahnung(en)**
We refer to our two previous letters (see enclosures), dated ... and ... with regard to the above-mentioned invoice, which is still overdue.	Wir beziehen uns auf unsere zwei vorhergehenden Briefe (siehe Anlagen) vom ... und ... bezüglich der oben genannten Rechnung, die noch offen steht.
As we have received neither an explanation nor a remittance ...	Da wir weder eine Erklärung noch eine Überweisung erhalten haben, ...
Request for explanation	**Bitte um eine Erklärung**
Why has our invoice not been paid?	Warum ist unsere Rechnung nicht bezahlt worden?
We would therefore welcome an explanation as to why payment is delayed.	Wir würden deshalb eine Erklärung für den Zahlungsverzug begrüßen.
Request for payment including deadline	**Bitte um Zahlung einschl. Fristsetzung**
Whatever the case may be ...	Wie dem auch sei ...
We must therefore request that you pay by 30 November 20.. at the latest.	Wir müssen Sie deshalb bitten, bis spätestens 30. November 20... zu zahlen.
We must insist that you remit the amount in question without delay.	Wir müssen darauf bestehen, dass der betreffende Betrag unverzüglich überwiesen wird.
We are setting you a final deadline for payment of 7 days.	Wir setzen Ihnen eine letzte Zahlungsfrist von 7 Tagen.
Consequences of non-payment	**Folgen der Nichtzahlung**
If payment is not made by 03 October 20.., we will stop all further deliveries and take the necessary steps to recover the sum owing.	Sollte die Zahlung bis zum 3. Oktober nicht geleistet werden, werden wir alle weiteren Lieferungen einstellen und die notwendigen Schritte einleiten, um den fälligen Betrag zu erhalten.
Should you fail to pay this invoice, we will have no choice but to discontinue our business relationship with your company.	Wenn Sie es versäumen, unsere Rechnung zu begleichen, haben wir keine andere Wahl, als unsere Geschäftsbeziehungen zu Ihrem Unternehmen einzustellen.
Suitable ending	**Angemessene Verabschiedung**
We look forward to receiving the sum in question in the next few days.	Wir würden uns freuen, die betreffende Summe in den nächsten Tagen zu erhalten.
Prompt payment is all that is needed to settle this matter.	Diese Angelegenheit kann durch eine umgehende Überweisung Ihrerseits geregelt werden.
If payment has already been made, please disregard this letter/fax/e-mail.	Sollte die Zahlung bereits erfolgt sein, betrachten Sie diesen Brief / dieses Fax / diese E-Mail bitte als gegenstandslos.
Enclosure(s)	**Anlage(n)**
Invoice(s) Letters dated ... and ...	Rechnung(en) Briefe vom ... und ...

14 Use the useful phrases to write a reminder in the form of a letter/fax/e-mail based on the following details.

Situation

(Fortsetzung von Aufgabe 7 auf Seite 169)

Sie (eigener Name) arbeiten in der Buchhaltung der Firma Sportbedarf Reimann GmbH in Köln. Vor sechs Wochen hat Ihre Firma Skiausrüstung an die schottische Firma Winter Gear Ltd in Aviemore geliefert und anschließend eine Rechnung geschickt. Trotz zweier Mahnungen haben Sie bis heute weder eine Erklärung noch eine Überweisung erhalten.

Aufgabe

Verfassen Sie eine letzte Mahnung (Brief, Fax oder E-Mail) an die schottische Firma unter Berücksichtigung folgender Einzelheiten:

- Ansprechpartner: Ms Sheena Murray, Einkaufsleiterin
- Behandlungsvermerk: Vertraulich
- Bezug auf Rechnung Nr. NM319 über 5.875,00 € vom... (Datum vor 6 Wochen)
- Bezug auf 1. und 2. Mahnung von vor 14 und 7 Tagen (Kopien liegen diesem Schreiben bei bzw. sind angehängt)
- Sie haben weder eine Erklärung noch eine Überweisung erhalten.
- Setzen Sie eine letzte Zahlungsfrist von 14 Tagen.
- Bei Nichtzahlung Stornierung künftiger Lieferungen und Androhung weiterer Schritte
- Bitte, dieses Schreiben als gegenstandslos zu betrachten, wenn Zahlung bereits erfolgt ist
- Angemessene Verabschiedung

15 Use the useful phrases to write a reminder in the form of a letter/fax/e-mail based on the following details.

Situation

(Fortsetzung Aufgabe 9 *Offers* auf Seite 153)

Sie (eigener Name) sind Sachbearbeiter/-in in der Buchhaltung der Firma World Navigator GmbH in Bochum. Ihre Firma hat eine Lieferung GPS-Geräte mit Rechnung-Nr. GPSIR-92 über 6.300,00 € (Datum vor 5 Wochen) an die Firma Whitefriar Trekking Ltd in Dublin, Irland geliefert. Auf Grund der guten Referenzen der irischen Firma waren die Zahlungsbedingungen 10 Tage 2 %, 30 Tage netto. Da zwei Tage nach Fälligkeit der Rechnung kein Geld auf Ihr Firmenkonto eingegangen war, haben Sie die irische Firma angerufen, und von der Einkaufsleiterin erfahren, die Zahlung sei unterwegs. Es sind inzwischen drei weitere Tage verstrichen, ohne dass die Rechnung bezahlt wurde.

Aufgabe

Verfassen Sie mit heutigem Datum eine Mahnung an die irische Firma unter Berücksichtigung folgender Punkte:

- Ihr Ansprechpartner ist Mrs Aileen O'Reilly, Einkaufsleiterin.
- Bezug auf Rechnung (Kopie beigefügt/angehängt)
- Bezug auf Telefonat von vor 3 Tagen
- Laut Kaufvertrag beträgt die Zahlungsfrist 30 Tage.
- Die Rechnung ist nunmehr 5 Tage überfällig.
- Sie bitten um eine Erklärung und unverzügliche Überweisung des fälligen Betrags.
- Bei Nichtzahlung Einstellung der Geschäftsbeziehungen
- Angemessene Verabschiedung

Complaints

1 **Sevda Yildiz, the purchasing director at Brix Mode GmbH in Bielefeld, is dissatisfied with a consignment of goods from Patrik K, a Swedish fashion company in Stockholm, so she phones Pehr Lindquist, the export sales director.**

2 25

Read or listen to the following phone call and, with a partner, put the pictures in the right order and use them to explain what happened. Begin like this: *The goods arrived in Germany ...*

PEHR: Lindquist?
SEVDA: Hello, it's Sevda Yildiz from Brix Mode in Bielefeld.
PEHR: Hello, Sevda! How are you?
SEVDA: Fine, thanks. And you?
PEHR: Fine. What can I do for you, Sevda?
SEVDA: Well, the reason I'm calling is to talk to you about the goods we've just received from you. We're very dissatisfied with them.
PEHR: Oh, dear! Wasn't it a consignment of jeans?
SEVDA: Yes, that's right.
PEHR: Can I just have the order number, please?
SEVDA: Yes, it's MW2838 dated the twelfth of February. That's exactly a month ago.
PEHR: Just a moment ... . Ah, yes, here we are. Five hundred pairs of men's and women's jeans in light blue, blue and dark blue. I can see here that they left our premises two weeks ago and were sent to you as air freight for delivery CIP Dortmund Airport.
SEVDA: Well, it's interesting that you should say that, Pehr, because we didn't get them until the day before yesterday.

PEHR: The day before yesterday! They should have arrived a week earlier than that!

SEVDA: Exactly, and when we unpacked them we saw that a number of things were wrong.

PEHR: Oh, no! What's wrong with them?

SEVDA: The sizes are all wrong and some of the jeans are dirty.

PEHR: Dirty! But when our freight forwarders picked up the consignment, they were in perfect condition. Something must have happened in transit.

SEVDA: Some of the boxes are different, too. Some have Patrik K on them and some have Stockholm Logistics.

PEHR: That's impossible! *All* the boxes had Patrik K on them. Stockholm Logistics is the name of our freight forwarders. Just a minute ... I remember now! There was a fire at their warehouse at the airport. It was in all the newspapers a few weeks ago. Perhaps they re-packed some of the goods in their own boxes after the fire and mixed them up.

SEVDA: That would make sense because we've always had good service from your company up to now.

PEHR: Look, we're extremely sorry about this, Sevda. I'll get in touch with Stockholm Logistics right away and we'll rush your original order to you by air. When it comes, please give back the goods you've just received to Stockholm Logistics, all right?

SEVDA: All right, but when will we get the jeans we ordered?

PEHR: In 24 hours, and if you want to keep any of the jeans you've just received, please keep them as a gesture of our good will for all the inconvenience.

SEVDA: OK, thanks.

PEHR: Anything else I can do for you, Sevda?

SEVDA: No thanks. All we need is the jeans so they're in stock for the summer season.

PEHR: You'll get them, don't worry. As I said, sorry about the inconvenience. I assure you it won't happen again!

SEVDA: OK, Pehr, that's great. Thank you. Bye.

PEHR: Bye.

2 Find words in the dialogue to match the following definitions.

1. not satisfied
2. delivery
3. building in which a company is located
4. transport company (*two words*)
5. on the way from one place to another (*two words*)
6. how big something is
7. to send very quickly
8. trouble, extra work
9. in the warehouse waiting to be sold (*two words*)
10. to promise

3 Jana Lorenz works in the purchasing department at Brix Mode GmbH in Bielefeld. Five weeks ago her company ordered a consignment of ladies' shoes from a Chinese supplier in Shanghai and was promised delivery within 30 days after receipt of order. The goods are now four days late, so she contacts the supplier. Read her email and match the sentence halves.

A complaint about a delay in delivery

To:	chen-yu-lan@632tradingchina.cn
Subject:	Delay in delivery of order no. LTS36B dated 13 February 20..
Cc:	sevda.yildiz@brixmode.de
Attachment(s):	

Dear Ms Chen Yu Lan

On 13 February 20.. we placed the above-mentioned order for ladies' T-shirts for delivery by 16 March.

The consignment is now four days overdue.

We would welcome your explanation of the delay, but must be sure that the consignment will reach our premises by 30 March at the latest, as several customers are now threatening to cancel their orders and look elsewhere.

We trust that we will hear from you in the very near future. Prompt delivery is all that is needed to settle this matter.

Yours sincerely

Jana Lorenz
Purchasing Department
Brix Mode GmbH

1	Brix Mode placed its order on	a	the delay.
2	The deadline for delivery was	b	as soon as possible.
3	This email was written on	c	cancel their orders.
4	So far the supplier has not explained	d	20 March.
5	Some German customers might	e	16 March.
6	Brix Mode wants the goods	f	13 February.

4 Match the German translations with points 1–5 in the box below.

Angemessene Verabschiedung | Bezug auf Verzögerung | Bitte um Erklärung | Bitte um Lieferung innerhalb einer bestimmten Frist | Folgen einer weiteren Verzögerung

5 Look at the e-mail to the Chinese company and in your exercise book make a note of as many of the points listed under the heading 'Structure of a complaint about delay in delivery' as possible.

Structure of a complaint about delay in delivery

A complaint about delay in delivery covers some or all of the following points:

1 Reference to delay
2 Request for explanation
3 Request for delivery by a given time
4 Consequences of further delay
5 Suitable ending

Useful phrases

Reference to delay	Bezug auf Verzögerung
On 1 November we placed an order with you for the above-mentioned items to be delivered within three weeks.	Am 1. November erteilten wir Ihnen einen Auftrag für die oben erwähnten Positionen, die innerhalb von drei Wochen geliefert werden sollten.
It was agreed that delivery was to be made within three weeks.	Es wurde vereinbart, dass die Lieferung innerhalb von drei Wochen erfolgen sollte.
Our order is now five days overdue.	Unser Auftrag ist jetzt fünf Tage überfällig.
Request for explanation	**Bitte um Erklärung**
We would welcome an explanation of the delay.	Wir würden eine Erklärung der Verzögerung begrüßen.
So far we have not been given a reason for the delay.	Bisher haben wir noch keine Begründung für die Verzögerung erhalten.
Please let us know why the goods have been delayed.	Bitte lassen Sie uns wissen, warum die Waren verspätet angekommen sind.
Request for delivery by a particular time	**Bitte um Lieferung zu einer bestimmten Frist**
Please let us know immediately when we will be able to take delivery of the goods.	Bitte teilen Sie uns sofort mit, wann wir mit der Lieferung der Waren rechnen können.
We must be certain that the consignment will reach our premises by 17 January at the latest.	Wir müssen sicher sein, dass die Sendung unsere Geschäftsräume spätestens bis zum 17. Januar erreicht.
Please ensure that we receive the goods within seven days.	Bitte stellen Sie sicher, dass wir die Waren innerhalb von sieben Tagen erhalten.
Consequences of further delay	**Folgen einer weiteren Verzögerung**
If this deadline is not kept we will be obliged to cancel this and all future orders ...	Wenn dieser Termin nicht eingehalten wird, sehen wir uns genötigt, diesen und alle weiteren Aufträge zu stornieren ...
... as several customers are threatening to cancel their orders and look elsewhere.	... da einige unserer Kunden drohen, ihre Bestellungen zu stornieren und sich anderweitig zu orientieren.
... since some of our customers have now cancelled their orders.	... da einige unserer Kunden ihre Aufträge jetzt storniert haben.
Suitable ending	**Angemessene Verabschiedung**
Prompt delivery is all that is needed to settle this matter.	Diese Angelegenheit kann durch eine umgehende Lieferung Ihrerseits geregelt werden.
We trust that we will be hearing from you in the very near future.	Wir vertrauen darauf, dass wir von Ihnen in Kürze hören.

6 Use the useful phrases to write an e-mail reminder based on the following details.

Situation

Sven Neumann ist Einkaufsleiter bei Intertrade Großhandel GmbH in Dortmund. Da eine Lieferung Haushaltsporzellan (*household crockery*) überfällig ist, mahnt er sie beim chinesischen Lieferanten, Man Sang Trading Limited in Hongkong, an.

Household crockery

Aufgabe

Schreiben Sie Svens E-Mail an Mr John Zheng (j.zheng@mansang.org) in der Exportabteilung unter Berücksichtigung folgender Punkte.

- Ware wurde vor 3 Wochen am ... mit Auftrag-Nr. HHC/46 bestellt.
- Lieferung ist inzwischen 7 Tage überfällig.
- Grund für Verspätung?
- Ihre Kunden drohen inzwischen, ihre Aufträge zu stornieren und die Ware von einem anderen Lieferanten zu beziehen.
- Letzte Frist für Lieferung: heute in 5 Tagen (*genauen Termin angeben!*)
- Angemessene Verabschiedung

7 Read Sevda's complaint to an Indian supplier and say if the statements are true or false. Correct the false statements.

A complaint

BRIX Mode GmbH
Feldstraße 42 • 33609 Bielefeld • Germany
Tel +49 521 4827764 Fax +49 521 4824760 info@brixmode.de

SY/AK
10 January 20..

Mr Sunil Mittal
Export Sales Director
J.P. Designs Incorporated
44 Mandir Marg
NEW DELHI
110 001
INDIEN

Dear Mr Mittal

Order no. IGTO 32249 for fashion tops dated 10 November 20..

The above-mentioned fashion tops arrived at our premises this morning as promised but on examining them we found that they were of poor quality. The sample tops sent to us were brightly coloured and wider with long sleeves and a low neck. The tops we have received are darker coloured, narrower and have short sleeves and a high neck.

We would welcome your explanation of these discrepancies.

Whatever the case may be, you will appreciate that we cannot sell these articles at the usual price and will only keep them if you reduce the price considerably.

We look forward to receiving your comments on this matter.

Yours sincerely
Brix Mode GmbH

S. Yildiz

Sevda Yildiz
Purchasing Director

Brix Mode GmbH • Bielefeld, Registergericht Bielefeld, HRB 82071, Geschäftsführerin: Karla Wenz

1 The tops arrived late.
2 The samples were better than the goods sent.
3 Brix Mode wants narrower tops.
4 Brix Mode wants sleeveless tops.
5 Brix Mode expects the Indian company to tell them what went wrong.
6 Brix Mode will do their best to sell the tops at the normal price.

8 J.P. Designs Incorporated also received a complaint about their fashion tops from another company. Use eight of the words in the box to fill in the gaps.

careful | bright | dark | high | late | careless | narrow | dirty | poor | short

E-MAIL

Dear Mr Mittal

The above-mentioned order, which should have arrived last week, came this morning seven days ... [1]. On checking the fashion tops, we were disappointed to find that the quality was ... [2] and some of the top looked unwashed and even ... [3]. We ordered bright colours but the tops are all ... [4] blue and grey. This year wide tops are fashionable but these are all ... [5]. We told your company representative to send us long-sleeved tops with a low neck. These all have ... [6] sleeves and a ... [7] neck.

We must insist that you send us the right goods without delay and would ask you be more ... [8] when dealing with our next order.

Yours sincerely
...

9 Match the German translations with points 1–7 in the box below.

Bitte um Erklärung | Bezug auf Waren | Angemessene Verabschiedung | Darstellung des Problems | Bitte um Ergreifung geeigneter Maßnahmen | Anlage(n) | Folgen für Käufer und Verkäufer

10 Look at the e-mail to the Indian company and in your exercise book make a note of as many of the points listed under the heading 'Structure of a complaint' as possible.

Structure of a complaint

A complaint covers some or all of the following points:

1 Reference to goods
2 Description of problem
3 Request for explanation
4 Consequences for the buyer and seller
5 Request for action
6 Suitable ending
7 Enclosure(s)/attachment(s)

Useful phrases

Reference to goods	Bezug auf Waren
The above-mentioned goods were delivered to us today, seven days later than expected.	Die oben erwähnten Waren wurden uns heute – sieben Tage nach dem vereinbarten Termin – geliefert.
We have just taken delivery of the above-mentioned consignment/goods/articles.	Wir haben soeben die oben erwähnte Sendung/Waren/Artikel erhalten.
We regret to inform you that we are dissatisfied with it/them.	Leider müssen wir Ihnen mitteilen, dass wir damit unzufrieden sind.
Description of problem	**Darstellung des Problems**
On examining the goods we found that ...	Bei Prüfung der Waren stellten wir fest, dass ...
... the contents were wet, (obviously) due to poor packing/rough handling in transit.	... der Inhalt war nass (offensichtlich) wegen mangelhafter Verpackung/unsachgemäßer Behandlung während des Transports.
... they are the wrong colour/size/shape, because they are ... instead of ... (as ordered).	... sie haben die falsche Farbe/Größe/Form, denn sie sind ... statt ... (laut Bestellung).
... (e.g. six) of the ... (e.g. 30) articles/tents/wardrobes ordered are (badly) damaged/dirty/discoloured.	... (z. B. sechs) der insgesamt ... (z. B. 30) bestellten (Artikel/Zelte/Schränke) sind (stark) beschädigt/verschmutzt/verfärbt.
... the quality and colour were not up to sample.	... Qualität und Farbe entsprechen nicht dem Muster.
We believe this was caused by rough handling in transit.	Wir glauben, dies wurde durch unsachgemäße Behandlung während des Transports verursacht.
We enclose photographs of these items for your information.	Wir fügen Fotos dieser Artikel zu Ihrer Information bei.
We are of the opinion that this is the result of poor packing (see photographs enclosed).	Wir sind der Meinung, dass dies das Ergebnis schlechter Verpackung ist (siehe beiliegende Fotos).
Request for explanation	**Bitte um Erklärung**
We would welcome your explanation of the damage.	Wir würden Ihre Erklärung des Schadens begrüßen.
Please explain why our order was so poorly executed.	Bitte erklären Sie, warum unser Auftrag so schlecht ausgeführt wurde.
Consequences for the buyer and seller	**Folgen für Käufer und Verkäufer**
Whatever the case may be, ...	Wie dem auch sei, ...
You will appreciate that ...	Sie werden dafür Verständnis haben, dass ...
... we cannot sell these articles at the normal price.	... wir diese Artikel nicht zum normalen Preis verkaufen können.
... we can only keep them if the price is reduced by 25%.	... wir sie nur behalten können, wenn der Preis um 25% reduziert wird.
If they do not arrive here by ... (e.g. 30 June) we will have to obtain them elsewhere.	Wenn sie bis ... (z. B. 30. Juni) nicht hier ankommen, werden wir sie woanders beziehen müssen.
Request for action	**Bitte um Ergreifung geeigneter Maßnahmen**
Whatever the case may be, we need ... urgently.	In jedem Fall benötigen wir ... dringend.
We must also/therefore ask you to send us replacements (for the damaged goods) by return, as these goods are needed urgently.	Wir müssen Sie auch/deshalb bitten, Ersatz (für die beschädigten Waren) zu schicken, da diese Waren dringend benötigt werden.
We would also point out that ...	Wir möchten Sie (auch) darauf hinweisen, dass ...
... we are only prepared keep the substandard items if a considerable reduction in price is granted.	... wir nur bereit sind, die minderwertige Ware zu behalten, wenn ein erheblicher Preisnachlass gewährt wird.

Suitable ending	Angemessene Verabschiedung
We look forward to receiving your comments on this matter without delay.	Wir erwarten Ihre unverzügliche Stellungnahme zu dieser Angelegenheit.
We feel sure you will appreciate that our future business relationship will depend on how this matter is dealt with.	Sie werden sicherlich dafür Verständnis haben, dass die Fortsetzung unserer Geschäftsbeziehung von der Regelung dieser Angelegenheit abhängig ist.
We trust you will deal with this matter without delay.	Wir vertrauen darauf, dass Sie sich unverzüglich mit dieser Angelegenheit befassen werden.
We expect to hear from you in the very near future.	Wir erwarten in Kürze, von Ihnen zu hören.
Enclosure(s)	**Anlage(n)**
Photograph(s)	Foto(s)

11 Use the useful phrases to write a complaint based on the following details.

Situation

(Fortsetzung von Aufgabe 7 *Enquiries* auf Seite 145) Sie (eigener Name) sind Einkaufsleiter/-in bei der FreiLuft Rhein GmbH in Bonn. Ihre Firma hatte mit Auftrag-Nr. EVCE3000 vom ... (*Datum vor vier Wochen*) 50 Zelte vom Typ Klondike beim britischen Lieferanten Apex Leisure Ltd bestellt. Die Sendung ist heute angekommen und weist verschiedene Mängel auf.

Tent

Aufgabe

Verfassen Sie mit heutigem Datum eine Beschwerde (Brief, E-Mail oder Fax) an die englische Firma unter Berücksichtigung folgender Punkte:

- Ihr Ansprechpartner ist Ms Emma Wade, Exportleiterin.
- Bezug auf Bestellung
- Statt orangefarbener Zelte sind graue geliefert worden.
- Sechs der insgesamt 50 bestellten Zelte sind schmutzig, wahrscheinlich infolge mangelhafter Verpackung (siehe Fotos).
- Bitte um Erklärung, warum Ihr Auftrag so schlecht ausgeführt wurde.
- Ware kann zum normalen Preis nicht verkauft werden.
- Sie sind bereit, die Zelte zu behalten, wenn der Preis um 20 % reduziert wird.
- Bitte um baldige Stellungnahme
- Angemessene Verabschiedung

12 Use the useful phrases to write a complaint based on the following details.

Situation

Die Firma „Jeans On The Rocks" GmbH in Essen (Sachsenstr. 27, 45128 Essen, Fax-Nr. 0049 201 9766507) hat heute von der chinesischen Firma Shenzhen Fashion Factory (Foreign Economic Building, 2 Yuan Dun Dong Street, Shenzhen, China 518000, Fax-Nr. 0086 10 544 8128, E-Mail: jjw@shenzhen.fashion.ch) eine Sendung Jeansjacken erhalten, die Anlass zu Beanstandungen gibt.

Jeans jacket

Aufgabe

Verfassen Sie mit heutigem Datum für die Einkaufsleiterin Ihrer Firma, Frau Mareike Sperling (E-Mail: mareike.sperling@jotr-essen.de), eine Mängelrüge (Brief, E-Mail oder Fax) an die Exportleiterin der chinesischen Firma, Ms Juanjuan Wan. Berücksichtigen Sie folgende Punkte.

> Heutiges Datum
> Bezug auf Lieferung (Auftrag Nr. JJ106/CH von vor 14 Tagen)
> Inhalt bei Ankunft nass wegen mangelhafter Verpackung
> Farbe und Qualität weichen erheblich von dem Muster ab (Fotos beigefügt).
> Bitte um umgehenden Ersatz, da Jeansjacken dringend benötigt werden
> Ohne beträchtliche Ermäßigung nicht bereit, die minderwertige Ware zu behalten
> Bitte um Stellungnahme
> Fortsetzung der Geschäftsbeziehung von der Regelung der Beschwerde abhängig
> Angemessene Verabschiedung

13 Use the useful phrases to write a complaint based on the following details.

Situation

Sie (eigener Name) sind Einkaufsleiter(in) bei der Firma Möbel Schwenk KG, Hagenstraße 12, 45894 Gelsenkirchen, Fax-Nr. 0049 209 8633420, E-Mail: Ihr Vorname. Ihr Nachname@moebel-schwenk.de. Vor einem Monat hatten Sie mit Auftrag-Nr. WDR/107A 100 Kleiderschränke (*wardrobes*) vom Typ „Highlands" bei der schottischen Firma First Class Furnishings, 47 Carlisle Street, Edinburgh EH2 8DF, Großbritannien, Fax-Nr. 0044 131 556 7244 bestellt. Die Ware ist gestern eingetroffen und gibt Anlass zur Beanstandung.

Wardrobe

Aufgabe

Verfassen Sie eine Mangelrüge (Brief, E-Mail oder Fax) an die britische Firma unter Berücksichtigung folgender Punkte:

> Heutiges Datum
> Ansprechpartner: Ms Fiona McTavish, Exportleiterin (E-Mail: fiona.mctavish@fcf.co.uk)
> Bezug auf Auftrag
> Erhalt der Sendung bestätigen
> Sendung kam mit fünf Tagen Verspätung an.
> Fünf hellbraune Kleiderschränke sind stark beschädigt, offenbar wegen unzureichender Verpackung (siehe Fotos)
> Fünfzig Kleiderschränke sind dunkelbraun statt hellbraun laut Bestellung.
> Bitte um Erklärung für schlechte Ausführung des Auftrags
> Sie hoffen, die schottische Firma hat dafür Verständnis, dass Ihre Firma die 50 dunkelbraunen Kleiderschränke nur mit einem Nachlass von 30% behalten kann.
> Bitte um umgehende Ersatzlieferung der beschädigten Kleiderschränke, weil sie dringend benötigt werden
> Bitte um unverzügliche Stellungnahme
> Zukünftige Geschäftsbeziehung hängt davon ab, wie Mangelrüge geregelt wird
> Angemessene Verabschiedung

7 Job applications

1 Look at the map and do the tasks below with a partner.

1. List as many of the English-speaking countries marked on the map as you can.
2. Say when you last used English outside the classroom. Describe where you were and why you spoke English.
3. Name some English-speaking countries you would like to visit or work in. Explain why you would like to go there.

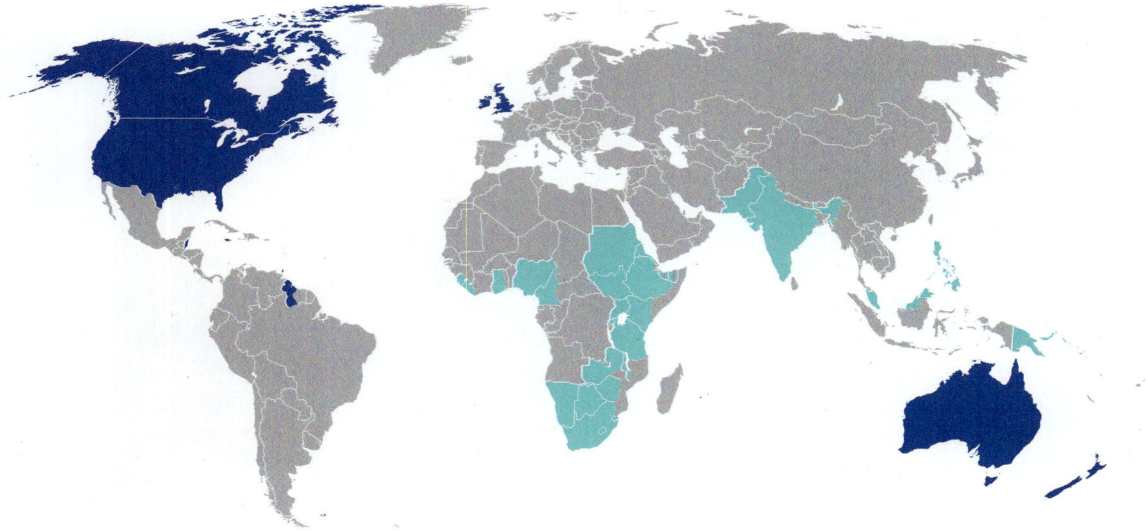

2 Study the online job advertisement on the right and complete the following statements with the correct answer.

1 The job is for
  a a young man.
  b a young woman.
  c a young man or woman.

2 Entry level work is
  a work at the entrance to the hotel.
  b work for someone new to the hotel business.
  c work in reception.

3 The hotel is
  a a long distance from London.
  b in London.
  c near London.

4 The applicant
  a need not have any experience.
  b must have some experience.
  c must have a lot of experience.

5 The employee will
  a get all meals free.
  b get free meals when at work.
  c pay for all meals.

6 To get this job the successful applicant must
  a be able to speak three languages.
  b be able to speak English and another language.
  c only be able to speak good English.

HOSPITALITY RECRUITMENT

HOME | CHECK YOUR E-MAIL | LATEST JOBS | REGISTER

JOB DESCRIPTION

Entry level hotel work (male or female)

We are looking for a full-time employee (37 hours a week) to work at a first-class hotel and conference venue in a major city in the north of England. Previous experience of hotel work is desirable but not necessary, and promotion prospects in this dynamic and exciting environment are excellent.

The successful applicant will receive training on the job and be paid £6.08 an hour for the first three months. We will then review your full performance and salary. A uniform and meals are provided during working hours.

We expect a team player with:
- a good command of English
- a good command of at least one other foreign language
- a high standard of personal appearance
- a passion for the customer care industry

Please send your application to the address below quoting reference no. RHYO 232:

Ms Debbie Wharton
Human Resources Manager
Best Western Monkbar Hotel
St. Maurice's Road
YORK
YO31 7JA
UK

3 Find words in the advertisement to match the following definitions.

1 someone who works for an employer
2 location
3 earlier, before now
4 needed
5 a higher position in the same company
6 very good
7 increase
8 breakfast, dinner and lunch
9 great interest and enthusiasm
10 the department of a company which gives people jobs and trains them

Applying for a job abroad

The most important part of a job application in an English-speaking country is your CV (curriculum vitae, American English: résumé). It should not be more than two pages long (12-point font) and should be tailored to fit each job application. As CVs are often uploaded on the internet, they should not contain any special effects.

Some employers also require a cover letter or e-mail in which the applicant explains why he or she particularly wants this job. Others require a short statement summarizing the applicant's skills.

It is not necessary to begin a CV with the heading CV or CURRICULUM VITAE.

4 Janina Witt is in the final year of a two-year commercial course at a vocational training college in Essen. She registers with a number of online recruitment agencies and decides to apply for the hotel job advertised. Look at her CV and make a list of the differences between an English and a German CV, including the following points:

- the points left out of an English CV
- the extra information in an English CV
- the order of an English CV

1 Make it easy for an employer to contact you by including your mobile number and e-mail. Make sure your e-mail address is acceptable to an employer (e.g. not lachdichkrumm@hihi.de).

2 The PROFILE section is the first thing an employer reads. Give a positive picture of yourself by listing your strongest points. This will make the employer read the rest of your CV. Remember: Most CVs are read in less than 60 seconds, so make sure your profile catches the reader's attention.

3 Check that the skills you list are what the employer is looking for. Use 'fluent', 'good command' or 'basic knowledge' to describe your language skills.

4 Begin in the present and work backwards. Leave out irrelevant information (e.g. primary school). Translate all German expressions into English.

5 This sections shows you know about the world of work. Make sure it is clear what types of employer you have worked for and what you did in each case.

6 Include any skills you have that may be relevant or interesting.

7 Include any activities which show what sort of person you are.

8 Make sure you write out the month as a word. Remember German starts with a capital 'G'.

9 The names of referees can be left out to save space.

A CV (curriculum vitae)

Janina Witt
Tulpenweg 15, 44892 Bochum, Germany
Landline: +49 234 588167 Mobile: +49 176 8873321
E-mail: janina.witt@web.de 1

2 **PROFILE**

My ambition is to use my experience in the hospitality industry at a large hotel in the UK. I am highly motivated, hard-working, responsible and reliable, and I am very interested in languages and other cultures.

3 **KEY SKILLS**

Native speaker of German
Fluent in English
Good command of Spanish
Good command of Serbian

4 **EDUCATION AND QUALIFICATIONS**

Since August 20..	Two-year, full-time commercial course at Robert Schumann Berufskolleg für Wirtschaft und Verwaltung der Stadt Essen (Robert Schumann Vocational Training College for Business and Administration in Essen), Germany to obtain higher education entrance qualifications (English and Spanish)
20.. – 20..	Städtische Realschule (selective state secondary school), Bochum

5 **WORK EXPERIENCE**

March – April 20..	Work placement at Porto Azzuro Aparthotel Malta in reception and housekeeping
September 20..	Work placement as shop assistant at Mango boutique, Essen
June – July 20..	Work placement at Hotel Zira in Novi Sad, Serbia in reception and back office

6 **RELEVANT SKILLS**

Good command of Microsoft Office
Swimming teacher for children of primary school age
First aid certificate

7 **EXTRA-CURRICULAR ACTIVITIES**

Ballroom dancing
Riding
Travel

8 **PERSONAL DETAILS**

Date of birth: 11 November 19..
Marital status: Single
Nationality: German

9 **REFERENCES**

Available on request

5 **Match the information from a CV (A–L) with the headings (1–6). There are two answers for each heading.**

1 PROFILE

2 KEY SKILLS

3 EDUCATION AND QUALIFICATIONS

4 WORK EXPERIENCE

5 RELEVANT SKILLS

6 EXTRA-CURRICULAR ACTIVITIES

A Full driving licence

B September 20.. Two-week placement at Softech Computers in workshop and shop.

C 20.. – 20.. Regular summer holiday job as play leader for primary school children

D June 20.. German school leaving certificate (Year 10)

E Member of Red Cross

F I wish to find a job in an English-speaking country where I can use my computer and language skills. I am highly motivated and extremely flexible.

G Fluent Polish / Good command of English and Russian

H 20.. – 20.. Duisburg state secondary school

I Experience of website design

J Badminton

K My goal is to gain experience of working in the US for at least six months. I have computer, language and administrative skills and am a reliable, flexible person.

L Fluent English / Basic knowledge of Spanish

6 **Make a list of your own skills and strong points under the headings in exercise 5. Invent more headings if necessary.**

TIME SPENT ABROAD

VOLUNTARY WORK

SPORTING ACHIEVEMENTS

7 **How do you refer to your education, training and skills in English? Find the English equivalent (a–j) for each German expression (1–8).**

1 Allgemeine Hochschulreife (Abitur)
2 Berufsschule, Berufskolleg, Gewerbliche Schule
3 Fachhochschulreife
4 Führerschein Klasse 3
5 Mittlere Reife
6 Realschule
7 Hauptschule
8 Gymnasium

a grammar school
b secondary school
c selective secondary school
d German university entrance qualifications
e German higher education entrance qualifications
f car licence
g (BE) vocational training college, (AE) vocational school
h German Class 10 School Leaving Certificate

8 Read Janina's cover letter and find the following information:

1. the location of the hotel
2. when Janina will be able to start work
3. what possibilities her course gives her
4. how she knows about the hospitality industry
5. what sort of atmosphere she likes to work in
6. what she sends with her letter

A cover letter

Tulpenweg 15
44892 Bochum
Germany

10 May 20..

Ms Debbie Wharton
Human Resources Manager
Best Western Monkbar Hotel
St. Maurice's Road
YORK
YO31 7JA
GROSSBRITANNIEN

Dear Ms Wharton

Vacancy for entry level hotel work, reference no. RHYO 232

With reference to your advertisement on the internet, I wish to apply for the above-mentioned post.

By June of this year I will have completed a two-year commercial course in business and adminstration at Robert-Schuman Vocational Training College in Essen, Germany. The course includes languages (English and Spanish), IT and a work placement with a local employer. It prepares students for a job in commerce or industry and also entitles them to attend a course in higher education.

My summer hotel jobs over the last two years have shown me that the hospitality industry is the field I wish to work in permanently. I enjoy working in a busy environment with people from all over the world and would love to have the chance to use the skills I have learned at college and on my work placements.

My CV is enclosed for your information and I am available for an interview at short notice.

I would be delighted if you would consider me for this post and hope to hear from you soon.

Janina Witt

Enc

9 Choose one of the jobs below and write:
– your own CV using the example on page 187 as a model
– an 80–100 word summary of your skills (job 1) or a cover letter (job 2)
Use the list of useful phrases on page 191 to help you.

Job 1

JOB DESCRIPTION
Entertainers /animators

Sun-sand-fun.com is looking for young German-speakers to train as all-round entertainers/animators at hotels in the Canary Islands.
Starting date: 01 July 20..

Requirements
You speak good English and Spanish. You are a top fit team player and a fun-loving person with a 'can-do' attitude. Previous experience is desirable but not necessary to do this job.

Training
We'll teach you how to entertain, dance, sing, act and give classes to young and old (e.g. aerobics, gymnastics, volleyball, ballroom dancing).

Locations
Lanzarote, Gran Canaria, Tenerife, Fuerteventura

Terms of employment
- Minimum age 18
- Board and lodging provided
- €500–600 per calendar month

Applications

Upload your *CV here: [ ] Browse...

* Supported file types are doc, docx, txt, rtf, pdf, wps

Explain in 80–100 words why we should employ you. Your statement:

Successful applicants will be invited to a face-to-face interview and casting in Cologne. When you have uploaded your CV, click NEXT... to fill in an online application form.

NEXT...

Job 2

JOB DESCRIPTION
Live-in au pair (male or female) required in Ireland

We're looking for a kind, reliable, honest, fun person to live in as part of our family for 6 to 24 months. We have one son aged 6½. We can offer you accommodation, meals, lots of free time, €340 per calendar month, and you'll be part of the family. You'll also be able to attend English courses at the local adult education college.

Please send your CV and cover letter explaining why you are suited to this post to:
Mrs Maureen O'Connor
42 Walkinstown Road
DUBLIN 12
IRELAND

We'd love to hear from you!

Useful phrases

Introduction	Einleitung
I was extremely interested to read your advertisement for the post of ...	Ich habe Ihre Anzeige für eine Stelle als ... mit großem Interesse gelesen.
I wish to gain experience in ... / make use of my foreign language skills.	Ich möchte Erfahrungen auf dem Gebiet von ... sammeln / von meinen Fremdsprachenkenntnissen Gebrauch machen.
I feel sure that your company/organization has the post I am looking for.	Ich bin sicher, dass Ihr Unternehmen / Ihre Organisation die Stelle hat, die ich suche.
I believe I am particularly suited for the post advertised because ...	Ich denke, dass ich für die ausgeschriebene Stelle besonders geeignet bin, weil ...
Skills	**Fähigkeiten**
As a native speaker of German/French/Spanish/Polish, I am also fluent in (spoken and written) ...	Als deutsche(r)/französische(r)/spanische(r)/polnische(r) Muttersprachler(in) beherrsche ich auch die ... Sprache (in Wort und Schrift).
I have a good/basic knowledge of ...	Ich habe (gute) Grundkenntnisse in ...
Previous experience	**Bisherige Erfahrung**
Before/After/During my course at ..., I completed a work placement at ... in the ... department.	Vor/Nach/Während meiner Ausbildung am ... habe ich ein Praktikum bei ... in der ... Abteilung absolviert.
My experience/work placement at ... has confirmed my interest in ...	Meine Erfahrungen haben / Mein Praktikum hat mein Interesse für ... bestätigt.
My course has enabled me to use/develop my skills in ...	Meine Ausbildung hat es mir ermöglicht, meine Fähigkeiten auf dem Gebiet von ... zu gebrauchen/entwickeln.
Availability	**Verfügbarkeit**
I am available for an interview at short notice / immediately / as from ...	Ich stehe für ein Vorstellungsgespräch kurzfristig / sofort /ab dem... zur Verfügung.
I would be able to start work any time after ...	Ich wäre in der Lage, jederzeit nach dem ... anzufangen.
Suitable ending	**Angemessene Verabschiedung**
I very much look forward to hearing from you at your earliest convenience.	Über Ihre zeitnahe Antwort würde ich mich sehr freuen.
I would be delighted if you would consider me for this post and hope to hear from you soon.	Ich würde mich sehr freuen, wenn Sie meine Bewerbung für diese Stelle berücksichtigen würden und hoffe, bald von Ihnen zu hören.

2 26

10 **Listen to two telephone interviews. First copy the table into your exercise book or onto your computer and then fill it in as you listen.**

	Tobias	Helena
1 Why this job?	...	...
2 Skills?	...	...
3 Strengths?	...	...
4 Weaknesses?	...	...
5 Future plans?	...	...
6 Own question(s)?	...	...

11 **Which applicant do you think should get the job? Explain why in 60–80 words.**

12 **Follow the steps below to role-play a job interview.**

1 Refer to the job advertisement for a live-in au pair in Ireland on page 190. Mrs Maureen O'Connor has received some interesting applications from young people in Germany, so she now telephones them to see which one is suitable.

2 Practise the telephone dialogue with a partner. Refer to Secretarial Activities, File B, Telephoning and voicemail, page 116 for telephone phrases.

Partner A: You (own name)
Turn to file 4 on page 211.

Partner B: Mrs Maureen O'Connor
Turn to file 23 on page 218.

3 Perform one of your dialogues in front of the class. The class should now judge which applicant is best suited for the job.

4 When you have finished, swap roles with your partner and do the role-play again.

TOP TEN INTERVIEW QUESTIONS

We asked 100 personnel managers: **'What are your top ten questions for recruitment interviews?'**

Here are the ten most popular questions.

1 Please take us through your CV.
2 Are you a team player?
3 Do you have any hobbies?
4 What are your strengths?
5 What are your weaknesses?
6 Why do you want to become a ...?
7 Why do you want this job?
8 Why should we employ you and not someone else?
9 What are your plans for the future?
10 Do you have any questions you'd like to ask?

Glossary of business terms

TYPES OF BUSINESS ORGANIZATION

In the **EU**, there are two basic types of company, the **private limited company** (GB: Ltd; German: *GmbH*) and the **public limited company** (GB: plc; German: AG). In the **USA** and **Canada** there are three types of company, as follows:

Incorporated company (Inc.) There is no exact equivalent of an incorporated company in the EU. 'Incorporated' simply means 'registered as a company'. It does not say anything about ownership or liability, or capitalization.

Close corporation (Corp.) This is the North American equivalent of the British Ltd and German *GmbH*. Close corporations have a small number of shareholders (here: *Gesellschafter/in*) and do not offer their shares on the stock market (*Börse*).

Open corporation (Corp.) The North American equivalent of the British PLC and German *AG*. Open corporations usually have numerous shareholders (here: *Aktienbesitzer/in*), often other corporations, and sell their shares on the stock market.

In **South Africa**, **Australia** and **New Zealand** the equivalents of the British Ltd and plc are **limited proprietary company** (Pty Ltd) and **proprietary company** (Pty).

TERMS OF DELIVERY

Incoterms 2010

As trade becomes more and more global, goods travel further and further, crossing geographical, cultural and language barriers on their way. For this reason is essential that importers and exporters agree to use the same terms of reference.

In 1936 the International Chamber of Commerce in Paris invented a set of International Commercial Terms (Incoterms) to define importers' and exporters' rights and obligations, such as transport costs, risk, insurance, customs duty, documentation, loading and unloading. Since then the Incoterms have been revised eight times to keep up with developments in the field of international trade and translated into many different languages. The last revision was in 2010. There are now eleven Incoterms, seven of which can be used for any mode or combined modes of transport, e.g. truck, train, ship or rail. The other four are used for ship or inland waterway transport only.

Rules for any mode or modes of transport

1
EXW (EX WORKS)
Ab Werk
The seller makes the goods available at his premises. The buyer bears all the costs and risks of transporting the goods to their destination.

2
FCA (FREE CARRIER)
Frei Frachtführer
The seller loads the goods on board the first carrier's vehicle. The buyer bears all the costs and risks of transporting the goods to their destination.

3

CPT (CARRIAGE PAID TO)

Frachtfrei bis

The seller bears all the costs and risks until the goods are handed over to the first carrier. He pays the transport costs, without insurance, for the main carriage to the named destination. The buyer insures the goods for the main carriage and bears all other costs.

4

CIP (COST AND INSURANCE PAID TO)

Frachtfrei versichert bis

The seller bears all the costs and risks until the goods are handed over to the first carrier. He pays the transport costs, including insurance, for the main carriage to the named destination. The buyer bears all other costs.

5

DAP (DELIVERED AT PLACE)

Geliefert benannter Ort

The seller bears all the costs and risks until the goods have reached their destination. The buyer is responsible for import duties and unloading the goods.

6

DAT (DELIVERED AT TERMINAL)

Geliefert Terminal

The seller bears all the costs and risks until the goods have reached the terminal and is also responsible for unloading them. The buyer bears all other costs.

7

DDP (DELIVERED DUTY PAID)

Geliefert Zoll bezahlt

The seller bears all the costs and risks until the goods have reached their destination, including import duties. The buyer is responsible for unloading the goods.

Rules for sea and inland waterway transport

8

FAS (FREE ALONGSIDE SHIP)

Frei Längsseite Schiff

The seller delivers the goods alongside the ship at the port of shipment. The buyer bears all the costs and risks of transporting the goods to their destination.

9

FOB (FREE ON BOARD)

Frei an Bord

The seller delivers the goods on board the ship at the port of shipment. The buyer bears all the costs and risks of transporting the goods to their destination.

10

CFR (COST AND FREIGHT)

Kosten und Fracht

The seller delivers the goods on board the ship at the port of shipment. He pays the transport costs, without insurance, for the main carriage to the port of destination. The buyer insures the goods for the main carriage and bears all other costs.

11

CIF (COST, INSURANCE AND FREIGHT (... named port of destination))

Kosten, Versicherung und Fracht

The seller bears all the costs and risks until the goods are delivered on board the ship at the port of shipment. He pays the transport costs, including insurance, to the named port of destination. The buyer bears all other costs.

INCOTERMS 2010

RULES FOR ANY MODE OR MODES OF TRANSPORT

Buyer = B
Seller = S

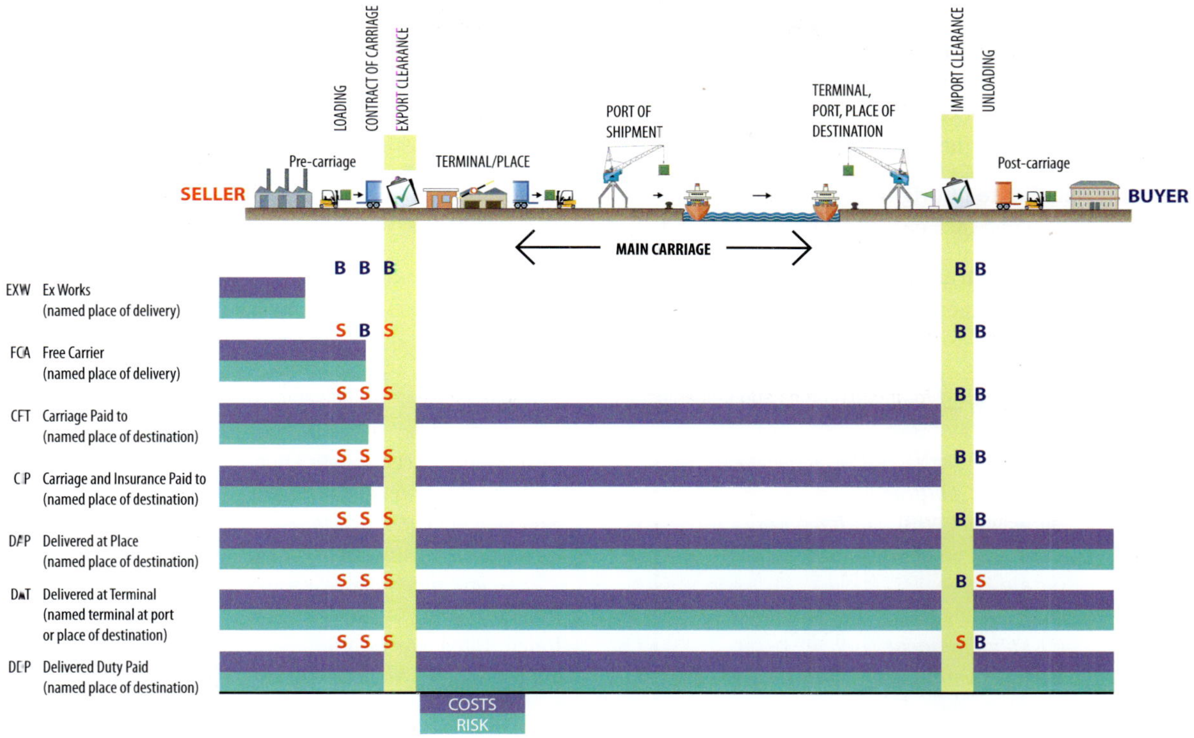

INCOTERMS 2010

RULES FOR SEA AND INLAND WATERWAY TRANSPORT

Buyer = B
Seller = S

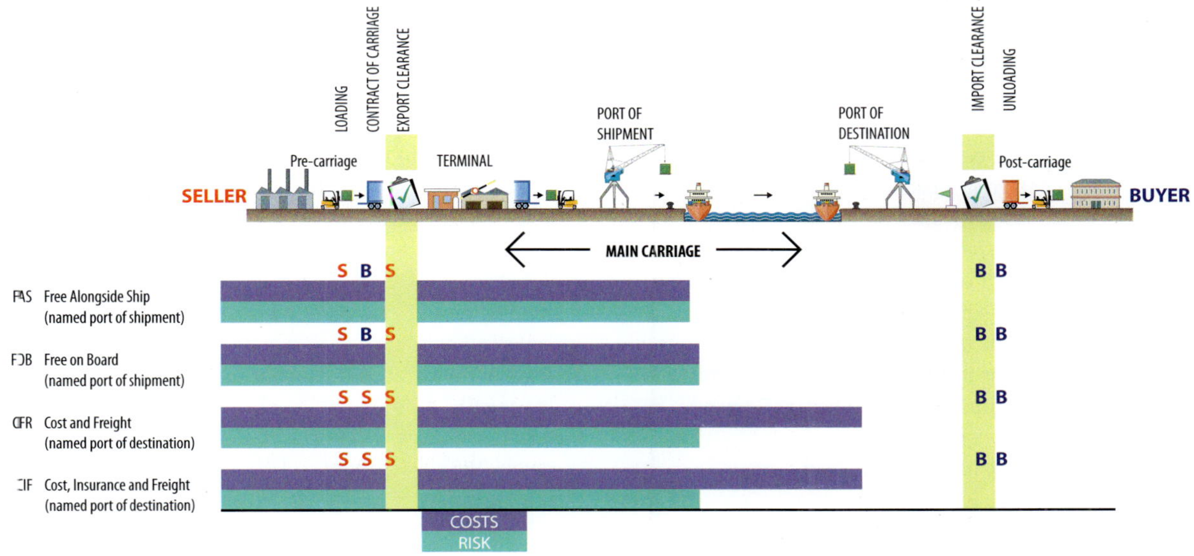

SHIPPING DOCUMENTS

Air waybill (AWB) The airline issues the air waybill to the consignor/exporter of the goods. It is a receipt for the goods and a contract of carriage. It is not a document of title (see Document of title). A copy accompanies the goods to their destination.

Bill of lading (B/L, plural Bs/L) The shipping company issues the bill of lading to the consignor/exporter of the goods. It is a document of title, a receipt for the goods and a contract of carriage. It is described as 'clean' if the goods are in apparent good order and 'foul' if they are not. A copy accompanies the goods to their destination.

Certificate of origin A certificate of origin shows which country the goods are from. It is issued by a chamber of commerce in the exporter's country.

Combined transport waybill This document is used for multi-modal transport, e.g. a container sent by road-sea-road.

English ⟶ German

advice of dispatch *Versandanzeige*
airfreight *Luftfracht*
air waybill (AWB) *Luftfrachtbrief*
approval: on approval *zur Ansicht, auf Probe*
bill of lading (B/L) *Seefrachtbrief, Konnossement*
bonded warehouse *Zollverschlusslager*
cargo *Ladung, Fracht*
cargo liner *Frachtschiff*
cargo space *Frachtraum*
certificate of origin (C/O) *Ursprungszeugnis*
chamber of (industry and commerce *(Industrie- und) Handelskammer*
combined transport waybill *kombinierter Warenbegleitschein*
commercial invoice *Handelsrechnung*
consignment note [road or rail] *Frachtbrief [Straßen- oder Bahn-]*
consignee *Empfänger/in*
consignor *Absender/in, Versender/in*
consular invoice *Konsularrechnung, Konsultatsfaktura*
contract of carriage *Beförderungsvertrag*
customs clearance *Zollabfertigung*
customs declaration *Zollinhaltserklärung*
customs invoice *Zollrechnung, Zollfaktura*
dangerous goods certificate *Gefahrgutbescheinigung*
delivery note *Lieferschein*
destination; port of destination *Bestimmungsort; Bestimmungshafen*
export licence *Exportlizenz*
forwarder's certificate of receipt (FCR) *Spediteurübernahmebescheinigung*
freight *Fracht*
freight rates *Frachttarife*
import licence *Einfuhrgenehmigung*
to take out insurance *eine Versicherung abschließen*
insurance certificate (IC) *Versicherungsschein, -police*
to insure goods against a risk *Ware gegen ein Risiko versichern*
to issue *ausstellen, ausfertigen*
loss; total or partial loss *Verlust; Gesamt- oder Teilverlust*
packing list *Packliste*
pro forma invoice (P/I) *Proforma-Rechnung*
rail consignment note *Bahnfrachtbrief*
receipt *Erhalt; Empfangsbescheinigung*
ro-ro (roll on-roll off) ferry/vessel *von Straßenfahrzeugen befahrbare/s Fähre/ Schiff*
shipping note (S/N) *Schiffszettel, Warenbegleitschein*
single administrative document *Einheitspapier*
warehouse *Lager*
waybill (WB) *Frachtbrief*

Commercial invoice This document is a request for payment. It contains details of the goods, the sum to be paid, the terms of delivery and payment and the buyer and seller's addresses.

Consignment note This document is for road or rail transport. It is issued to the consignor/exporter of the goods by the railway or haulage company. It is a receipt for the goods and a contract of carriage. It is not a document of title. A copy accompanies the goods to their destination.

Document of title The holder of a document of title owns the goods described in it. A document of title can be bought or sold without moving the goods from one place to another. It is often used in international trade. A bill of lading is a document of title to a consignment of goods transported by sea.

Insurance certificate This is an extract from the insurance policy. It contains details of the insurer and the insured, the goods insured and the sum for which they are insured. It includes details of the risks covered, the time for which they are covered and any geographical restrictions, e.g. the route to be taken by the ship or plane.

Packing list The packing list is put both inside the container with the goods and on the outside of the container. It lists the goods in the container.

Pro-forma invoice This document shows how much the goods will or would cost. It is not a request for payment. It contains details of the goods, the price, the terms of delivery and payment and the buyer and seller's addresses. It is normally used for a quotation, for payment in advance, for goods sent on approval or to open a letter of credit (Akkreditiv).

Shipping note (S/N) A document signed by the ship's chief officer when goods are taken on board.

Shipping documents This is all the documentation used when exporting goods (commercial invoice, bill of lading, insurance certificate, certificate of origin, etc).

Single administrative document This is a single document describing a consignment of goods issued by the customs authorities. It makes importing and exporting goods within the EU easier. It contains copies for the importer and exporter, the importer's and exporter's customs authorities and for transit through other countries.

PACKAGING

Here is a list of the most common types of packaging used when transporting goods.

German ⟶ English

Ballen *bale*
Beutel *bag (small)*
Dose *can; tin*
Fass *barrel*
Flasche *bottle*
Karton *carton*
Kasten *box*
Kiste *box; crate*
Korb *basket*
Laderost *pallet*
Luftpolstertasche *bubble envelope*
Paket *carton; packet*
Pallette *pallet*
Rolle *roll*
Sack *sack*
Schachtel *box*
Seecontainer *sea container*
Tasche *bag (big); pouch (small)*
Tonne *barrel; drum*
Tube *tube*
Umschlag *envelope*

TERMS OF PAYMENT

payment in advance	*Vorauszahlung/Vorkasse*
cash with order (CWO)	*Barzahlung bei Auftragserteilung*
payment by irrevocable and confirmed documentary (letter of) credit	*Zahlung durch unwiderrufliches und bestätigtes Dokumentenakkreditiv*
documents against payment (D/P) / cash against documents (CAD)	*Kasse gegen Dokumente*
cash on delivery (COD)	*gegen Nachnahme*
30% with order, 70% on completion	*30% bei Auftragserteilung, 70% bei Fertigstellung*
$\frac{1}{3}$ with order, $\frac{1}{3}$ on delivery, $\frac{1}{3}$ within 30 days after delivery	*$\frac{1}{3}$ bei Auftragserteilung, $\frac{1}{3}$ bei Lieferung, $\frac{1}{3}$ innerhalb von 30 Tagen nach Lieferung*
payment within 30/60/90 days from date of invoice	*Zahlung innerhalb von 30/60/90 Tagen nach Rechnungsdatum*
10 days 2%, 30 days net	*Zahlung innerhalb 10 Tagen abzüglich 2 % Skonto oder innerhalb 30 Tagen netto*
payment on receipt of goods	*Zahlung bei Erhalt der Waren*
payment on receipt of invoice	*Zahlung bei Rechnungserhalt*
documents against (three months') acceptance (D/A)	*Dokumente gegen (Dreimonats)akzept*
open account terms with monthly / quarterly settlement	*offenes Zahlungsziel mit monatlicher/ vierteljährlicher Abrechnung*

This diagram shows how attractive the different terms of payment are for the importer and exporter.

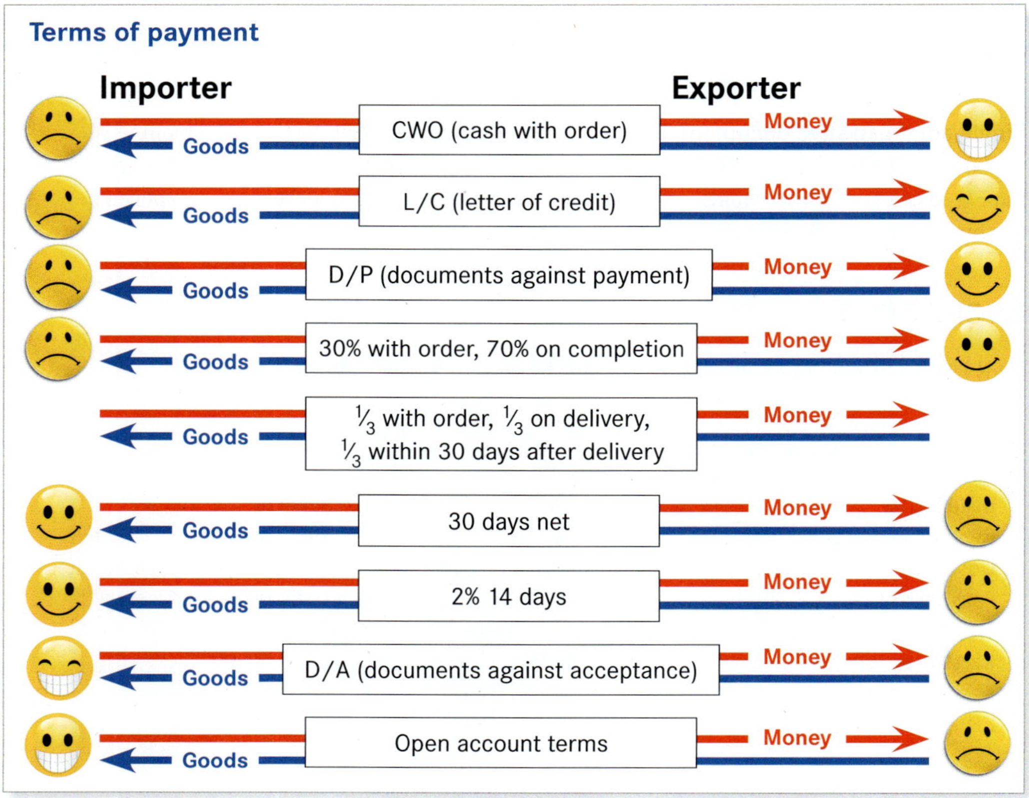

Methods of payment in foreign trade

The most common methods of payment are:

Bank transfer *(Überweisung)* Since the creation of the Single Euro Payments Area (SEPA) in 2008 it has been possible to make international bank transfers electronically between the banks of member states as quickly and cheaply as for domestic transfers. To make an international transfer it is necessary to know the payee's Bank Identifier Code (BIC) and International Bank Account Number (IBAN).

Bill of exchange (B/E) *(Wechsel/Tratte)* A bill of exchange (draft) is a promise by the buyer to pay the seller a sum of money on an agreed date. It is an instrument of payment used in international trade, e.g with a letter of credit or documentary collection.

Cheque *(Scheck)* Cheques (AE: checks) are widely used in North America. They are still used in the United Kingdom, Ireland, and France but losing popularity in favour of electronic means of payment.

Documentary collection *(Dokumenteninkasso)* In this case there is no guarantee of payment. The seller's bank forwards the shipping documents to the buyer's bank and pays the seller when it has received the money from the buyer's bank. With documents against payment (D/P), the buyer's bank gives the buyer the shipping documents if the buyer pays for them immediately. With documents against acceptance (D/A), the buyer's bank gives the buyer the shipping documents if the buyer promises to pay for them later (e.g. 30, 60 or 90 days later). In both cases the seller waits longer for payment than with a documentary credit.

Documentary credit *(Dokumentenakkreditiv)* Payment by confirmed and irrevocable documentary credit is the safest method of payment in international trade. In simple terms, the buyer's bank promises to pay the seller's bank if the seller gives his bank the shipping documents for the goods. The buyer's bank stipulates exactly which documents the seller must give to his bank (e.g. the transport document [bill of lading or air waybill or consignment note], the commercial invoice, the certificate of origin, the insurance certificate etc.). The seller gives these documents to his bank. The bank checks them and, if they are correct, pays the seller. The seller's bank now sells the documents to the buyer's bank. The buyer's bank sells the documents to the buyer. The buyer uses them to collect the goods at the port / airport / terminal.

A letter of credit can be *confirmed* and *irrevocable*. If it is *confirmed*, the seller's bank promises to pay the seller as long as the seller gives it documents stipulated by the buyer's bank. If the documentary credit is *irrevocable*, none of the details of the credit can be changed, e.g. the name of the ship, the route, the quantity of goods etc.

See also the diagram on page 200: A documentary credit step by step.

Draft *(Tratte)* (→ Bill of exchange)

PayPal This is an online payment system which can be used in and between many countries all over the world. In China PayPal can only be used for domestic payments.

SWIFT The Society for Worldwide Interbank Financial Telecommunication (SWIFT) is an international network used to transfer funds all over the world. It has data centres in the United States, the Netherlands and Switzerland.

A documentary credit step by step

1 The buyer and seller agree to pay by documentary credit.
2 The buyer instructs his bank to open a documentary credit in the exporter's favour.
3 The buyer's bank opens the documentary credit and instructs the seller's bank to inform the seller which documents are needed.
4 The seller's bank tells the seller which documents he needs.
5 The seller ships the goods.
6 The seller presents the documents stipulated in the documentary credit to his bank.
7 The seller's bank checks the documents and, if they are as stipulated, pays the seller as agreed.
8 The seller's bank sells the documents to the buyer's bank.
9 The buyer's bank sells the documents to the buyer.
10 The buyer uses the documents to collect the goods.

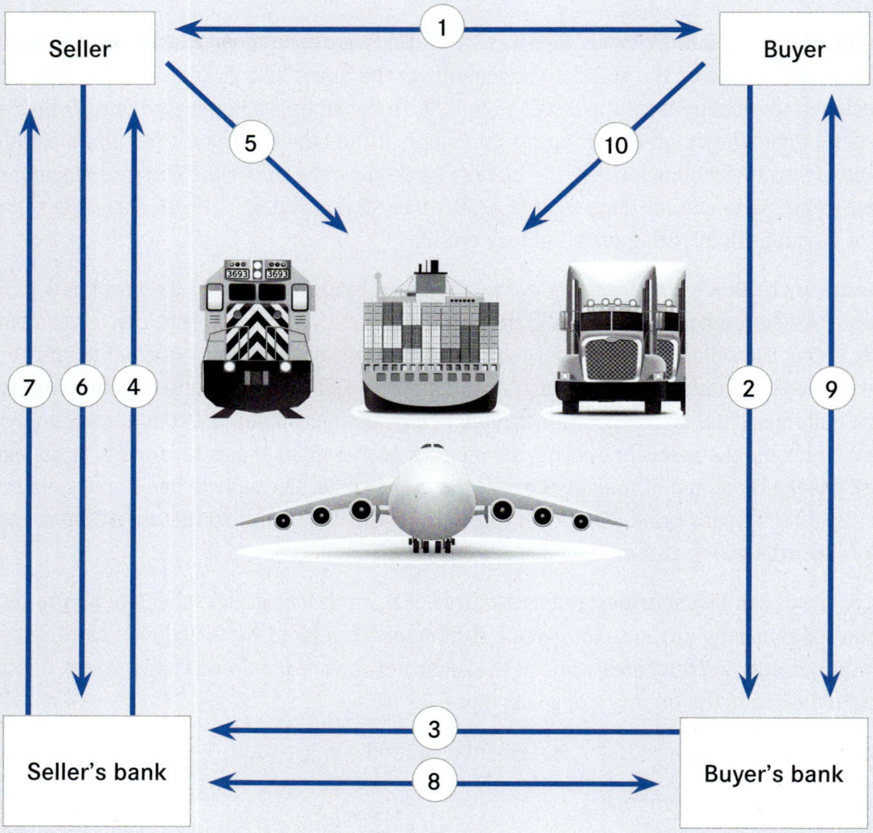

COMMON ABBREVIATIONS

English → German

a/c account *Konto*
a.m. *vormittags* (→ **p.m.**)
AOB any other business *Sonstiges, Verschiedenes [Tagesordnung]*
approx. approximate(ly) *ungefähr*
asap as soon as possible *so bald wie möglich*
attn attention *zu Händen (von) (z. Hd.)*
Ave. *(BE)* **Av.** *(AE)* Avenue *Allee*
AWB air waybill *Luftfrachtbrief*
B/E bill of exchange *Wechsel*
B/L bill of lading *Seefrachtbrief, Konnossement*
bn billion *Milliarde USA*
Bros brothers *Gebrüder*
BST British Summer Time *britische Sommerzeit*
CAD cash against documents *Zahlung gegen Dokumente*
cc carbon copy *Kopie, Durchschrift*
CC Chamber of Commerce *Handelskammer*
CEO Chief Executive Officer *Vorstandsvorsitzende/r*
cf. *vergleiche (vgl.)*
c/o care of *bei [Adresse], zu Händen (von)*
C/O certificate of origin *Ursprungszeugnis*
COD cash on delivery *Zahlung bei Lieferung*
cr credit *Haben; Kredit* (→ **deb**)
CWO cash with order *Zahlung bei Auftragserteilung/Bestellung*
D/A documents against acceptance *Dokumente gegen Wechselakzept*
deb debit *Soll, Debet* (→ **cr**)
dep. departure *Abreise, Abfahrt, Abflug*
Dept department *Abteilung*
D/P documents against payment *Dokumente gegen Zahlung*
Enc(s) enclosure(s) *Anlage(n)*
E&OE errors and omissions excepted *Irrtümer und Auslassungen vorbehalten*
est. established; estimated *gegründet; geschätzt*
ETA estimated time of arrival *voraussichtliche Ankunftzeit*
excl. excluding *ausschließlich, ohne*
ft foot, feet [length] *Fuß [30,48 cm]*
FYI(O) for your information (only) *(nur) zu Ihrer Information*
gal(s). gallon(s) *Gallone(n) [GB: 4,546 l, USA:3,785 l]*
GDP gross domestic product *Bruttoinlandsprodukt*
GMT Greenwich Mean Time *Greenwicher Zeit*
GNP gross national product *Bruttosozialprodukt*
HGV heavy goods vehicle *(Schwer-) Lastfahrzeug*
h.p. horsepower *Pferdestärke(n) (PS) [Kfz]*
IC insurance certificate *Versicherungsschein*
i.e. *das heißt (d. h.)*
incl. including *einschließlich, mit*
IOU I Owe You *Schuldanerkenntnis, Schuldschein*
K thousand *tausend*
lb(s) pound(s) [weight] *Pfund [0,454 kg]*
L/C (plural: Ls/C) letter of credit *Akkreditiv*
m million(s) *Million(en)*
max maximum *Höchst-*
MD Managing Director *Geschäftsführer*
min. minimum *Mindest-*
misc miscellaneous *Verschiedenes*
mpg miles per gallon *Meilen pro Gallone*
mph miles per hour *Meilen pro Stunde*
n/a non-applicable; not available *nicht zutreffend; nicht verfügbar*
no. (nos) number(s) *Nummer(n), Nr.*
oz ounce(s) [weight] *Unze(n) [28,35 g]*
p.a. per annum *pro Jahr*
PA personal assistant
P/A power of attorney *Vertretungsvollmacht*
pd paid *bezahlt*
pls please *bitte*
p.m. nachmittags (→ **a.m.**)
PO Box post office box *Postfach*
pp on behalf of *im Auftrag (i. A.)*

P&P postage and packing *Porto und Verpackung*
PS postscript *Postskriptum, Nachsatz*
PTO please turn over *bitte wenden (b.w.)*
qtly quarterly *vierteljährlich*
Rd Road *Straße (Str.)*
R&D research and development *Forschung und Entwicklung*
ref. reference *Bezug,Bezugszeichen*
reg(d). registered *eingetragen; eingeschrieben [Post]*
rep representative *Vertreter/in*
ro-ro roll-on roll-off *von Straßenfahrzeugen befahrbar [Schiff]*
RRP recommended retail price *unverbindliche Preisempfehlung*
sae stamped addressed envelope *frankierter und adressierter Rückumschlag*
S/N shipping note(s) *Schiffszettel, Warenbegleitschein(e)*
sq square *Quadrat(-)*
Sq. Square *Platz*
St Street *Straße*
SWIFT Society for Worldwide Interbank Financial Telecommunication *Gesellschaft für internationalen Bankverkehr*
TM trademark *(eingetragenes) Warenzeichen*
VAT value added tax *Mehrwertsteuer (MwSt.)*
via by way of [named place] *über [Ortsangabe]*
vol. volume *Volumen; Band [Buch]*
wk(s) week(s) *Woche(n)*
yd(s) yard(s) [length] *Yard(s) [91,4 cm]*

Appendix

204	Exam practice
210	Files
220	Skills
236	Grammar summary
252	Basic word list
258	Unit word list
288	A–Z word list
307	Irregular verbs

Exam practice

EXAM 1

Aufgabenteil A: Stichwortbrief

1 Making an enquiry

Situation: Sie (eigener Name) arbeiten bei Garten und Mehr, Beusselstr. 169, 10553 Berlin. Im Segment „exklusive Outdoor-Möbel" (*exclusive outdoor furniture*) zählt Ihre Firma zu den führenden Unternehmen und möchte das Sortiment an Holztischen und Stühlen erweitern. Beim Studium eines Fachmagazins fanden Sie eine Anzeige des irischen Gartenmöbelherstellers Woods of Ireland, Forrest Hill Industrial Estate, Belfast BT 41 2SJ.

Ihre Aufgabe: Schreiben Sie mit dem Aktenzeichen GM/0563 nach folgenden Angaben an den irischen Hersteller:

- Nehmen Sie Bezug auf die Anzeige.
- Stellen Sie kurz Ihre Firma vor.
- Fordern Sie einen aktuellen Katalog an, um detaillierte Informationen über Materialien, Größen, Herstellungsmethoden zu erlangen.
- Erbitten Sie auch eine aktuelle Preisliste sowie die Liefer- und Zahlungsbedingungen einschl. aller Rabatte.
- Fragen Sie nach der Lieferzeit.
- Bitten Sie um eine baldige Antwort.

2 Writing an offer

Situation: Sie sind jetzt Marie/Martin O'Donnell und arbeiten beim irischen Gartenmöbelhersteller Woods of Ireland, Forrest Hill Industrial Estate, Belfast BT 41 2SJ.

Ihre Aufgabe: Beantworten Sie mit dem heutigen Datum die Anfrage von Garten und Mehr, Beusselstr. 169, 10553 Berlin.

- Betreff: Anfrage Nr. GM/0563
- Bedanken für die Anfrage
- Erwähnen Sie, dass Woods of Ireland eine breite Palette von hochwertigen Produkten herstellt und weisen Sie darauf hin, dass ein Katalog mit zweckdienlichen Informationen sowie die aktuelle Preisliste beigefügt sind.
- Erwähnen Sie, dass alle im Katalog aufgeführten Produkte auf Lager sind.
- Nennen Sie Ihre Liefer- und Zahlungsbedingungen:
  - EXW Belfast, incl. Verpackung;
  - Bezahlung ohne Abzug innerhalb 30 Tagen; 1,5 % Skonto innerhalb 15 Tagen.
- Lieferung innerhalb einer Woche nach Bestellung
- Verabschieden Sie sich höflich mit dem Hoffen auf einen Auftrag.

Aufgabenteil B: Textaufgabe

A small victory for Indonesian shoe factory workers

by Evie Rose

Almost 4,500 employees at an Indonesian factory which makes sports shoes for Nike have won a court battle to get payment for working almost 600,000 hours of unpaid overtime over a period of two years. A local union, Serikat Pekerja National (SPN), negotiated with the owners of the PT Nikomas shoe plant in the town of Serang for almost a year for compensation for workers. In an out-of-court settlement, the factory owners have agreed to pay the workers US$1 million.

The amount to be paid was worked out based on an agreement signed last year by Indonesian textile, clothing and footwear unions and the major factories which supply the big-name sportswear brands. These include Nike, Adidas and Puma. The agreement guarantees the workers the right to form unions and the freedom to bargain collectively.

Although the sum of money to be paid looks large, the chairman of the trade union, Bambang Wirahyoso, says that the PT Nikomas really owes the workers a lot more than US$1 million. "It is common knowledge that the employees have been doing overtime without pay for 18 years. Unfortunately, Indonesian laws mean that the workers can only claim for the last two years."

"Even though, it is better than nothing," he continues. "It means that other Asian factory owners who produce goods for multinationals will also have to pay their workers for doing overtime. The suppliers who have contracts with Adidas and Puma are next on our list," says Wirahyoso.

Jim Keady, director of the United States NGO "Education for Justice", who became involved in the case following complaints from workers, says, "This is great news. Indonesian-based sportswear factories often forbid their workers to join unions. It is considered normal for employees to work long hours, seven days a week without overtime pay or other benefits. That looks likely to change."

Most of the shoe workers in Indonesia are teenagers and unmarried women aged 17 to 30 who are paid the minimum wage of $2.50 a day. The daily liveable wage in Indonesia is $4.00 to $4.50. It is hoped that, after the victory in Serang, workers' wages will be increased.

The last word goes to an employee. "On an average day, I can produce four pairs of shoes which each cost over $100 in the shops," she says. "I would love to buy these shoes but they are too expensive for me." (398 words)

Annotations:

l. 7 out-of-court settlement: money that is paid to sb, or an agreement that is made to stop sb going to court
l. 11 to bargain collectively: to have discussions between a trade/labour union and an employer about the pay and working conditions of the union members
l. 15 to claim: to demand or ask for sth because you believe it is your legal right to have it
l. 19 NGO: non-governmental organization (a charity, association, etc. that is independent of government and business)

Assignments:

Read and do the following assignments carefully. Use your own words as much as possible.

1 Explain the background to the report as described in the first and second paragraphs.
2 Say why the amount of compensation is less than it might be.
3 Describe the changes which are likely to come about in Asia as a result of SPN's victory.
4 Comment on the worker's statement. (lines 27–29)

EXAM 2

Aufgabenteil A: Stichwortbrief

Writing a reminder

Situation: Sie (eigener Name) arbeiten bei der Buchhaltung der Firma Socken und Puschen, Lehenerstr. 56, 79106 Freiburg. Vor acht Wochen hat Ihre Firma eine Lieferung Hausschuhe mit beigefügter Rechnung an die englische Firma Homewear plc geschickt. Trotz einer 1. Mahnung haben Sie bis heute weder eine Überweisung noch irgendeine Erklärung erhalten.

Ihre Aufgabe: Schreiben Sie mit heutigen Datum eine zweite Mahnung nach folgenden Angaben an Homewear plc, 299 Evershot Road, London N4 6DG:

> Ansprechpartner: Ms Lauren Maxwell, Einkaufsleiterin
> Bezug auf Rechnung Nr. HW431über 4.482,00 € vom (*Datum vor acht Wochen*)
> Bezug auf 1. Mahnung von vor 14 Tagen (Kopie liegt bei)
> Es ging keine Überweisung oder irgendeine Erklärung ein.
> Setzen Sie eine weitere Zahlungsfrist von 14 Tagen.
> Bei Nichtzahlung Androhung weiterer Schritte
> Hinweis, den Brief als gegenstandslos zu betrachten, falls Zahlung inzwischen erfolgt ist.
> Höfliche Verabschiedung

Aufgabenteil B: Textaufgabe

Read the following assignments carefully, then read the text on the opposite page. Do the tasks using your own words as much as possible.

Assignments:

1 Describe youth unemployment figures in the EU in the years 2008 to 2011 and say how things have developed specifically in Spain and Greece.
2 Describe developments in Germany, explaining the differences in youth unemployment levels in eastern and western parts of the country.
3 What does John Monks mean when he talks about a 'lost generation of young workers'? (lines 19–20)
4 Comment on Martin Klein's situation and his personal solution to the problem of underemployment in Europe. (lines 24–29)

The crisis of Europe's young unemployed

by Lisa Frey, Frankfurt am Main

The recession is hitting hard. According to the latest figures, 45 million people in the EU are unemployed with young people being hit hardest. It has been calculated that for every unemployed person over the age of 25, two young people aged between 15 and 24 are without work.

According to the 2011 figures from Eurostat, youth unemployment across Europe has increased by 25% in three years, rising from 14.6% in 2008 to 20.4%.

Figures are different depending on where you are. In Spain, youth employment has doubled since 2008 and now stands at 46% while the unemployment rate for young people in Greece jumped from 24% in 2008 to 38% in 2011. The prognosis is that figures for these countries will worsen over the next few months.

The Netherlands and Germany are the only two European countries with youth unemployment rates below 10%.

Focussing on Germany, the number of young unemployed people fell in January, 2011 with only 6.5% of 15- to 25-year-olds without work. There is, however, a huge difference between figures in eastern and western Germany. More than 20 years after the fall of the Berlin Wall, the unemployment rate in the east is 10.8%, twice as high as in the west.

John Monks, general secretary of the European Trade Union Confederation in Brussels, says, "Long-term unemployment among European youth is leading to a lost generation of young workers. Many highly-qualified young people are doing temporary work or part-time jobs involving less than 20 hours per week. The pay is often less than €400 per month but the young are taking on these low-paid jobs to keep their heads above water - and to get a job of any sort. It is well-known that employment gaps on a CV look bad."

An alternative to underemployment in Europe is to look for qualified work abroad. Martin Klein, a 24-year-old with a degree in economics who has been working as a hospital porter since he graduated last year, says: "Hundreds of graduates are chasing after the same jobs. It doesn't matter how many applications you send off, there is no chance to get work. You often don't even get a reply to your application. I've decided to emigrate to New Zealand where I have relatives. I don't want to leave home, but I don't have any other choice." (392 words)

Annotations:

l. 6 Eurostat: The statistical office of the European Union situated in Luxembourg. Its task is to provide the European Union with statistics at European level that enable comparisons between countries and regions.
l. 22 to keep one's head above water (idiom): to deal with a difficult situation, especially one in which you have financial problems

EXAM 3

Aufgabenteil A: Stichwortbrief

Writing a letter of complaint

Situation: Sie (eigener Name) sind Einkaufsleiter(in) des Großhandels Heim und Herd, Südallee, Industriepark Höchst, 65929 Frankfurt am Main.

Vor fünf Wochen haben Sie bei der Firma Lightworks, 17 Hillend Street, Glasgow G65 9JX dreißig Stehlampen (*standard lamps*) der Marke „Highlight" bestellt (Auftrag Nr. 903/02). Die Lieferung ist gestern mit zwei Wochen Verspätung angekommen; bei der Überprüfung stellten Sie einige Probleme fest.

Ihre Aufgabe: Schreiben Sie nach folgenden Angaben eine Beschwerde an Lightworks mit dem heutigen Datum.

- Ansprechpartner: Mr Robert Douglas
- Bezug auf o.g. Auftrag
- Bestätigen Sie die Ankunft einer Lieferung.
- Weisen Sie auf die Verspätung hin.
- Reklamieren Sie, dass statt 30 Stehlampen nur 25 geliefert wurden.
- Außerdem mussten Sie beim Öffnen der Kisten feststellen, dass fünf von diesen 25 Stehlampen stark zerkratzt sind (Hinweis auf beigefügtes Foto).
- Ihre Vermutung: Die Ware war nicht ordnungsgemäß verpackt, denn bei den fünf beschädigten Lampen fehlten die üblichen Styroporkügelchen (*polystyrene balls*).
- Sie erklären sich bereit, die beschädigte Ware bei einem Preisnachlass von 25% zu behalten.
- Höfliche Verabschiedung mit der Bitte um zeitnahe Stellungnahme.

Aufgabenteil B: Textaufgabe

Read the following assignments carefully, then read the text on the opposite page. Do the tasks using your own words as much as possible.

Assignments:

1 Describe megacities and say why they are needed.
2 Compare the ideas of optimistic and pessimistic experts when they describe megacities.
3 What does the author of the text mean when he writes that Chengdu 'appears to be getting it right'? (line 18)
4 Comment on the local authority's attitudes to 'urban squalor' and to homeless people. (lines 21–27)

The rise and rise of the city

by Hamish Craig, London

What do Cairo, Egypt and Lagos, Nigeria have in common with New York City, London and Moscow? All of them are megacities - metropolitan areas with a population of more than 10 million people.

At the end of 2010, the world's population reached 7 billion. According to the UN, 3.2 billion were living in cities at that time. Forecasts indicate that this number will rise to nearly 5 billion by the year 2030, when three out of five people will live in cities. In 2011, there were 21 megacities. By 2030, Asia will have at least 10 megacities; there will also be a rise in the number of megacities in Africa and South America.

Experts are in two minds regarding megacities. Optimists talk about stable and prosperous city states, where a good infrastructure leads to improvements in living standards. Pessimists predict antisocial environments where huge numbers of people fight over scarce resources. They bring up the environmental issues - pollution, smog and traffic congestion - and they also point to disease-ridden slums and the social effects caused by gentrification which leads to homelessness.

Chengdu, in the Sichuan area of China, appears to be getting it right. In 2012, the city was home to more than 14 million inhabitants. The local government is doing its best to avoid most of the negative effects of urbanization.

One example is the city's zero-tolerance approach to urban squalor. "We have patrols monitoring the city," the mayor, Ge Honglin, explains. "They look for things like broken advertising hoardings, missing manhole covers and other minor problems. As soon as these things are reported, they are fixed. We also have a special system for monitoring homeless people," Ge continues. "They are taken to the assistance centre, where they are given food and shelter and money to take them back to their home town. We have invested money in rural areas and made improvements so that people do not feel the need to move into the city."

One of the biggest challenges faced by every megacity is establishing a sense of community. Chengdu is also doing well on this front and managing to keep its sense of cultural identity. Ancient districts which were flattened in the last century have been carefully recreated and, in 2011, Chengdu put on an art and architecture exhibition which included traditional techniques and rural themes.

Predictions say that Chengdu will be home to 20 million people by 2018. (402 words)

Annotations:

l. 4 metropolitan: connected with a large or capital city

l. 16 gentrification: changing an area so that it is suitable for people from a higher social class than before

l. 21 squalor: dirty and unpleasant conditions

l. 22 hoardings: huge boards used for advertising; billboards

Files

FILE 1 Unit 1, Exercise 4A, p. 40

From:	Debbie Wharton, HR Manager <debbie@monkbar-hotel-york.com>
To:	Janina Witt <janina.witt@web.de>
Date:	10 June 20.., 09:10
Subject:	First day induction

Dear Janina

We are very much looking forward to your arrival and being part of our team.

I realize you will be on your own when you arrive in York, so if you have any problems before you start your job at the Monkbar Hotel, please contact me on my mobile. Feel free to call me at any time.

On your first day please wear sensible flat black shoes, black trousers and a white blouse. You will be given all other items of clothing needed.

On Monday 12th July 20.. we will discuss the following:

- Fire exits & fire evacuation points
- Staff toilets
- Still room (to make teas & coffees)
- Kitchen, where we get lunch, cutlery, etc. ...
- Working hours

The points listed are important and I will go through all of them in detail before you start work. If there are any questions before you get here, please do not hesitate to email me at: Debbie@monkbar-hotel-york.com or ask me when you arrive.

Yours sincerely
Debbie

Debbie Wharton
HR Manager

Direct Line: (44) 01904 523710
Personal Mobile: (44) 07525 392844

FILE 2 Unit 5, Task options, exercise C, p. 84

Partner A

You are from a city which once hosted the Olympics (e.g. London, Torino or Athens). You do not speak any German, but you are very concerned for the economic welfare of the German state where the Pan-European Games will be held. You want the following:

- The new venue(s) and anything else which is built for the games should be used after the games are over. If your state already has enough football stadiums, for example, it would be foolish to build another one.
- You prefer infrastructure projects (e.g. new transport lines) to building projects, because you believe they create more long-term jobs and help the economy in the long term.
- You think the games should be paid for by putting extra taxes on alcohol and cigarettes for the next 12 years.

role card

FILE 3 Secretarial activities, File C, exercise 5, p. 121

Partner B

You are Rob Heldof. It is 10 a.m. You're staying at the Hotel Santa Teresa in Rio with Katie (your girlfriend) when your mobile rings. It is Natasha Merck, the famous German model. She is in Rio, too. You are surprised and ask what brings her to Rio. She explains and suggests some times to meet. You are busy the first times she suggests (Katie wants to go shopping), so you suggest 3 p.m. tomorrow at the Corcorvado (statue of Christ).

role card

FILE 4 Commercial correspondence, File 7, Exercise 12, p. 192

Partner A
You *(your own name)*

- Answer the phone with the words 'Ja, hallo?'
- Confirm that you are ... (*own name*).
- Say you will be happy to answer her questions.
- Give your own answers to Maureen's questions.
- Ask your own question(s).
- Thank Maureen for calling.

role card

FILE 5 Unit 5, exercise 4, p. 80

Partner C (flight attendant)

To the questions, you should answer that

- all flights are non-smoking and passengers have to wait until after leaving the terminal to smoke;
- food and drink is available on board the flight but only once the plane is in the air;
- the flight will arrive in Glasgow at 15.36 local time;
- the weather is quite rainy and windy today and that passengers should therefore expect some turbulence during the flight;
- there will be no films showing on this flight because it is only a short-haul flight and it will not be long before they are in Glasgow anyway.

Ask the passenger to:

- place his/her bag in the overhead locker because it is too large to go under the seat;
- do up his/her seatbelt;
- take off his/her headphones and put them in his bag and then turn off any electrical equipment he may have with him/her.

role card

FILE 6 Unit 3, Focus, Exercise 3, p. 57

Percentage of 13- to 20-year-olds
who think the brand is important, by product

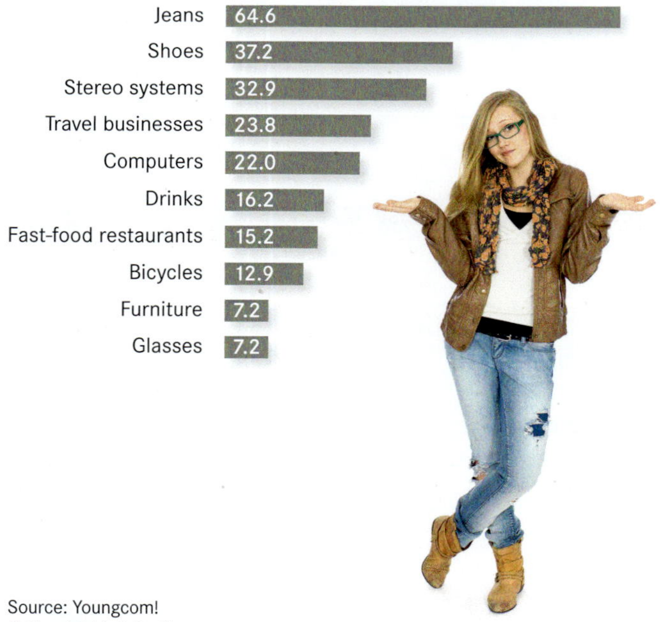

Source: Youngcom!
© Handelsblatt-Grafik

FILE 7 Unit 7, Focus, p. 97

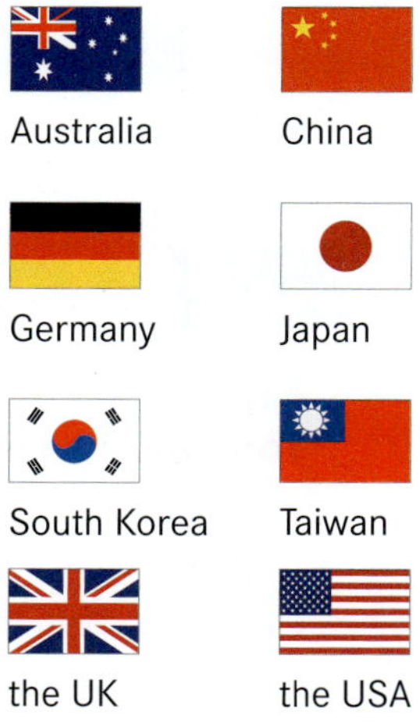

FILE 8 Secretarial activities, File E, exercise 3, p. 129

Partner B

You are the booking clerk at Hotel Vanadisvägen in Stockholm, Sweden. You take a telephone booking from Michael/Michaela Lorenz. Pass on the following details:

Dates:	Available
Rooms:	Available
Meals:	Half board costs €30 per person per day.
Conference room:	Only large conference room (20 seats) available. €50 per day.
Internet:	Free wifi throughout the hotel
Payment:	All major credit cards accepted
Questions:	All rooms are en suite rooms with a shower
	Free parking (underground car park)
	Special discount of 10% if the booking is made today

role card

FILE 9 Unit 5, Task options, exercise C, p. 84

Partner D

You are the only participant in the discussion who actually lives in the state where the games are going to be held. You want the following:

- The new venue should be located between the largest cities in the region so that people from all over will use it. You think an urban location would only benefit one city.
- As little taxpayer money as possible should be spent on the games. You do not want a lot of new building projects, unless they benefit the economy in the long term.
- You think the games should be paid for by taking money from other state funds – law enforcement, education, street and infrastructure repair, etc. – for the next 15 years.

role card

FILE 10 Unit 6, exercise 5B, p. 94

Partner C

You believe that it is necessary to cut costs.
You want to keep the customer service department in-house.
Your plan:

- Let the full-time employees go.
- Offer the same workers freelance work, without benefits like health insurance, etc.
- Offer them more flexibility, e.g. work part-time or from home.
- If some do not accept the offer, find other local freelancers.

role card

FILE 11 Unit 5, Task options, exercise C, p. 84

Partner C

You are from a European 'development' commission. You do not speak any German, but you want the German host state to invest in as many building and infrastructure projects as possible. You believe that any and all development projects will help the state economically and improve the quality of life there.

You think the games should be paid for by raising income taxes for the next 10 years. The tax would be called the 'Games Tax'. After the games are over in five years, it could be called the 'European Solidarity Tax'.

role card

FILE 12 Unit 6, exercise 5B, p. 94

Partner B

You believe that the only way the company can survive is to outsource your customer service department. All your competitors are saving money this way.

You also believe global outsourcing makes the world a fairer place. Why should workers here have such luxury when workers in poorer countries have it so hard?

You argue from the perspective of the workers overseas. They need work, and they deserve it just as much as people here.

role card

FILE 13 Unit 5, exercise 4, p. 80

Partner B (passenger)

Sie möchten wissen

- ob man hier rauchen darf;
- was für Getränk- und Essmöglichkeiten es auf diesem Flugzeug gibt;
- um wie viel Uhr Sie in Glasgow ankommen werden;
- wie das Wetter während des Fluges sein wird;
- ob es heute irgendeine Filme anzuschauen gibt.

Sie entschuldigen sich

- wenn Sie erfahren, dass Ihr Koffer zu groß ist, unter den Stuhl gestellt zu werden – Sie dachten, dass er klein genug war;
- wenn der/die Flugbegleiter/in Sie darauf aufmerksam macht, dass Sie noch nicht angeschnallt sind;
- wenn der/die Flugbegleiter/in Sie darum bittet, Ihre Kopfhörer in Ihr Koffer zu stecken und alle elektronische Geräte auszuschalten.

role card

FILE 14 Unit 2, Exercise 3, p. 49

Scoring for questionnaire

Results

20–30 points
You believe in a top-down system where the boss takes responsibility for all things. You are inflexible and see no need for team work. You see a clear division between work and leisure time.

10–19 points
You try to balance work and leisure time evenly but basically prefer to be at home. You are flexible up to a point but you do not identify strongly with your company.

0–9 points
You believe in a bottom-up system where employees take decisions together. You believe that human relationships at work and in your private life are very important. You want to get the best out of people, so you do not try to criticize them. You are flexible and sociable and want your company to get good results.

FILE 15 Secretarial activities, File C, exercise 3, p. 121

Partner B

You are Rob Heldof. It is 4 p.m. on Thursday afternoon and you have just woken up and are still jet lagged. You get a phone call from Britt Elsner, the famous German talk show host. She wants to make an appointment with you to go on her talk show on Friday morning, so you get your diary and look at Friday, 2 May. The time she first suggests is too early for you. You ask who else is on the show and after some discussion agree a much later time to come on the show. Make sure you do not agree to her first two or three suggestions!

role card

FILE 16 Secretarial activities, File B, exercise 8, p. 117

Partner B

You are Nina Wittstock, the CEO of Top Act Event Management. Today you phone a famous American rapper called DJ 60 Cent. Follow the steps below to play your role. (Partner A has steps 1, 3, 5 and 7.)

2 Say who you are and ask to speak to DJ 60 Cent.
4 Ask if he has received the contract.
6 React with enthusiasm and say it was nice talking to him.
8 Finish the call.

role card

FILE 17 Unit 5, Task options, exercise C, p. 84

Partner B

You are from another European country and do not speak any German. You are very concerned about the environment. You want the following:

- The new venue should be easily accessible by public transport. It should displace as little wildlife as possible-better to have it in an urban area that is already developed.
- Any new building projects should be done in an environmentally friendly way.
- You think the games should be paid for by putting extra taxes on petrol and air travel for the next 8 years.

role card

FILE 18 Unit 6, exercise 5B, p. 94

Partner A

You believe the following things:
- Firing your workers would be unfair. They helped build the company!
- Firing them would be unwise. Quality would suffer. Excellent customer service must be the top priority and your full-timers do it best.
- People in poorer countries work for 'slave wages'. You don't want to support this.
- Overseas companies have cultures that are different from yours. This would create problems with communication and productivity.

role card

FILE 19 Secretarial activities, File C, exercise 4, p. 121

Partner B

You are Rob Heldof. It is 10.30 a.m. and you have already checked out of your hotel in Düsseldorf. Your flight to Rio leaves Düsseldorf Airport at 1.30 p.m. and you have to check in by 11.30 a.m. You have just bought a pair of designer sunglasses at a shop in Düsseldorf and you and your girlfriend Katie are about to go to the airport by car. You get a phone call from Father Hubert, who wants you to autograph a T-shirt for charity. Explain why you cannot meet where he suggests and agree to meet him in the airport's VIP Lounge at about 11 a.m.

role card

FILE 20 Secretarial activities, File E, exercise 4, p. 130

Role B (Travelwise Hotel)

You are the booking clerk at the Travelwise Hotel in Sydney, Australia. You take a telephone enquiry from Helena Sawicki. Pass on the following details:

Dates:	Available
Rooms:	Available
Meals:	Half board costs AUD 50 (*Australian dollars*) per person per day.
Conference room:	Conference room (30 seats) available. AUD 25 per day.
Internet:	Surcharge of AUD 2 per day for wifi
Payment:	All major credit cards accepted
Questions:	Spa available with a gym Outdoor pool (Olympic size)

Role B (Fair Deal Hotel)

You are the booking clerk at the Fair Deal Hotel in Sydney, Australia. You take a telephone enquiry from Helena Sawicki. Pass on the following details:

Dates:	Available
Rooms:	Available
Meals:	No meals served by hotel. Good takeaway food nearby (pizza, curry, Chinese food).
Conference room:	Conference room (30 seats) available 50 metres away. AUD 20 per day.
Internet:	No wifi
Payment:	All major credit cards accepted
Questions:	Gym 100 metres away. AUD 15 per week per person. Tropical Paradise indoor swimming pool 500 metres away with a sauna. AUD 50 per person per day.

role card

FILE 21 Commercial correspondence, File 2, Exercise 11, p. 146

Memo

An: ...
Von: ...

Datum: ...
Betreff: ...

FILE 22 Secretarial activities, File F, exercises 3 + 4, p. 133

Role A (with Dr. Alexander Mieberg)

Background

You are Jonathan Sykes.

- You have just flown over to Düssel-dorf from the UK.
- You had a bad flight with a lot of turbulence.
- You would like a cup of tea – white, no sugar.
- You are happy with your hotel in Neuss. It is very comfortable.
- You exchange business cards.

Role B (With Sevda Yildiz)

Background

You are Amanda Lakely.

- You have just flown from Paris to Düsseldorf at the last minute to attend the Igedo fashion fair.
- Your flight was half an hour late but otherwise it was fine.
- You would like a glass of mineral water.
- You thank Sevda for booking you a hotel. You had no time to book a hotel yourself.
- You exchange business cards.

role card

FILE 23 Commercial correspondence, File 7, Exercise 12, p. 192

Partner B (Mrs Maureen O'Connor)

- Ask if you are speaking to (*Partner A's first name and surname*).
- Explain that you have received A's application and are very interested, but have a few questions.
- Ask about A's own family (brothers, sisters, nephews, nieces – how old?).
- Ask if A likes children.
- Ask about A's hobbies, strengths and weaknesses.
- Ask if A has been to an English-speaking country before.
- Ask how long A would like to stay in Ireland.
- Ask if A would like to go to English classes.
- As about A's plans for the future.
- Ask if A has any questions.
- Finish the telephone conversation politely.

role card

FILE 24 Unit 5, exercise 4, p. 80

Partner A (passenger)

You must translate what is said by your friend and the flight attendant. Use phrases such as 'he/she asked whether...' or 'is my friend able to...'. Do not worry about getting each bit of vocabulary correct; the most important thing is to get your meaning across, even if that means describing the object you're talking about!

role card

FILE 25 Unit 2, exercise 4B, p. 54

Al Winters

- You thought Miele had forgotten you.
- It's eight o'clock in the morning and you haven't opened your store or checked your e-mail yet.
- You need to get a pen to write down the details.
- You ask about delivery.
- You ask for a phone number for Miele.

role card

Skills

REZEPTION

Lesen schwieriger Texte

Texte werden zu unterschiedlichen Zwecken gelesen. Manchmal braucht man nur zu wissen, worum es geht, dann reicht in der Regel ein aufmerksames Überfliegen des Textes. Oft müssen gezielt Informationen herausgesucht werden, dann kommt es darauf an, die richtigen Schlüsselwörter zu finden. Will man sich gründlich mit einem Text auseinandersetzen, um z. B. Fragen zu beantworten oder einen Aufsatz dazu zu schreiben, ist gründliches, möglicherweise zweimaliges Lesen erforderlich.

Grobverständnis: Sich einen schnellen Überblick über einen Text verschaffen

Manchmal werden Sie im Buch aufgefordert, einen Text schnell zu lesen, um das Thema grob zu erfassen.

1. Schritt: Suchen Sie nach Anhaltspunkten, die Ihnen Aufschluss über den Textinhalt geben: Titel und Zwischenüberschriften, fett gedruckte Wörter, Bilder und Bildunterschriften.

2. Schritt: Sind Sie noch unsicher, lesen Sie die ersten und letzten Sätze jedes Absatzes. Bleiben Sie nicht an Einzelwörtern, schwierigen Zitaten usw. hängen.

Suche nach Einzelinformationen im Text

Bei vielen Textverständnisfragen oder Aufgaben vom Typ *True or false* geht es darum, schnell bestimmte Informationen im Text zu finden und nicht jedes Mal den ganzen Text neu zu lesen.

1. Schritt: Suchen Sie den Text nach Schlüsselbegriffen für die gesuchten Informationen ab. Geht es etwa um die Meinung des Autors zu einem bestimmten Thema, halten Sie nach Wörtern wie *think, believe, opinion* usw. Ausschau. Geht es um Informationen zu einem Thema, rufen Sie sich ein paar Schlüsselbegriffe in Erinnerung, nach denen Sie Ausschau halten. Manchmal hilft es, sich den gesuchten Begriff als gedrucktes Wort vor dem geistigen Auge vorzustellen.

2. Schritt: Gehen Sie falls nötig mit dem Finger die Zeilen entlang, während Sie suchen. Wenn Sie sich wie oben beschrieben vorbereitet haben, springen Ihnen die gesuchten Begriffe sofort ins Auge.

Detailverständnis: Gründliches Lesen

Lesen Sie nicht einfach drauflos. Ein paar einfache Schritte helfen Ihnen, den Text besser zu verstehen, ohne sich in Details zu verlieren.

1. Schritt: Der erste Schritt sollte darin bestehen, sich einen groben Überblick vom Textinhalt zu verschaffen (siehe oben). So werden Sie unklare Stellen besser in den Gesamtzusammenhang einordnen können. Es ist hilfreich, sich die wichtigsten Stichwörter kurz zu notieren. Zu dem Text *The future of global shipping* auf S. 71 etwa könnten Sie nach kurzem Überfliegen aufschreiben: *The text is about environmentally friendly alternatives to conventional ships.*

2. Schritt: Machen Sie sich die Struktur des Textes bewusst. Wo ist die Einleitung? Welcher Teil enthält die Hauptinformationen, und wie sind sie aufgebaut (Zwischenüberschriften, Absätze usw.)? Achten Sie auf Strukturwörter wie *only, but while, that's why, while, however* usw., mit denen der Verfasser seine Argumentation gliedert.

3. Schritt: Lesen Sie den Text nun aufmerksam. Notieren Sie sich Schlüsselstellen, z. B: *Container ships carry huge amount of cargo; they're cheap but also environmental concerns; new technology can make shipping greener, etc.* Schlagen Sie Wörter beim ersten Lesen nur nach, wenn die Bedeutung des ganzen Satzes an ihnen hängt. Oft lässt sich die wesentliche Bedeutung durch den Kontext erschließen.

4. Schritt: Notieren Sie sich den Textinhalt in strukturierter Form, etwa einer Mind Map oder einer Liste (Themen, pro/kontra). Fügen Sie auch Formulierungen hinzu, die Ihnen später helfen, sich in eigenen Worten über den Textinhalt zu äußern. Schlagen Sie jetzt das notwendige Vokabular nach.

> Note Making S. 225, Mind Mapping S. 225

Umgang mit unbekannten Vokabeln

Fragen Sie sich bei neuen Vokabeln immer, ob sie für das Verständnis des Zusammenhangs unbedingt notwendig sind. Nachschlagen kostet Zeit und hilft oft nicht beim Verständnis des wirklich Wichtigen.

Erschließen der Bedeutung aus dem Kontext

> Ein Wort, das unbekannt scheint, kann z. B. mit einem anderen, Ihnen bekannten Wort verwandt sein (Ableitungen wie *aggressor* von *aggressive*). Oder das Wort hat einen bekannten Wortstamm und ein angehängtes Wortteil, mit dessen Hilfe Sie die Bedeutung erkennen können (*formal* – ***in****formal, clockwise* – ***anti****clockwise, change* – *change****able****, stupid* – *stupid****ity***). Manche Wörter haben Ähnlichkeiten mit einem deutschen Wort (vgl. etwa *initial* und „Initialen", *potential* und „potenziell").

> Sind Sie sich immer noch nicht sicher, kann der Satzzusammenhang Aufschluss geben. Machen Sie sich zunächst die Wortart bewusst: Suchen Sie nach einem Substantiv? Wofür steht das gesuchte Substantiv wahrscheinlich – für ein Gebäude? Eine Person? Handelt es sich um ein Adjektiv, das die Situation näher beschreibt oder jemanden charakterisiert?
Schauen Sie sich den folgenden Absatz an und versuchen Sie die Bedeutung der fett gedruckten Wörter aus dem Zusammenhang zu erschließen:
Business is bad at the moment and we don't expect it to ***rally*** *for at least a year. All the signals are very* ***inauspicious****, I'm afraid.*
Auch wenn man *rally* und *inauspicious* nicht kennt, kann man aus dem Kontext erschließen, dass *rally* ein Verb ist, das eine positive Entwicklung beschreibt und *inauspicious* ein Adjektiv mit negativer Bedeutung ist.

Umgang mit dem einsprachigen Wörterbuch

Machen Sie sich mit Ihrem Wörterbuch vertraut, so dass Sie die Symbole, Abkürzungen und die Lautschrift verstehen und die Hilfen, die vorne und hinten im Wörterbuch oder auf Zusatzseiten angeboten werden, nutzen können. Auf der folgenden Seite sehen Sie ein Beispiel eines typischen Wörterbucheintrags.

Wörterbucheintrag

uncountable = unzählbares Nomen

North American English = Aussprachevariante

Wortart

Erste Bedeutung

Verweis auf einen anderen Eintrag

verb/noun + 'to' infinitive = zusammengesetzter Ausdruck, in dem das Verb von *to* + Infinitiv gefolgt wird

alarm /ə'lɑːm; *NamE* ə'lɑːrm/ *noun, verb*
■ *noun* **1** [U] fear and anxiety that sb feels when sth dangerous or unpleasant might happen: *'What have you done?' Ellie cried in alarm.* ◇ *I felt a growing sense of alarm when he did not return that night.* ◇ *The doctor said there was no cause for alarm.* ⇨ note at FEAR **2** [C, usually sing.] a loud noise or a signal that warns people of danger or of a problem: *She decided to* ***sound the alarm*** (= warn people that the situation was dangerous). ◇ *I hammered on all the doors to* ***raise the alarm***. – see also FALSE ALARM **3** [C] a device that warns people of a particular danger: *a* ***burglar/fire/smoke alarm***. ◇ *The cat* ***set off the alarm*** (= made it start ringing). ◇ *A car* ***alarm went off*** *in the middle of the night* (= started ringing). **4** = ALARM CLOCK: *The* ***alarm went off*** *at 7 o'clock.* IDM **a'larm bells ring/start ringing** if you say that **alarm bells are ringing**, you mean that people are starting to feel worried and suspicious
■ *verb* **1** to make sb anxious or afraid SYN WORRY: [VN] *The captain knew there was an engine fault but didn't want to alarm the passengers.* [also VN **to** inf] ⇨ note at FRIGHTEN **2** [VN] to fit sth such as a door with a device that warns people when sb is trying to enter illegally

Zweite Bedeutung

countable = zählbares Nomen

idiom = Redewendung

Synonym

verb/noun = zusammengesetzter Ausdruck aus Verb und Nomen

- Notieren Sie sich alle Wörter, deren Bedeutung Sie suchen, und schlagen Sie dann alle hintereinander nach.
- Lesen Sie nicht den gesamten Eintrag, sondern beschränken Sie sich auf die Verwendung Ihres Stichworts in der gesuchten Wortart (z. B. Sie suchen *alarm* als Verb, also ignorieren Sie den ersten Teil des oben stehenden Eintrags). Den entsprechenden Abschnitt mit allen zusammengesetzten Ausdrücken und den Beispielsätzen, die Ihnen helfen zu unterscheiden, in welchen Zusammenhängen welche Bedeutung zutrifft, müssen Sie dann allerdings gründlich lesen.
- Schauen Sie sich auch die Einträge in der unmittelbaren Umgebung Ihres Stichworts an, um eine Vorstellung von dem Wortfeld zu bekommen.
- Notieren Sie sich die passende Bedeutung, damit Sie sie nicht wieder vergessen.

Lernen neuer Vokabeln

Es gibt verschiedene Möglichkeiten, Vokabeln zu lernen – suchen Sie sich die, die Ihnen am besten liegt. Eines gilt jedoch für alle Methoden: Wörter prägen sich am besten ein, wenn man nicht nur das Stichwort aufschreibt, sondern auch noch dazugehörige Ausdrücke, Synonyme, Gegenteile, verwandte Wörter und Verwendungsbeispiele, evtl. auch Aussprachehinweise. Besonders wichtig sind zusammengesetzte Ausdrücke. Dazu gehören auch *phrasal verbs* (*set about, put off* usw.). Der Eintrag für das Stichwort *pay* könnte z. B. so aussehen:

pay (noun)	–	*Bezahlung, Gehalt, Lohn*
payslip	–	*Gehaltsabrechnung*
pay day	–	*Zahltag*
pay-off	–	*Abfindung*
pay (verb)	–	*zahlen*
pay for sth	–	*etw bezahlen*
pay off	–	*auszahlen*
pay as you go (phone)	–	*Prepaid(-Handy)*

Natürlich brauchen Sie nicht gleich komplette Wörterbucheinträge aufzuschreiben. Überlegen Sie sich jedoch, welche Ableitungen Ihnen zu dem neuen Wort schon bekannt sein könnten oder in welchem zusammengesetzten Ausdruck es Ihnen begegnet ist. Lassen Sie Platz für spätere Hinzufügungen, so dass die Einträge nach und nach „wachsen".

Karteikarten: Sie benötigen Karteikarten und einen Karteikasten mit mehreren Abteilungen. Schreiben Sie das englische Wort mit den dazugehörigen Ergänzungen auf eine Seite einer Karteikarte und die deutschen Bedeutungen auf die Rückseite. Sobald Sie ein Wort wissen, wandert es von der ersten in die zweite Abteilung des Karteikastens. Die Wörter in der zweiten Abteilung schauen Sie sich in größeren Abständen nochmal an, um diejenigen, die Sie wissen, dann in die dritte Abteilung fürs Langzeitgedächtnis abzulegen. Was Sie nicht wissen, kommt zurück in die erste Abteilung, die Sie sich möglichst oft anschauen sollten.

Vokabelheft: Wenn Sie im Unterricht neue Vokabeln mitschreiben wollen, bietet sich ein Vokabelheft an. Benutzen Sie ein zweispaltiges Heft, damit Sie eine Spalte leicht bedecken können. Gestalten Sie das Lernen weniger schematisch, indem Sie die Seiten, die Sie lernen wollen, zufällig auswählen und ab und zu mal Deutsch-Englisch statt Englisch-Deutsch lernen.

Wortfamilien: Fertigen Sie Listen mit Wortfamilien an, um sich zusammen mit einem neuen Wort auch noch seine Ableitungen einzuprägen (*approve - approval - approving - disapprove - disapproval*).

Wortfelder: Die beste Methode, Wortfelder, also zusammenhängende Wortgruppen zu einem Thema zu lernen, sind Mind Maps, also grafisch angelegte Wortnetze. Diese Methode ist gut geeignet, um den Themenwortschatz für eine Klassenarbeit zu lernen. Um den Schlüsselbegriff herum werden einzelne Oberbegriffe für die wichtigsten Aspekte des Themas angeordnet. Um jeden Oberbegriff werden nun die dazugehörigen Vokabeln herumgeschrieben.

> Mind Mapping S. 225

Vokabeltrainer: Wer gerne am Computer lernt, findet problemlos einen geeigneten Vokabeltrainer im Handel. Solche Software enthält meistens vielerlei Übungen, die das Vokabellernen unterhaltsam und spielerisch gestalten. Achten Sie darauf, dass es sich um eine Software handelt, die auf Ihre Schulart abgestimmt ist. Es gibt auch zahlreiche kostenlose Online-Vokabeltrainer im Internet.

Das Hörverständnis üben

Um gesprochenes Englisch zu verstehen, z. B. in Unterhaltungen, Telefongesprächen, Vorstellungsgesprächen, im Fernsehen u. a., sollten Sie sich gut auf die jeweilige Situation vorbereiten. Oft beeinträchtigen der Akzent, Hintergrundgeräusche und andere Störungen das Verständnis so, dass man sich auf das Wichtigste konzentrieren muss. Eignen Sie sich die unten beschriebene Methode an, wenn Sie die Hörverständnisaufgaben in *Focus on Business* bearbeiten. Damit lassen sich Barrieren bei schwierigen Hörtexten leicht abbauen.

Vor dem Hören

- Lesen Sie die gesamte Aufgabenstellung sorgfältig durch. Nutzen Sie alle Hilfen, die Ihnen zur Verfügung stehen - Abbildungen, Überschriften usw.
- Schreiben Sie wenn möglich **Schlüsselbegriffe** auf und rufen Sie sich, wenn genug Zeit ist, kurz wichtige Wortfelder zum Thema in Erinnerung.

Während des Hörens

- Hören Sie sich den gesamten Hörtext zunächst in Ruhe an, um zu verstehen, worum es geht. Machen Sie in dieser Phase keine Notizen.
- Achten Sie bei einem zweiten Hören nur auf die für die Aufgabe wichtigen Informationen. Konzentrieren Sie sich nicht auf einzelne Wörter und Ausdrücke, die Sie nicht verstehen.

- Achten Sie auf Ausdrücke, die den logischen Gedankengang verdeutlichen, z. B. *however, in my view, in conclusion* usw. Sie helfen Ihnen, den roten Faden nicht zu verlieren.
- Notieren Sie Informationen nur **stichpunktartig**, nie in ganzen Sätzen. Dabei kann ein Raster sehr hilfreich sein. In diesem Beispiel handelt es sich um den Wandel der Geschlechterrollen in unserer Gesellschaft:

	changed role	*reasons*	*consequences*
men			
women			

- Verwenden Sie Zeichen, Abkürzungen und Wortverkürzungen, um beim Notieren Zeit zu sparen:

Zeichen		Abkürzungen		Wortverkürzungen	
=	*the same as*	e.g.	*for example*	govt	*government*
≠	*not the same as*	km	*kilometres*	impt	*important*
+	*and*	w., w/o	*with, without*	kids	*children*

Nach dem Hören

- Formulieren Sie Ihre Stichpunkte so schnell wie möglich aus – vielleicht können Sie später Ihre Aufzeichnungen nicht mehr lesen oder Ihre Wortverkürzungen nicht mehr verstehen.
- Versuchen Sie, alle Fragen zu beantworten. Wenn Sie einige Informationen nicht verstanden haben, stellen Sie eine begründete Vermutung an.

Suche nach Informationen im Internet

Das Internet bietet riesige Ressourcen für die Recherche, z. B. für Aufsätze oder Präsentationen, aber es ist wichtig zu wissen, wo und wie man am besten sucht.

1. Schritt: Notieren Sie, wonach Sie genau suchen, und halten Sie passende Suchbegriffe fest. Ohne eine solche Vorgabe, die so spezifisch wie möglich sein sollte, gerät man vom Suchen leicht ins Surfen.

2. Schritt: Überlegen Sie sich, wo Sie mit der Suche beginnen sollten. Es ist sinnvoll, sich mit der Zeit einen Grundstock an englischsprachigen Ressourcen zusammenzustellen, z. B. *online encyclopedias* (etwa www.encyclopedia.com), *online dictionaries* (z. B. www.leo.org), *facts and figures about different countries* (etwa https://www.cia.gov/library/publications/the-world-factbook/), *news sites* (z. B. www.bbc.co.uk), *science and technology sites* (etwa www.howstuffworks.com).

3. Schritt: Suchen Sie sich die beste Suchmaschine und geben Sie möglichst spezifische Suchbegriffe ein. Machen Sie sich mit allen Suchfunktionen vertraut. Schränken Sie die Sprache der angezeigten Ergebnisseiten auf Englisch ein.

4. Schritt: Achten Sie darauf, nur verlässliche Quellen zu benutzen. Im Durchschnitt ist das Internet nicht sehr zuverlässig, da jeder Nutzer beliebige Informationen einstellen kann. Prüfen Sie immer, wer für die jeweiligen Inhalte verantwortlich ist, und verlassen Sie sich nicht auf die nächstbeste Information.

5. Schritt: Bevor Sie einzelne Artikel Satz für Satz lesen, überfliegen Sie sie. Sind nur einzelne Abschnitte für Ihr Thema relevant, suchen Sie sich diese heraus und ignorieren Sie die übrigen Teile. > Grobverständnis S. 220

6. Schritt: Anstatt ganze Textabschnitte in Ihr Dokument herüberzukopieren, machen Sie sich gezielt Notizen. Speichern Sie die Seite unter Ihren Favoriten, wenn Sie später noch einmal darauf zurückkommen oder Materialien bzw. Zitate von der Seite verwenden möchten. > Note Making S. 225

PRODUKTION

Note Making

Es ist sinnvoll, sich beim Lesen und Hören eines Textes Notizen zu machen. So können Sie später leichter auf die Informationen zurückgreifen.

Beim Lesen

Auf den ersten Blick scheint es ziemlich leicht, sich beim Lesen eines Textes Notizen zu machen. Trotzdem fällt es vielen schwer, sich wirklich kurze, sinnvolle Stichpunkte zu notieren. Oft führt die Sorge, etwas Wichtiges auszulassen, dazu, dass ganze Sätze des Originaltextes abgeschrieben werden. Damit verliert man nicht nur Zeit, sondern es wird später auch schwierig, seinen Text in eigenen Worten zu formulieren.

Hier einige Tipps, damit Sie diese Falle umgehen:

- Geben Sie Ihren Notizen eine Überschrift, die Ihr Thema klar umreißt, z. B. *Effects of genetic engineering on the environment.*
- Gehen Sie den Text durch und filtern Sie die wesentlichen Unterthemen heraus, die Sie als Überschriften verwenden können. Denken Sie daran, unter den Überschriften genug Platz für Ihre Stichpunkte zu lassen. > Detailverständnis S. 220
- Halten Sie Ausschau nach Signalen wie Hervorhebungen, Wiederholungen und bedeutungstragenden Adjektiven wie *huge, incredible, devastating* usw. Diese zeigen, was der Verfasser für wichtig hält.
- Notieren Sie nur Stichwörter, nicht ganze Sätze.
- Verdeutlichen Sie den logischen Aufbau der Informationen, z. B. indem Sie bestimmte Punkte in einer Liste untereinanderschreiben, Themen durch Leerzeilen voneinander abheben oder die wichtigsten Begriffe unterstreichen.
- Kontrollieren Sie, ob Sie alle notwendigen Informationen zusammengetragen haben. Vergessen Sie nicht, dass sie oft über den gesamten Text verstreut sind.

Beim Hören

In diesem Fall ist es schwieriger Notizen zu machen, da man oft sehr schnell schreiben muss. Man muss sich auf das Wesentliche konzentrieren und sollte Abkürzungen verwenden, damit man den Faden nicht verliert. > Das Hörverständnis üben S. 223

Mind Mapping

Eine Mind Map ist eine sinnvolle Methode, Begriffe und Angaben übersichtlich in einem Netz um einen Oberbegriff herum anzuordnen. Sie eignet sich z. B. zum Vokabellernen, zum Brainstorming, zum Ideensammeln und zur Vorbereitung eines Aufsatzes oder einer Präsentation.

> Umgang mit unbekannten Vokabeln S. 221

Materialien: Ein großes Blatt (z. B. DIN A3), farbige Stifte.

1. Schritt: Schreiben Sie den Oberbegriff (wenn es um Wortfelder geht) bzw. das Thema (wenn es um eine Ideensammlung geht) deutlich und groß in die Mitte.

2. Schritt: Schreiben Sie die wichtigsten Begriffe zum Thema um den Oberbegriff herum; sie sollten durch starke „Äste" mit dem Oberbegriff verbunden sein.

3. Schritt: Fügen Sie nach demselben Prinzip weitere Wörter und Ideen zu den einzelnen Unterthemen hinzu. Je spezieller, desto kleiner die Verzweigungen, d.h. der Weg vom Thema nach außen führt vom Allgemeinen zum Speziellen. Sie können jederzeit und überall neue Ideen hinzufügen.

4. Schritt: Heben Sie wichtige Begriffe durch farbige Markierungen und Symbole hervor.

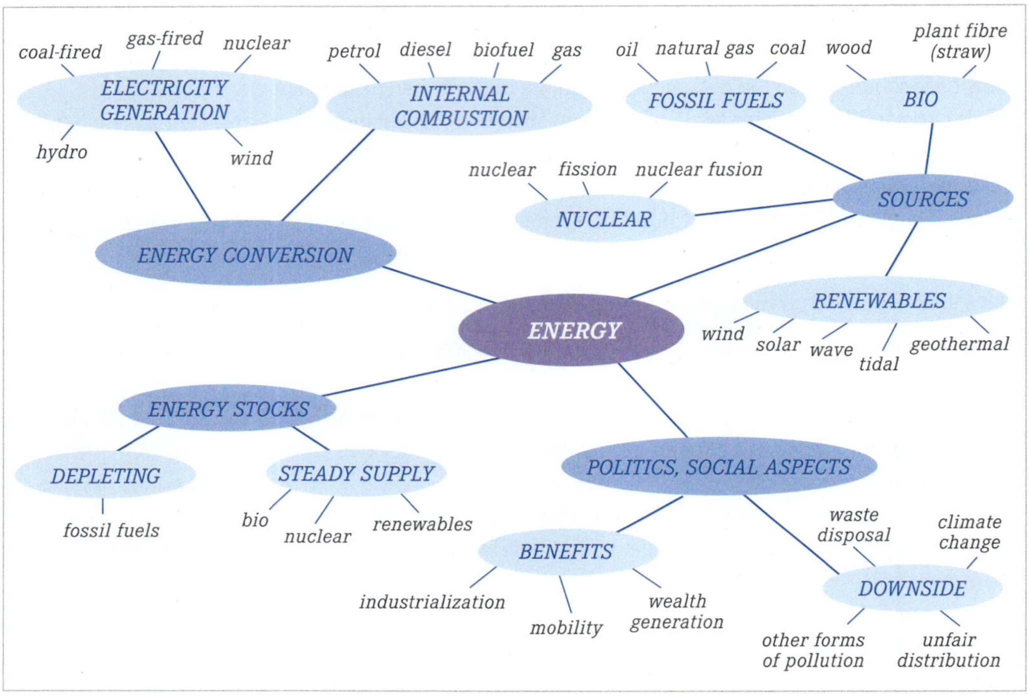

Fragen zum Text beantworten

> Lesen schwieriger Texte S. 220

Bevor Sie mit dem Schreiben beginnen, vergewissern Sie sich, dass Sie den gesamten Text verstanden haben. (Nicht jedes Wort ist wichtig - überlegen Sie sich, ob Sie die Bedeutung des Satzes auch verstehen, ohne jedes Wort zu kennen.) Lesen Sie die Aufgabenstellung immer genau, um zu verstehen, worauf es bei der Beantwortung genau ankommt - ein häufiger Fehler ist das „Vorbeischreiben" an der Frage. Achten Sie auch darauf, keine Informationen zu „verpulvern", die Sie möglicherweise für die Beantwortung einer anderen Frage benötigen.

- Wenn Sie im Buch nichts anstreichen dürfen, machen Sie sich Notizen in Form von Stichpunkten und Listen, anstatt ganze Sätze aus dem Text herauszuschreiben. In der Klassenarbeit bzw. Prüfung sollten Sie die wichtigsten Passagen im Text markieren. Am besten markieren Sie alles, was für eine Textverständnisfrage wichtig ist, mit einer bestimmten Farbe, und nehmen dann eine andere Farbe für die nächste Textverständnisfrage.
- Verwenden Sie in der Antwort die Zeitform der Fragestellung.

- Verwenden Sie so viele Synonyme und Umschreibungen der Begriffe und Formulierungen aus dem Text wie möglich, z. B. *recently - in recent years; violent crime - crime involving violence; think - believe; to a great extent - greatly; when she was a child - in her childhood* usw.
- Suchen Sie Signale im Text wie Hervorhebungen, Wiederholungen und bedeutungstragende Adjektive und Adverbien wie *absolutely, unbelievably, amazing*. Dies sind Signale dafür, was der Verfasser für wichtig hält.
- Versuchen Sie nicht, Ihre eigene Meinung einzubringen, wenn dies nicht in der Fragestellung gefordert ist.

Formulierungen für das Schreiben über den Text

- *According to the author, ...*
- *The article goes on to say that ...*
- *The text says that ...*
- *The author makes the point that ...*

Aus dem Text zitieren

Wenn Sie wirklich einmal eine wichtige Aussage aus dem Text zitieren möchten, um einen Punkt zu unterstreichen, so tun Sie dies nicht, indem Sie einfach die Formulierung des Textes übernehmen, sondern zeigen Sie, dass Sie bewusst zitieren und dies auch sprachlich deutlich machen können. Zitieren Sie in Ihrer Antwort höchstens einmal aus dem Text.

Zitate in die Antwort einbauen

- *To quote the author, ...*
- *According to the article, the high cost makes hosting these events 'a liability rather than an asset'.*
- *David Lambert criticizes people who give the 'feel-good-factor' as a reason for hosting events, and poses the question: 'Does bankruptcy feel good?'*

Eine Stellungnahme (*comment*) schreiben

Bei einer Stellungnahme geht es darum, Ihre Meinung zu einem bestimmten Thema darzulegen. Wichtig ist, dass Ihre Meinung begründet und mit Beispielen belegt ist.

1. Schritt: Machen Sie sich genau bewusst, worüber Sie schreiben sollen. Lesen Sie die Aufgabenstellung mehrmals durch.

2. Schritt: Machen Sie sich Notizen. Ordnen Sie Ihre Stichwörter übersichtlich an, z. B. in einer Mind Map, einer Liste oder einer Übersicht. > Note Making S. 225, Mind Mapping S. 225

3. Schritt: Schreiben Sie einen Einleitungssatz, der sich auf die Aufgabenstellung beziehen sollte.

4. Schritt: Behandeln Sie jedes Argument in einem Absatz. Handelt es sich um ein Pro-/Kontra-Thema, können Sie erst die Pro- und dann die Kontra-Argumente anführen. Verdeutlichen Sie Ihre Argumentation durch die Verwendung von Strukturwörtern; hierzu siehe die Liste auf der hinteren Umschlagklappe dieses Buches (*Language for writing*). > Einen Text sinnvoll gliedern S. 230

5. Schritt: Bringen Sie Ihre Argumentation in einem prägnanten Schlusssatz auf den Punkt.

Eine Stellungnahme einleiten

- *In the following I shall deal with the problem/subject/issue of ...*
- *I would like to discuss ...*
- *I intend to present arguments in favour of ... and against ...*

Eine Stellungnahme abschließen

- *All in all, I think it can be said that ...*
- *In conclusion, I would like to say that ...*
- *I would like to conclude by saying that ...*

Einen Text zusammenfassen

Die Fähigkeit, einen gelesenen Text zusammenzufassen, ist nicht nur wichtig, um den Text richtig zu verstehen, sondern sie hilft auch bei anderen Situationen, in denen Sie Informationen aus einem Text auf das Wesentliche reduzieren müssen. Zu solchen Situationen gehören z. B. die Beantwortung von Textverständnisfragen oder eine Mediation.

> Fragen zum Text beantworten S. 226, Mediation S. 234

1. Schritt: Lesen Sie den Text so oft wie möglich, bis Sie sicher sind, alles verstanden zu haben.

> Detailverständnis S. 220, Umgang mit unbekannten Vokabeln S. 221

2. Schritt: Fassen Sie in ein oder zwei einleitenden Sätzen zusammen, worum es in dem Text geht, z. B.: *The text is an extract from a radio phone-in show which is looking at people's attitudes to the EU.*

3. Schritt: Machen Sie sich bewusst, welche Informationen für den Leser wichtig sind, indem Sie *Wh*-Fragen beantworten: *Who? What? When? Where? Why?*, z. B.:
- > *Who: Dr Peter Brown from Manchester University*
- > *What: has been doing research into corruption in the EU*

4. Schritt: Machen Sie sich Notizen in Form von Stichwörtern. > Note Making S. 225

5. Schritt: Schreiben Sie Ihren Text. Beachten Sie dabei folgende Punkte:
- > Lassen Sie Unwesentliches weg. Dazu gehören etwa Beispiele, Aufzählungen, Namen, Zitate usw.
- > Verwenden Sie so weit wie möglich Ihre eigenen Worte.
- > Vermeiden Sie es, zu dem Text Stellung zu nehmen. Dies gehört in der Regel nicht zur Aufgabenstellung.
- > Denken Sie daran, Zitate in indirekte Rede umzuwandeln. > Reported speech S. 241

6. Schritt: Kontrollieren Sie Ihren Text auf Fehler und vergewissern Sie sich, dass Sie alle wichtigen Aspekte des Textes berücksichtigt haben.

Einen Bericht schreiben

Ein Bericht fasst die Hauptinformationen einer Präsentation, einer Sitzung, eines Geschäftsvorhabens oder über ein wichtiges Ereignis wie einen Streik, einen Unfall oder die Folgen einer Naturkatastrophe zusammen.

- > Ein Bericht ist die **objektive Darstellung** eines Vorgangs oder einer Situation. Daher enthalten Berichte oft Antworten auf folgende Fragen:
  - ***What*** *event took place? /* ***What*** *situation came about?*
  - ***Where*** *and* ***when*** *did it take place?*
  - ***Who*** *was involved in the event or situation?*
  - ***Why*** *and* ***how*** *did the event take place or the situation arise?*
- > Berichte haben einen **förmlicheren Stil**. Eine objektive Haltung wird durch den Gebrauch des **Passivs**, insbesondere des **unpersönlichen Passivs** *(It was suggested that ..., The sales department was reported to have ...)* und durch eine wertfreie Darstellungsweise zum Ausdruck gebracht. > Impersonal passive S. 244
- > Beginnen Sie immer mit einer knappen Einleitung, in der Sie das **Ziel** Ihres Berichts aufzeigen.
- > Lassen Sie alles Unwesentliche weg! Beziehen Sie nur so viele Informationen ein, wie der Leser braucht, um zu verstehen, was Sie ihm sagen wollen.
- > Verwenden Sie Überschriften, um Ihren Bericht klar zu strukturieren.

Einen Aufsatz schreiben

Im Laufe der Oberstufe, in der Abschlussprüfung und auch später, z. B. im Studium, werden Sie immer wieder Aufsätze zu unterschiedlichsten Themen schreiben müssen. Es ist sinnvoll, sich von Anfang an einige Regeln zu eigen zu machen, um das Vorgehen möglichst zu automatisieren und sich gleich auf den Inhalt konzentrieren zu können. Dies ist besonders wichtig, wenn es – wie in der Abschlussprüfung – auf die Zeit ankommt.

1. Schritt: Verschaffen Sie sich Klarheit über Ihr Thema. Welche Aspekte gehören dazu, welche nicht?

2. Schritt: Machen Sie ein Brainstorming, indem Sie alle Ideen aufschreiben, die Ihnen zum Thema in den Kopf kommen. Wichtig: Die Ideen sollten Sie gleich in eine Struktur bringen, um nicht in einem Wust von ungeordnetem Gekritzel zu enden. Zur Strukturierung eignen sich z. B. Listen oder Mind Maps.

> Note Making S. 225, Mind Mapping S. 225

3. Schritt: Überlegen Sie sich einen Aufbau für Ihren Text. Dies kann z. B. in Form einer Mind Map geschehen. Eine andere Möglichkeit ist eine Übersicht (*outline*) wie die folgende:

Should old towns be closed to private vehicles?

Einleitung: Umreißen des Themas
Hauptteil: Ausführung zum Thema, z. B.:

- **1.** *Disadvantages for business*
  - **1.1** *Job losses*
    - **1.1.1** *retail trade*
    - **1.1.2** *fewer tourists*
      - **1.1.2.1** *less money for tourist attractions*
      - **1.1.2.2** *job losses in cafés, etc.*
  - **1.2** *What about town centre residents, delivery vehicles, etc.?*
- **2.** *Advantages, positive effects on town and people*

...

Schluss: Zusammenfassung, Fazit

4. Schritt: Schreiben Sie Ihren Text. Lassen Sie Platz für Korrekturen, Änderungen oder Ergänzungen. Wichtig: Verdeutlichen Sie Ihre Argumentation durch die Verwendung von Strukturwörtern; hierzu siehe die Liste auf der hinteren Umschlagklappe dieses Buches (*Language for writing*) und den Abschnitt auf der nächsten Seite „Einen Text sinnvoll gliedern".

5. Schritt: Überprüfen Sie Ihren Entwurf auf:

- **Rechtschreibfehler** (z. B. gleichlautende Wörter wie *there/their, meet/meat* usw.)
- **Grammatikfehler** (z. B. Gebrauch der Zeitformen; *-ly*-Endung für Adverbien)
- **Wortwahl** (z. B. Wiederholungen; *False friends* wie „aktuell" ≠ *actual*, „eventuell" ≠ *eventual*, „spenden" ≠ *spend*)
- **Satzbau** (z. B. unvollständige Antworten, die mit *Because* beginnen)
- **Gedankenführung** (z. B. Klarheit des Ausdrucks; Verwendung von Strukturwörtern wie *However, On the other hand, In addition, As a result* usw.)

Einen Text sinnvoll gliedern

Wann immer es darum geht, einen zusammenhängenden Text zu schreiben, sei es eine Antwort auf eine Frage zum Text, einen Aufsatz, eine Zusammenfassung o. Ä., ist es ganz wichtig, die Gedanken in einen logischen Zusammenhang zu bringen, damit der Leser den Faden nicht verliert. Dies alles gilt ebenso für mündliche Präsentationen, nur werden Sie dabei Ihre Materialien nicht Wort für Wort ablesen, sondern frei sprechen. Daher ist es wichtig, Formulierungen für die Gliederung auch mündlich parat zu haben.

Die wichtigsten Strukturwörter finden Sie auf der hinteren Umschlagklappe dieses Buches (*Language for writing*). Im Folgenden sehen Sie einige Beispiele, wie man diese Formulierungen in einen Text einbauen kann.

Argumente gliedern

> *In his text 'The world's changing energy supplies' Knapp discusses many aspects of energy and the environment. Firstly, he states that ... Secondly / Then he goes on to say that ... Another point he makes is that ... Finally, ...*

Eine Begründung anführen

> *Due to / Because of / As a result of all the discussions about renewable sources of energy ...*

> *Renewable energy has been talked about a lot. Therefore, the public ...*

> *Renewable energy has been talked about a lot, so the public ...*

Aspekte ergänzen

> *Brian Knapp states that many renewable sources of energy include high development costs. In addition, / Moreover, he points out that these energy forms still only offer a small amount of the world's rising energy requirements.*

> *In addition to / Besides / As well as mentioning the high development costs of many renewable forms of energy, Knapp points out that these energy forms still only offer a small amount of the world's rising energy requirements.*

Einen Gegensatz ausdrücken

> *Although the demand for cheap energy is continuing to rise, our current main sources of energy – fossil fuels – are running out.*

> *In spite of the rising demand for cheap energy, our current main sources of energy are running out.*

> *While / Whereas the demand for cheap energy is continuing to rise, our current main sources of energy are running out.*

> *Our current main sources of energy are running out. However, / But nevertheless, the demand for cheap energy is continuing to rise.*

> *On the one hand, our current main sources of energy are running out; on the other hand, the demand for cheap energy is continuing to rise.*

Beispiele anführen

> *The writer is of the opinion that nuclear fusion is a safe energy source compared with other energy sources, for example / for instance / such as / e.g. ...*

Ein Fazit ziehen

> *As a consequence, / All in all, / Consequently, Brian Knapp thinks that ...*

> *To sum up, / To conclude, I would like to say that ...*

Diese Strukturwörter (*connectors*) sollten Sie sich so zu eigen machen, dass Sie sie möglichst in jedem Text verwenden. Dadurch gewöhnen Sie sich eine genaue und logische Ausdrucksweise an. Achten Sie auch beim Lesen von Texten auf Strukturwörter; so können Sie der Gedankenführung leichter folgen.

Die Arbeitsergebnisse präsentieren

Die Fähigkeit, wirkungsvoll vor einem Publikum zu referieren, ist wichtig im Berufsleben und zunehmend auch in der Schule. Dabei kommt es nicht nur auf den Inhalt an, sondern auch darauf, wie anschaulich Sie den Inhalt „verpacken", d.h. dass Sie Ihren Vortrag leicht nachvollziehbar gliedern, abwechslungsreich gestalten und lebendig illustrieren.

Vor der Präsentation

1. Schritt: Bereiten Sie Ihr Thema gründlich vor und machen Sie sich dabei schon Notizen auf Englisch.

2. Schritt: Prüfen Sie Ihre Stichpunkte sprachlich und vergewissern Sie sich, dass Sie alles richtig aussprechen (anhand der Lautschrift in einem Wörterbuch oder der Aussprachebeispiele in gängigen Online-Wörterbüchern oder auf Wörterbuch-CD-ROMs).

3. Schritt: Überlegen Sie sich, wie Sie Ihren Vortrag interessanter und lebendiger machen können (Anschauungsmaterial, Audiobeispiele, Anekdoten usw.).

4. Schritt: Organisieren Sie alle Hilfsmittel, die Sie benötigen (OHP, Flipchart usw.).

5. Schritt: Üben Sie die Präsentation, am besten vor Zuhörern.

Während der Präsentation

1. Schritt: Steigen Sie nicht gleich mitten ins Thema ein, sondern geben Sie einen Überblick über Ihre Präsentation.

2. Schritt: Machen Sie es den Zuhörern leicht, indem Sie sich klar ausdrücken, kurze Sätze benutzen und langsam sprechen.

3. Schritt: Die Zuhörer bleiben am ehesten interessiert, wenn Sie Ihre Präsentation so abwechslungsreich wie möglich gestalten: Ziehen Sie zwischendurch Anschauungsmaterial (OHP, Beamer usw.) heran und teilen Sie Handouts aus. Wenn Sie Folien benutzen, halten Sie sie klar und übersichtlich, anstatt sie mit Grafiken zu überladen.

4. Schritt: Achten Sie auf Ihre Körpersprache: Wenden Sie sich dem Publikum zu, halten Sie Blickkontakt mit den Zuhörern, sprechen Sie langsam und deutlich und benutzen Sie Gesten, um den Inhalt zu verdeutlichen.

5. Schritt: Fassen Sie zum Schluss das Wichtigste zusammen. Bedanken Sie sich bei den Zuhörern für ihre Aufmerksamkeit und ermuntern Sie sie, Fragen zu stellen.

Interpretation von Grafiken, Diagrammen und Tabellen

Wie im Falle von Cartoons ist es auch bei Grafiken, Diagrammen und Tabellen sinnvoll, einen Grundstock an Formulierungen zur Beschreibung und Interpretation parat zu haben. Halten Sie die folgenden Schritte ein, um Ihre Antwort sinnvoll zu gliedern:

1. Schritt: **Beschreibung der Vorlage.** Hier geht es nicht darum, alle Details aufzuzählen, sondern zu beschreiben, worum es in der Vorlage geht und welche Daten dargestellt werden.

2. Schritt: **Zusammenfassung der dargestellten Tendenzen, Entwicklungen bzw. Größen.** Welche Schlussfolgerungen ergeben sich aus den Daten? Kann man zusammenfassend ein Ergebnis oder Fazit formulieren?

Typen von Diagrammen

Tabelle (*table*)

	USA	UK
1995	495	105
2005	718	85

Kurvendiagramm (*graph, line graph*)

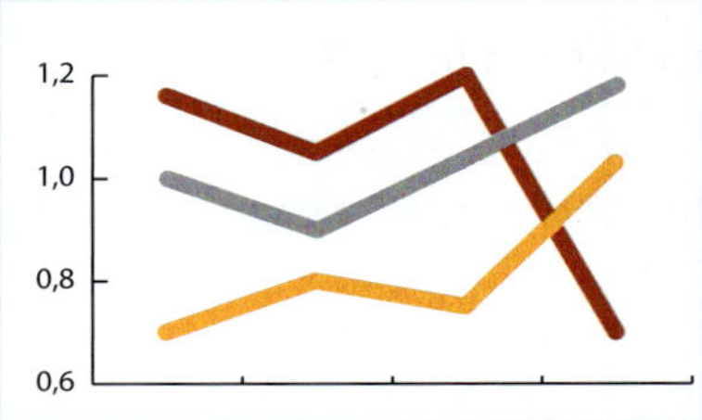

Balkendiagramm (*bar chart*)

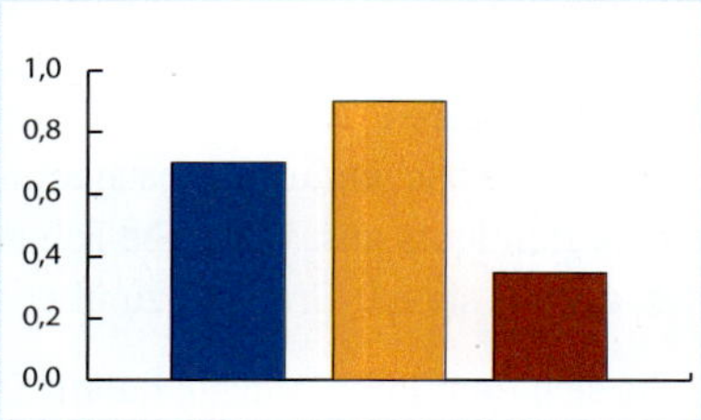

Kreis-/Tortendiagramm (*pie chart*)

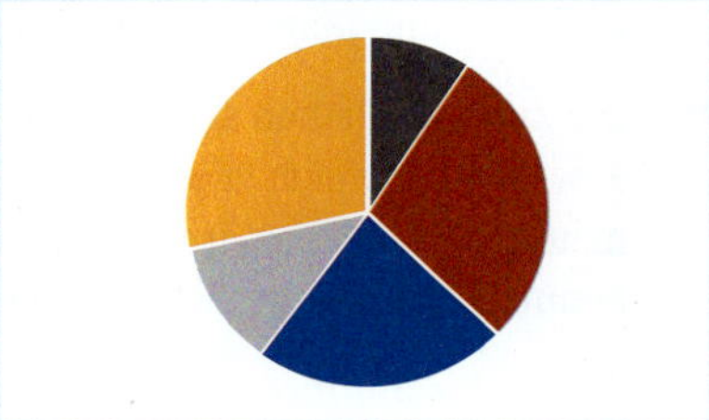

Sprechen über Zahlen und Mengenangaben (*values, amounts*)

- > *more / less than ...*
- > *no less than ...*
- > *eighty-five per cent (said that ...)*
- > *On the other hand, almost ...*

Sprechen über Proportionen (*proportions, shares, percentages*)

- > *(over) half of ...*
- > *more / less than one third / quarter of ...*
- > *the (vast) majority of ...*
- > *a mere third of ...*

Sprechen über Entwicklungen (*developments*) und Tendenzen (*tendencies*)

- > *a huge / sharp increase / decrease*
- > *a small / slight raise / dip*
- > *levels out, remains constant*
- > *drastically, gradually, sharply, steadily*
- > *rises / increases / hits a maximum*
- > *drops / decreases / falls / plunges*
- > *over a period of ...*
- > *between 2000 and 2008*

INTERAKTION

Gruppengespräche und Diskussionen führen

Ob es um Gruppengespräche, Diskussionen oder Rollenspiele geht: Machen Sie das Beste daraus, indem Sie die folgenden Punkte beherzigen.

> Lernen Sie die Formulierungen auf der hinteren Umschlagklappe dieses Buches (*Language for discussion*). Klappen Sie diese während des Unterrichts aus. Die Formulierungen helfen Ihnen, sich klar und logisch auszudrücken.
> Bereiten Sie sich inhaltlich vor, indem Sie sich einzelne Aspekte des Themas noch einmal in Stichworten ins Gedächtnis rufen und Schlüsselbegriffe auf Englisch notieren.
> Legen Sie sich, wenn genügend Zeit ist, ein paar Fragen/Antworten zum Thema zurecht.
> Bleiben Sie immer ruhig und denken Sie nach, bevor Sie sprechen.
> Bleiben Sie beim Thema und schweifen Sie nicht ab.
> Gehen Sie auf Ihre Gesprächspartner ein und halten Sie Blickkontakt.
> Beteiligen Sie sich und hören Sie nicht bloß still zu: Gruppenarbeit ist eine hervorragende Gelegenheit zum freien Sprechen.

Melden Sie sich auch immer mal wieder spontan zu Wort und lassen Sie Ausdrücke einfließen, die Interesse, Überraschung, Skepsis usw. äußern – so etwas macht das Gespräch gleich viel lebendiger:

Sich zu Wort melden	
> *Can I just say that ... ?*	> *Well, if you ask me ...*
Jemand anderen ins Gespräch einbringen	
> *What do you think, Sven / Svenja?*	
Verständnis, Erstaunen usw. ausdrücken	
Ach so. / Ah ja.	*I see. / Right. / Oh, right.*
Oh je!	*Oh dear!*
Echt?	*Really?*
Gut. / Okay.	*Fine.*
Alles klar.	*OK then.*
Das ist doch wohl nicht dein Ernst!	*You're kidding!*

Ein Interview führen

Ein Interview ist eine Unterhaltung zwischen Ebenbürtigen, das heißt der Person, die Fragen stellt (*the interviewer*) und der, die sie beantwortet (*the interviewee*). Es ist kein Verhör. Die Wendungen unten werden Ihnen helfen, nicht in diese Falle zu tappen.

1. Schritt: Beginnen Sie, indem Sie sich bei dem zu Befragenden dafür bedanken, dass er/sie sich die Zeit genommen hat, Ihre Fragen beantworten zu wollen.

2. Schritt: Machen Sie sich im Voraus ein Konzept zur Reihenfolge Ihrer Fragen, aber bleiben Sie flexibel. Seien Sie darauf vorbereitet, Fragen zu vertauschen oder wegzulassen, je nach den Antworten des Befragten. Wenn Sie zu unnachgiebig sind, könnte sich Ihr Interview in ein Quiz verwandeln!

3. Schritt: Seien Sie niemals aggressiv oder aufdringlich. Wenn der Befragte eine Frage nicht beantworten möchte, bringen Sie Ihre Frage anders zum Ausdruck. Wenn er/sie immer noch nicht bereit ist zu antworten, fahren Sie fort.

4. Schritt: Beenden Sie das Interview mit einer positiven Anmerkung, beispielsweise indem Sie sagen, wie interessant Sie es fanden. Vergessen Sie nicht, sich bei dem Befragten nochmals dafür zu bedanken, dass er/sie sich die Zeit genommen hat.

Interviewer

> *May I start/end by asking you your views on ...?*
> *Can/May I go on to ask you about ...?*
> *Do you mind if we turn to ... now?*

> *I (quite) see what you mean.*
> *That's interesting. I didn't know / wasn't aware that ...*
> *Yes, I was just about to turn to the question of ...*
> *It's funny/interesting you say that because I wanted to ask you ...*

> *So what you are getting at is ...*
> *Am I correct/right in thinking that ...?*

> *Tell me more.*
> *Yes, but I'm sure you'd agree that ...*

> *Sorry to break in / interrupt you, but ...*
> *If I may just go back (for a moment) to ...*

Interviewee

> *What I mean is ...*
> *What I'm getting at / trying to say is ...*
> *In other words, ...*

> *Take ... for instance. In my opinion/view, ...*
> *To give you an example of this / of what I'm getting at, ...*

> *From my point of view, the fact is that ...*
> *It seems to me that ...*

MEDIATION

Mediation

Schriftliche Mediation bedeutet das sinngemäße Übertragen von Texten in eine andere Sprache für jemanden, der das Original nicht versteht. Wichtig bei einer Mediation ist immer die Konzentration auf das Wesentliche, im Unterschied zur Übersetzung. Einzelheiten sind bei einer Mediation ebenso zweitrangig wie stilistische Feinheiten.

1. Schritt: Lesen Sie genau, **für welche Situation** Sie den Text zusammenfassen müssen und **für wen**. Meist bestimmt die jeweilige Situation, worauf es ankommt.

2. Schritt: Lesen Sie den gesamten Text durch, ohne sich dabei auf Einzelwörter zu konzentrieren. Ignorieren Sie unbekannte Vokabeln wenn möglich, oft sind sie für das Verständnis des Hauptinhalts nicht wesentlich.

3. Schritt: Lesen Sie nochmals, worauf es in der Aufgabenstellung ankommt und in welcher Form die Lösung abgefasst sein soll. Wenn es einzelne Fragen gibt, markieren Sie die für die jeweiligen Fragen wichtigen Textpassagen in unterschiedlichen Farben.

4. Schritt: Fassen Sie die Hauptpunkte des Textes zusammen. Drücken Sie sich klar und verständlich aus; vereinfachen Sie die Sprache des Originals, indem Sie sich darauf konzentrieren, **was** gesagt wird, nicht **wie** es gesagt wird.

5. Schritt: Lesen Sie Ihren Text nochmals durch und vergewissern Sie sich, dass der Inhalt des Originals angemessen und verständlich ausgedrückt ist.

Übersetzung

Im Gegensatz zur Mediation ist bei der Übersetzung jedes Wort des Originaltextes wichtig. Oft muss im Deutschen jedoch eine andere Satzkonstruktion gewählt werden. Besonders knifflig sind z. B. die folgenden Konstruktionen; übersetzen Sie die Beispielsätze ins Deutsche:

> **Partizipialkonstruktionen**
> z. B. *The jobs done by women are often badly paid. / Some people say that feminism has been a great success pointing to the progress in the last 30 years.*

> **Konstruktionen mit Gerundium**
> z. B. *I avoided looking at her. / She achieved her aims by working very hard.*

> **Passivkonstruktionen**
> z. B. *He was offered a good job. / He is said to be rich.*

Außerdem muss häufig die Wortart geändert werden, z. B. *There is a need to ...* (Es ist notwendig, zu ...) oder *She used to work in France.* (Früher arbeitete sie in Frankreich.).

Eine weitere Schwierigkeit sind kleinere Partikel und Ausdrücke, die sich vom Deutschen oft unterscheiden, z. B. *after all, as, as to, as for, at all, at least, however, neither ... nor, not ... either, not ... until, unless.*

1. Schritt: Lesen Sie den gesamten Text einmal zügig durch.

2. Schritt: Lesen Sie den Text nun Wort für Wort und schlagen Sie schwierige Wörter nach. Vergewissern Sie sich, dass Sie den Satzbau jedes Satzes richtig erfasst haben (siehe die Liste schwieriger Konstruktionen oben).

3. Schritt: Fertigen Sie eine Rohfassung an, die Sie am besten doppelzeilig schreiben, um Korrekturen einfügen zu können.

4. Schritt: Bevor Sie die Reinschrift anfertigen, prüfen Sie Ihren Text auf:
Rechtschreib- und Grammatikfehler (z. B. Partizipien, Gerundien, Zeitenfolge)
Ausdruck (z. B. Sätze, an denen man noch das englische Original erkennt)
Verständlichkeit (z. B. zu lange oder verschachtelte Sätze)
Vollständigkeit (ausgelassene Wörter oder Satzteile).

Grammar summary

THE SIMPLE PRESENT

1 I **go** to meetings twice a week.
2 We **live** in Bavaria.
3 Mr Brown **teaches** us English every day.
4 I **don't like** conference calls.
5 **Does** he **like** travelling?

> Man gebraucht das **simple present** für regelmäßige, sich wiederholende Ereignisse oder Handlungen (1, 3) und für Dauerzustände (2, 4, 5).
> Mit Ausnahme der 3. Person Singular (*he, she, it*) hat das **simple present** dieselbe Form wie der Infinitiv (1, 2).
⚠ Die **3. Person Singular** endet auf *-(e)s* (3).
> Ist **kein Hilfsverb** im Satz vorhanden, werden **Verneinung** und **Fragen** mit der entsprechenden Form von *to do* gebildet (4, 5).

Das **simple present** wird häufig mit den folgenden **Zeitangaben** benutzt:

> *always, never, often, rarely, seldom, sometimes*
> *generally, mostly, normally, regularly, usually*
> *every day/week/month/..., every morning/afternoon/...*
> *on Mondays/Tuesdays/..., on weekdays*
> *in (the) summer/winter/...*
> *at Christmas/Easter, at weekends*

THE PRESENT PROGRESSIVE

1 I'**m calling** to say that Ben's ill.
2 He'**s working** from home today.
3 The computer **isn't working**.
4 **Are** you **eating** lunch?

> Man benutzt das **present progressive** (auch **present continuous** genannt) für Vorgänge oder Handlungen, die im Moment des Sprechens oder Schreibens passieren und noch nicht abgeschlossen sind (1, 3, 4).
> Es wird auch für vorübergehende Situationen gebraucht (2).
> Das **present progressive** wird mit dem Präsens von *to be* und der *-ing*-Form des Vollverbs gebildet.
> Da beim **present progressive** immer ein Hilfsverb vorhanden ist, wird die **Verneinung** mit *not/n't* gebildet (3).
> Fragen werden durch Umstellung gebildet (4).

Das **present progressive** wird oft mit den folgenden **Zeitangaben** benutzt:

at the moment, at present, now, this week/month, currently

⚠ Diese Verben bilden normalerweise **keine progressive-Form**:

be, believe, doubt, feel (meinen), *hate, hear, imagine, know, like/dislike, love, mean, notice, prefer, realize, recognize, remember, see* (begreifen), *seem, suppose, think* (meinen), *understand, want, wish*

THE SIMPLE PAST

1 We **wanted** to go to the USA last year.
2 She **went** on a business trip to London.
3 Jasmin **did not enjoy** her holiday in Rimini last summer.
4 Where **did** you **go** last year?

> Man benutzt das **simple past**, um über Vergangenes zu berichten.
> Das **simple past** wird auch gebraucht, wenn man sagen will, **wann** etwas geschehen ist (1, 3, 4).
> Bei **regelmäßigen** Verben wird das **simple past** durch das Anhängen von *-ed* an den Infinitiv gebildet (1).
⚠ Die unregelmäßigen Verben haben eine Sonderform (2), die man sich merken – auswendig lernen! – muss. > Irregular Verbs (S. 307)
> Ist **kein Hilfsverb** im Satz vorhanden, bildet man die **Verneinung** und **Fragen** mit *did/didn't* (3, 4).

Das **simple past** wird häufig mit den folgenden **Zeitangaben** benutzt:

> *yesterday, the day before yesterday, the week/month/... before last*
> *last night/week/month/summer/December/Easter/...*
> *two/three/... hours/days/years/... ago*
> *in 2005 / in the 20th century ...*
> *at that time, in those days*

THE PAST PROGRESSIVE

1 The boss **was talking** to Heather **during the presentation**.
2 The businessmen **were exchanging** business cards when a fire alarm (suddenly) **rang**.
3 I **wasn't doing** anything particular when he **arrived**.
4 **Were** you **having** breakfast when I **phoned**?

> Wenn man ausdrücken möchte, dass eine Handlung zu einem bestimmten Zeitpunkt oder während eines bestimmten Zeitraumes in der Vergangenheit **im Gange** war, benutzt man das **past progressive** (auch **past continuous** genannt) (1).
> Das **past progressive** wird auch benutzt, um zu verdeutlichen, dass eine Handlung im Gange war, als ein neues Ereignis (plötzlich) eintrat (2–4).
> Man bildet das **past progressive** mit *was/were* und der *-ing*-Form des Vollverbs (1).
> Die **Verneinung** wird mit *was not / wasn't* bzw. *were not / weren't* gebildet (3).
> **Fragen** bildet man durch Umstellung (4).
⚠ Einige Verben haben normalerweise **keine progressive-Form** (siehe die Liste unter **present progressive**).

THE PRESENT PERFECT

1 I'**ve bought** a new computer.
2 I **haven't seen** the new office yet.
3 How long **have** you **had** a laptop?
4 We'**ve had** snow **for** two weeks.
5 She'**s had** a cold **since** December.

> Wenn man ausdrücken will, dass etwas geschehen ist, ohne dass der genaue Zeitpunkt des Ereignisses wichtig ist, wird das **present perfect** benutzt (1, 2).
> Man gebraucht das **present perfect** auch, um zu sagen, seit wann oder wie lange ein Zustand oder eine Handlung schon andauert (3–5). Dafür wird sehr oft *for* bzw. *since* verwendet. (Im Deutschen steht dafür „seit" plus Gegenwart.)
> Das **present perfect** wird mit *have/has* und der 3. Form des Vollverbs gebildet (1, 4, 5).
⚠ Die unregelmäßigen Verben haben eine Sonderform (1, 2), die man auswendig lernen muss.

> Irregular verbs (S. 307)

> Die **Verneinung** wird durch das Einfügen von *not/n't* nach *have/has* gebildet (2).
> **Fragen** bildet man durch Umstellung (3).

Das **present perfect** wird oft mit den folgenden Zeitangaben benutzt:

> *already, still (not), (not) yet*
> *(not) ever, just, lately, never, recently*
> *so far this week/month/..., till/until now*

THE PRESENT PERFECT PROGRESSIVE

1 I'**ve been learning** English since I was ten.
2 They'**ve not been speaking** to each other lately.
3 **Has** he **been planning** the meeting for long?

> Das **present perfect progressive** (auch **present perfect continuous** genannt) benutzt man für Handlungen und Vorgänge, die in der Vergangenheit begonnen haben und zum Zeitpunkt des Sprechens bzw. Schreibens noch nicht beendet sind.
> Das **present perfect progressive** wird mit *have/has been* und der *-ing*-Form des Vollverbs gebildet (1).
> Die **Verneinung** bildet man durch das Einfügen von *not/n't* unmittelbar nach *have/has* (2).
> **Fragen** werden durch Umstellung gebildet (3).
⚠ Einige Verben haben normalerweise **keine progressive-Form** (siehe die Liste unter **present progressive**, S. 237).

THE PAST PERFECT

1 Laura couldn't pay. She **had forgotten** her purse.
2 Nina **had** already **left** the coffee bar by the time I arrived.
3 When I visited John in hospital, he **had been** there for ten days.

> Mit Hilfe des **past perfect** drückt man aus, dass zwei Handlungen oder Vorgänge in der Vergangenheit aufeinander folgten (1, 2). Die Handlung, die zeitlich voranging, steht im **past perfect**.
> Das **past perfect** wird auch verwendet, um auszudrücken, dass ein Zustand vor einem Zeitpunkt der Vergangenheit begann und zu diesem Zeitpunkt noch andauerte (3).

⚠ Wenn zwei oder mehrere kurze Handlungen in der Vergangenheit direkt aufeinander folgen, wird für alle Handlungen das **simple past** verwendet:
*The cat **ran** out when Joanne **opened** the door.*

THE PAST PERFECT PROGRESSIVE

1 Rod **had been preparing** for his interview for three weeks when he got another job offer.
2 When I found Mary, I could see that she **had been crying**.

> Das **past perfect progressive** (auch **past perfect continuous** genannt) wird verwendet, wenn man ausdrücken will, dass eine Handlung oder ein Vorgang vor einem Zeitpunkt in der Vergangenheit begonnen hatte und bis (oder fast bis) zu diesem Zeitpunkt andauerte.

THE FUTURE

A will

1 In the future people **will use** public transport more often.
2 We can only hope that everyone **will accept** this shift in attitudes.
3 You've forgotten your purse? Don't worry. I**'ll lend** you some money.
4 Ms Smith **will not be** at the meeting this afternoon.
5 I **won't come** either.
6 **Will** he **get** the job?

> Das **will future** benutzt man, um Vorhersagen zu machen (1) oder Vermutungen über die Zukunft zu äußern (2).
> Man benutzt es auch, wenn man sich spontan zu etwas entschließt, Angebote oder Versprechen macht (3).
> Das **will future** wird mit *will* + Infinitiv des Vollverbs gebildet. Es hat für alle Personen die gleiche Form (1–3).
> Die **Verneinung** bildet man durch das Einfügen von *not* unmittelbar nach *will* (4). Im gesprochenen Englisch sagt man häufig *won't* (5).
> **Fragen** werden durch Umstellung gebildet (6).

Das **will future** kommt häufig mit den folgenden einleitenden Verben und Ausdrücken vor:

> *believe, expect, forecast, hope, imagine, suppose, think*
> *It's clear/obvious that ..., There's no doubt that ...*

B going to

1 Look at these clouds. It**'s going to rain** soon.
2 This time I**'m going to get** good marks in the class test.
3 Tom **isn't going to work** at the club any more.
4 When **are** you **going to take** your driving test?

> Das **going to future** benutzt man für Ereignisse und Situationen, die nach Meinung des Sprechers bald eintreten werden (weil es bereits Anzeichen dafür gibt) (1).
> Es wird auch für Pläne und Absichten gebraucht (2).
> Das **going to future** wird mit *am/is/are* + *going to* + Infinitiv gebildet (1, 2).
> Die **Verneinung** bildet man durch das Einfügen von *not/n't* unmittelbar nach *am/is/are* (3).
> **Fragen** werden durch Umstellung gebildet (4).

⚠ Der **Gebrauch des Futurs** hängt in gewissem Maße von der Absicht oder Sichtweise des Sprechers ab. Dies gilt insbesondere für das **going to future** und für zukünftige Ereignisse. Daher ist es im Zweifelsfall ratsam, das neutralere **will future** zu benutzen.

C The present progressive / The simple present

1 We'**re leaving** the house at 10.30.
2 The bus **goes** at 11 o'clock.

> Man kann das **present progressive** auch **mit einer Zeitbestimmung der Zukunft** (*at 10.30, this afternoon, on Sunday*) für bereits feststehende Pläne und Verabredungen verwenden (1).
> Genau wie im Deutschen wird auch im Englischen das **simple present mit einer Zeitangabe** benutzt, um fest terminierte Vorgänge (Fahrpläne, Stundenpläne, Programme usw.) anzugeben (2).

MODAL AUXILIARY VERBS

1 He **can speak** several languages.
2 You **must accept** your new situation.
3 We **needn't go** to work today.
4 **May** I **interrupt** you?

> Um zu sagen, was geschehen kann, muss, darf, soll usw., benutzt man ein modales Hilfsverb in Verbindung mit einem Vollverb (1-4).

⚠ Im Englischen steht ein Hilfsverb - anders als im Deutschen - nie ohne Vollverb:
- Lena kann Spanisch. ⟶ *Lena can speak Spanish.* NICHT: ~~Lena can Spanish.~~

> Modale Hilfsverben - nicht jedoch die Ersatzverben (siehe unten) - haben bei allen Personen immer die gleiche Form, einschließlich der 3. Person Singular (keine *-s*-Endung) (1, 2).
> Die **Verneinung** wird durch das Einfügen von *not/n't* unmittelbar nach dem Hilfsverb gebildet (3).
> **Fragen** bildet man durch Umstellung (4).
> Abgesehen von *could* (wenn damit eine Fähigkeit ausgedrückt werden soll) kann man modale Hilfsverben nur im Präsens und - mit einer geeigneten Zeitangabe - mit zukünftiger Bedeutung benutzen, zum Beispiel:
- *You **can go** home now.* (Präsens)
  *You **can go** home an hour early tomorrow.* (Futur)
- *I **must write** these letters now.* (Präsens)
  *I **must write** a long report next week.* (Futur)

⚠ Um andere Zeitformen bei modalen Hilfsverben zu bilden, z. B. die Vergangenheit, muss ein geeignetes Ersatzverb gebraucht werden:

must *The provider **had to block** access to the internet last December.*
can *I **couldn't start** the car yesterday.* (Fähigkeit)
*We **weren't allowed to go** home early last Friday.* (Erlaubnis)

Übersicht der modalen Hilfsverben nach Funktion

Funktion	Modale(s) Hilfsverb(en)	
Fähigkeit	*He* ***can*** *speak several languages.* *The first satellites* ***could*** *only transmit sound.*	
Möglichkeit	*With your qualifications you* ***could*** *work abroad.* *The boss* ***may*** *come in at any moment.* *He* ***might*** *ask you what you are doing.*	
Bitte	***Can*** *I have a word with Ms Sims, please?* ***Could*** *I speak to Ms Sims, please?* ***May*** *I interrupt you?* ***Might*** *I ask you a personal question?*	(neutral) (höflich) (betont höflich) (äußerst höflich)
Erlaubnis	*You* ***can*** *go in now.* *The boss is free. You* ***may*** *go in now.*	(neutral) (gefällig)
Verbot	*We* ***mustn't*** *be late for work tomorrow.*	
Pflicht	*You* ***must*** *wear a hard hat in the factory.*	
Wahl	*Most shop workers* ***needn't*** *work on Sundays.*	
Empfehlung	*You* ***should*** *get better qualifications.* *You* ***ought to*** *get better qualifications.* *You* ***must*** *get better qualifications.*	(neutral) (betont) (streng)

REPORTED SPEECH

A Aussagesätze

1 Some people **claim** that 'servant' robots **are putting** people out of work.
2 The speaker **reminded** his audience that there **were** some jobs robots **couldn't do**.

> Wenn man einem Dritten berichten möchte, was während eines Gespräches gesagt wurde, benutzt man die **indirekte Rede**.

> Bei Verwendung der indirekten Rede benutzt man ein einleitendes Verb wie *claim, say, remind, answer, think, mention* usw., um zu verdeutlichen, dass eine Äußerung wiedergegeben wird.
Steht das einleitende Verb in der Vergangenheit - also *said, answered, mentioned* usw. -, dann verschieben sich die Zeiten wie folgt:

direkte Rede		indirekte Rede
simple present *she works hard*	→	**simple past** *she worked hard*
present progressive *she is working hard*	→	**past progressive** *she was working hard*
simple past *she worked hard*	→	**past perfect** *she had worked hard*
past progressive *she was working hard*	→	**past perfect progressive** *she had been working hard*
present perfect *she has worked hard*	→	**past perfect** *she had worked hard*

present perfect progressive *she has been working hard*	→	**past perfect progressive** *she had been working hard*
past perfect *she had worked hard*		(keine Verschiebung) –
past perfect progressive *she had been working hard*		(keine Verschiebung) –
will *she will work hard*	→	**would** *she would work hard*
am/is/are going to *she is going to work hard*	→	**was/were going to** *she was going to work hard*
would/might etc. *she would work hard*		(keine Verschiebung) –
would have/might have etc. *she had been working hard*		(keine Verschiebung) –

⚠ Die modalen Hilfsverben werden folgendermaßen verschoben:

Modalverb	Bedeutung	indirekte Rede
can	Fähigkeit	*could, was/were able to*
can	Erlaubnis	*was/were allowed to*
may	Möglichkeit	*might*
may	Erlaubnis	*was/were allowed to*
must	Pflicht	*had to*
mustn't	Verbot	*was/were not allowed to*
needn't	freie Wahl	*did not/didn't have to*

> Außer wenn man über ein Gespräch berichtet, das am selben Tag stattgefunden hat, müssen fast alle **Zeit**- und einige **Ortsangaben** entsprechend der folgenden Tabelle geändert werden. (Angaben, die nicht aufgeführt sind, bleiben unverändert.)

direkte Rede		indirekte Rede
today	→	*on that day*
tomorrow	→	*the next day*
yesterday	→	*the day before*
the day after tomorrow	→	*two days later*
the day before yesterday	→	*two days before*
next day/Friday/week/Christmas/...	→	*the following day/Friday/week/Christmas/...*
last Friday/week/summer/...	→	*the Friday/week/summer/... before*
two years/months/weeks/... ago	→	*two years/months/weeks/... before*
now, at present	→	*then*
at the moment	→	*at that moment*
at this time	→	*at that time*
here	→	*there*
in this place	→	*at that place*
this	→	*that*
these	→	*those*

B Fragesätze

1 A member of the audience **asked what had led** to the widespread use of robots in factories.
2 She **wanted to know if/whether** her job **was endangered**.

> Bei indirekten **Fragen** unterscheidet man zwischen Fragen mit Fragewort (1) und Fragen ohne Fragewort (2).
> Bei Fragen **mit Fragewort** wird das Fragewort übernommen (1).
> Bei Fragen **ohne Fragewort** benutzt man *if* bzw. *whether* (= ob), um zu verdeutlichen, dass es sich um eine Frage handelt (2).
> Alle anderen Änderungen erfolgen wie bei den Aussagesätzen (siehe **Aussagesätze** S. 242).

C Bitten, Aufforderungen und Befehle

1 Lucy **asked the engineer to show her** the robot.
2 He **told her not to go** too close to it.

> **Bitten** werden meist durch *asked* (= bitten) (1), **Aufforderungen** und **Befehle** durch *told* (= sagen) (2) eingeleitet.
> Bei **positiven Sätzen** erscheint das Verb als *to* + Infinitiv (1).
> Bei **negativen Sätzen** wird *not* unmittelbar vor *to* gesetzt (2).

⚠ Die beiden Verben *to tell* und *to ask* stehen immer mit einem Objekt, das die angesprochene Person erwähnt (1, 2). Ist dies vom Kontext her nicht erkennbar, wird einfach ein passender Begriff eingesetzt:

> *Ben said, 'Don't enter the studio when the red light is on.'*
> *Ben* ***told everybody*** *not to enter the studio when the red light was on.*

THE PASSIVE

1 Measures **are being introduced** to reduce traffic pollution.
2 Pollution **is caused by** some thoughtless people.

> Ist der Verursacher einer Handlung unbekannt oder zweitrangig, benutzt man das Passiv. Im Vordergrund steht also das Ergebnis des Vorgangs (1).
> Möchte man den Verursacher doch angeben, benutzt man einen *by agent* (2).
⚠ Der Verursacher wird mit *by* – auf keinen Fall mit *from* – eingeleitet.
> Das Passiv wird mit einer Zeitform von *to be* und der 3. Form des Vollverbs gebildet:

Zeit	Zeitform von *to be*	3. Form
simple present	*am / is / are*	*caused*
present progressive	*am / is / are being*	*introduced*
simple past	*was / were*	*buried*
past progressive	*was / were being*	*built*
present perfect	*has / have been*	*installed*
will-Futur	*will be*	*blocked*
going to-Futur	*am / is / are going to be*	*sacked*

> Beim Gebrauch von modalen Hilfsverben wird nach folgendem Muster verfahren:

bei Aussagen	Hilfsverb + *to be* + 3. Form	*must be displayed*
bei Fragen	Hilfsverb + Subjekt + *to be* + 3. Form	*Can ... be persuaded?*

⚠ Das Verb *to be* bleibt im Infinitiv immer unverändert.

THE IMPERSONAL PASSIVE

1 **It is said that** petrol will soon cost more.
2 He **is thought** to have completed the training course.

> Das **impersonal passive** wird vor allem dann benutzt, wenn man sich objektiv bzw. unbeteiligt ausdrücken möchte. Daher kommt diese Struktur oft in Polizeiberichten, seriösen Zeitungsartikeln usw. vor.

> Bei Verben des Berichtens, Denkens usw. benutzt man häufig das Satzmuster:
It is/was/... + 3. Form des einleitenden Verbs + *that*-Satz (1).
Hier sind weitere Beispiele dieses Musters:

Aktiv	*Some **say** that companies which cause pollution should be heavily fined.*
Passiv	***It is said that** companies which cause pollution should be heavily fined.*
Aktiv	*Experts **recommended** that more be spent on public transport.*
Passiv	***It was recommended** that more be spent on public transport.*

> Um das Subjekt des *that*-Satzes zu betonen, kann man folgendes Muster benutzen:
Subjekt + *is/was/...* + 3. Form + *to be* + andere Satzteile (2):

Aktiv	*Many **believe** that the minister is thinking of raising fuel taxes.*
Passiv	*The minister **is believed to be** thinking of raising fuel taxes.*

⚠ Der *by agent* wird in solchen Passivsätzen folgendermaßen verwendet:

Aktiv	*The speaker felt that the idea was too radical.*
Passiv	*The idea was felt to be too radical **by** the speaker.*

IF-SENTENCES

1 If we **invest** in new technology, a lot of people **will lose** their jobs.
2 A lot of people **will lose** their jobs if we **invest** in new technology.
3 If more people **took part** in re-training schemes, they **wouldn't have to worry** about finding new employment.
4 We **won't have** political censorship if we **don't start** to censor the internet.
5 **Will** we soon **have** political censorship if we **start** to censor the internet?

> Ein **Konditionalsatz** besteht aus zwei Teilen: dem ***if*-Teil** und dem **Hauptteil**.
Der ***if*-Teil** drückt eine **Bedingung** aus, der Hauptteil eine **Folge**.
> Bei **Konditionalsätzen** kommen folgende **Zeitmuster** am häufigsten vor:

Typ I	*If + simple present*	+	*will*-Futur
Typ II	*If + simple past*	+	*would* + Infinitiv
Typ III	*If + past perfect*	+	*would have* + 3. Form des Verbs

> Der *if*-Teil kann hinter dem Hauptteil stehen. In diesem Fall steht kein Komma dazwischen (2, 4, 5).
> Je nach Sinn kann der *if*-Teil, der Hauptteil oder beide Teile des Satzes **verneint** werden (3, 4).
> Bei **Fragen** kann nur der **Hauptteil** zu einer Frage geformt werden. Dann steht dieser Teil **an erster Stelle** (5).

> *if*-Sätze werden gemäß der **Wahrscheinlichkeit** der zu erwartenden Folge eingesetzt:
Typ I: Folge (fast) sicher.
*If we **invest in** new technology, a lot of people **will lose** their jobs.*
D.h. viele Leute werden (vermutlich) ihre Stellen verlieren, da wir (sehr wahrscheinlich) in die neue Technologie investieren werden.
Typ II: Folge theoretisch möglich, aber kaum wahrscheinlich.
*If we **invested in** new technology, a lot of people **would lose** their jobs.*
D.h. es ist kaum zu erwarten, dass viele Leute ihre Stellen verlieren werden, da wir (wahrscheinlich) nicht in die neue Technologie investieren werden.
Typ III: Folge unmöglich, da die Bedingung nicht erfüllt wurde und bereits in der Vergangenheit liegt.
*If we **had invested in** new technology, a lot of people **would have lost** their jobs.*
D.h. der Sprecher weiß schon, dass keiner den Job verloren hat, da wir in die neue Technologie nicht investiert haben.

GERUND/INFINITIVE

1 Max **enjoys visiting** his customers.
2 Can you **afford to buy** that new computer software?
3 Cem and Julie **continued to meet** even though they were no longer business partners.
4 Cem and Julie **continued meeting** even though they were no longer business partners.
5 Alison **normally likes meeting** clients, but **today** she would **prefer to stay** in the office.

> Nach einigen Verben folgt immer die *-ing*-Form **(gerund)** (1).
Am wichtigsten sind:

admit, avoid, consider, deny, enjoy, finish, give up, imagine, mention, (not) mind (etwas/nichts dagegen haben), *miss, practise, recommend, risk, stop, suggest*

> **Nach einigen Verben** folgt immer der Infinitiv **(infinitive)** (2).
Die **wichtigsten** Verben dieser Gruppe sind:

afford, choose, decide, expect, hope, manage, mean, plan, promise, refuse, want

⚠ Nach den Verben *begin, continue, intend* und *start* kann der **Infinitiv** oder die ***-ing*-Form beliebig benutzt werden** (3, 4).

> Einige Verben werden **je nach Bedeutung** entweder mit dem **Infinitiv** oder mit der ***-ing*-Form** benutzt. Die **wichtigsten** Verben dieser Gruppe sind:

like, dislike, love, hate, prefer

> Wenn von einer **allgemeingültigen Situation** die Rede ist, folgt auf diese Verben die ***-ing*-Form**. Handelt es sich aber um eine **Ausnahmesituation**, dann verwendet man den **Infinitiv** (5).

advise, allow, encourage, forbid, permit, recommend
Handelt es sich um einen **konkreten Einzelfall**, wird mit diesen Verben ein **Objekt + Infinitiv** verwendet.
*I strongly **advise you to** be more polite to people.*
Wenn es sich aber um eine **allgemeine Situation** handelt, dann steht das nachfolgende Verb in der ***-ing*-Form**.
*Most firms don't **allow smoking** in their offices.*

forget/remember

Die Struktur ***forget/remember* + *-ing*-Form** bezieht sich auf die Vergangenheit. Sie drückt etwa die Idee „Ich werde nie vergessen ..." aus.

⚠ „Vergangenheit" bezieht sich hier nicht auf *forget/remember*, sondern auf das nachfolgende Verb.

*I still **remember getting** my first job.*

*I'll never **forget going** to the Japanese headquarters last year.*

Die Struktur ***forget/remember* + Infinitiv** dagegen bezieht sich auf die Zukunft. Sie drückt etwa die Idee aus „Ich darf nicht vergessen, etwas zu tun" bzw. „Ich habe noch etwas zu tun, weil ich es bis jetzt vergessen habe".

*Dad, please **remember / don't forget to pick me up** from the station.*

*Oh dear. I **forgot / didn't remember to pick Sally up** from the station.*

regret

Die Struktur ***regret* + *-ing*-Form** drückt Bedauern über eine vergangene Situation bzw. einen vergangenen Vorfall aus. Häufig geht es dabei um verpasste Chancen.

*I really **regret leaving** school without any qualifications.*

*I know they will **regret buying** such a big, expensive car.*

Die Struktur ***regret* + Infinitiv** – fast immer mit einem Verb des Mitteilens wie *inform, say, tell* kombiniert – drückt eine schlechte Nachricht aus.

*I **regret to say** that I can't attend the meeting tomorrow.*

*We **regret to inform** you that the vacancy has now been filled.*

stop

Bedeutet ***stop*** „aufhören, etwas zu tun", steht das nachfolgende Verb in der ***-ing*-Form**.

Bedeutet ***stop*** aber „kurz anhalten, um etwas anderes zu tun", folgt ein Verb im **Infinitiv**.

*For heaven's sake **stop shouting** at me.*

*I'm a little late because I **stopped to give** somebody a lift.*

try

Bedeutet ***try*** „etwas ausprobieren", steht das nachfolgende Verb in der ***-ing*-Form**.

Bedeutet ***try*** aber „sich anstrengen, etwas zu tun", folgt ein Verb im **Infinitiv**.

*I **tried phoning** Ellie, but she wasn't at home.*

*We'll **try to repair** your computer by the weekend.*

ADJECTIVES AND ADVERBS

1 John has a **new** printer.
2 He always buys **expensive** equipment.
3 My computer has become **very slow**.
4 That CD sounds **terrible**.
5 We can make printouts **quickly** and **cheaply**.

> Um **Personen** oder **Sachen** näher zu beschreiben, benutzt man **Adjektive** (1–4).
> Adjektive stehen **unmittelbar** vor Substantiven oder **unmittelbar nach** einer Form von *be* (bzw. *become* oder *seem*, die *be* ersetzen können) (3).
> **Adjektive** können mit Verben wie *feel, look* (aussehen), *sound, smell* und *taste* eine **sinnliche Wahrnehmung** ausdrücken (4).
> Um einen **Tätigkeitsverb** näher zu beschreiben, setzt man ein Adverb **unmittelbar hinter das Verb** bzw. Verb + Objekt (5).

⚠ Im Englischen können ein Verb und sein Objekt - anders als im Deutschen - nicht durch ein Adverb getrennt werden. Also NICHT: ~~We can make quickly printouts~~. (siehe **Word order** unten)

> Adverbien werden auch benutzt, um **Adjektive, andere Adverbien** und **ganze Sätze** näher zu bestimmen:
*MP3 players have become **surprisingly cheap**.* (Adverb + Adjektiv)
*My fax machine prints out **terribly slowly**.* (Adverb + Adverb)
***Luckily** Gerd left a message on my mailbox.* (Satzadverb)

> Die meisten Adverbien werden durch Anhängen von *-ly* an das Adjektiv gebildet (5). Eine kleine Anzahl von Adverbien hat dieselbe Form wie Adjektive; die häufigsten sind *fast, hard, early late, long, daily*.

COMPARISON OF ADJECTIVES AND ADVERBS

1 A hundred years ago life was **slower** and people may have been **happier**.
2 Which technological innovation is the **most/least important**?
3 Today you can copy data **more easily than** ever before.

> **Einsilbige** und **zweisilbige Adjektive**, die auf *-y* enden - zum Beispiel *easy, happy* und *lucky* -, werden mit *-(i)er/-(i)est* gesteigert (1).

> **Mehrsilbige Adjektive** und **Adverbien**, die auf *-ly* enden, werden mit *more/most* gesteigert (2, 3).
⚠ Die Adverbien, die dieselbe Form wie das entsprechende Adjektiv haben (*fast, hard, early* usw.), werden mit *-er/-est* gesteigert.

> Um Personen oder Sachen im Satz miteinander zu vergleichen, gibt es folgende Möglichkeiten:

Kein Unterschied	*as good as*	genau so gut wie
Unterschied	*not as good as*	nicht so gut wie
Unterschied	*better than*	besser als

WORD ORDER

positions of adverbs of time, place and frequency

1 She stays in hotels **every week**.
2 The company is based in a small town **outside of Frankfurt**.
3 **Last year** we went to an Italian restaurant for our department Christmas party.
4 Paul and Emily went to **the USA last year**.
5 She **always finishes** work early on Fridays.
6 He **is never** in the office when I call.
7 I like to work at home **now and then**.
8 Gina acted **strangely at the trade show last week**.

> Zeitangaben (Wann?) und Ortsangaben (Wo?, Wohin?) stehen in der Regel am Satzende (1, 2).

> Um die Zeit eines bestimmten Ereignisses hervorzuheben, kann man die Zeitangabe an die erste Stelle setzen (3).

> Stehen eine Zeitangabe und eine Ortsangabe zusammen am Satzende, dann gilt die Reihenfolge Ort vor Zeit (alphabetisch merken: O vor Z!) (4).

> Besteht eine Häufigkeitsangabe aus einem Wort, z.B. *always, often, sometimes*, steht sie unmittelbar vor dem Vollverb (5).

> Lautet das Vollverb *to be*, steht das Adverb direkt dahinter (6).

- Besteht die Häufigkeitsangabe aus mehreren Wörtern, z.B. *every day, now and then*, steht sie wie eine Zeitangabe am Satzende (7).
- Adverbien der Art und Weise stehen in der Regel am Satzende. Kommen noch Zeit- oder Ortsadverbien hinzu, lautet die Reihenfolge: Art und Weise - Ort - Zeit (AOZ) (8).

RELATIVE CLAUSES AND CONTACT CLAUSES

1 Car manufacturers are designing cars **which/that** can use hydrogen fuel cells.
2 Wildernesses are being spoiled by tourists **who/that** want to go to 'unspoiled' places.
3 Tony filled in a job satisfaction questionnaire **(which/that)** he found on the internet.
4 Fred Foley is a business tycoon **whose** fortune amounts to over €400 million.
5 Call centre employees, most **of whom** come from India, work long hours.
6 Some non-GM crops are attacked by pests **against which** they have no resistance.

- Relativsätze werden benutzt, um den Hauptsatz durch zusätzliche Informationen genauer zu bestimmen.
- Für **Sachen** benutzt man das Relativpronomen *which* bzw. *that* (1) und für Personen *who* bzw. *that* (2).
- Steht das Relativpronomen für das **Objekt des Hauptsatzes**, dann kann man es weglassen (3). Solche Relativsätze heißen **contact clauses**.
- Um **Besitz** bzw. **Zugehörigkeit** anzuzeigen, gebraucht man *whose* unmittelbar vor dem **Substantiv** bei Personen und Sachen (4).
- Steht eine **Präposition** vor dem **Relativpronomen**, wird *whom* für Personen und *which* für Sachen benutzt (5, 6). In solchen Fällen ist der Gebrauch von *that* nicht möglich.

DEFINING AND NON-DEFINING RELATIVE CLAUSES

1 The first Europeans **who** settled in Australia came from Britain.
2 Sydney, **which** is famous for its unusually designed opera house, is situated on the south-eastern coast of Australia.

- Im **ersten Beispielsatz** ist der Sinn des Hauptsatzes *The first Europeans came from Britain* ohne den Relativsatz *who settled in Australia* offensichtlich falsch bzw. unvollständig. Relativsätze dieser Art - die wesentlich für das Verständnis des gesamten Satzes sind - nennt man **defining relative clauses** (notwendige oder bestimmende Relativsätze).
- Im **zweiten Beispielsatz** ist die Aussage des Hauptsatzes *Sydney is situated on the south-eastern coast of Australia* ohne den Relativsatz völlig verständlich, weil der Relativsatz *which is famous for its unusually designed opera house* eine zusätzliche, also nebensächliche, Information enthält. Daher werden solche Relativsätze ***non-defining relative clauses*** (nicht notwendige oder nicht bestimmende Relativsätze) genannt.
  ⚠ Notwendige Relativsätze werden immer **ohne** trennende **Kommas** benutzt. Dies signalisiert, dass sie fester Bestandteil der Hauptaussage sind.

PARTICIPLE CONSTRUCTIONS

1 Malaria, preventable with a treated bed net **costing** less than one pound, is endemic.
2 Many men believe that any work **involved** with cooking is a woman's chore.
3 **Losing** more and more people to AIDS, Africa now needs effective help more urgently than ever before.

4 **Burdened** with declining life expectancy, large parts of Africa are caught in a poverty trap.
5 **Having fetched** water from a river for many years, some women in developing countries are now happy to be able to use the Hippo Roller.
6 **Despite facing** extreme destitution, many rural residents haven't given up hope.
7 Donors should invest in projects that help local inhabitants become self-supporting, **thereby making** sure that the money isn't wasted.
8 Poor infrastructure is a key barrier to economic growth in Nepal, **thus causing** huge additional costs to the transport of commercial goods.
9 Life is becoming hard in the developing countries, **with** many small farmers **going** out of business.
10 AIDS represents a major challenge to sub-Saharan Africa, currently **killing** more than two million people every year.

Die englische Sprache ist geprägt durch die häufige Verwendung von Partizipialkonstruktionen. Diese ermöglichen einen eleganteren Sprachfluss.

> Partizipialkonstruktionen verkürzen Relativsätze; dabei kann entweder das **present participle** (1) oder das **past participle** (2) verwendet werden.

> Sie werden auch verwendet, um adverbiale Nebensätze zu vekürzen. In diesen Fällen unterscheidet man zwischen Partizipialkonstruktionen ohne Konjunktion (3–5) und solchen mit Konjunktion (6–9). In Sätzen ohne Konjunktion ist der Inhalt des Satzes auch ohne eine solche klar. Dagegen sind Konjunktionen nötig, um zu verhindern, dass der logische Zusammenhang des Satzes verloren geht. Zum Beispiel wird der Inhalt von Satz 6 unklar, wenn die Konjunktion *despite* ausgelassen wird.

> Wie bei der Verkürzung von Relativsätzen kommen auch bei der Verkürzung von adverbialen Nebensätzen das **present participle** (3, 6–9) und das **past participle** (4) zur Anwendung. Darüber hinaus wird hier auch noch das **perfect participle** verwendet (5), und zwar um die Vorzeitigkeit der Handlung im Nebensatz auszudrücken. *(Nachdem sie jahrelang Wasser aus dem Fluss geholt hatten, ...)*

> Schließlich verknüpft man mit einer Partizipialkonstruktion zwei Hauptsätze zu einem einzigen Satz, und zwar ausnahmslos mittels **present participle** (10).

COUNTABLE AND UNCOUNTABLE NOUNS

1	Visit our website for more **information** on our firm.	NICHT ~~informations~~
2	Have you read the paper today? The political **news** is interesting.	NICHT ~~news are~~
3	Where can I get some **advice**?	NICHT ~~an advice~~

> Einige wichtige **Substantive** sind **zählbar im Deutschen, nicht jedoch im Englischen**. Diese Substantive können also nicht ohne weiteres mit dem unbestimmten Artikel *a*/*an* oder mit einem Zahlwort benutzt werden.
Hier ist eine Liste solcher Wörter, die Sie auswendig lernen sollten:

advice, baggage, damage, data, equipment, evidence, furniture, information, knowledge, luck, luggage, machinery, news, progress, research, rubbish, work (housework, homework)

> Um diese Substantive im Plural zu verwenden, muss *some, a bit of* bzw. *a piece of* hinzugefügt werden (3).

SOME AND *ANY*

1 **Some** departments prefer to hold regular weekly meetings.
2 They haven't got **any** women working in their company.
3 Have you got **any** information about arrival times?
4 Can I have **some** more coffee, please?
5 Would you like **some** mineral water?
6 There's **something** I need to do but I can't remember what it is.
7 He can't find that letter **anywhere**. Maybe **somebody** took it.

> Wir verwenden *some* in **bejahten Aussagen** (1) und *any* in **verneinten Aussagen** (2) und **„echten" Fragen** (3).
> Drückt die Frage eine höfliche **Bitte** (4) bzw. ein **Angebot** (5) aus, worauf eine positive Antwort erwartet wird, verwenden wir ebenfalls *some*.
> Wir verwenden die Zusammensetzungen von *some* and *any* - also *somebody/someone, something, somewhere, anybody/anyone, anything* und *anywhere* - in genau derselben Art und Weise (6-7).

THE DEFINITE ARTICLE

1 **Sociologists** say that **violence** is increasing among young people.
2 Is **the current trend** partly caused by **the violent films** they watch?
3 **Most sentences** are not tough enough.
4 Nearly **half the prisoners** in **British prisons** are under 25.
5 **Spring** is my favourite season but **the spring** we're having this year is more like **winter**.
6 We had **breakfast** late this morning so we came to work **by car** instead of **by bus**.
7 They are thinking of legalizing soft drugs in **the Netherlands**.

> Hat ein Substantiv eine allgemeine, uneingeschränkte Bedeutung - also „alle ohne Ausnahme" - dann steht es ohne Artikel (1, 5).
> Ist die Bedeutung eines Substantives auf bestimmte Fälle eingeschränkt, benutzt man den Artikel (2, 5).
> Ferner wird der Artikel in den folgenden Fällen und Wendungen im Englischen - z. T. anders als im Deutschen - nicht gebraucht:
- bei *most* in der Bedeutung „die meisten" (3),
- bei öffentlichen Gebäuden im allgemeinen Sinn (4),
- bei Mahlzeiten (6),
- bei Verkehrsmitteln (6),
- bei Straßennamen,
- bei Tageszeiten, Wochentagen, Monaten und Jahreszeiten im allgemeinen Sinn (5).

> Der Artikel wird verwendet nach *all* und *half* (4) und mit den Pluralnamen von Staaten (7).
⚠ Der bestimmte Artikel steht im Englischen (viel) seltener als im Deutschen. Daher: *When in doubt, leave it out!*

THE INDEFINITE ARTICLE

1 Yesterday I met **a woman** who works for **a friend** of my father's.
2 We'll have to buy **a** new **computer**.
3 That's **an** interesting **idea**.
4 Jane's **an accountant**? I thought she was **a sales rep**.
5 My father has been **a non-smoker** all his life.
6 How much does petrol cost **a liter**?
7 We have planning meetings four times **a month**.

> Der unbestimmten Artikel a/an steht bei einer einzelnen, nicht näher bestimmten Person (1), einer Sache (2), oder einem Begriff (3).
> Anders als im Deutschen verwenden wir im Englischen den unbestimmten Artikel in folgenden Fällen:
- bei Berufsangaben (4),
- bei Angaben über Nationalität, Religion, Politik oder Gruppenzugehörigkeit (5)
- bei Maß- (6), Verpackungs-, und Zeitangaben (7)
- bei den folgenden Wendungen:

to be in a hurry	in Eile sein, es eilig haben
to come to an end	enden
to have a bath/shower/...	sich baden/duschen/...
to have a go	es ausprobieren
to have a turn at (+ -ing-Form)	an der Reihe sein, etwas zu tun
to make a noise	Lärm machen
to take a seat	Platz nehmen
for a change	zur Abwechslung
for a long/short time	lange/kurze Zeit
in a loud/quiet voice	mit lauter/ruhiger Stimme
What a pity!	Wie schade!
without a break	ohne Pause

⚠ Bei *half, quite, rather* und *such* wird der unbestimmte Artikel nachgestellt:
> The meeting starts in half **an** hour.
> We had quite **a** successful year in 2005.
> Jack can be rather **an** idiot sometimes.
> We've never had such **a** big order.

Basic word list

Diese Liste enthält ca. 900 Grundwörter, die in **Focus on Business 4th Edition** als bekannt vorausgesetzt werden. Nicht aufgeführt, jedoch vorausgesetzt sind einige sehr elementare Wörter wie einfache Präpositionen, Pronomen, Farben, Zahlen, Tage, Jahreszeiten, Staaten usw. sowie internationale Wörter wie z. B. *hotel*, *restaurant*, *e-mail*.

able: to **be ~ to** können
about um, über, ungefähr
above über, oben, oberhalb
abroad im/ins Ausland
absolute(ly) absolut, völlig
to **accept** akzeptieren, annehmen
accident Unfall
across (hin)über; quer durch
active aktiv
activity Tätigkeit, Beschäftigung
actual(ly) eigentlich, tatsächlich
to **add** hinzufügen
to **address** adressieren, anreden; Adresse, Anrede
advice Rat(schlag)
afraid: I'm ~ leider
after nach
afternoon Nachmittag
afterwards nachher, danach
again wieder
against gegen
age Alter, Zeitalter
ago vor
to **agree** zustimmen, sich einigen, vereinbaren
ahead voraus, vorn
air Luft
airline Fluggesellschaft
airport Flughafen
all alle
to **allow** erlauben, gestatten
to **allow:** to **be ~ed to** etw dürfen
almost fast, beinah
alone allein(e)
along entlang, weiter, vorwärts
already schon, bereits
also auch, außerdem
although obwohl
always immer
amazing erstaunlich, fantastisch
ambulance Krankenwagen
among unter, zwischen
amusing lustig
angry böse, zornig, ärgerlich
animal Tier
another noch eine/r/s, ein/e andere/r/s
to **answer; answer** (be)antworten; Antwort, Lösung
any irgendetwas, irgendwelche
anybody (irgend)jemand, jeder
anymore: not ~ nicht mehr
anyone jede/r
anything (irgend)etwas
anyway trotzdem, sowieso
anywhere irgendwo
apartment Wohnung
apple Apfel
to **argue** sich streiten; argumentieren
around ungefähr, zirka; um (... herum)
to **arrive** ankommen, eintreffen
as well (as) ebenso (wie)
to **ask** fragen, bitten
at least zumindest, wenigstens
to **attack; attack** angreifen; Angriff
to **attend** teilnehmen, besuchen, absolvieren
aunt Tante
away weg, entfernt
back Rücken; zurück
bad(ly) schlecht
bag Tasche, Tüte
to **bake** backen
basic Grund-, Haupt-, grundsätzlich
basically im Prinzip, im Grunde
bathroom Badezimmer
beach Strand
beautiful(ly) schön, herrlich
because weil, da
to **become** werden
bed Bett
beer Bier
before vor, vorher, zuvor, bevor
to **begin** anfangen, beginnen
behind hinter, hinten
to **believe** glauben, meinen
below unter(halb), unten
between zwischen
beyond darüber hinaus
bicycle Fahrrad
big groß
bike (Fahr-, Motor-)Rad
birthday Geburtstag
bit: a ~ ein wenig, etwas
body Körper
to **book; book** buchen; Buch
bored: to **be/get bored** sich langweilen
boring langweilig
born geboren
boss Chef/in
both beide
bottle Flasche
box Kiste, Kasten, Karton
boy Junge
boyfriend Freund
bread Brot
breakfast Frühstück
bright hell, strahlend, glänzend
brilliant glänzend, genial, super
to **bring** bringen, mitbringen
brother Bruder
to **build** (auf)bauen
building Gebäude
to **burn** (ver)brennen
business Geschäft(e), Unternehmen, Wirtschafts-
busy beschäftigt, verkehrsreich, besetzt
but aber, sondern
to **buy** kaufen
calendar Kalender
to **call; call** (an)rufen; Anruf
to **call:** to **be ~ed** heißen
caller Anrufer/in
can können; Dose
car Auto
card Karte
careful(ly) vorsichtig, sorgfältig
to **carry** tragen, befördern
to **catch** fangen; packen; erreichen
to **cause; cause** hervorrufen, verursachen; Ursache, Grund
central zental
centre Mitte, Mittelpunkt, Zentrum
certain(ly) sicher(lich), gewiss, bestimmt
chance Gelegenheit, Chance
to **change; change** wechseln, (sich ver)ändern, umsteigen; Veränderung
to **chat; chat** (mit jdm) plaudern, sich unterhalten; Schwätzchen
cheap billig, preiswert
cheese Käse
to **check** (über)prüfen, kontrollieren
child, children Kind, Kinder
choice Wahl, Auswahl
to **choose** wählen, aussuchen
Christmas Weihnachten
city Stadt
class Klasse, Kurs, Unterricht
to **clean; clean** putzen, säubern; sauber

clear(ly) klar, deutlich
clever(ly) klug, gescheit, raffiniert
to **climb** klettern, steigen
to **close** schließen, zumachen
clothes Kleidung, Kleider
coast Küste
cold Kälte; kalt
to **collect** (ein)sammeln; abholen
college Hochschule, Berufsschule, Universität
colour Farbe
colourful bunt, farbenfroh
to **come** kommen, geliefert werden
comfortable bequem, angenehm, komfortabel
common üblich, verbreitet, gemeinsam
to **communicate** sich verständigen, kommunizieren
communication Kommunikation, Verständigung
to **complete; complete(ly)** abschließen, ausfüllen, vervollständigen; völlig, vollständig, komplett
conference Tagung, Konferenz
context Zusammenhang, Kontext
to **continue** weitergehen, fortsetzen, weitermachen
contract Vertrag
conversation Gespräch, Unterhaltung
to **cook** kochen, braten
cool kühl, cool
to **copy; copy** kopieren, abschreiben; Kopie, Exemplar
to **correct; correct(ly)** berichtigen; richtig, genau
corridor Gang, Flur
to **cost; cost** kosten; Kosten
to **count** zählen
country Land, Staat
countryside Land(schaft), Natur
couple (Ehe-)Paar
couple: a ~ ein paar, einige
course Kurs, Studiengang
course: of ~ natürlich, selbstverständlich
crazy verrückt
creative kreativ, schöpferisch
crowd Menge, Menschenmasse
customer Kunde/Kundin
to **cut** schneiden
to **cycle** radeln
daily täglich
to **dance; dance** tanzen; Tanz
danger Gefahr
dangerous gefährlich
date Datum, Verabredung
daughter Tochter
day Tag
dear liebe/r
to **decide** (sich) entscheiden, beschließen, sich entschließen
decision Entscheidung, Beschluss
deep tief
to **describe** beschreiben
desert Wüste
detail Einzelheit, Detail, Angabe(n)
to **develop** (sich) entwickeln
development Entwicklung
dialogue Dialog
diary Tagebuch, Terminkalender
dictionary Wörterbuch
to **die** sterben
difference Unterschied
different(ly) verschieden, unterschiedlich
difficult schwierig, schwer
difficulty Schwierigkeit
dinner Abendessen
direct(ly) **direkt**
direction Richtung
direction: to **give ~s** den Weg beschreiben
to **discuss** diskutieren, besprechen, erörtern
to **do** tun, machen
doctor Arzt/Ärztin
dog Hund
door Tür
double doppelt, Doppel-
down her-/hinunter
to **dress** sich kleiden, sich anziehen
to **drink; drink** trinken; Getränk
to **drive** fahren
driver Fahrer/in
during während
each jede/r/s, jeweils
each: ~ other einander
early früh
to **earn** verdienen
Easter Ostern
eas(il)y einfach, leicht
to **eat** essen
edition Ausgabe
effect Auswirkung, Effekt
egg Ei
either: ~ ... or entweder ... oder
either: not ... ~ auch nicht, auch kein/e
else sonst (noch), andere/r/s
empty leer
to **end; end** (be)enden; Ende, Schluss
engine Motor
to **enjoy** genießen, gefallen
to **enjoy doing sth** etw gern tun
enough genug
even sogar, noch
event Ereignis, Veranstaltung
ever je(mals)
every jede/r/s
everybody jede/r
everyone jede/r
everything alles
everywhere überall(hin)
exact(ly) genau, exakt
exam Prüfung
example Beispiel
example: for ~ zum Beispiel
excellent ausgezeichnet, hervorragend
except außer
excited (freudig) aufgeregt
exciting aufregend, spannend
to **excuse; excuse** entschuldigen; Ausrede
to **exercise; exercise** üben, trainieren; Übung, Training
exercise book (Schul-)Heft
to **expect** erwarten
expensive teuer
to **explain** erklären, erläutern
expression Ausdruck
extreme(ly) äußerst, extrem
eye Auge
fact Tatsache
factory Fabrik
fair Messe; fair, gerecht
fairly ziemlich
to **fall; fall** sinken, fallen; Rückgang
false falsch
family Familie
famous berühmt
fantastic fantastisch, großartig
far weit
farm Bauernhof
farmer Bauer/Bäuerin
fascinating faszinierend
fast schnell
fat dick
father Vater
favourite Lieblings-
to **feel** (sich) fühlen, glauben
feeling Gefühl, Ansicht
few wenige
few: a ~ einige, ein paar
field Feld
to **fight; fight** (be)kämpfen; Kampf
to **file; file** ablegen; Ordner, Akte
to **fill** (aus-, be-)füllen; übernehmen; erledigen
to **fill: ~ in** ausfüllen
final letzte/r/s, End-
finally endlich, schließlich, zuletzt
financial(ly) finanziell
to **find (out)** (heraus)finden, feststellen
fine gut, schön, in Ordnung
finger Finger
to **finish; finish** zu Ende bringen, (be-, ab)schließen; Schluss
fire Feuer, Brand
first name Vorname
fish Fisch
flat Wohnung; flach
floor Etage
flower Blume, Blüte
to **fly** fliegen

following folgende/r/s
food Essen, Lebensmittel
foot, feet Fuß, Füße
to **forget** vergessen
forward vorwärts, nach vorn
free frei, umsonst
freedom Freiheit
fresh frisch
friend Freund/in
friendly freundlich
front: in ~ vorne, davor
front: in ~ of vor
fruit Obst, Frucht
full(y) voll, völlig
fun Spaß
funny lustig, seltsam
furniture Möbel
further weiter/e/s
future Zukunft, zukünftige/r/s
game Spiel
garden Garten
gate Tor; Flugsteig
general(ly) allgemein, generell
to **get** bekommen, werden, gelangen
to **get on** vorankommen
to **get up** aufstehen
giant Riese; riesig
girl Mädchen
girlfriend Freundin
to **give** geben, schenken
to **give up** aufgeben, aufhören mit
glad froh
glass Glas
to **go** gehen, fahren
to **go on** weitermachen, fortfahren
good gut
goodbye auf Wiedersehen
grammar Grammatik
grandchildren Enkelkinder
great groß, großartig, toll
group Gruppe
to **grow** (an)wachsen
to **grow up** aufwachsen
guest Gast
hair Haar, Haare
half Hälfte, halb
ham Schinken
hand Hand
hand: on the one ~, on the other ~ einerseits, andererseits
to **happen** passieren, geschehen
happy glücklich, zufrieden
hard hart, schwer, schwierig
harmless harmlos
to **have to** müssen
head Kopf
health Gesundheit(szustand)
healthy gesund
to **hear** hören
heart Herz, Zentrum
heavy schwer
to **help; help** helfen; Hilfe
helpful hilfreich, hilfsbereit
here hier
high hoch
to **hold** halten
holiday Ferien, Urlaub, Feiertag
home zu/nach Hause, Zuhause
homework Hausaufgaben
to **hope; hope** hoffen; Hoffnung
hour Stunde
house Haus
how wie
however doch, jedoch, aber; egal wie
hungry hungrig
ice Eis
idea Idee, Gedanke, Vorstellung
if wenn, falls
ill krank
immediate(ly) unmittelbar, umgehend, sofort
important wichtig
to **improve** (sich) verbessern
indoors drinnen
to **inform** informieren, unterrichten
inside in, innen, hinein
to **interest; interest** interessieren; Interesse
interested: to **be ~ in** interessiert sein an, sich interessieren für
interesting interessant
to **introduce** einführen, vorstellen, bekanntmachen
introduction(s) Einleitung, Einführung, Vorstellung, Bekanntmachen
to **invite** einladen
island Insel
jacket Jacke, Jackett
jam Marmelade, Konfitüre
job Arbeit, Stelle, Arbeitsplatz
to **join** verbinden, beitreten, sich anschließen
journey Fahrt, Reise
just einfach, gerade
to **keep** bleiben, halten, behalten, aufbewahren, etw weiter tun
kids Kinder
kind Sorte; freundlich
king König
kitchen Küche
to **know** wissen, kennen
knowledge Wissen, Kenntnis
lady Dame
lake See
to **land; land** landen; Land
language Sprache
large groß, bedeutend
last: at ~ endlich
to **last; last** dauern; letzte/r/s
late spät
to **lead** führen
to **learn** lernen
to **leave** (ver-, hinter-, da)lassen, weggehen, abfahren
to **lend** leihen
less weniger
to **let** lassen
letter Brief, Buchstabe
to **lie** liegen
life Leben
lift Aufzug
light hell, leicht; Licht
to **like; like** mögen, gern haben; (ähnlich) wie
line Linie, Zeile, Leitung
to **list; list** auflisten; Liste
to **listen (to)** (zu-, an)hören
little klein, wenig
little: a ~ ein bisschen
to **live** leben
lonely einsam
long lang, lang
to **look; look** ansehen, aussehen; Blick
to **look after** sich kümmern um
lorry Lastwagen
to **lose** verlieren
lot: a ~ (of) viel, viele
lots of viel, viele
to **love; love** lieben, sehr gern mögen; Liebe
lovely hübsch, nett
low niedrig
luck Glück
luckily glücklicherweise
lucky glücklich
lucky: to **be ~** Glück haben
lunch Mittagessen
lunch break Mittagspause
madam gnädige Frau
magazine Zeitschrift
main Haupt-, hauptsächliche/r/s
to **make** machen
man, men Mann, Männer
many viele
map Stadtplan, Landkarte
to **market; market** vermarkten; Markt
married verheiratet
may dürfen, können
maybe vielleicht
to **mean** bedeuten, heißen, meinen
meaning Bedeutung, Sinn
meat Fleisch
to **meet** treffen, kennen lernen
meeting Sitzung, Besprechung, Konferenz
member Mitglied
message Nachricht, Botschaft
midday Mittag
middle mittlere/r/s
midnight Mitternach
might könnte
mile Meile
milk Milch
minute Minute
mirror Spiegel

to **miss** vermissen, verpassen
missing fehlend
mistake Fehler
to **mix; mix** mischen; Mischung
model Modell, Beispiel
moment Moment, Augenblick
moment: at the ~ im Augenblick
money Geld
month Monat
more mehr
morning Morgen
most der/die/das meiste, die meisten
mostly größtenteils
mother Mutter
motorbike Motorrad
mountain Berg
to **move** (sich) bewegen, umziehen, verlegen, versetzen
much viel
must müssen
must not nicht dürfen
to **name; name** (be)nennen; Name
nature Nature
near nahe, in der Nähe von
nearly beinahe, fast
necessary notwendig, nötig
to **need; need** brauchen, benötigen; Bedarf, Bedürfnis
neighbour Nachbar/in
neither keines (von beiden), auch nicht
never nie(mals)
new neu
news Neuigkeit(en), Nachricht(en)
newspaper Zeitung
next nächste/r/s, danach
nice schön, nett
night Nacht
nobody niemand
none keine/r/s
normal(ly) normal(erweise)
north (nach) Norden, Nord
to **note; note** notieren, zur Kenntnis nehmen; Notiz
nothing nichts
to **notice** beachten, bemerken
now nun, jetzt
nowhere nirgends
number Zahl, (Telefon-) / Nummer
obvious(ly) offensichtlich, klar, deutlich, natürlich
occasional(ly) gelegentlich
to **offer; offer** (an)bieten; Angebot
office Büro, Amt
often oft, häufig
oil Öl
old alt
once einmal; sobald
only nur
to **open; open** (sich) öffnen, eröffnen; offen
opinion Meinung
opportunity Gelegenheit
opposite Gegenteil; gegenüber(liegend)
or oder
order: in ~ to um ... zu
to **order; order** bestellen; Bestellung, Auftrag, Reihenfolge
ordinary gewöhnlich, normal
other andere/r/s, weitere/r/s
otherwise sonst, ansonsten
ought to sollte
outside Außenseite; außerhalb von, draußen
over über, vorüber
to **own; own** besitzen; eigene/r/s
page Seite
paint Farbe
pair Paar
paragraph Absatz, Abschnitt
parents Eltern
part Teil
particular bestimmt, besondere/r/s, speziell
particularly besonders, vor allem, insbesondere
partner Partner, Gesellschafter/in
past Vergangenheit; vorbei (an), hinter
path Weg, Pfad
to **pay; pay** (be)zahlen; Bezahlung, Gehalt
people Leute, Menschen
per cent Prozent
perfect vollkommen, perfekt
perhaps vielleicht
period Zeit(raum), Frist
permanent(ly) dauerhaft, bleibend
person Person
to **phone; phone** telefonieren, anrufen; Telefon
photo Foto
phrase Ausdruck, Redewendung
to **pick up** abholen
picture Bild
piece Stück, Teil
place Stelle, Platz, Ort
to **plan; plan** planen; Plan
plane Flugzeug
planet Planet
to **play** spielen
pleasant angenehm, freundlich, nett
please bitte
pleased froh, erfreut
pleasure Vergnügen
pocket Tasche,
to **point; point** zeigen, richten; Punkt, Argumente, Seite
police Polizei
pool Schwimmbad, Pool
poor arm, schlecht
popular beliebt, populär
possible möglich, denkbar
possibly möglicherweise
post Post
pound Pfund
practice Praxis, Verfahrensweise
to **practise** üben, trainieren
to **prefer** vorziehen, lieber mögen
to **prepare** (sich) vorbereiten
present Gegenwart, Geschenk
pretty hübsch; ziemlich
price Preis
private privat, persönlich
probably wahrscheinlich
programme (TV-, Radio-)Sendung, Programm, Plan
to **promise; promise** versprechen; Versprechen
proper(ly) richtig, ordnungsgemäß
to **protect** schützen, beschützen
pub Kneipe
to **pull** ziehen
pupil Schüler/in
to **put** setzen, stellen, legen
to **put on** anziehen
quality Qualität, Eigenschaft
queen Königin
question Frage
quick(ly) schnell
quiet(ly) still, ruhig, leise
quite ziemlich, ganz
to **race; race** rennen; Rennen
to **rain; rain** regnen; Regen
rather ziemlich
to **reach; reach** erreichen; Reichweite
to **read** lesen, vorlesen
ready bereit
real(ly) echt, wirklich, sehr
to **receive** erhalten, empfangen
recent jüngst, aktuell
recently neulich, kürzlich, in letzter Zeit
regular(ly) regelmäßig
to **relax** sich entspannen
to **remember** sich an etw erinnern, daran denken
to **rent; rent mieten; Miete**
to **reply; reply** antworten; Antwort
to **report; report** berichten; Bericht
to **reserve** reservieren, buchen
rest Rest
result Folge, Ergebnis
to **return** zurückkehren, zurückgeben, -senden
rich reich, wohlhabend
right richtig; rechts; Recht
to **risk; risk** riskieren; Risiko
river Fluss
road Straße
role Rolle
room Zimmer, Raum
round rund; (um/in ...) herum
rule Regel, Vorschrift
to **run** laufen, rennen

sad traurig
safe sicher
safety Sicherheit
to **sail; sail** segeln, zur See fahren; Segel
salad Salat
salt Salz
same gleiche/r/s, der-, die-, dasselbe
to **say** sagen
school Schule
sea Meer, See
season Saison
seat Sitz, Platz
second-hand gebraucht, aus zweiter Hand
secretary Sektretär/in
to **see** sehen
to **seem** scheinen
to **sell** verkaufen
to **send** senden, schicken
sentence Satz
serious(ly) ernst(haft)
several etliche, einige, mehrere
shelf Regal
ship Schiff
shirt Hemd
shoe Schuh
to **shop; shop** einkaufen; Laden, Geschäft
short kurz
should sollte
shoulder Schulter
to **show** zeigen
sightseeing Besichtigungen
to **sign; sign** unterschreiben, unterzeichnen; Zeichen, Schild
silly albern, doof
simple (simply) einfach, schlicht
since seit, seitdem, da, weil
to **sing** singen
sir mein Herr
to **sit** sitzen
to **sit down** sich setzen
size Größe
slow(ly) langsam
small klein
to **smell; smell** riechen; Duft, Geruch
to **smile; smile** lächeln; Lächeln
to **smoke;smoke** rauchen; Rauch
snow Schnee
so so, also
soap Seife
some etwas, einige, irgendein
somebody jemand
something etwas
sometimes manchmal
somewhere irgendwo(hin)
son Sohn
song Lied
soon bald
(I'm) sorry (es) tut mir leid
sort Art, Sorte
to **sound; sound** klingen; Klang
soup Suppe
to **speak** sprechen
special besondere/r/s, Sonder-
spend *(Zeit)* verbringen, *(Geld)* ausgeben
sport Sport(art)
stairs Treppe
to **stand** stehen
star Stern, Star
to **start; start** beginnen, eröffnen; Anfang
station Bahnhof
to **stay** bleiben, wohnen
still noch immer
to **stop** aufhören, anhalten
storm Sturm, Unwetter
story Geschichte
straight direkt, gerade
strange seltsam
stranger Fremde/r
street Straße
strong stark
to **study** lernen, studieren, sich etw genau ansehen, durchlesen
subject Thema; (Schul-)Fach; Betreff
success Erfolg
successful(ly) erfolgreich
such solche/r/s
sudden(ly) plötzlich
sugar Zucker
summer Sommer
sun Sonne
to **suppose** glauben, annehmen, vermuten
sure sicher, freilich
to **surprise; surprise** überraschen; Überraschung
sweet süß
sweets Süßigkeiten
to **swim** schwimmen
table Tisch; Tabelle
to **take** (an-, ein-, mit)nehmen, dauern
to **talk** reden, sprechen
tall groß, hoch
task Aufgabe
tea Tee
to **tell** sagen
tent Zelt
terrible furchtbar, schrecklich
than als
to **thank** danken
thanks danke
that dies; der, die, das; dass; jene/r/s
then dann
there da, dort, dorthin
therefore deshalb
these diese
thief Dieb
thing Sache, Ding
to **think (of)** denken (an), halten von
this dies, diese/r/s
those jene
though obwohl, doch
through durch, hindurch
time Zeit, Mal
title Titel, Anrede, Bezeichnung
today heute
together zusammen
tomorrow morgen
tonight heute Abend
too zu, auch
toothpaste Zahncreme
top Spitze, Anfang; Spitzen-, oberste/r/s
total(ly) völlig, total, Gesamt
towards gegen, auf ... zu, (in) Richtung
town Stadt
toy Spielzeug
traffic Verkehr
train Zug
trainee Auszubildende/r
to **translate** übersetzen
to **travel; travel** reisen, fahren; Reisen
tree Baum
trip Reise, Ausflug
trouble Problem(e), Schwierigkeiten, Mühe(n)
truck Lastwagen
true wahr
to **try** versuchen, probieren
twice zweimal
twin Zwilling, Zwillings-
to **type; type** tippen; Art, Sorte, Typ
ugly häßlich
under unter
to **understand** verstehen, begreifen
unfortunately leider, unglücklicherweise
unfriendly unfreundlich
unhappy unzufrieden, unglücklich
unhealthy ungesund
unit Einheit, Lektion, Stück
university Universität
unless wenn nicht; es sei denn, dass
unnecessary unnötig
until bis
unusual ungewöhnlich, unüblich
to **use; use** gebrauchen, benutzen; Verwendung, Gebrauch
useful nützlich
usual(ly) normal(erweise), gewöhnlich
vegetable Gemüse
very sehr
via über, per
village Dorf
to **visit; visit** besuchen, besichtigen; Besuch, Besichtigung

visitor Besucher/in
to **wait** warten
waiter, waitress Kellner/in
to **wake up** aufwachen
to **walk; walk** (zu Fuß) gehen; Spaziergang, Fußweg
wall Wand
to **want** wollen, mögen
warm warm
to **warn** warnen
to **watch** zusehen, beobachten, anschauen
way Weg, Methode
way: this ~ hier entlang
weak schwach
to **wear** tragen
week Woche
weekday Wochentag
weekend Wochenende
weight Gewicht
to **welcome; welcome** willkommen heißen; willkommen
well also; gut
what was, welche/r/s
whatever was auch immer
wheel Rad
when wenn, als, wann
where wo, wohin
whether ob
which welche/r/s
while während, solange; Weile
who wer, die, der
whoever wer auch immer
whole ganze/r/s
why warum, weshalb
why: that's ~ deshalb, darum
will will, wollen, werden; Wille
to **win** gewinnen, siegen
to **wish; wish** wünschen; Wunsch
with mit, bei
within innerhalb, binnen, in
without ohne
woman, women Frau
to **wonder (about); wonder** sich (etw) fragen; Wunder
wonderful wunderbar
word Wort
to **work; work** arbeiten, funktionieren; Arbeit
world Welt
to **worry; worry** sich Sorgen machen; Sorge
to **write (down)** (auf-, ab)schreiben
wrong falsch
year Jahr
yesterday gestern
yet schon, bereits
young jung

Unit word list

Dieses Wörterverzeichnis enthält alle Wörter in **Focus on Business 4th Edition** in der Reihenfolge ihres Auftretens. Nicht aufgeführt sind die Wörter aus der *Basic word list* sowie internationale Wörter wie *hotel*, *e-mail* usw.
Das Vokabular des *Refresher Course* und *Main Course* wird für die *Secretarial Activities* sowie für den Abschnitt *Commercial Correspondence* vorausgesetzt. Wörter, die in den Hörverständnis-übungen vorkommen, sind mit einem orangefarbenen Balken, und Wörter, die in den *Partner files* vorkommen, mit einem blauen Balken gekennzeichnet.

REFRESHER COURSE

UNIT A

page 6

experience [ɪk'spɪəriəns]	Erfahrung
work experience ['wɜːk ɪkspɪəriəns]	Praktikum
archive ['ɑːkaɪv]	Archiv
comment ['kɒment]	Kommentar
to **contact sb** ['kɒntækt]	sich mit jdn in Verbindung setzen
tired ['taɪəd]	müde
to **be in a hurry** [bi ɪn ə 'hʌri]	es eilig haben
Wait a minute [ː'weɪt ə mɪnɪt]	Moment mal!
student ['stjuːdnt]	Schüler/in, Berufsschüler/in
college ['kɒlɪdʒ]	Berufsschule, Berufsfachschule
employer [ɪm'plɔɪə]	Arbeitgeber/in
interview ['ɪntəvjuː]	Vorstellungsgespräch
work placement ['wɜːk pleɪsmənt]	Praktikum
store [stɔː]	Geschäft, Laden
retail ['riːteɪl]	Einzelhandel
purchasing ['pɜːtʃəsɪŋ]	Einkauf, Beschaffung
department [dɪ'pɑːtmənt]	Abteilung
stock [stɒk]	Ware(n)
customer service [ˌkʌstəmə 'sɜːvɪs]	Kundendienst, Kundenbetreuung
to **handle sth** ['hændl]	etw bearbeiten
query ['kwɪəri]	Anfrage
accounts [ə'kaʊnts]	Buchhaltung
financial [faɪ'nænʃl]	Finanz-, finanziell
surprising [sə'praɪzɪŋ]	erstaunlich
behind the scenes [bɪˌhaɪnd ðə 'siːnz]	hinter den Kulissen
rare(ly) ['reə]	selten
personnel [ˌpɜːsə'nel]	Personal
employee [ɪm'plɔɪiː]	Angestellte/r, Beschäftigte/r
job advertisment ['dʒɒb ədvɜːtɪsmənt]	Stellenanzeige
to **update** [ˌʌp'deɪt]	auf den neusten Stand bringen, aktualisieren
records ['rekɔːdz]	Daten, Akten, Unterlagen
form letter ['fɔːm letə]	Formbrief, Serienbrief
to **photocopy** ['fəʊtəʊkɒpi]	fotokopieren
paperwork ['peɪpəwɜːk]	Unterlagen
to **answer the phone** [ˌɑːnsə ðə 'fəʊn]	ans Telefon gehen
not yet [nɒt 'jet]	noch nicht
honest ['ɒnɪst]	ehrlich
folks [fəʊks]	Leute
I'm off to bed [ːaɪm ˌɒf tə 'bed]	Ich gehe dann mal ins Bett.

page 7

staff [stɑːf]	Personal, Belegschaft
to **treat** [triːt]	behandeln
administrative [əd'mɪnɪstrətɪv]	Verwaltungs-
to **organize** ['ɔːgənaɪz]	organisieren
advantage [əd'vɑːntɪdʒ]	Vorteil
disadvantage [ˌdɪsəd'vɑːntɪdʒ]	Nachteil
in your opinion [ɪn ˌjɔːr ə'pɪniən]	deiner/Ihrer Meinung nach
view [vjuː]	Ansicht
to **replace** [rɪ'pleɪs]	ersetzen, austauschen
in italics [ɪn ɪ'tælɪks]	kursiv
similar ['sɪmələ]	ähnlich
company ['kʌmpəni]	Unternehmen, Gesellschaft, Firma
to **deal with sth** ['diːl wɪð]	etw erledigen, etw bearbeiten
complaint [kəm'pleɪnt]	Reklamation, Beschwerde
purchase ['pɜːtʃəs]	Kauf
to **involve** [ɪn'vɒlv]	mit sich bringen, einbeziehen, beinhalten
the public [ðə 'pʌblɪk]	die Öffentlichkeit
concerning [kən'sɜːnɪŋ]	betreffend
notice ['nəʊtɪs]	Hinweis, Bekanntmachung
to **contain** [kən'teɪn]	enthalten
latest ['leɪtɪst]	neueste/r/s
gap [gæp]	Lücke, Zwischenraum
printed ['prɪntɪd]	gedruckt

page 8

present ['preznt]	Gegenwart
occasionally [ə'keɪʒənəli]	gelegentlich
now and then [ˌnaʊ ən 'ðen]	ab und zu

accounts manager [ə'kaʊnts mænɪdʒə]	Leiter/in der Buchhaltung
purchasing manager ['pɜːtʃəsɪŋ mænɪdʒə]	Einkaufsleiter/in
personnel assistant [ˌpɜːsə'nel əsɪstənt]	Personalassistent/in
employee records [ɪm'plɔɪiː rekɔːdz]	Personalakte
sales [seɪlz]	Verkauf, Vertrieb
sales assistant ['seɪlz əsɪstənt]	Verkäufer/in
to **serve sb** [sɜːv]	jdn bedienen
accounts assistant [ə'kaʊnts əsɪstənt]	Buchhaltungsassistent/in
representative [ˌreprɪ'zentətɪv]	Vertreter/in
personnel manager [ˌpɜːsə'nel mænɪdʒə]	Personalchef/in
purchasing assistant ['pɜːtʃəsɪŋ əsɪstənt]	Einkaufsassistent/in
coffee break ['kɒfi breɪk]	Kaffeepause

page 9

keyboard ['kiːbɔːd]	Tastatur
cash register ['kæʃ redʒɪstə]	Registrierkasse
negative ['negətɪv]	verneinend
mobile phone [ˌməʊbaɪl 'fəʊn]	Mobiltelefon, Handy
at present [ət 'preznt]	gegenwärtig
currently ['kʌrəntli]	derzeit, zur Zeit
to **hate** [heɪt]	hassen, überhaupt nicht mögen

page 10

to **make friends** [meɪk 'frendz]	Freunde finden, Freundschaft(en) schließen
boss [bɒs]	Chef/in
to **look forward to sth** [ˌlʊk 'fɔːwəd tə]	sich auf etw freuen
photocopier ['fəʊtəʊkɒpiə]	Fotokopierer
enjoyable [ɪn'dʒɔɪəbl]	angenehm, schön
law firm ['lɔː fɜːm]	Anwaltskanzlei
high street ['haɪ striːt]	Hauptgeschäftsstraße
translation [træns'leɪʃn]	Übersetzung
appropriate [ə'prəʊpriət]	passend, angemessen

UNIT B

page 11

gap year ['gæp jɪə]	*das Jahr zwischen Schulabgang und Studienbeginn*
school-leaver [ˌskuːl 'liːvə]	Schulabgänger/in
to **take time off** [teɪk ˌtaɪm 'ɒf]	sich frei nehmen
full-time [ˌfʊl 'taɪm]	Vollzeit-
mixture ['mɪkstʃə]	Mischung
casual work [ˌkæʒuəl 'wɜːk]	Gelegenheitsarbeit(en)
to **go places** [ˌgəʊ 'pleɪsɪz]	herumkommen
youth [juːθ]	Jugend
reason ['riːzn]	Grund
ticket ['tɪkɪt]	Fahrkarte, (Flug-)Ticket
fare [feə]	Fahrpreis
spending money ['spendɪŋ mʌni]	Taschengeld
to **save** [seɪv]	sparen
skill [skɪl]	Fähigkeit, Fertigkeit
training ['treɪnɪŋ]	Ausbildung
to **make ends meet** [meɪk ˌendz 'miːt]	über die Runden kommen
shy [ʃaɪ]	schüchtern
to **get along with sb** [ˌget ə'lɒŋ wɪð]	mit jdm zurechtkommen
self-confident [ˌself 'kɒnfɪdənt]	selbstbewusst, selbstsicher
to **afford sth** [ə'fɔːd]	sich etw leisten
imagination [ɪˌmædʒɪ'neɪʃn]	Phantasie
planning ['plænɪŋ]	Planung
exotic [ɪg'zɒtɪk]	exotisch
faraway [ˌfɑːrə'weɪ]	weit entfernt, fern, entlegen
youth hostel ['juːθ hɒstl]	Jugendherberge
instructor [ɪn'strʌktə]	Lehrer/in
initiative [ɪ'nɪʃətɪv]	Eigeninitiative, Initiative
determination [dɪˌtɜːmɪ'neɪʃn]	Entschlossenheit
to **be scared** [bi 'skeəd]	Angst haben
CV (= curriculum vitae) *(BE)* [ˌsiː 'vi / kəˌrɪkjələm 'viːtaɪ]	Lebenslauf
crowd [kraʊd]	Menge, Menschenmasse
to **stand out from the crowd** [stænd ˌaʊt frəm ðə 'kraʊd]	aus der Menge herausstechen

page 12

to **match sth** [mætʃ]	etw zuordnen, zu etw passen
contributor [kən'trɪbjuːtə]	Verfasser/in (eines Beitrags)
foreign ['fɒrən]	Auslands-, ausländisch, fremd
experience [ɪk'spɪəriəns]	Erlebnis
wealthy ['welθi]	wohlhabend, reich
luxury ['lʌkʃəri]	Luxus
preparation [ˌprepə'reɪʃn]	Vorbereitung
backpacker ['bækpækə]	Rucksacktourist/in
cash [kæʃ]	Bargeld
according to [ə'kɔːdɪŋ tə]	gemäß, nach, zufolge
to **intend** [ɪn'tend]	beabsichtigen
instead of [ɪn'sted əv]	anstatt
potential [pə'tenʃl]	potentiell, künftig
low-paid [ˌləʊ 'peɪd]	Niedriglohn-
colleague ['kɒliːg]	Kollege/-in
voluntary ['vɒləntri]	freiwillig
character ['kærəktə]	Charakter
applicant ['æplɪkənt]	Bewerber/in
to **be likely to do sth** [bi 'laɪkli tə]	etw wahrscheinlich tun werden

page 13

round-the-world trip [ˌraʊnd ðə ˌwɜːld 'trɪp]	Weltreise
horrible ['hɒrəbl]	schrecklich, fürchterlich
accommodation [əˌkɒmə'deɪʃn]	Unterkunft

skiing instructor ['ski:ɪŋ ɪnstrʌktə]	Skilehrer/in
to **be fun** [bi 'fʌn]	Spaß machen
return flight [rɪˌtɜ:n 'flaɪt]	Hin- und Rückflug
first aid [ˌfɜ:st 'eɪd]	Erste Hilfe
apprenticeship [ə'prentɪʃɪp]	Lehre, Ausbildung

page 14

bracket ['brækɪt]	Klammer
irregular [ɪ'regjələ]	unregelmäßig
reply [rɪ'plaɪ]	Antwort
water sports ['wɔ:tə spɔ:ts]	Wassersportarten
crocodile ['krɒkədaɪl]	Krokodil
to **photograph** ['fəʊtəgrɑ:f]	fotografieren
kangaroo [ˌkæŋgə'ru:]	Känguru
to **ride sth** [raɪd]	auf etw reiten
camel ['kæml]	Kamel
to **pick** [pɪk]	pflücken
grapes [greɪps]	Trauben
dolphin ['dɒlfɪn]	Delphin
frequency ['fri:kwənsi]	Häufigkeit
to **run out of sth** [ˌrʌn 'aʊt əv]	kein ... mehr haben

page 15

foreign language [ˌfɒrən 'læŋgwɪdʒ]	Fremdsprache
missing ['mɪsɪŋ]	vermisst
break [breɪk]	Pause
to **take a break** [ˌteɪk ə 'breɪk]	eine Pause machen
career [kə'rɪə]	Karriere, Laufbahn

UNIT C

page 16

nervous ['nɜ:vəs]	nervös
proper(ly) ['prɒpə]	richtig
impression [ɪm'preʃn]	Eindruck
congratulations (on sth) [kənˌgrætʃʊ'leɪʃnz]	herzlichen Glückwunsch (zu etw)
adult ['ædʌlt]	Erwachsene/r
formal ['fɔ:ml]	formell, förmlich
conservative [kən'sɜ:vətɪv]	konservativ
casual ['kæʒuəl]	leger
to **fit in** [ˌfɪt 'ɪn]	sich anpassen, sich einfügen
to **express** [ɪk'spres]	ausdrücken, zum Ausdruck bringen
individuality [ˌɪndɪˌvɪdʒu'æləti]	Individualität
comfortable ['kʌmftəbl]	bequem
professional [prə'feʃənl]	professionell
sleep [sli:p]	Schlaf
meeting ['mi:tɪŋ]	Besprechung, Sitzung
to **pass** [pɑ:s]	vorübergehen
energy ['enədʒi]	Energie
arrival [ə'raɪvl]	Ankunft
worker ['wɜ:kə]	Arbeiter/in
lazy ['leɪzi]	nachlässig, faul
disorganized [dɪs'ɔ:gənaɪzd]	chaotisch
to **make sure** [ˌmeɪk 'ʃʊə]	sicherstellen, sich vergewissern
trial run ['traɪəl rʌn]	Probelauf
Good luck! [ˌgʊd 'lʌk]	Viel Glück!
conversation [ˌkɒnvə'seɪʃn]	Gespräch
to **call sb** [kɔ:l]	jdn anreden
job title ['dʒɒb taɪtl]	Berufsbezeichnung
responsibility [rɪˌspɒnsə'bɪləti]	Aufgabenbereich, Zuständigkeit
to **fill in** [ˌfɪl 'ɪn]	ausfüllen
Well done! [ˌwel 'dʌn]	Gut gemacht!
notes [nəʊts]	Notizen
to **take notes** [ˌteɪk 'nəʊts]	sich Notizen machen
to **take sth in** [ˌteɪk 'ɪn]	etw aufnehmen
to **make sense** [ˌmeɪk 'sens]	sinnvoll/logisch sein
stupid ['stju:pɪd]	albern, dumm
slack [slæk]	flau, untätig
to **keep busy** [ˌki:p 'bɪzi]	sich beschäftigen
access ['ækses]	Zugriff, Zugang
workplace ['wɜ:kpleɪs]	Arbeitsplatz
first name ['fɜ:st neɪm]	Vorname

page 17

suitable ['su:təbl]	geeignet, passend
on time [ɒn 'taɪm]	pünktlich
to **dress the part** [ˌdres ðə 'pɑ:t]	sich der Rolle entsprechend kleiden
to **find your way around** [faɪnd jɔ: ˌweɪ 'raʊnd]	sich zurechtfinden
to **succeed** [sək'si:d]	Erfolg haben
advice [əd'vaɪs]	Rat, Ratschlag/Ratschläge
to **impress** [ɪm'pres]	beeindrucken
to **learn on the job** [ˌlɜ:n ɒn ðə 'dʒɒb]	lernen am Arbeitsplatz
to **grow up** [ˌgrəʊ 'ʌp]	erwachsen werden
individual [ˌɪndɪ'vɪdʒuəl]	individuell
style [staɪl]	Stil
to **advise** [əd'vaɪz]	raten
travel time ['trævl taɪm]	Fahrzeit
route [ru:t]	Weg, Strecke, Route
to **avoid** [ə'vɔɪd]	vermeiden
to **concentrate** ['kɒnsntreɪt]	sich konzentrieren
to **miss** [mɪs]	versäumen, verpassen
to **suggest** [sə'dʒest]	vorschlagen
to **research sth** [rɪ'sɜ:tʃ]	Nachforschungen über etw anstellen, etw recherchieren
firm [fɜ:m]	Firma

page 18

opposite ['ɒpəzɪt]	engegengesetzt, gegensätzlich
underlined [ˌʌndə'laɪnd]	unterstrichen
bored [bɔ:d]	gelangweilt
hard-working [ˌhɑ:d 'wɜ:kɪŋ]	fleißig
work routine ['wɜ:k ru:ti:n]	Arbeitsablauf
clever ['klevə]	intelligent, klug
to **create** [kri'eɪt]	schaffen, kreieren, (Eindruck) hinterlassen

accidentally [ˌæksɪ'dentəli]	unabsichtlich
organization chart [ˌɔːɡənaɪ'zeɪʃn tʃɑːt]	Organigramm
interviewer ['ɪntəvjuːə]	*Person, die ein Vorstellungsgespräch führt*

page 19

to **take part in** sth [ˌteɪk 'pɑːt ɪn]	an etw teilnehmen
induction [ɪn'dʌkʃn]	Einführung
managing director [ˌmænɪdʒɪŋ də'rektə]	Geschäftsführer/in
talk [tɔːk]	Vortrag, Rede
tour [tʊə]	Rundgang
salary ['sæləri]	Gehalt, Lohn
head of department [ˌhed əv dɪ'pɑːtmənt]	Abteilungsleiter/in
business card ['bɪznəs kɑːd]	Visitenkarte
toilet ['tɔɪlət]	Toilette
mouse [maʊs]	Maus
broken ['brəʊkən]	kaputt
pen [pen]	Stift
to **lend** [lend]	leihen
notepad ['nəʊtpæd]	Notizblock
to **crash** [kræʃ]	abstürzen
support [sə'pɔːt]	Unterstützung, Kundendienst
cup [kʌp]	Tasse

page 20

secretary ['sekrətri]	Sekretär/in
to **rewrite** [ˌriː'raɪt]	neu schreiben, umformulieren
apostrophe [ə'pɒstrəfi]	Apostroph
to **train** sb [treɪn]	jdn schulen, jdn ausbilden
assistant [ə'sɪstənt]	Assistent/in
surname ['sɜːneɪm]	Nachnahme
credit card ['kredɪt kɑːd]	Kreditkarte
to **steal** [stiːl]	stehlen
thief, thieves [θiːf, θiːvz]	Dieb, Diebe
parking space ['pɑːkɪŋ speɪs]	Parkplatz
to **park** [pɑːk]	parken

UNIT D

page 21

dispute [dɪ'spjuːt]	Streit, Disput
to **get** sb **down** [ˌɡet 'daʊn]	jdn bedrücken, jdn deprimieren
supervisor ['suːpəvaɪzə]	Vorgesetzte/r
to **give** sb **a hard time** [ɡɪv ə ˌhɑːd 'taɪm]	jdm das Leben schwer machen
awful ['ɔːfl]	furchtbar
to **make** sb's **life a misery** [meɪk ˌlaɪf ə 'mɪzəri]	jdm das Leben schwer machen
incompetent [ɪn'kɒmpɪtənt]	inkompetent
embarrassing [ɪm'bærəsɪŋ]	peinlich
shocked [ʃɒkt]	schockiert
in private [ɪn 'praɪvət]	unter vier Augen
chair [tʃeə]	Stuhl
to **dispatch** [dɪ'spætʃ]	versenden
by mistake [baɪ mɪ'steɪk]	irrtümlich
lorry ['lɒri]	Lastwagen, Lkw
load [ləʊd]	Ladung
furious ['fjʊəriəs]	wütend
to **find out** [ˌfaɪnd 'aʊt]	(es) herausfinden, (es) erfahren
to **enter** sth ['entə]	etw eingeben
to **blame** sb [bleɪm]	jdm die Schuld geben
sb's **fault** [fɔːlt]	jds Schuld
to **prove** [pruːv]	beweisen
though [ðəʊ]	allerdings, aber, jedoch
to **put up with** sth [ˌpʊt 'ʌp wɪð]	sich etw gefallen lassen
treatment ['triːtmənt]	Behandlung
to **hand** sth **in** [ˌhænd 'ɪn]	etw einreichen
resignation [ˌrezɪɡ'neɪʃn]	Kündigung
to **defend** [dɪ'fend]	verteidigen
to **complain** [kəm'pleɪn]	sich beschweren
for instance [fə'r ɪnstəns]	zum Beispiel
What's the point? [ˌwɒts ðə 'pɔɪnt]	Welchen Sinn soll das haben?
to **take** sb's **side** [ˌteɪk 'saɪd]	für jdn Partei ergreifen
management ['mænɪdʒmənt]	Geschäftsführung
to **stick together** [ˌstɪk tə'ɡeðə]	zusammenhalten
official [ə'fɪʃl]	offiziell
grievance procedure ['ɡriːvəns prəsiːdʒə]	Beschwerdeverfahren
to **deal with** sth ['diːl wɪð]	mit etw umgehen
harassment ['hærəsmənt]	Schikane, Mobbing
to **put** [pʊt]	*hier:* formulieren, sagen
to **bully** ['bʊli]	mobben, tyrannisieren
mark [mɑːk]	Zeichen, Kreuz
extra training [ˌekstrə 'treɪnɪŋ]	Fortbildung
in the end [ɪn ði 'end]	schließlich, letztendlich
It's up to you [ˌɪts ˌʌp tə 'juː]	Die Entscheidung liegt bei dir.
victim ['vɪktɪm]	Opfer

page 22

statement ['steɪtmənt]	Aussage
to **fire** sb ['faɪə]	jdn (fristlos) entlassen, jdn feuern
previous ['priːviəs]	vorige/r/s, vorherige/r/s
to **criticize** ['krɪtɪsaɪz]	kritisieren
private ['praɪvət]	privat, eigene/r/s
to **follow** ['fɒləʊ]	folgen
leaflet ['liːflət]	Faltblatt
to **face** sth [feɪs]	vor etw stehen
physical ['fɪzɪkl]	körperlich
unwanted [ˌʌn'wɒntɪd]	unerwünscht
sexual ['sekʃuəl]	sexuell
to **take** sth **down** [ˌteɪk 'daʊn]	etw aufnehmen
discount ['dɪskaʊnt]	Rabatt, Nachlass
to **keep up with** sth [ˌkiːp 'ʌp wɪð]	sich über etw auf dem Laufenden halten
technology [tek'nɒlədʒi]	Technik, Technologie
to **fall off** sth [ˌfɔːl 'ɒf]	von etw herunterfallen

page 23

headache ['hedeɪk] — Kopfschmerzen
flight [flaɪt] — Flug
delayed [dɪ'leɪd] — verspätet
to **score** [skɔ:] — *(Tor)* schießen, erzielen
goal [gəʊl] — *(Fußball etc.:)* Tor

page 24

sales representative ['seɪlz reprɪzentətɪv] — (Handels-)Vertreter/in
cost accounting ['kɒst əkaʊntɪŋ] — Kalkulation, Kostenrechnung
apart from [ə'pɑ:t frəm] — außer, abgesehen von
to **start** [stɑ:t] — *(Auto:)* anspringen
to **give sb a lift** [ˌgɪv ə 'lɪft] — jdn (mit dem Auto) mitnehmen
technician [tek'nɪʃn] — Techniker/in

page 25

to **teach oneself sth** [ti:tʃ] — sich etw beibringen
guitar [gɪ'tɑ:] — Gitarre
briefcase ['bri:fkeɪs] — Aktenkoffer
to **borrow sth** ['bɒrəʊ] — sich etw ausleihen
to **respect** [rɪ'spekt] — respektieren

UNIT E

page 26

business idea ['bɪznəs aɪdɪə] — Geschäftsidee
column ['kɒləm] — Kolumne
to **go into business** [ˌgəʊ ɪntə 'bɪznəs] — sich selbständig machen
mobile ['məʊbaɪl] — mobil
to **detail** ['di:teɪl] — *(Auto:)* gründlich waschen, reinigen
to **shine** [ʃaɪn] — glänzen
show [ʃəʊ] — Ausstellung
owner ['əʊnə] — Besitzer/in, Inhaber/in
vehicle ['vi:əkl] — Fahrzeug
thorough(ly) ['θʌrə] — gründlich
wax [wæks] — Wachs
polish ['pɒlɪʃ] — Politur
as good as new [əz ˌgʊd əz 'nju:] — (so gut) wie neu
repair [rɪ'peə] — Reparatur
qualified ['kwɒlɪfaɪd] — ausgebildet, mit Abschluss
spray painter ['spreɪ peɪntə] — Lackierer/in
restoration [ˌrestə'reɪʃn] — Restaurierung, Aufarbeitung
to **repair** [rɪ'peə] — reparieren
torn [tɔ:n] — zerschlissen
seat [si:t] — Sitz
scratched [skrætʃt] — zerkratzt, verkratzt
paint [peɪnt] — Farbe, Lack
second-hand [ˌsekənd 'hænd] — gebraucht
van [væn] — Transporter, Kleinbus
garage ['gærɑ:ʒ] — Autowerkstatt
equipment [ɪ'kwɪpmənt] — Geräte, Ausstattung
to **store** [stɔ:] — lagern
to **design** [dɪ'zaɪn] — gestalten
to **print** [prɪnt] — drucken
market ['mɑ:kɪt] — Markt
enthusiasm [ɪn'θju:ziæzəm] — Begeisterung, Enthusiasmus
however [haʊ'evə] — allerdings, jedoch
homework ['həʊmwɜ:k] — Hausaufgaben
to **commit oneself to sth** [kə'mɪt tə] — sich auf etw einlassen, sich auf etw festlegen
basics ['beɪsɪks] — grundsätzliche Dinge
to **apply to sth** [ə'plaɪ tə] — für etw gelten
business start-up [ˌbɪznəs 'stɑ:t ʌp] — Unternehmensgründung
to **research** [rɪ'sɜ:tʃ] — untersuchen, recherchieren, erforschen
informal [ɪn'fɔ:ml] — informell, zwanglos, locker
research [rɪ'sɜ:tʃ] — Nachforschungen, Recherche
figure ['fɪgə] — Zahl
to **charge** [tʃɑ:dʒ] — *(Preis)* verlangen
area ['eəriə] — Gegend
expenses [ɪk'spensɪz] — Kosten, Auslagen
to **get started** [ˌget 'stɑ:tɪd] — loslegen
turnover ['tɜ:nəʊvə] — Umsatz *(UK)*
to **achieve** [ə'tʃi:v] — erzielen
in order to [ɪn 'ɔ:də tə] — um ... zu
to **separate** ['seprət] — trennen
fixed assets [ˌfɪkst 'æsets] — Sachanlagen, Sachwerte
to **last** [lɑ:st] — halten
supplies [sə'plaɪz] — Verbrauchsgüter
cleaning supplies ['kli:nɪŋ səplaɪz] — Reinigungsmittel
soap [səʊp] — Seife
fuel ['fju:əl] — Treibstoff
to **draw sth up** [ˌdrɔ: 'ʌp] — etw erstellen
business plan ['bɪznəs plæn] — Geschäftsplan
to **include** [ɪn'klu:d] — einbeziehen
to **seek** [si:k] — suchen
small business [ˌsmɔ:l 'bɪznəs] — Kleinbetrieb, Kleinunternehmen
advisor [əd'vaɪzə] — Berater/in
success [sək'ses] — Erfolg

page 27

advertisment [əd'vɜ:tɪsmənt] — Anzeige, Annonce
vintage car [ˌvɪntɪdʒ 'kɑ:] — Oldtimer
car hire ['kɑ: haɪə] — Autovermietung
chauffeur-driven ['ʃəʊfə drɪvn] — mit Chauffeur
wedding ['wedɪŋ] — Hochzeit
scratch [skrætʃ] — Kratzer
advertising ['ædvətaɪzɪŋ] — Werbung
market research [ˌmɑ:kɪt rɪ'sɜ:tʃ] — Marktforschung
to **perform** [pə'fɔ:m] — ausführen, durchführen
exchange [ɪks'tʃeɪndʒ] — Austausch, Tausch
goods [gʊdz] — Güter, Ware(n)
total ['təʊtl] — Gesamt-
value ['vælju:] — Wert
service ['sɜ:vɪs] — Dienstleistung
tool [tu:l] — Werkzeug
machine [mə'ʃi:n] — Maschine
product ['prɒdʌkt] — Produkt, Erzeugnis

page 28

vacuum cleaner ['vækjuəm kli:nə] — Staubsauger

page 29

computing [kəm'pju:tɪŋ] — Informatik
to **handle sth** ['hændl] — etw erledigen
to **require** [rɪ'kwaɪə] — erfordern, benötigen
to **handle sth** ['hændl] — mit etw umgehen, etw bewältigen
illegal [ɪ'li:gl] — illegal, verboten
package ['pækɪdʒ] — Paket
network ['netwɜ:k] — Netzwerk
to **get into trouble** [ˌget ɪntə 'trʌbl] — in Schwierigkeiten geraten, sich Ärger einhandeln
fee [fi:] — Gebühr
at all [ət 'ɔ:l] — überhaupt
adequate ['ædɪkwət] — angemessen
arrangements [ə'reɪndʒmənts] — Vorkehrungen, Maßnahmen
to **back sth up** [ˌbæk 'ʌp] — *(Daten)* sichern
data ['deɪtə] — Daten
to **put sb out of business** [ˌpʊt aʊt əf 'bɪznəs] — jdn in den Bankrott treiben
substitute ['sʌbstɪtju:t] — Ersatz(-)
to **increase** ['ɪŋkri:s] — erhöhen
to **reduce** [rɪ'dju:s] — senken, reduzieren
luckily ['lʌkɪli] — glücklicherweise
bill [bɪl] — Rechnung

page 30

litre ['li:tə] — Liter
can [kæn] — Dose
tube [tju:b] — Tube
to **give sb (a piece of) advice** [ˌgɪv əd'vaɪs] — jdm etw raten, jdm einen Ratschlag erteilen
delivery [dɪ'lɪvəri] — Lieferung
countable ['kaʊntəbl] — zählbar
uncountable [ˌʌn'kaʊntəbl] — unzählbar

UNIT F

page 31

original(ly) [ə'rɪdʒənl] — ursprünglich
accountancy [ə'kaʊntənsi] — Buchhaltung, Rechnungswesen
to **email** ['i:meɪl] — mailen
vintage clothes [ˌvɪntɪdʒ 'kləʊðz] — edle/klassische Second-Hand-Kleidung
charity shop ['tʃærəti ʃɒp] — *Laden einer Wohltätigkeitsorganisation*
car boot sale [ˌkɑ: 'bu:t seɪl] — Trödel, Flohmarkt
grandparents ['grænpeərənts] — Großeltern
fashion ['fæʃn] — Mode
to **advertise sth** ['ædvətaɪz] — etw anbieten
item ['aɪtəm] — Artikel
to **receive** [rɪ'si:v] — erhalten
profit ['prɒfɪt] — Gewinn
stock [stɒk] — Ware, Bestand
to **attach** [ə'tætʃ] — *(E-Mail:)* anhängen
spreadsheet ['spredʃi:t] — Tabellenkalkulationsdatei
to **go wrong** [ˌgəʊ 'rɒŋ] — einen Fehler machen
wish [wɪʃ] — Wunsch
to **wonder** ['wʌndə] — sich fragen
to **be delighted** [bi dɪ'laɪtɪd] — sich freuen
price [praɪs] — Preis
structure ['strʌktʃə] — Struktur
to **happen** ['hæpən] — passieren
supplier [sə'plaɪə] — Lieferant, Zulieferer
case [keɪs] — Fall
worth [wɜ:θ] — Wert
wide [waɪd] — groß, weit
marketplace ['mɑ:kɪtpleɪs] — Marktplatz
to **realize sth** ['rɪəlaɪz] — etw erkennen, wissen
solution [sə'lu:ʃn] — Lösung
sale [seɪl] — Verkauf
willing ['wɪlɪŋ] — bereit, willens
area ['eəriə] — Gebiet, Bereich, Feld
handmade [ˌhænd'meɪd] — handgemacht
jewellery ['dʒu:əlri] — Schmuck
military ['mɪlətri] — Militär(-)

page 32

summary ['sʌməri] — Zusammenfassung
for free [fə 'fri:] — umsonst
to **concern sb** [kən'sɜ:n] — jdm Sorgen machen
leather ['leðə] — Leder
trainers ['treɪnəz] — Turnschuhe
quality ['kwɒləti] — Qualität

page 33

in stock [ɪn 'stɒk] — vorrätig, auf Lager
to **fail** [feɪl] — (Unternehmen:) Pleite gehen
to **return sth** [rɪ'tɜ:n] — etw zurückgeben
factory ['fæktəri] — Fabrik

page 34

bank account ['bæŋk əkaʊnt] — Bankkonto, Girokonto
to **apply for sth** [ə'plaɪ fə] — etw beantragen
careers advisor [kə'rɪəz ədvaɪzə] — Berufsberater/in
to **close a business** [ˌkləʊz ə 'bɪznəs] — ein Geschäft aufgeben

page 35

mixed [mɪkst] — gemischt
keen [ki:n] — begeistert
gear [gɪə] — Ausrüstung
seller ['selə] — Verkäufer
ever since [ˌevə 'sɪns] — seitdem
helmet ['helmɪt] — Helm
refund ['ri:fʌnd] — (Kosten-)Erstattung
to **ban sb** [bæn] — jdn sperren
lesson ['lesn] — Lektion

MAIN COURSE

UNIT 1

page 36

commercial course [kəˌmɜːʃl ˈkɔːs]	kaufmännische Ausbildung
vocational training college *(BE)* [vəʊˌkeɪʃənl ˈtreɪnɪŋ kɒlɪdʒ]	Berufsschule, Berufskolleg, Gewerbliche Schule
library [ˈlaɪbrəri]	Bibliothek
horse racing [ˈhɔːs reɪsɪŋ]	Pferderennen
culture [ˈkʌltʃə]	Kultur
bookshop [ˈbʊkʃɒp]	Buchhandlung
parliament [ˈpɑːləmənt]	Parlament
member of parliament (MP) [ˌmembər əf ˈpɑːləmənt]	Parlamentsabgeord-nete/r
extraordinarily [ɪkˈstrɔːdnrəli]	außergewöhnlich
to register with sth [ˈredʒɪstə wɪð]	sich bei etw anmelden
project [ˈprɒdʒekt]	Projekt
youth centre [ˈjuːθ sentə]	Jugendzentrum
local [ˈləʊkl]	örtlich, ortsansässig, lokal
to **train sb** [treɪn]	jdn trainieren
speech bubble [ˈspiːtʃ bʌbl]	Sprechblase
capital [ˈkæpɪtl]	Hauptstadt

page 37

to set up a business [set ˌʌp ə ˈbɪznəs]	ein Unternehmen gründen
venture [ˈventʃə]	Vorhaben, Unternehmen, Wagnis, Gründung
expatriot [ˌeksˈpætriət]	*jd, der im Ausland lebt*
Briton [ˈbrɪtn]	Brite/Britin
to **qualify** [ˈkwɒlɪfaɪ]	einen/seinen/ihren Abschluss machen
diving [ˈdaɪvɪŋ]	Tauchen
diving instructor [ˈdaɪvŋ ɪnstrʌktə]	Tauchlehrer/in
the English Channel [ði ˌɪŋglɪʃ ˈtʃænl]	der Ärmelkanal
underwater [ˌʌndəˈwɔːtə]	unter Wasser, Unterwasser-
paradise [ˈpærədaɪs]	Paradies
delightful(ly) [dɪˈlaɪtfl]	herrlich
in a flash [ɪn ə ˈflæʃ]	im Nu
to **fall ill** [ˌfɔːl ˈɪl]	erkranken, krank werden
to **stand in for sb** [ˌstænd ˈɪn fə]	jdn vertreten, jds Platz einnehmen
rudimentary [ˌruːdɪˈmentri]	bruchstückhaft
to give sth a try [ˌgɪv ə ˈtraɪ]	etw ausprobieren
a roaring success [ə ˌrɔːrɪŋ səkˈses]	ein voller Erfolg
time flew [ˌtaɪm ˈfluː]	die Zeit verging wie im Flug
fisherman [ˈfɪʃəmən]	Fischer
to **lay idle** [ˌleɪ ˈaɪdl]	*(Boot:)* (ungenutzt) im Hafen liegen
unemployment [ˌʌnɪmˈplɔɪmənt]	Arbeitslosigkeit
teenage [ˈtiːneɪdʒ]	im Teenageralter
to paint sth up [ˌpeɪnt ˈʌp]	etw (neu) anmalen, streichen
paperwork [ˈpeɪpəwɜːk]	Formalitäten, Büroarbeit
to calculate [ˈkælkjuleɪt]	ausrechnen, berechnen, kalkulieren
business licence [ˈbɪznəs laɪsns]	Gewerbeschein, Gewerbeerlaubnis
premises [ˈpremɪsɪz]	Geschäftsräume
deposit [dɪˈpɒzɪt]	Kaution
to convert [kənˈvɜːt]	umbauen, umwandeln
to set sth up [ˌset ˈʌp]	etw einrichten
to advertise (sth) [ˈædvətaɪz]	(für etw) Werbung machen
enquiry [ɪnˈkwaɪəri]	Anfrage
to pour in [ˌpɔːr ˈɪn]	*(Aufträge etc.)* (in großer Zahl) eingehen
desperately [ˈdespərətli]	verzweifelt, unbedingt
in time [ɪn ˈtaɪm]	rechtzeitig
to go bankrupt [ˌgəʊ ˈbæŋkrʌpt]	Pleite gehen
to refuse [rɪˈfjuːz]	sich weigern, ablehnen
loan [ləʊn]	Darlehen, Kredit
cash flow [ˈkæʃ fləʊ]	Einnahmen, Geldzufluss
desperate [ˈdespərət]	verzweifelt
to lend sb sth [lend]	jdm etw leihen
at last [ət ˈlɑːst]	endlich
to take off [ˌteɪk ˈɒf]	abheben, losgehen
pretty [ˈprɪti]	ziemlich
weak [wiːk]	schwach, schlecht

page 38

to belong to sb [bɪˈlɒŋ tə]	jdm gehören
permission [pəˈmɪʃn]	Erlaubnis, Genehmigung
sum [sʌm]	Summe, Betrag
to run sth [rʌn]	etw führen, etw betreiben
background [ˈbækgraʊnd]	Herkunft
bar chart [ˈbɑː tʃɑːt]	Balkendiagramm, Säulendiagramm
pie chart [ˈpaɪ tʃɑːt]	Tortendiagramm
to present [prɪˈzent]	vorstellen, präsentieren

page 39

background [ˈbækgraʊnd]	Hintergrund
briefing [ˈbriːfɪŋ]	Informationen
emigration [ˌemɪˈgreɪʃn]	Auswanderung
immigration [ˌɪmɪˈgreɪʃn]	Einwanderung
migration [maɪˈgreɪʃn]	Migration
citizen [ˈsɪtɪzn]	Bürger/in
member state [ˈmembə steɪt]	Mitgliedsstaat
century [ˈsentʃəri]	Jahrhundert
to settle down [ˌsetl ˈdaʊn]	sich niederlassen
in general [ɪn ˈdʒenrəl]	im Allgemeinen
move [muːv]	Bewegung
in addition [ɪn əˈdɪʃn]	außerdem
population [ˌpɒpjuˈleɪʃn]	Bevölkerung
to shrink [ʃrɪŋk]	schrumpfen
current [ˈkʌrənt]	aktuell
increase [ˈɪŋkriːs]	Zunahme, Steigerung
decrease [ˈdiːkriːs]	Abnahme, Rückgang
to estimate [ˈestɪmeɪt]	schätzen
to emigrate [ˈemɪgreɪt]	auswandern
to immigrate [ˈɪmɪgreɪt]	einwandern

to **rise (by)** [raɪz]	steigen, ansteigen (um)
labour ['leɪbə]	Arbeit, Arbeitskraft
labour market ['leɪbə mɑ:kɪt]	Arbeitsmarkt
diagram ['daɪəgræm]	Grafik, Diagramm
available [ə'veɪləbl]	verfügbar, erhältlich
wage [weɪdʒ]	Lohn, Gehalt
level ['levl]	Niveau
section ['sekʃn]	Abschnitt

page 40

to **turn to** ['tɜ:n tə]	*(Seite)* aufschlagen
sensible ['sensəbl]	vernünftig, *(Schuhe:)* bequem, robust
trousers ['traʊzəz]	Hose
blouse [blauz]	Bluse
item of clothing [ˌaɪtəm əf 'kləʊðɪŋ]	Kleidungsstück
fire exit ['faɪər eksɪt]	Notausgang
fire evacuation point [ˌfaɪər ɪvækju'eɪʃn pɔɪnt]	Sammestelle/-punkt bei Feueralarm
still room ['stɪl ru:m]	Teeküche
cutlery ['kʌtləri]	Besteck
working hours [ˌwɜ:kɪŋ 'aʊəz]	Arbeitszeiten
to **hesitate** ['hezɪteɪt]	zögern
Yours sincerely [jɔ:z sɪn'sɪəli]	Mit freundlichen Grüßen
Human Resources (HR) [ˌhju:mən rɪ'sɔ:sɪz]	Personalabteilung
Human Resources Manager [ˌhju:mən rɪ'sɔ:sɪz mænɪdʒə]	Personalleiter/in
shift [ʃɪft]	Schicht
early shift ['ɜ:li ʃɪft]	Frühschicht
day shift ['deɪ ʃɪft]	Tagschicht
late shift ['leɪt ʃɪft]	Spätschicht
from abroad [frəm ə'brɔ:d]	aus dem Ausland
fire alarm ['faɪər əlɑ:m]	Feueralarm
car park ['kɑ: pɑ:k]	Parkplatz
to **be missing** [bi 'mɪsɪŋ]	fehlen
health and safety [ˌhelθ ənd 'seɪfti]	Arbeitsschutz
regulations [ˌregju'leɪʃnz]	Vorschriften, Bestimmungen
clearly ['klɪəli]	deutlich
to **mark** [mɑ:k]	kennzeichnen
to **push** [pʊʃ]	stoßen, drücken
bar [bɑ:]	Stange, Hebel
dining room ['daɪnɪŋ ru:m]	Speisesaal
to **vary** ['veəri]	variieren, unterschiedlich sein
to **get sb down for sth** [ˌget 'daʊn fə]	jdn für etw vorsehen
to **imagine sth** [ɪ'mædʒɪn]	sich etw vorstellen
to **apply for sth** [ə'plaɪ fə]	sich für/auf etw bewerben
(job) application [ˌæplɪ'keɪʃn]	Bewerbung
cover letter ['kʌvə letə]	Anschreiben, Begleitschreiben
to **advertise a job** [ˌædvətaɪz ə 'dʒɒb]	eine Stelle ausschreiben
preference ['prefrəns]	Vorliebe
volunteer [ˌvɒlən'tɪə]	Freiwillige/r, ehrenamtlich Tätige/r
hotel maid [həʊ'tel meɪd]	Zimmermädchen
room attendant ['ru:m ətendənt]	Raumpfleger/in
worker ['wɜ:kə]	Arbeiter/in

page 41

society [sə'saɪəti]	Gesellschaft
virgin ['vɜ:dʒɪn]	Jungfrau
group [gru:p]	Konzern
inventor [ɪn'ventə]	Erfinder
brand [brænd]	Marke
empire ['empaɪə]	Reich
billion ['bɪliən]	Milliarde
to **include** [ɪn'klu:d]	umfassen
approximately [ə'prɒksɪmətli]	ungefähr, zirka
to **plant** [plɑ:nt]	pflanzen, anpflanzen
technically speaking ['teknɪkli spi:kɪŋ]	genau genommen, fachsprachlich
sole trader [ˌsəʊl 'treɪdə]	Einzelunternehmer/in
to **share** [ʃeə]	teilen
unlimited [ʌn'lɪmɪtɪd]	unbegrenzt, unbeschränkt
liability [ˌlaɪə'bɪləti]	Haftung
to **bear sth** [beər]	etw tragen
rabbit ['ræbɪt]	Kaninchen
to **fail** [feɪl]	Pleite gehen, es nicht schaffen, scheitern
mail order [ˌmeɪl 'ɔ:də]	Versandhandel
major ['meɪdʒə]	groß, bedeutend
record label ['rekɔ:d leɪbl]	Plattenfirma
to **sign sb up** [ˌsaɪn 'ʌp]	jdn unter Vertrag nehmen
unknown [ˌʌn'nəʊn]	unbekannt
private limited company (Ltd) *(UK)* [ˌpraɪvət ˌlɪmɪtɪd 'kʌmpəni]	Gesellschaft mit beschränkter Haftung (GmbH)
limited ['lɪmɪtɪd]	begrenzt, beschränkt
responsibility [rɪˌspɒnsə'bɪləti]	Verantwortung, Haftung
investment [ɪn'vestmənt]	Einlage
in contrast [ɪn 'kɒntrɑ:st]	im Gegensatz (dazu)
electrician [ɪˌlek'trɪʃn]	Elektriker/in
to **burn down** [ˌbɜ:n 'daʊn]	abbrennen
damage ['dæmɪdʒ]	Schaden
property ['prɒpəti]	Eigentum
to **fear** [fɪə]	fürchten, befürchten
amount [ə'maʊnt]	Menge, Betrag
cash [kæʃ]	Geld, Bargeld, liquide Mittel
to **fund** [fʌnd]	finanzieren
to **form** [fɔ:m]	bilden
public limited company (plc) *(UK)* [ˌpʌblɪk ˌlɪmɪtɪd 'kʌmpəni]	Aktiengesellschaft (AG)
share [ʃeə]	Aktie
stock exchange ['stɒk ɪkstʃeɪndʒ]	Börse
chairman ['tʃeəmən]	Vorsitzende/r
shareholder ['ʃeəhəʊldə]	Aktionär/in

page 42

to **be prepared to do sth** [bi prɪ'peəd tə]	bereit sein, etw zu tun
to **invest** [ɪn'vest]	investieren
to **finance** ['faɪnæns]	finanzieren
head [hed]	Leiter/in, Chef/in
loss [lɒs]	Verlust
to **take a decision** [,teɪk dɪ'sɪʒn]	eine Entscheidung fällen
limited liability company (LLC) *(US)* [,lɪmɪtɪd ,laɪə'bɪləti kʌmpəni]	Gesellschaft mit beschränkter Haftung (GmbH)
circle ['sɜːkl]	Kreis
corporation (Corp./Inc.) *(US)* [,kɔːpə'reɪʃn]	Aktiengesellschaft (AG)
director [də'rektə]	Vorstandsmitglied
proprietary limited company (Pty Ltd) *(Aus, NZ)* [prə,praɪətri ,lɪmɪtɪd 'kʌmpəni]	Gesellschaft mit beschränkter Haftung (GmbH)

page 43

bankruptcy ['bæŋkrʌpsi]	Konkurs, Pleite
serious ['sɪəriəs]	ernstzunehmend
solar power [,səʊlə 'paʊə]	Solarenergie, Solarstrom
trekking ['trekɪŋ]	Wandern
mountaineering [,maʊntə'nɪərɪŋ]	Bergsteigen
politics ['pɒlətɪks]	Politik
to **generate** ['dʒenəreɪt]	erzeugen
environmentally friendly [ɪn,vaɪrən,mentəli 'frendli]	umweltfreundlich
distant ['dɪstənt]	entfernt, fern, entlegen
close [kləʊs]	eng
to **import** [ɪm'pɔːt]	importieren, einführen
dress [dres]	Kleid
to **cut off the phone** [kʌt ,ɒf ðə 'fəʊn]	das Telefon abstellen

page 44

live-in job [,lɪv 'ɪn dʒɒb]	*Arbeitsstelle mit Kost und Logis*
to **be about to do sth** [bi ə'baʊt tə]	im Begriff sein, etw zu tun; etw tun wollen/werden
waiting ['weɪtɪŋ]	Kellnern
reception [rɪ'sepʃn]	Rezeption, Empfang
housekeeping ['haʊskiːpɪŋ]	Hauswirtschaft
seasonal ['siːzənl]	Saison-
employment [ɪm'plɔɪmənt]	Anstellung, Beschäftigung, Arbeit
to **last** [lɑːst]	dauern
to **ring** [rɪŋ]	anrufen
to **backpack** ['bækpæk]	mit dem Rucksack reisen
chefing ['ʃefɪŋ]	Tätigkeiten als Koch/Köchin
position [pə'zɪʃn]	Posten, Stellung, Stelle
smart [smɑːt]	*(Kleidung:)* elegant, schick
skirt [skɜːt]	Rock
face-to-face [,feɪs tə 'feɪs]	persönlich
permanent ['pɜːmənənt]	*(Stelle:)* unbefristet
heel [hiːl]	*(Schuh:)* Absatz
to **role-play** ['rəʊl pleɪ]	mit verteilten Rollen spielen
to **take it in turns** [,teɪk ɪt ɪn 'tɜːnz]	sich abwechseln
reliable [rɪ'laɪəbl]	zuverlässig
helpful ['helpfl]	hilfsbereit
sociable ['səʊʃəbl]	gesellig
board game ['bɔːd geɪm]	Brettspiel
theatre ['θɪətə]	Theater
strength [streŋθ]	Stärke
weakness ['wiːknəs]	Schwäche
excitement [ɪk'saɪtmənt]	Aufregung, Spannung
to **get married** [,get 'mærid]	heiraten
pay [peɪ]	Bezahlung, Lohn
included [ɪn'kluːdɪd]	inbegriffen, enthalten

page 45

lately ['leɪtli]	in letzter Zeit
to **disturb** [dɪ'stɜːb]	stören
instruction [ɪn'strʌkʃn]	Anweisung, Anleitung
to **greet** [griːt]	begrüßen
to **write sth out** [,raɪt 'aʊt]	etw ausstellen
receipt [rɪ'siːt]	Quittung, Beleg
mainly ['meɪnli]	hauptsächlich
concert ['kɒnsət]	Konzert
exhibition [,eksɪ'bɪʃn]	Ausstellung
seat [siːt]	Platz
opera ['ɒprə]	Oper
tip [tɪp]	Trinkgeld
supervisor ['suːpəvaɪzə]	Vorgesetzte/r
for ages [fər 'eɪdʒɪz]	eine Ewigkeit
to **mention** ['menʃn]	erwähnen
to **go fishing** [,gəʊ 'fɪʃɪŋ]	angeln/fischen gehen
to **sail out to sea** [seɪl ,aʊt tə 'siː]	aufs Meer hinausfahren
to **laze about** [,leɪz ə'baʊt]	faulenzen, herumfaulenzen
to **borrow sth from sb** ['bɒrəʊ]	sich etw von jdm leihen

UNIT 2

page 46

to **label** ['leɪbl]	beschriften, etikettieren
caption ['kæpʃn]	Bildunterschrift
punctual(ly) ['pʌŋktʃuəl]	pünktlich
to **bow** [baʊ]	sich verbeugen
to **exchange** [ɪks'tʃeɪndʒ]	austauschen
to **shake hands** [,ʃeɪk 'hændz]	sich die Hand geben, die Hände schütteln
to **queue** [kjuː]	sich anstellen, anstehen
to **press** [pres]	drücken
to **demonstrate** ['demənstreɪt]	vorführen, zeigen

page 47

friendliness ['frendlinəs]	Freundlichkeit
unfriendliness [ʌn'frendlinəs]	Unfreundlichkeit
helpfulness ['helpflnəs]	Hilfsbereitschaft
politeness [pə'laɪtnəs]	Höflichkeit
custom ['kʌstəm]	Brauch, Sitte
topic ['tɒpɪk]	Thema

meanwhile ['mi:nwaɪl]	in der Zwischenzeit
timetable ['taɪmteɪbl]	Fahrplan
crowded ['kraʊdɪd]	überfüllt, vollgestopft
whenever [wen'evə]	immer, wenn; jedesmal, wenn
wherever [weər'evə]	überall, wo
passenger ['pæsɪndʒə]	Fahrgast, Passagier
strict [strɪkt]	streng
division [dɪ'vɪʒn]	Trennung
leisure ['leʒə]	Freizeit
to **clock in/out** [ˌklɒk 'ɪn/'aʊt]	die Uhr stechen
to **carry on** [ˌkæri 'ɒn]	weitermachen
landline ['lændlaɪn]	Festnetztelefon
to **ring** [rɪŋ]	klingeln, läuten
export sales director [ˌekspɔ:t 'seɪlz dərektə]	Vertriebsleiter/in Export
to **deliver** [dɪ'lɪvə]	liefern
host [həʊst]	Gastgeber
guest of honour [ˌgest əv 'ɒnə]	Ehrengast
furthest from sth ['fɜ:ðɪst frəm]	am weitesten von etw entfernt
at the top table [ət ðə ˌtɒp 'teɪbl]	am Kopfende des Tisches
importance [ɪm'pɔ:tns]	Bedeutung, Wichtigkeit
to **propose a toast** [prəˌpəʊz ə 'təʊst]	einen Toast ausbringen
to **raise sth** [reɪz]	etw erheben, hochheben

page 48

public transport [ˌpʌblɪk 'trænspɔ:t]	öffentliche Verkehrsmittel
reason ['ri:zn]	Motiv, Grund, Beweggrund
machine [mə'ʃi:n]	Gerät, Maschine
happiness ['hæpinəs]	Glück, Zufriedenheit
step [step]	Schritt
questionnaire [ˌkwestʃə'neə]	Fragebogen
to **compare** [kəm'peə]	vergleichen
to **prepare sth** [prɪ'peə]	etw erstellen
punctuality [ˌpʌŋktʃu'æləti]	Pünktlichkeit
efficiency [ɪ'fɪʃnsi]	Effizienz
to **do overtime** [ˌdu: 'əʊvətaɪm]	Überstunden machen
straight [streɪt]	sofort, gleich
to **meet socially** [ˌmi:t 'səʊʃəli]	sich privat treffen
social event [ˌsəʊʃl ɪ'vent]	geselliges Treffen
to **disagree with sb** [ˌdɪsə'gri: wɪð]	anderer Meinung als jd sein, jdm nicht zustimmen
public(ly) ['pʌblɪk]	öffentlich

page 49

on one's own [ɒn wʌnz 'əʊn]	allein
fixed [fɪkst]	fest
pleasure ['pleʒə]	Vergnügen
separate ['seprət]	getrennt
to **combine** [kəm'baɪn]	verbinden, kombinieren
expert ['ekspɜ:t]	Fachmann, Experte/-in
concerned [kən'sɜ:nd]	betroffen, beteiligt
conflict ['kɒnflɪkt]	Streit(igkeiten), Konflikt
on a regular basis [ɒn ə ˌregjələ 'beɪsɪs]	regelmäßig
score [skɔ:]	Ergebnis, Punkte(stand)
top-down system [ˌtɒp 'daʊn sɪtəm]	hierarchisches System
to **take responsibility** [ˌteɪk rɪˌspɒnsə'bɪləti]	Verantwortung übernehmen/tragen
to **balance** ['bæləns]	ausgleichen, ins Gleichgewicht bringen
evenly ['i:vnli]	ausgeglichen, gleichmäßig
to **identify with sb/sth** [aɪ'dentɪfaɪ wɪð]	sich mit jdm/etw identifizieren
bottom-up [ˌbɒtəm 'ʌp]	von unten nach oben
human ['hju:mən]	menschlich
relationship [rɪ'leɪʃnʃɪp]	Beziehung

page 50

to **found** [faʊnd]	gründen
income ['ɪnkʌm]	Einkommen
to **dislike** [dɪs'laɪk]	nicht mögen
search engine ['sɜ:tʃ endʒɪn]	Suchmaschine
nowadays ['naʊədeɪz]	heutzutage
garage ['gærɑ:ʒ]	Garage
relaxed [rɪ'lækst]	locker
gym [dʒɪm]	Fitnessklub
to **mind** [maɪnd]	etwas dagegen haben
to **be happy to do sth** [bi 'hæpi tə]	etw gern tun
manufacturer [ˌmænju'fæktʃərə]	Hersteller
provider [prə'vaɪdə]	Anbieter
to **do research** [du: rɪ'sɜ:tʃ]	recherchieren, Nachforschungen anstellen
Chief Executive Officer (CEO) [ˌtʃi:f ɪg'zekjətɪv ɒfɪsə]	Vorstandsvorsitzende/r
president ['prezɪdənt]	Präsident/in
location [ləʊ'keɪʃn]	Standort
profit margin ['prɒfɪt mɑ:dʒɪn]	Gewinnspanne
to **be located in ...** [bi ləʊ'keɪtɪd ɪn]	in ... ansässig sein, seinen/ihren Sitz in ... haben
headquarters [ˌhed'kwɔ:təz]	Zentrale
head office [ˌhed 'ɒfɪs]	Zentrale
parent company [ˌpeərənt 'kʌmpəni]	Muttergesellschaft
subsidiary [səb'sɪdiəri]	Tochtergesellschaft
agent ['eɪdʒənt]	Vertreter, Vertretung
pure [pjʊə]	rein
wool [wʊl]	Wolle
steel [sti:l]	Stahl
to **export** [ɪk'spɔ:t]	exportieren, ausführen

page 51

household ['haʊshəʊld]	Haushalt, Haushalts-
appliance [ə'plaɪəns]	Gerät, Haushaltsgerät
to **break down** [ˌbreɪk 'daʊn]	kaputtgehen
washing machine ['wɒʃɪŋ məʃi:n]	Waschmaschine
cream [kri:m]	Rahm

unwittingly [ʌn'wɪtɪŋli] ohne es zu ahnen
social ['səʊʃl] gesellschaftlich
back-breaking ['bæk breɪkɪŋ] äußerst anstrengend
time-consuming ['taɪm kənsju:mɪŋ] zeitraubend
to **heat** [hi:t] erhitzen
goal [gəʊl] Ziel
to **liberate** ['lɪbəreɪt] befreien
pill [pɪl] Pille
right to work [ˌraɪt tə 'wɜ:k] Recht auf Arbeit
to **diversify** [daɪ'vɜ:sɪfaɪ] verbreitern, auffächern, diversifizieren
range (of products) [reɪndʒ] Sortiment, Angebot, Palette
to **manufacture** [ˌmænju'fæktʃə] herstellen, fertigen
core business ['kɔ: bɪznəs] Kerngeschäft
labour-saving ['leɪbə seɪvɪŋ] arbeitssparend
device [dɪ'vaɪs] Gerät, Apparat
insurance [ɪn'ʃʊərəns] Versicherung
medical insurance [ˌmedɪkl ɪn'ʃʊərəns] Krankenversicherung
pension scheme ['penʃn ski:m] betriebliche Altersversorgung, Rentenversicherung
housing ['haʊzɪŋ] Wohnungen, Wohnraum, Unterkunft
contented [kən'tentɪd] zufrieden
loyal ['lɔɪəl] treu, loyal
life expectancy ['laɪf ɪkspektənsi] Lebenserwartung
limited partnership [ˌlɪmɪtɪd 'pɑ:tnəʃɪp] Kommanditgesellschaft (KG)
shareholder ['ʃeəhəʊldə] Teilhaber/in, Gesellschafter/in
founder ['faʊndə] Gründer/in
publicly owned [ˌpʌblɪkli 'əʊnd] börsennotiert
pressure ['preʃə] Druck
to **increase** [ɪn'kri:s] steigern, erhöhen
quarter ['kwɔ:tə] Quartal
to **force** [fɔ:s] zwingen
to **buy sth up** [ˌbaɪ 'ʌp] etw aufkaufen
competitor [kəm'petɪtə] Konkurrent/in
to **expand** [ɪk'spænd] ausweiten
production facilities [prə'dʌkʃn fəsɪlətiz] Produktionsstätte(n), Werk(e)
unlike [ˌʌn'laɪk] anders als, im Gegensatz zu
to **minimize** ['mɪnɪmaɪz] auf ein Minimum beschränken, minimieren
outsourcing ['aʊtsɔ:sɪŋ] Auslagern
low-wage country [ˌləʊ weɪdʒ 'kʌntri] Niedriglohnland
plant [plɑ:nt] Werk, Betrieb, Anlage
control [kən'trəʊl] Steuerung
sales [seɪlz] Verkaufsumsatz

page 52

heading ['hedɪŋ] Überschrift
first-rate [ˌfɜ:st 'reɪt] erstklassig
condition [kən'dɪʃn] Bedingung
long-term [ˌlɒŋ 'tɜ:m] langfristig
chart [tʃɑ:t] Tabelle
to **be based on sth** [bi 'beɪst ɒn] auf etw basieren
to **produce** [prə'dju:s] produzieren, herstellen, fertigen
to **employ** [ɪm'plɔɪ] beschäftigen, anstellen
in capitals [ɪn 'kæpɪtls] in Großbuchstaben
close [kləʊs] nahe, in der Nähe

page 53

request [rɪ'kwest] Anfrage, Wunsch, Bitte
dealer ['di:lə] Händler
adapter [ə'dæptə] Passstück, Adapter
connection [kə'nekʃn] Verbindung, Anschluss
supply [sə'plaɪ] *(Strom, Wasser etc.:)* Anschluss, Versorgung
installation guide [ˌɪnstə'leɪʃn gaɪd] Aufbauanleitung
excerpt ['eksɜ:pt] Auszug, Ausschnitt
to **connect** [kə'nekt] anschließen, verbinden
hose [həʊz] Schlauch
water intake hose ['wɔ:tər ɪnteɪk həʊz] Wasserzulaufschlauch
to **attach** [ə'tætʃ] anschließen, anbringen
valve [vælv] Ventil
hardware store ['hɑ:dweə stɔ:] Eisenwarenhandlung, Baumarkt
source [sɔ:s] Quelle
to **function** ['fʌŋkʃn] funktionieren
out of stock [ˌaʊt əf 'stɒk] nicht lieferbar, nicht vorrätig
design [dɪ'zaɪn] Konstruktion
to **supply** [sə'plaɪ] liefern, anbieten
to **include** [ɪn'klu:d] beifügen
proprietor [prə'praɪətə] Inhaber/in
All rights reserved [ːɔ:l ˌraɪts rɪ'zɜ:vd] Alle Rechte vorbehalten.

page 54

to **refer to sth** [rɪ'fɜ: tə] in etw nachschlagen
accessories [ək'sesəriz] Zubehör
urgent ['ɜ:dʒənt] dringend, eilig
matter ['mætə] Angelegenheit, Sache
to **structure** ['strʌktʃə] strukturieren
apology [ə'pɒlədʒi] Entschuldigung
explanation [ˌeksplə'neɪʃn] Erläuterung, Erklärung
polite [pə'laɪt] höflich
ending ['endɪŋ] Schluss, Ende
to **take turns** [ˌteɪk 'tɜ:nz] sich abwechseln
anyway ['eniweɪ] wie dem auch sei
suggestion [sə'dʒestʃən] Vorschlag
at short notice [ət ˌʃɔ:t 'nəʊtɪs] kurzfristig
to **consider sth** [kən'sɪdə] etw berücksichtigen
to **get to know sb** [ˌget tə 'nəʊ] jdn kennenlernen
convenient [kən'vi:niənt] passend, praktisch, angenehm
to **solve** [sɒlv] lösen
query ['kwɪəri] Frage

page 55

building contractor ['bɪldɪŋ kəntræktə]	Bauunternehmer/in, Bauunternehmen
mechanic [mɪ'kænɪk]	Mechaniker/in
cashier [kæ'ʃɪə]	Kassierer/in
hairdresser ['heədresə]	Friseur/in
radio station ['reɪdiəʊ steɪʃn]	Radiosender
medium-sized ['mi:diəm saɪzd]	mittelgroß, mittelständisch
bricklayer ['brɪkleɪə]	Maurer/in
block of flats [ˌblɒk əv 'flæts]	Mietshaus, Wohnblock
extension [ɪk'stenʃn]	Anbau
far afield [ˌfɑ:r ə'fi:ld]	weit weg
surrounding area [səˌraʊndɪŋ 'eərɪə]	Umgebung
noisy ['nɔɪzi]	laut
mask [mɑ:sk]	Maske
hygienic [haɪ'dʒi:nɪk]	hygienisch
altogether [ˌɔ:ltə'geðə]	insgesamt
shape [ʃeɪp]	Form
fresh [freʃ]	frisch
frozen foods [ˌfrəʊzn 'fu:dz]	Tiefkühlkost
meat [mi:t]	Fleisch
chicken ['tʃɪkɪn]	Huhn
fish fingers [ˌfɪʃ 'fɪŋgəz]	Fischstäbchen
to **supply sb** [sə'plaɪ]	jdn beliefern
van [væn]	Lieferwagen
canteen [kæn'ti:n]	Kantine
hospital ['hɒspɪtl]	Krankenhaus
distance ['dɪstəns]	Entfernung
regional ['ri:dʒənl]	regional
to **be pleased to do sth** [bi 'pli:zd tə]	etw gern tun
specific [spə'sɪfɪk]	speziell, spezifisch
branch [brɑ:ntʃ]	Filiale, Niederlassung
credit ['kredɪt]	Kredit
investment [ɪn'vestmənt]	Geldanlage
equally ['i:kwəli]	gleichermaßen
deal [di:l]	Geschäft
sky [skaɪ]	Himmel
limit ['lɪmɪt]	Grenze
The sky's the limit [:ðe ˌskaɪz ðe 'lɪmɪt]	Nach oben sind keine Grenzen gesetzt.
corporate ['kɔ:pərət]	Unternehmens-, Geschäfts-
government ['gʌvənmənt]	Regierung, öffentliche Verwaltung
motorway ['məʊtəweɪ]	Autobahn
to **spare** [speə]	erübrigen

page 56

to **link** [lɪŋk]	verbinden
clause [klɔ:z]	Nebensatz, Satzteil
to **invent** [ɪn'vent]	erfinden
tiring ['taɪərɪŋ]	anstrengend
to **appear** [ə'pɪə]	auftauchen, erscheinen
demand [dɪ'mɑ:nd]	Nachfrage
to **provide** [prə'vaɪd]	zur Verfügung stellen, anbieten
health insurance ['helθ ɪnʃʊərəns]	Krankenversicherung
social package [ˌsəʊʃl 'pækɪdʒ]	Sozialleistungen
facilities [fə'sɪlətiz]	Anlage(n)
to **cut down on sth** [ˌkʌt 'daʊn ɒn]	etw kürzen, einsparen
concern [kən'sɜ:n]	Konzern
talks [tɔ:ks]	Gespräche, Verhandlungen
fear [fɪə]	Angst
to **disappear** [ˌdɪsə'pɪə]	verschwinden
easy-going [ˌi:zi 'gəʊɪŋ]	angenehm, locker
sales director ['seɪlz dərektə]	Verkaufsleiter/in
to **suffer from sth** ['sʌfə frəm]	an etw leiden
illness ['ɪlnəs]	Krankheit
to **recover** [rɪ'kʌvə]	sich erholen
to **go public** [ˌgəʊ 'pʌblɪk]	an die Börse gehen
steadily ['stedɪli]	stetig, kontinuierlich

UNIT 3

page 57

to **recognize** ['rekəgnaɪz]	erkennen, wiedererkennen
good value for money [gʊd ˌvælju: fə 'mʌni]	preiswert
influence ['ɪnfluəns]	Einfluss
taste [teɪst]	Geschmack
to **care about sb/sth** ['keər əbaʊt]	sich um jdn/etw kümmern, am Herzen liegen
environment [ɪn'vaɪrənmənt]	Umwelt
to **associate** [ə'səʊʃiət]	verbinden, assoziieren
to **brainwash sb** ['breɪnwɒʃ]	jdn einer Gehirnwäsche unterziehen
honest ['ɒnɪst]	ehrlich
athletics [æθ'letɪks]	Sport, Leichtathletik
athlete ['æθli:t]	Sportler/in
exception [ɪk'sepʃn]	Ausnahme
toothpaste ['tu:θpeɪst]	Zahncreme
victim ['vɪktɪm]	Opfer
to **admit** [əd'mɪt]	zugeben
Shame on you [:'ʃeɪm ɒn ju:]	Schäm dich!
awareness [ə'weənəs]	Bewusstsein
glasses ['glɑ:sɪz]	Brille
stereo system ['steriəʊ sɪstəm]	Stereoanlage
survey ['sɜ:veɪ]	Umfrage
item ['aɪtəm]	Artikel, Gegenstand
to **survey sb** ['sɜ:veɪ]	jdn befragen

page 58

duchess ['dʌtʃəs]	Herzogin
grocery store ['grəʊsəri stɔ:]	Lebensmittelgeschäft
to **picture** ['pɪktʃə]	abbilden
responsible [rɪ'spɒnsəbl]	verantwortlich, zuständig
investigation [ɪnˌvestɪ'geɪʃn]	Forschung, Ermittlung(en)
process ['prəʊses]	Verfahren, Ablauf, Prozess
strategy ['strætədʒi]	Strategie
to **promote sth** [prə'məʊt]	etw bewerben

to **distribute** [dɪ'strɪbju:t]	vertreiben
to **set a price** [ˌset ə 'praɪs]	einen Preis festlegen/ festsetzen
product launch ['prɒdʌkt lɔ:ntʃ]	Produkteinführung
Product Development (PD) [ˌprɒdʌkt dɪ'veləpmənt]	Produktentwicklung
Research and Development (R&D) [rɪˌsɜ:tʃ ən dɪ'veləpmənt]	Forschung(s-) und Entwicklung(s-abteilung)
shaped [ʃeɪpt]	geformt, Form-
product brief ['prɒdʌkt bri:f]	Produktbeschreibung
packaging ['pækɪdʒɪŋ]	Verpackung
novelty ['nɒvlti]	Neuheit
excited about sth [ɪk'saɪtɪd əbaʊt]	von etw begeistert
to **schedule** ['ʃedju:l]	*(Termin)* ansetzen
schedule ['ʃedju:l]	Terminkalender
excuse [ɪk'skju:s]	Ausrede
to **familiarize oneself with sth** [fə'mɪliəraɪz wʌnself wɪð]	sich mit etw vertraut machen
target group ['tɑ:gɪt gru:p]	Zielgruppe
to **define** [dɪ'faɪn]	definieren, festlegen
to **carry sth out** [ˌkæri 'aʊt]	etw durchführen
to **determine** [dɪ'tɜ:mɪn]	ermitteln, bestimmen
to **market** ['mɑ:kɪt]	vermarkten
share [ʃeə]	Anteil
to **be conceived for sb** [bi kən'si:vd fə]	für jdn gedacht sein
concept ['kɒnsept]	Idee, Konzept
Unique Selling Point/ Proposition (USP) [juˌni:k 'selɪŋ pɔɪnt/ prɒpəzɪʃn]	Alleinstellungsmerkmal
aspect ['æspekt]	Aspekt, Seite
to **ship** [ʃɪp]	versenden
to **display** [dɪ'spleɪ]	ausstellen, präsentieren
preparation [ˌprepə'reɪʃn]	Zubereitung
standpoint ['stændpɔɪnt]	Standpunkt

page 59

crazy ['kreɪzi]	verrückt
heart [hɑ:t]	Herz
shamrock ['ʃæmrɒk]	Kleeblatt
star [stɑ:]	Stern
sex [seks]	Geschlecht
female ['fi:meɪl]	weiblich, Frau
male [meɪl]	männlich, Mann
education [ˌedʒu'keɪʃn]	Schulbildung
secondary school ['sekəndri sku:l]	weiterführende Schule, Hauptschule
habit ['hæbɪt]	Gewohnheit
wrap [ræp]	Folie
sticker ['stɪkə]	Aufkleber
label ['leɪbl]	Etikett
purpose ['pɜ:pəs]	Zweck
question mark ['kwestʃən mɑ:k]	Fragezeichen
to **summarize** ['sʌməraɪz]	zusammenfassen
to **figure out** [ˌfɪgər 'aʊt]	herausfinden
to **come up with sth** [ˌkʌm 'ʌp wɪð]	sich etw einfallen lassen, sich etw ausdenken
to **brainstorm** ['breɪnstɔ:m]	Ideen sammeln
pumpkin ['pʌmpkɪn]	Kürbis
primarily [praɪ'merəli]	hauptsächlich, vorrangig
to **double** ['dʌbl]	sich verdoppeln
realistic [ˌri:ə'lɪstɪk]	realistisch
sample ['sɑ:mpl]	Muster, Probe
to **bake** [beɪk]	backen
oven ['ʌvn]	Ofen, Herd
consumer [kən'sju:mə]	Verbraucher/in
stem [stem]	Stengel, Stiel
to **burn** [bɜ:n]	anbrennen
bear [beə]	Bär
to **turn out great** [ˌtɜ:n aʊt 'greɪt]	sehr gut gelingen
upright ['ʌpraɪt]	aufrecht
square [skweə]	quadratisch
uniform ['ju:nɪfɔ:m]	einheitlich, Einheits-

page 60

to **confirm** [kən'fɜ:m]	bestätigen
to **congratulate sb on sth** [kən'grætʃuleɪt]	jdn für etw beglückwünschen
productive [prə'dʌktɪv]	produktiv
to **glow** [gləʊ]	leuchten
wallpaper ['wɔ:lpeɪpə]	Tapete
security service [sɪ'kjʊərəti sɜ:vɪs]	Wachdienst
to **light up** [ˌlaɪt 'ʌp]	aufleuchten
pricing ['praɪsɪŋ]	Preisgestaltung

page 61

billboard ['bɪlbɔ:d]	Reklametafel, Plakatwand
brochure ['brəʊʃə]	Prospekt
full-page [ˌfʊl 'peɪdʒ]	ganzseitig
poster ['pəʊstə]	Plakat
leaflet ['li:flət]	Faltblatt, Informationsblatt
clever ['klevə]	klug, geschickt
disgusting [dɪs'gʌstɪŋ]	ekelhaft
glamorous ['glæmərəs]	glanzvoll
agency ['eɪdʒənsi]	Agentur
advertising agency ['ædvətaɪzɪŋ eɪdʒənsi]	Werbeagentur
advertising space ['ædvətaɪzɪŋ speɪs]	Werbefläche(n), Werbezeit(en), Anzeigenraum
to **appeal to sb** [ə'pi:l tə]	für jdn attraktiv sein, jdn ansprechen
media ['mi:diə]	Medien
to **advertise sth** ['ædvətaɪz]	für jdn attraktiv sein, jdn ansprechen
to **write copy** [ˌraɪt 'kɒpi]	texten, Werbetexte verfassen
to **decorate** ['dekəreɪt]	einrichten, gestalten
to **inspire** [ɪn'spaɪə]	anregen
creativity [ˌkri:eɪ'tɪvəti]	Kreativität
print [prɪnt]	Druck
work of art [ˌwɜ:k əv 'ɑ:t]	Kunstwerk
to **be on display** [bi ˌɒn dɪ'spleɪ]	ausgestellt sein/werden, zu sehen sein
broad(ly) [brɔ:d]	breit
department store [dɪ'pɑ:tmənt stɔ:]	Warenhaus
account services [ə'kaʊnt sɜ:vɪsɪz]	Kontakt

advertising campaign ['ædvətaɪzɪŋ kæmpeɪn]	Werbekampagne
account executive [ə'kaʊnt ɪgzekjətɪv]	Kontakter/in, Berater/in
to **coordinate** [kəʊ'ɔ:dɪneɪt]	koordinieren
brief [bri:f]	Dossier, Anweisungen
typical ['tɪpɪkl]	typisch
to **brew** [bru:]	sich zusammenbrauen, gären
creative (department) [kri'eɪtɪv]	Kreation
to **propose** [prə'pəʊz]	vorschlagen
to **feature** ['fi:tʃə]	vorkommen, eine Rolle spielen
mermaid ['mɜ:meɪd]	Meerjungfrau
longing(ly) ['lɒŋɪŋ]	sehnsüchtig

page 62

seductive(ly) [sɪ'dʌktɪv]	verführerisch
to **remove** [rɪ'mu:v]	(Kleidung:) ausziehen
underwear ['ʌndəweə]	Unterwäsche
shot [ʃɒt]	*(Film:)* Einstellung, Aufnahme
myth [mɪθ]	Mythos, Märchen, Legende
unoriginal [ˌʌnə'rɪdʒənl]	herkömmlich, unoriginell
effective [ɪ'fektɪv]	wirkungsvoll, effektiv
to **make an impact** [ˌmeɪk ən 'ɪmpækt]	einen Eindruck hinterlassen
twinkle ['twɪŋkl]	Zwinkern
to **shoot** [ʃu:t]	*(Film:)* drehen, Aufnahmen machen
dozen ['dʌzn]	Dutzend
graphic artist [ˌgræfɪk 'ɑ:tɪst]	Grafiker/in
buyer ['baɪə]	Einkäufer/in
copy editor ['kɒpi edɪtə]	Redakteur/in
to **exist** [ɪg'zɪst]	es geben, existeren
to **have sth in common** [həv ˌɪn 'kɒmən]	etw geminsam haben
effectiveness [ɪ'fektɪvnəs]	Wirksamkeit, Effektivität
customer satisfaction [ˌkʌstəmə ˌsætɪs'fækʃn]	Kundenzufriedenheit
whirlwind ['wɜ:lwɪnd]	Wirbelwind, Trubel
strategist ['strætədʒɪst]	Stratege/-in
among [ə'mʌŋ]	(mitten) in
chaos ['keɪɒs]	Chaos
to **strategize** ['strætədʒaɪz]	(die strategisch besten Lösungen) finden
method ['meθəd]	Methode, Art (und Weise)
health-conscious ['helθ kɒnʃəs]	gesundheitsbewusst
target audience [ˌtɑ:gɪt 'ɔ:diəns]	Zielpublikum, -gruppe
to **be considered sth** [bi kən'sɪdəd]	als etw gelten
along with [ə'lɒŋ wɪð]	zusammen mit
pillar ['pɪlə]	Säule
to **purchase** ['pɜ:tʃəs]	kaufen
channel ['tʃænl]	Sender
cable channel ['keɪbl tʃænl]	Kabelsender
audience ['ɔ:diəns]	Publikum
component [kəm'pəʊnənt]	Bestandteil, Komponente
application [ˌæplɪ'keɪʃn]	Anwendung
industry ['ɪndəstri]	Branche
constant ['kɒnstənt]	konstant, gleichbleibend
shopping mall ['ʃɒpɪŋ mɔ:l]	Einkaufszentrum, -passage
commercial [kə'mɜ:ʃl]	Werbespot
to **enquire about sth** [ɪn'kwaɪər əbaʊt]	sich nach etw erkundigen
boring ['bɔ:rɪŋ]	langweilig

page 63

various ['veəriəs]	unterschiedlich
copywriter ['kɒpiraɪtə]	Werbetexter/in
client ['klaɪənt]	Kunde/Kundin
to **limit** ['lɪmɪt]	beschränken
explicit(ly) [ɪk'splɪsɪt]	ausdrücklich, wörtlich

page 64

featuring ['fi:tʃərɪŋ]	*(Film:)* mit
to **have a hard time** [həv ə ˌhɑ:d 'taɪm]	es schwer haben, schwerfallen
mythology [mɪ'θɒlədʒi]	Mythologie
magic ['mædʒɪk]	Zauberei, Magie
attention [ə'tenʃn]	Aufmerksamkeit
to **attract sb's attention** [əˌtrækt sʌmwʌnz ə'tenʃn]	jds Aufmerksamkeit wecken/fesseln
comical ['kɒmɪkl]	komisch, lustig
to **arouse** [ə'raʊz]	wecken, erregen
desire (for sb/sth) [dɪ'zaɪə]	Verlangen, Wunsch (nach jdm/etw)
to **act** [ækt]	handeln
action ['ækʃn]	Handlung, Aktion, Maßnahme(n)
model ['mɒdl]	Modell
engaging [ɪn'geɪdʒɪŋ]	fesselnd
benefit ['benɪfɪt]	Nutzen, Vorteil
to **get sb involved in sth** [ˌget ɪn'vɒlvd ɪn]	jdn an etw beteiligen, jdn in etw einbeziehen
to **approve of sth** [ə'pru:v əv]	etw gut finden
to **encourage** [ɪn'kʌrɪdʒ]	fördern

page 65

to **touch** [tʌtʃ]	berühren, anfassen
screen [skri:n]	Bildschirm
headphones ['hedfəʊnz]	Kopfhörer
peace [pi:s]	Frieden
to **check sb/sth out** [ˌtʃek 'aʊt]	sich jdn/etw ansehen
sun roof ['sʌn ru:f]	Schiebedach
remote [rɪ'məʊt]	Fern-
seat heating ['si:t hi:tɪŋ]	Sitzheizung
to **be sick** [bi 'sɪk]	sich übergeben (müssen)

page 66

disappointed (with sb/sth) [ˌdɪsə'pɔɪntɪd]	enttäuscht (von jdm/etw)
Dear Sir or Madam [dɪə ˌsɜ: ɔ: 'mædəm]	Sehr geehrte Damen und Herren
policy ['pɒləsi]	Politik, Vorgehensweise, Regelung
disapproval [ˌdɪsə'pru:vl]	Missbilligung

playable [ˌpleɪəbl]	abspielbar
principle ['prɪnsəpl]	Prinzip, Grundsatz
to **hold** [həʊld]	gelten
whichever [wɪtʃ'evə]	wer/was (auch immer), egal welche/r/s
to **turn to sb** ['tɜːn tə]	sich an jdn wenden
to **file** [faɪl]	einreichen
commerce ['kɒmɜːs]	Handel
means [miːnz]	Mittel

page 67

to **launch sth** [lɔːntʃ]	etw auf den Markt bringen
aimed at sb ['eɪmd ət]	an jdn gerichtet, für jdn
to **turn sth into sth** ['tɜːn ɪntə]	etw zu etw machen
to **design** [dɪ'zaɪn]	entwerfen, gestalten
to **pay attention** [ˌpeɪ ə'tenʃn]	aufmerksam sein
competition [ˌkɒmpə'tɪʃn]	Wettbewerb
to **focus on sth** ['fəʊkəs ɒn]	sich auf etw konzentrieren
to **grab** [græb]	packen, greifen
This will have to do [ˌðɪs wɪl ˌhæv tə 'duː]	Das muss reichen.
to **go ahead** [ˌgəʊ ə'hed]	anfangen, loslegen
to **deal with sb/sth** ['diːl wɪð]	es mit jdm/etw zu tun haben
reputation [ˌrepju'teɪʃn]	Ruf
unwilling to do sth [ʌn'wɪlɪŋ tə duː]	nicht bereit, etw zu tun
budget ['bʌdʒɪt]	Budget, Haushalt, Etat
to **hire sb** ['haɪə]	jdn engagieren, beauftragen, einstellen
brief [briːf]	Auftrag
to **turn sth down** [ˌtɜːn 'daʊn]	etw ablehnen
to **take sb on** [ˌteɪk 'ɒn]	jdn annehmen, übernehmen
contract ['kɒntrækt]	Vertrag, *hier:* Auftrag

UNIT 4

page 68

to **sort sth** [sɔːt]	etw einsortieren, einordnen
energy source ['enədʒi sɔːs]	Energiequelle
category ['kætəgəri]	Kategorie
fuel ['fjuːəl]	Brennstoff, Kraftstoff
renewable [rɪ'njuːəbl]	erneuerbar
prompt [prɒmpt]	Stichwort
to **damage** ['dæmɪdʒ]	schaden, (be)schädigen
to **pollute** [pə'luːt]	verschmutzen
to **release** [rɪ'liːs]	freisetzen
carbon (dioxide) ['kɑːbən]	Kohlenstoff, Kohlendioxid
to **run out** [ˌrʌn 'aʊt]	versiegen, sich erschöpfen
nation ['neɪʃn]	Staat, Nation

page 69

energy requirements ['enədʒi rɪkwaɪəmənts]	Energiebedarf, -verbrauch
emission [ɪ'mɪʃn]	Emission
cycling ['saɪklɪŋ]	Fahrradfahren
conservation [ˌkɒnsə'veɪʃn]	Einsparung, Sparen
consumption [kən'sʌmpʃn]	Verbrauch, Konsum
sustainable [sə'steɪnəbl]	nachhaltig
lifestyle ['laɪfstaɪl]	Lebensweise, Lebensführung
biofuel [ˌbaɪəʊ'fjuːəl]	Biokraftstoff
waste [weɪst]	Müll, Abfall
turbine ['tɜːbaɪn]	Turbine
harmful ['hɑːmfl]	schädlich
carbon-neutral [ˌkɑːbən 'njuːtrəl]	CO_2-neutral
emirate ['emɪərət]	Emirat
to **cover** ['kʌvə]	bedecken
hectare ['hekteə]	Hektar
high-density [ˌhaɪ 'densəti]	dicht bevölkert
entirely [ɪn'taɪəli]	völlig, ausschließlich
urban ['ɜːbən]	städtisch, Stadt-
demand [dɪ'mɑːnd]	Bedarf
resident ['rezɪdənt]	Bewohner/in, Einwohner/in
to **model sth on sth** ['mɒdl ɒn]	etw einer Sache zum Vorbild nehmen, etw einer Sache nachbilden
architecture ['ɑːkɪtektʃə]	Architektur
to **drape** [dreɪp]	einhüllen, verhüllen
fabric ['fæbrɪk]	Gewebe, Stoff, Tuch
sunlight ['sʌnlaɪt]	Sonnenlight
electricity [ɪˌlek'trɪsəti]	Strom, Elektrizität
canal [kə'næl]	Kanal
alongside [əˌlɒŋ'saɪd]	neben, entlang
pedestrian [pɪ'destriən]	Fußgänger/in
heat [hiːt]	Hitze
to **average sth** ['ævərɪdʒ]	etw durchschnittlich erreichen
shade [ʃeɪd]	Schatten
construction material [kən'strʌkʃn mətɪəriəl]	Baumaterial, Baustoff
considerably [kən'sɪdərəbli]	erheblich, beträchtlich
to **provide** [prə'vaɪd]	bieten
solar collector [ˌsəʊlə kə'lektə]	Sonnenkollektor
throughout [θruː'aʊt]	überall, in ganz
means of travel [ˌmiːnz əf 'trævl]	Fortbewegungsart/-mittel
fully automated [ˌfʊli 'ɔːtəmeɪtɪd]	vollautomatisch
rapid(ly) ['ræpɪd]	schnell, rasch
transit ['trænzɪt]	Beförderung, Transport
alternative [ɔːl'tɜːnətɪv]	Alternative
palm [pɑːm]	Palme
mangrove ['mæŋgrəʊv]	Mangrove
plantation [plæn'teɪʃn]	Anpflanzung, Plantage
belt [belt]	Gürtel
raw material [ˌrɔː mə'tɪəriəl]	Rohstoff(e)
developer [dɪ'veləpə]	Entwickler/in
to **supplement** ['sʌplɪment]	ergänzen
revenue ['revənjuː]	Einnahmen
tiny ['taɪni]	winzig
exporter [ɪk'spɔːtə]	Exporteur

to **envisage** [ɪn'vɪzɪdʒ]	vorhaben
drop [drɒp]	Tropfen
mirror ['mɪrə]	Spiegel
breeze [bri:z]	Wind
gulf [gʌlf]	*(Meer:)* Golf

page 70

solar-powered [ˌsəʊlə 'paʊəd]	solarbetrieben
desalination plant [ˌdi:ˌsælɪ'neɪʃn plɑ:nt]	Entsalzungsanlage
wastewater ['weɪstwɔ:tə]	Abwasser
to **purify** ['pjʊərɪfaɪ]	klären
to **grow** [grəʊ]	anbauen
to **contribute** [kən'trɪbju:t]	beitragen
stage [steɪdʒ]	Abschnitt, Etappe, Stadium, Schritt
to **set the tone** [ˌset ðə 'təʊn]	den Ton/Takt vorgeben
entire [ɪn'taɪə]	gesamte/r/s
construction [kən'strʌkʃn]	Bau
state-of-the-art [ˌsteɪt əv ði 'ɑ:t]	auf dem neuesten Stand der Technik
power plant ['paʊə plɑ:nt]	Kraftwerk
to **require** [rɪ'kwaɪə]	erfordern, verlangen, benötigen
to **conserve** [kən'sɜ:v]	sparen, einsparen
to **contrast** [kən'trɑ:st]	einander gegenüberstellen
to **comment on sth** ['kɒment ɒn]	etw kommentieren
issue ['ɪʃu:]	Frage, Streitpunkt, Problem
findings ['faɪndɪŋz]	Ergebnisse
eco-friendly ['i:kəʊ frendli]	umweltfreundlich
environmental [ɪnˌvaɪrən'mentl]	Umwelt-
similarity [ˌsɪmə'lærəti]	Ähnlichkeit
measure ['meʒə]	Maßnahme
to **take measures** [ˌteɪk 'meʒəz]	Maßnahmen ergreifen
infrastructure ['ɪnfrəstrʌktʃə]	Infrastruktur

page 71

shipping ['ʃɪpɪŋ]	Schiffstransport, Schifffahrt, Schiffs-
inexpensive [ˌɪnɪk'spensɪv]	preisgünstig
to **transport** [træn'spɔ:t]	befördern, transportieren
shipping container ['ʃɪpɪŋ kənteɪnə]	Versandcontainer
cargo ['kɑ:gəʊ]	Fracht
world's cargo [ˌwɜ:ldz 'kɑ:gəʊ]	weltweites Frachtaufkommen, Welthandel
trillion ['trɪljən]	Billion
trade [treɪd]	Handel, Handelsverkehr
earth [ɜ:θ]	Erde
concern [kən'sɜ:n]	Befürchtung, Bedenken, Sorge
to **address sth** [ə'dres]	sich mit etw befassen
to **feature sth** ['fi:tʃə]	etw zum Gegenstand haben
innovative ['ɪnəveɪtɪv]	innovativ
maritime ['mærɪtaɪm]	Schifffahrts-
rail [reɪl]	Bahn
aviation [ˌeɪvi'eɪʃn]	Luftfahrt
greenhouse gas [ˌgri:nhaʊs 'gæs]	Treibhausgas(e)
to **tackle sth** ['tækl]	etw angehen, etw in Angriff nehmen
port [pɔ:t]	Hafen
to **leave port** [ˌli:v 'pɔ:t]	auslaufen
vessel ['vesl]	Schiff
to **reveal** [rɪ'vi:l]	enthüllen
weapon ['wepən]	Waffe
climate ['klaɪmət]	Klima
climate change ['klaɪmət tʃeɪndʒ]	Klimawandel
kite [kaɪt]	Drachen
ton [tʌn]	Tonne
to **eliminate** [ɪ'lɪmɪneɪt]	unterbinden, eliminieren
to **cut** [kʌt]	senken
average ['ævərɪdʒ]	Durchschnitt
variety [və'raɪəti]	Vielzahl, Vielfalt
conventional [kən'venʃənl]	herkömmlich, konventionell
engine ['endʒɪn]	Motor, Maschine
to **design** [dɪ'zaɪn]	konstruieren
remarkably [rɪ'mɑ:kəbli]	erstaunlich
critically ['krɪtɪkli]	äußerst
endangered [ɪn'deɪndʒəd]	bedroht
fin [fɪn]	Flosse
to **harness** ['hɑ:nɪs]	nutzen
wave energy ['weɪv enədʒi]	Wellenenergie
rigid ['rɪdʒɪd]	starr
solar panel [ˌsəʊlə 'pænl]	Solarmodul
hydrogen ['haɪdrədʒən]	Wasserstoff
to **store** [stɔ:]	speichern, lagern
fuel cell ['fju:əl sel]	Brennstoffzelle
by-product ['baɪ prɒdʌkt]	Neben-, Abfallprodukt
vapour ['veɪpə]	Dampf
hull [hʌl]	(Schiffs-)Rumpf
to **empty** ['empti]	leeren, löschen
to **balance** ['bæləns]	im Gleichgewicht halten

page 72

intake ['ɪnteɪk]	Zufuhr, Aufnahme
discharge ['dɪstʃɑ:dʒ]	Ablassen
plant [plɑ:nt]	Pflanze
virus ['vaɪrəs]	Virus
bacteria [bæk'tɪəriə]	Bakterien
ocean ['əʊʃn]	Ozean, Weltmeer
extensive [ɪk'stensɪv]	ausgedehnt, beträchtlich
ecological [ˌi:kə'lɒdʒɪkl]	ökologisch, Umwelt-
marine [mə'ri:n]	Meeres-
capacity [kə'pæsəti]	Fassungsvermögen, Zuladung
to **sacrifice** ['sækrɪfaɪs]	opfern
vehicle ['vi:əkl]	Fahrzeug
roll-on roll-off vessel [rəʊl ˌɒn rəʊl 'ɒf vesl]	Fähre, RoRo-Schiff
to **serve** [sɜ:v]	dienen
inspiration [ˌɪnspə'reɪʃn]	Anregung
converter [kən'vɜ:tə]	Wandler
propulsion [prə'pʌlʃn]	Antrieb
popularity [ˌpɒpju'lærəti]	Beliebtheit
hazard ['hæzəd]	Gefahr

in terms of [ɪn 'tɜ:mz əv]	was ... angeht
monetary ['mʌnɪtri]	finanziell, Geld-
either ['aɪðə]	jede/r/s (von beiden)
to signify ['sɪgnɪfaɪ]	bedeuten, bezeichnen
percentage [pə'sentɪdʒ]	Anteil, Prozentsatz
contribution [ˌkɒntrɪ'bju:ʃn]	Beitrag
to preserve [prɪ'zɜ:v]	schützen, bewahren
grade [greɪd]	Note
classmate ['klɑ:smeɪt]	Klassenkamerad/in

page 73

accurate(ly) ['ækjərət]	genau
huge [hju:dʒ]	gewaltig, riesig
uniqueness [ju'ni:knəs]	Einzigartigkeit
relative ['relətɪv]	relativ
ease [i:z]	Leichtigkeit, Einfachheit
versatility [ˌvɜ:sə'tɪləti]	Vielseitigkeit
vast majority [ˌvɑ:st mə'dʒɒrəti]	(bei weitem) größter Teil, Löwenanteil

page 74

increasingly [ɪn'kri:sɪŋli]	zunehmend
to unify ['ju:nɪfaɪ]	vereinigen
man-made ['mæn meɪd]	von Menschen verursacht
to appear [ə'pɪə]	scheinen
atmosphere ['ætməsfɪə]	Atmosphäre
global warming [ˌgləʊbl 'wɔ:mɪŋ]	Erderwärmung
pattern ['pætn]	Muster, Verhalten
to rise [raɪz]	steigen
sea level ['si: levl]	Meeresspiegel
natural disaster [ˌnætʃrəl dɪ'zɑ:stə]	Naturkatastrophe
to predict [prɪ'dɪkt]	voraussagen, vorhersagen
eventually [ɪ'ventʃuəli]	letztendlich, schließlich
significant [sɪg'nɪfɪkənt]	bedeutend, erheblich
effect [ɪ'fekt]	Auswirkung
well-being ['wel bi:ɪŋ]	Wohlbefinden
heatwave ['hi:tweɪv]	Hitzewelle
to claim [kleɪm]	fordern
the sick [ðə 'sɪk]	die Kranken
the elderly [ði 'eldəli]	die Alten
shortage ['ʃɔ:tɪdʒ]	Mangel, Knappheit
farmland ['fɑ:mlænd]	Ackerland
to dry up [ˌdraɪ 'ʌp]	austrocknen
coastal ['kəʊstl]	Küsten-
to resettle [ˌri:'setl]	umsiedeln
measure ['meʒə]	Maß
to account for sth [ə'kaʊnt fə]	etw ausmachen
to suggest [sə'dʒest]	hinweisen auf, hindeuten auf
environmental friendliness [ɪnˌvaɪrənˌmentl 'frendlinəs]	Umweltfreundlichkeit
to implement ['ɪmplɪmənt]	einführen, umsetzen
scale [skeɪl]	Umfang
to support [sə'pɔ:t]	untermauern
conclusion [kən'klu:ʒn]	Fazit, Schluss
brief(ly) [bri:f]	kurz
to lower ['ləʊə]	senken
to influence ['ɪnfluəns]	beeinflussen
ordinary ['ɔ:dnri]	normal

page 75

race car ['reɪs kɑ:]	Rennwagen
technical ['teknɪkl]	technisch
chassis ['ʃæsi]	Fahrgestell
speed [spi:d]	Geschwindigkeit
miles per hour (mph) [ˌmaɪlz pər 'aʊə]	Meilen pro Stunde
petrol ['petrəl]	Benzin
mode [məʊd]	Modus, Art
rocket ['rɒkɪt]	Rakete
to pass [pɑ:s]	vorbeifahren, überholen
to overtake [ˌəʊvə'teɪk]	überholen
mileage ['maɪlɪdʒ]	Spritverbrauch
miles per gallon (mpg) [ˌmaɪlz pɜ: 'gælən]	Meilen pro Gallone
win [wɪn]	Sieg
awesome ['ɔ:səm]	fantastisch
Just kidding [ː,dʒʌst 'kɪdɪŋ]	Kleiner Scherz.
to picture sb ['pɪktʃə]	sich jdn vorstellen
to consider sth sth [kən'sɪdə]	etw für etw halten
racing ['reɪsɪŋ]	Rennen, Renn-
wheel [wi:l]	Rad
to power ['paʊə]	antreiben
to maximize ['mæksɪmaɪz]	maximieren
performance [pə'fɔ:məns]	Leistung
bloody ['blʌdi]	verdammt
button ['bʌtn]	Knopf, Taste
gorgeous ['gɔ:dʒəs]	(wunder)schön, prächtig
looks [lʊks]	(gutes) Aussehen
environmentalist [ɪnˌvaɪrən'mentəlɪst]	Umweltschützer/in
to beat [bi:t]	schlagen
drawback ['drɔ:bæk]	Nachteil, Schattenseite
context ['kɒntekst]	Zusammenhang
capable ['keɪpəbl]	fähig
present ['preznt]	gegenwärtig, aktuell
to be supposed to do sth [bi sə'pəʊzd tə du:]	etw tun sollen
agriculture ['ægrɪkʌltʃə]	Landwirtschaft
medicine ['medsn]	Medizin
transportation [ˌtrænspɔ:'teɪʃn]	Beförderung, Transport(wesen)

page 76

section ['sekʃn]	Abschnitt
authority [ɔ:'θɒrəti]	Behörde
mayor [meə]	Bürgermeister/in
to put sth into action [ˌpʊt ɪntu 'ækʃn]	etw in die Tat umsetzen
city council ['sɪti kaʊnsl]	Stadtverwaltung
incentive [ɪn'sentɪv]	Anreiz
Chamber of Commerce [ˌtʃeɪmbər əf 'kɒmɜ:s]	Handelskammer
to remind sb [rɪ'maɪnd]	jdn (an etw) erinnern
to waste [weɪst]	verschwenden, vergeuden
valuable ['væljuəbl]	wertvoll
resource [rɪ'sɔ:s]	Ressource, Rohstoff
to fade [feɪd]	nachlassen, schwächer werden
volume ['vɒlju:m]	Volumen, Menge
instruction [ɪn'strʌkʃn]	Anweisung, Aufforderung
in case of fire [ɪn ˌkeɪs əf 'faɪə]	im Brandfall

level ['levl] (Öl-, Wasser-)Stand
name tag ['neɪm tæg] Namensschild
at all times [ət ˌɔːl 'taɪmz] ständig
to **handle sth** ['hændl] mit etw hantieren, etw anfassen
fine [faɪn] Geldstrafe

UNIT 5

page 77

to **rely on sth** [rɪ'laɪ ɒn] auf etw angewiesen sein
tourism ['tʊərɪzəm] Tourismus
to **be located in ...** [bi ləʊ'keɪtɪd ɪn] in ... liegen
creation [kri'eɪʃn] Schaffung
economic [ˌiːkə'nɒmɪk] wirtschaftlich
prosperity [prɒ'sperəti] Wohlstand
native ['neɪtɪv] Einheimische/r, einheimisch
job training ['dʒɒb treɪnɪŋ] Berufsausbildung
pollution [pə'luːʃn] Verschmutzung
congestion [kən'dʒestʃən] Stau(s)
crowding ['kraʊdɪŋ] Übervölkerung
destruction [dɪ'strʌkʃn] Zerstörung
lack [læk] Mangel
affordable [ə'fɔːdəbl] preiswert
overpriced [ˌəʊvə'praɪst] überteuert
parking charge ['pɑːkɪŋ tʃɑːdʒ] Parkgebühr
rubbish ['rʌbɪʃ] Müll
farming ['fɑːmɪŋ] Landwirtschaft
to **discover** [dɪ'skʌvə] entdecken
mass [mæs] Masse
profession [prə'feʃn] Beruf
concrete ['kɒŋkriːt] Beton
critical ['krɪtɪkl] kritisch
mainland ['meɪnlænd] Festland
holiday-maker ['hɒlədeɪ meɪkə] Urlauber/in
to **fall in love with sb/sth** [ˌfɔːl ɪn 'lʌv wɪð] sich in jdn/etw verlieben
racist ['reɪsɪst] rassistisch
mind you [ˌmaɪnd 'juː] allerdings
railway ['reɪlweɪ] Eisenbahn
primary ['praɪməri] Haupt-, primär, hauptsächlich
secondary ['sekəndri] sekundär, Folge-
destination [ˌdestɪ'neɪʃn] Reiseziel
to **strike up a conversation** [straɪk ˌʌp ə kɒnvə'seɪʃn] eine Unterhaltung beginnen
challenge ['tʃælɪndʒ] Herausforderung, (schwierige) Aufgabe
the locals [ðə 'ləʊkls] die Einheimischen
to **rank** [ræŋk] einstufen
ranking ['ræŋkɪŋ] Einstufung, Bewertung
dependent on [dɪ'pendənt ɒn] abhängig von

page 78

impact ['ɪmpækt] Auswirkung, Folge, Einfluss
long-haul flight [ˌlɒŋ hɔːl 'flaɪt] Langstreckenflug
eco-warrior ['iːkəʊ wɒriə] Öko-Aktivist/in
tune [tjuːn] Song, Lied
loads of ['ləʊdz əv] eine Menge
tan [tæn] Sonnenbräune
Let's face it [ˌlets 'feɪs ɪt] Seien wir ehrlich.
say [seɪ] zum Beispiel
rainforest ['reɪnfɒrɪst] Regenwald
supplies [sə'plaɪz] Vorrat, Vorräte
polar ice cap [ˌpəʊlər 'aɪs kæp] Polkappe
rate [reɪt] Tempo
to **remove sth** [rɪ'muːv] etw entfernen
whilst [waɪlst] während
community [kə'mjuːnəti] Gemeinde, Gemeinschaft
to **save sb/sth** [seɪv] jdn/etw retten
whale [weɪl] Wal
ski-resort area [ˌskiː rɪzɔːt 'eəriə] Skigebiet
emotional [ɪ'məʊʃənl] Gefühls-, gefühlsmäßig
level ['levl] Ebene
to **break** [breɪk] brechen
skiing ['skiːɪŋ] Skilaufen
impossible [ɪm'pɒsəbl] unmöglich
conscience ['kɒnʃəns] Gewissen
to **consider sth** [kən'sɪdə] etw in Betracht ziehen
practical ['præktɪkl] praktisch
catch 22 [ˌkætʃ twenti 'tuː] Dilemma, ausweglose Situation
to **destroy** [dɪ'strɔɪ] zerstören
to **depend on sth** [dɪ'pend ɒn] von etw abhängig sein
scientist ['saɪəntɪst] (Natur-)Wissenschaftler/in
snow [snəʊ] Schnee
to **melt** [melt] schmelzen
orphanage ['ɔːfənɪdʒ] Waisenhaus
business studies ['bɪznəs stʌdiz] Betriebswirtschaft(slehre)
guilty ['gɪlti] schuldig
to **step** [step] betreten
integral part [ˌɪntɪgrəl 'pɑːt] fester Bestandteil
to **suppress** [sə'pres] verdrängen, unterdrücken
to **integrate** ['ɪntɪgreɪt] integrieren
to **get around** [ˌget ə'raʊnd] sich fortbewegen, herumkommen
to **negate** [nɪ'geɪt] aufheben
to **resolve** [rɪ'zɒlv] lösen, auflösen

page 79

viewpoint ['vjuːpɔɪnt] Standpunkt, Blickwinkel
cover flap ['kʌvə flæp] Umschlagklappe
to **be in favour of sth** [bi ɪn 'feɪvər əv] für etw sein
reservations [ˌrezə'veɪʃnz] Bedenken
fiercely ['fɪəsli] äußerst, heftig
to **object to sth** [əb'dʒekt tə] etwas gegen etw haben
to **not care** [nɒt 'keə] egal sein
consequence ['kɒnsɪkwəns] Folge, Konsequenz
unable [ʌn'eɪbl] nicht in der Lage, unfähig
geographic [ˌdʒiːə'græfɪk] geographisch
diversity [daɪ'vɜːsəti] Verteilung

to **consist of sth** [kən'sɪst əv] aus etw bestehen
to **operate** ['ɒpəreɪt] (geschäftlich) tätig sein
aircraft ['eəkrɑ:ft] Flugzeug(e)
regardless [rɪ'gɑ:dləs] ungeachtet
length [leŋθ] Länge, Dauer
overnight [ˌəʊvə'naɪt] über Nacht

page 80

overall [ˌəʊvər'ɔ:l] gesamt
dominance ['dɒmɪnəns] Vorherrschaft, Dominanz
to **remain** [rɪ'meɪn] bleiben
to **level out** [ˌlevl 'aʊt] sich einpendeln
to **triple** ['trɪpl] sich verdreifachen
to **decrease** [dɪ'kri:s] zurückgehen, abnehmen
dramatic(ally) [drə'mætɪk] dramatisch
unexpected(ly) [ˌʌnɪk'spektɪd] unerwartet
sharp(ly) [ʃɑ:p] steil
marked(ly) ['mɑ:kɪdli] deutlich, merklich
gently ['dʒentli] sanft
slight(ly) [slaɪt] leicht
cross [krɒs] Kreuz
to **refer to sth** [rɪ'fɜ: tə] auf etw verweisen, sich auf etw beziehen
currency ['kʌrənsi] Währung
crisis ['kraɪsɪs] Krise
tournament ['tʊənəmənt] Turnier
proportion [prə'pɔ:ʃn] Anteil
likely ['laɪkli] wahrscheinlich
projection [prə'dʒekʃn] Prognose
to **interpret** [ɪn'tɜ:prɪt] dolmetschen
to **clear sth up** [ˌklɪər 'ʌp] etw klären
flight attendant ['flaɪt ətendənt] Flugbegleiter/in
vocabulary [və'kæbjələri] Wortschatz
to **get sth across** [ˌget ə'krɒs] etw klarmachen, etw vermitteln
meaning ['mi:nɪŋ] Sinn, Bedeutung
rainy ['reɪni] regnerisch
windy ['wɪndi] windig
turbulence ['tɜ:bjələns] Turbulenzen
short-haul flight [ˌʃɔ:t hɔ:l 'flaɪt] Kurzstreckenflug
to **place** [pleɪs] legen
overhead locker [ˌəʊvəhed 'lɒkə] Gepäckfach (über den Sitzen)
seatbelt ['si:tbelt] Sicherheitsgurt

page 81

sporting event ['spɔ:tɪŋ ɪvent] Sportereignis, -veranstaltung
championship ['tʃæmpiənʃɪp] Meisterschaft
Olympic [ə'lɪmpɪk] olympisch
match [mætʃ] Spiel, Partie
stadium ['steɪdiəm] Stadion
tennis court ['tenɪs kɔ:t] Tennisplatz
racetrack ['reɪstræk] Rennbahn
ski slope ['ski: sləʊp] Skipiste
world cup [ˌwɜ:ld 'kʌp] Weltpokal
to **boost** [bu:st] stärken, Auftrieb geben
to **benefit** ['benɪfɪt] nützen, Nutzen bringen
economy [ɪ'kɒnəmi] Wirtschaft
Olympics [ə'lɪmpɪks] Olympische Spiele
to **affect sb/sth** [ə'fekt] sich auf jdn/etw auswirken
to **be aware of sth** [bi ə'weər əv] etw wissen, sich einer Sache bewusst sein
minority [maɪ'nɒrəti] Minderheit
committee [kə'mɪti] Komitee, Ausschuss
to **host sth** [həʊst] etw ausrichten
to **attract** [ə'trækt] anziehen, anlocken
magically ['mædʒɪkli] wie durch Zauberhand
obscene [əb'si:n] unverschämt
taxpayer ['tækspeɪə] Steuerzahler/in
prestigious [pre'stɪdʒəs] renommiert, angesehen
liability [ˌlaɪə'bɪləti] Belastung
asset ['æset] Vorteil, etwas Gutes
to **convince** [kən'vɪns] überzeugen
organizer ['ɔ:gənaɪzə] Organisator/in
to **underestimate** [ˌʌndər'estɪmeɪt] unterschätzen
deficit ['defɪsɪt] Verlust, Defizit
history ['hɪstri] (die) Geschichte
to **defy sth** [dɪ'faɪ] sich über etw hinwegsetzen
law [lɔ:] Gesetz
law of nature [ˌlɔ: əv 'neɪtʃə] Naturgesetz
to **end up with sth** [ˌend 'ʌp wɪð] am Ende mit etw dastehen
debt [det] Schuld(en)
to **pay sth off** [ˌpeɪ 'ɒf] etw abbezahlen

page 82

to **turn out** [ˌtɜ:n 'aʊt] sich herausstellen
whopping ['wɒpɪŋ] gewaltig, saftig
budget deficit ['bʌdʒɪt defɪsɪt] Haushaltsdefizit
to **coincide with sth** [ˌkəʊɪn'saɪd wɪð] mit etw zusammenfallen
growth [grəʊθ] Wachstum
economic growth [i: kəˌnɒmɪk 'grəʊθ] Wirtschaftswachstum
Gross Domestic Product (GDP) [ˌgrəʊs dəˌmestɪk 'prɒdʌkt] Bruttoinlandsprodukt (BIP)
author ['ɔ:θə] Verfasser/in, Autor/in
calculation [ˌkælkju'leɪʃn] Berechnung
retailer ['ri:teɪlə] Einzelhändler/in
district ['dɪstrɪkt] Bezirk, Bereich, Viertel
to **hold** [həʊld] *(Veranstaltung etc.)* abhalten
fall [fɔ:l] Rückgang
temporary ['temprəri] vorübergehend, befristet
to **gain** [geɪn] erwerben, gewinnen, sammeln
employable [ɪm'plɔɪəbl] anwendbar, praktisch einsetzbar
study ['stʌdi] Untersuchung, Studie
evidence ['evɪdəns] Nachweis(e), Beweis(e)
recovery [rɪ'kʌvəri] Erholung
insignificant [ˌɪnsɪg'nɪfɪkənt] unbedeutend
money pit ['mʌni pɪt] Kostenfalle, Millionengrab
to **maintain sth** [meɪn'teɪn] etw unterhalten, instandhalten
to **demolish** [dɪ'mɒlɪʃ] abreißen

bird's nest [ˌbɜːdz 'nest]	Vogelnest
ghost town ['gəʊst taʊn]	Geisterstadt
former ['fɔːmə]	ehemalige/r/s
to seat (1000) [siːt]	Platz für (1000) Menschen bieten
attendance [ə'tendəns]	Zuschauerzahl
advocate ['ædvəkət]	Befürworter
inevitably [ɪn'evɪtəbli]	zwangsläufig
intangible [ˌɪn'tændʒəbl]	immateriell
to make way for sth [meɪk 'weɪ fə]	für etw Platz machen

page 83

to claim [kleɪm]	behaupten
to profit ['prɒfɪt]	profitieren
to seem [siːm]	scheinen
venue ['venjuː]	Veranstaltungsort, -stätte
sold out [ˌsəʊld 'aʊt]	ausverkauft
merchandise ['mɜːtʃəndaɪs]	Handelsware, hier: Fanartikel, Lizenzartikel
beneficial to [ˌbenɪ'fɪʃl tə]	nützlich, gewinnbringend für
damaging ['dæmɪdʒɪŋ]	schädlich

page 84

state [steɪt]	Staat, Land
roughly ['rʌfli]	ungefähr
to compete [kəm'piːt]	(in Wettbewerben) antreten
wheelchair ['wiːltʃeə]	Rollstuhl
racing ['reɪsɪŋ]	Rennen
synchronized swimming [ˌsɪŋkrənaɪzd 'swɪmɪŋ]	Synchronschwimmen
water polo ['wɔːtə pəʊləʊ]	Wasserbal
gymnastics [dʒɪm'næstɪks]	Turnen
parallel bars [ˌpærəlel 'bɑːz]	Barren
pommel horse ['pɒml hɔːs]	Seitpferd
to earmark sth for sth ['ɪəmɑːk]	etw für etw vorsehen
facilities [fə'sɪlətiz]	Einrichtungen, Anlagen
to undertake [ˌʌndə'teɪk]	unternehmen, in Angriff nehmen
concerned [kən'sɜːnd]	besorgt, beunruhigt
accessible [ək'sesəbl]	erreichbar, zugänglich
to displace [dɪs'pleɪs]	verdrängen, vertreiben
wildlife ['waɪldlaɪf]	Tiere (in freier Wildbahn)
tax [tæks]	Steuer, Abgabe
welfare ['welfeə]	Wohl
foolish ['fuːlɪʃ]	töricht, dumm, unklug
in the long term [ɪn ðə ˌlɒŋ 'tɜːm]	langfristig, auf lange Sicht
cigarette [ˌsɪgə'ret]	Zigarette
commission [kə'mɪʃn]	Kommission
solidarity tax [ˌsɒlɪ'dærəti tæks]	Solidaritätszuschlag
participant [pɑː'tɪsɪpənt]	Teilnehmer/in
funds [fʌndz]	Gelder
law enforcement [ˌlɔː ɪn'fɔːsmənt]	Strafverfolgung

page 85

guest house ['gest haʊs]	Pension
pension ['penʃn]	Rente
pensioner ['penʃənə]	Rentner/in
to make sb's life a misery [ˌmeɪk ˌlaɪf ə 'mɪzəri]	jdm das Leben zur Hölle machen
dead [ded]	tot
immigration officer [ɪmɪ'greɪʃn ɒfɪsə]	Grenzbeamte/r
to enter ['entə]	betreten, einreisen
valid ['vælɪd]	gültig
entry visa ['entri viːzə]	Einreisevisum
to enquire [ɪn'kwaɪə]	fragen, sich erkundigen
passport ['pɑːspɔːt]	Reisepass
drug [drʌg]	Droge
substance ['sʌbstəns]	Substanz

UNIT 6

page 86

developing country [dɪˌveləpɪŋ 'kʌntri]	Entwicklungsland
economic sector [iːkəˌnɒmɪk 'sektə]	Wirtschaftssektor
dominant ['dɒmɪnənt]	vorherrschend
distribution [ˌdɪstrɪ'bjuːʃn]	Verteilung
per capita [pə 'kæpɪtə]	pro Kopf
industry ['ɪndəstri]	Industrie

page 87

to rise [raɪz]	aufsteigen, aufstreben
spirituality [ˌspɪrɪtʃu'æləti]	Spiritualität
poverty ['pɒvəti]	Armut
to gain [geɪn]	erlangen
independence [ˌɪndɪ'pendəns]	Unabhängigkeit
indeed [ɪn'diːd]	in der Tat
to industrialize [ɪn'dʌstriəlaɪz]	industrialisieren
textiles ['tekstaɪlz]	Textilien
most notably [ˌməʊst 'nəʊtəbli]	vor allem
to close sth down [ˌkləʊz 'daʊn]	etw *(Fabrik etc.)* schließen
operation [ˌɒpə'reɪʃn]	Betrieb
migration [maɪ'greɪʃn]	Abwanderung, Verlagerung
investment [ɪn'vestmənt]	Investitionen
pharmaceutical [ˌfɑːmə'suːtɪkl]	Pharma-
manufacture [ˌmænju'fæktʃə]	Herstellung, Fertigung
pharmaceuticals [ˌfɑːmə'suːtɪklz]	Arzneimittel
substandard [ˌsʌb'stændəd]	minderwertig
drug [drʌg]	Medikament, Arzneimittel
high-skill [ˌhaɪ 'skɪl]	hochqualifiziert
speciality [ˌspeʃi'æləti]	Spezialität, Spezialgebiet

page 88

world marketplace [ˌwɜːld 'mɑːkɪtpleɪs]	Weltmarkt
enormous [ɪ'nɔːməs]	gewaltig, enorm
finance services ['faɪnæns sɜːvɪsɪz]	Finanzdienstleitungen
accounting [ə'kaʊntɪŋ]	Buchhaltung
off-shore [ˌɒf 'ʃɔː]	Auslands-
brain [breɪn]	Gehirn

lotus blossom ['ləʊtəs blɒsəm]	Lotosblüte
rural ['rʊərəl]	ländlich, bäuerlich
to **survive** [sə'vaɪv]	überleben
optimism ['ɒptɪmɪzəm]	Zuversicht, Optimismus
to **suffer sth** ['sʌfə]	etw erleiden
recession [rɪ'seʃn]	Rezession
to **project** [prə'dʒekt]	prognostizieren, vorhersagen

page 89

rise [raɪz]	Aufstieg, Anstieg
data entry ['deɪtə entri]	Dateneingabe
clerk [klɑ:k]	Angestellte/r
mind-numbing ['maɪnd nʌmɪŋ]	stumpfsinnig, todlangweilig
wife [waɪf]	(Ehe-)Frau
water buffalo ['wɔ:tə bʌfələʊ]	Wasserbüffel
rupee [ru:'pi:]	Rupie
unthinkable [ʌn'θɪŋkəbl]	undenkbar
to **outsource** ['aʊtsɔ:s]	(Arbeit) auslagern
grateful ['greɪtfl]	dankbar
corporation [ˌkɔ:pə'reɪʃn]	Konzern
a bunch of [ə 'bʌntʃ əv]	eine Menge
purchasing power ['pɜ:tʃəsɪŋ paʊə]	Kaufkraft
to **drive sth** [draɪv]	etw ankurbeln
winner ['wɪnə]	Gewinner/in

page 90

labour intensive [ˌleɪbər ɪn'tensɪv]	arbeitsintensiv
material [mə'tɪəriəl]	materiell
medic ['medɪk]	Arzt/Ärztin
exceptional [ɪk'sepʃənl]	außergewöhnlich
to **maintain** [meɪn'teɪn]	behalten, beibehalten

page 91

hourly wage [ˌaʊəli 'weɪdʒ]	Stundenlohn
internal [ɪn'tɜ:nl]	intern
external [ɪk'stɜ:nl]	extern
to **lay sb off** [ˌleɪ 'ɒf]	jdn entlassen, jdm betriebsbedingt kündigen
to **meet (sth)** [mi:t]	*(Bedarf, Norm etc.)* erfüllen, befriedigen, enstprechen
to **adapt (to sth)** [ə'dæpt]	sich anpassen (an etw)
competitive [kəm'petətɪv]	*(Preis:)* günstig
public sector [ˌpʌblɪk 'sektə]	öffentliche Hand, öffentlicher Dienst
application management [ˌæplɪ'keɪʃn mænɪdʒmənt]	Anwendungsentwicklung
geek [gi:k]	Nerd, Freak
suit [su:t]	Anzug, Hosenanzug, Kostüm, *hier:* Anzugträger
to **go way beyond sth** [gəʊ ˌweɪ bɪ'jɒnd]	weit über etw hinausgehen

page 92

anxious(ly) ['æŋkʃəs]	besorgt, beunruhigt, ängstlich
to **predict** [prɪ'dɪkt]	vorhersehen, abschätzen
flexibility [ˌfleksə'bɪləti]	Flexibilität
to **pass a law** [ˌpɑ:s ə 'lɔ:]	ein Gesetz verabschieden
minor ['maɪnə]	klein, unbedeutend
data storage ['deɪtə stɔ:rɪdʒ]	Datenspeicherung, Speicherplatz
freelancer ['fri:lɑ:nsə]	Freiberufler/in
at the bottom [ət ðə 'bɒtəm]	(ganz) unten
food chain ['fu:d tʃeɪn]	Nahrungskette
retirement [rɪ'taɪəmənt]	Ruhestand
schedule ['ʃedju:l]	Terminplan
client base ['klaɪənt beɪs]	Kundenstamm
quotation [kwəʊ'teɪʃn]	Zitat
overseas [ˌəʊvə'si:z]	Auslands-
to **fulfil** [fʊl'fɪl]	erfüllen

page 93

to **visualize** ['vɪʒuəlaɪz]	bildlich darstellen, visualisieren
cause and effect [ˌkɔ:z ənd ɪ'fekt]	Ursache und Wirkung
domestically [də'mestɪkli]	im Inland

page 94

routine [ru:'ti:n]	Tagesablauf, Routine
to **motivate** ['məʊtɪveɪt]	motivieren
freelance ['fri:lɑ:ns]	selbständig, freiberuflich
decent ['di:snt]	anständig, ordentlich
vacation [və'keɪʃn]	Urlaub
to **make sth up** [ˌmeɪk 'ʌp]	etw ausmachen, bilden
to **cut costs** [ˌ kʌt 'kɒsts]	Kosten senken
tempting ['temptɪŋ]	verlockend
to **sack sb** [sæk]	jdn entlassen, rausschmeißen
unfair [ˌʌn'feə]	unfair
unwise [ˌʌn'waɪz]	unklug
to **suffer** ['sʌfə]	leiden
top priority [ˌtɒp praɪ'ɒrəti]	oberste Priorität
slave [sleɪv]	Sklave
to **support sb/sth** [sə'pɔ:t]	jdn/etw unterstützen
productivity [ˌprɒdʌk'tɪvəti]	Produktivität
perspective [pə'spektɪv]	Perspektive
to **deserve sth** [dɪ'zɜ:v]	etw verdienen
benefits ['benɪfɪts]	Zusatzleistungen, Vergünstigungen

page 95

chances are [ˌtʃɑ:nsɪz 'ɑ:]	sehr wahrscheinlich
to **interview** ['ɪntəvju:]	ein Vorstellungsgespräch führen
written correspondence [ˌrɪtn kɒrɪ'spɒndəns]	Schriftverkehr
dress [dres]	Kleiderordnung, Kleidung
to **dress up** [ˌdres 'ʌp]	sich elegant kleiden
to **appreciate** [ə'pri:ʃieɪt]	schätzen, zu schätzen wissen
effort ['efət]	Bemühen, Bemühungen
to **take place** [ˌteɪk 'pleɪs]	stattfinden
tidy ['taɪdi]	aufgeräumt, ordentlich
at sb's end [ət sʌmbədiz 'end]	bei jdm
lighting ['laɪtɪŋ]	Beleuchtung, Licht
attractive [ə'træktɪv]	attraktiv

to pass sth out [ˌpɑːs 'aʊt]	etw verteilen
corner ['kɔːnə]	Ecke
to distribute [dɪ'strɪbjuːt]	verteilen
nevertheless [ˌnevəðə'les]	nichtsdestotrotz, dennoch
to approach sb [ə'prəʊtʃ]	auf jdn zugehen, jdn ansprechen
to give the impression that ... [ˌgɪv ði ɪm'preʃn ðət]	den Eindruck erwecken, dass ...
to quit [kwɪt]	kündigen
to pick sth [pɪk]	sich etw aussuchen
to relate to sth [rɪ'leɪt tə]	sich auf etw beziehen
challenging ['tʃælɪndʒɪŋ]	(heraus)fordernd, schwierig

page 96

fluent(ly) ['fluːənt]	*(Sprache:)* fließend
entrepreneur [ˌɒntrəprə'nɜː]	Unternehmer/in
attraction [ə'trækʃn]	Anziehungspunkt
educated ['edʒukeɪtɪd]	(gut) ausgebildet
expansion [ɪk'spænʃn]	Expansion
to turn sth over to sb/sth [ˌtɜːn 'əʊvə tə]	etw an jdn/etw übergeben
condition [kən'dɪʃn]	Zustand, Bedingung
despite [dɪ'spaɪt]	trotz
comparison [kəm'pærɪsn]	Steigerung (von Adjektiven)
patient ['peɪʃnt]	geduldig
to report sb/sth [rɪ'pɔːt]	jdn/etw melden

UNIT 7

page 97

integrated circuit [ˌɪntɪgreɪtɪd 'sɜːkɪt]	integrierter Schaltkreis, Mikrochip
display [dɪ'spleɪ]	Bildschirm, Display
touch control module [ˌtʌtʃ kən'trəʊl mɒdjuːl]	Touchscreen-Steuermodul
to assemble [ə'sembl]	montieren, zusammenbauen
minerals ['mɪnərəlz]	Mineralien, Bodenschätze
semi-conductor ['semɪ kəndʌktə]	Halbleiter
to mine [maɪn]	abbauen, fördern
mine [maɪn]	Bergwerk, Mine
possession [pə'zeʃn]	Besitz, Besitztum

page 98

cotton ['kɒtn]	Baumwolle
garment ['gɑːmənt]	Kleidungsstück
hanger ['hæŋə]	Kleiderbügel
rack [ræk]	Kleiderstange
sewing machine ['səʊɪŋ məʃiːn]	Nähmaschine
fashionista [fæʃə'nɪstə]	Modefan, Modefreak
to linger ['lɪŋgə]	im Raum stehen
earnings ['ɜːnɪŋz]	Einnahmen
to contribute [kən'trɪbjuːt]	einen/seinen/ihren Beitrag leisten
to harvest ['hɑːvɪst]	ernten
pesticide ['pestɪsaɪd]	Schädlingsbekämpfungsmittel
to spray [spreɪ]	sprühen
crop [krɒp]	Pflanzen (auf einem Feld), Ernte
fortunate ['fɔːtʃənət]	glücklich, vom Glück begünstigt

page 99

to maintain [meɪn'teɪn]	(nach wie vor) behaupten
child labor (AE) ['tʃaɪld leɪbə]	Kinderarbeit
to head [hed]	(in Richtung von etw) gehen, fahren
diligent(ly) ['dɪlɪdʒənt]	gewissenhaft, fleißig
to grow sth [grəʊ]	etw anbauen
textile ['tekstaɪl]	Textil-
massive ['mæsɪv]	riesig
multiple ['mʌltɪpl]	vielfach
to transform [træns'fɔːm]	verwandeln
laborer (AE) ['leɪbərə]	Arbeiter/in
cloth [klɒθ]	Stoff
discounted [dɪs'kaʊntɪd]	billig, Billig-
to pass sth on [ˌpɑːs 'ɒn]	etw weitergeben, -leiten
to surround [sə'raʊnd]	umgeben
legal age [ˌliːgl 'eɪdʒ]	gesetzliches Mindestalter
monthly ['mʌnθli]	monatlich
minimum wage [ˌmɪnɪməm 'weɪdʒ]	Mindestlohn
barely ['beəli]	kaum
squalid ['skwɒlɪd]	ärmlich, menschenunwürdig
hunger ['hʌŋgə]	Hunger
dockworker ['dɒkwɜːkə]	Hafenarbeiter
to load [ləʊd]	verladen, laden
to unload [ˌʌn'ləʊd]	entladen
rack [ræk]	Regal
federal ['fedərəl]	Bundes-
annual(ly) ['ænjuəl]	jährlich
to throw [θrəʊ]	werfen
to beg the question [ˌbeg ðə 'kwestʃən]	die Frage aufwerfen
to cross [krɒs]	überqueren
border ['bɔːdə]	(Landes-)Grenze
flowchart ['fləʊtʃɑːt]	Flussdiagramm
supply chain [sə'plaɪ tʃeɪn]	Lieferkette

page 100

to stuff one's pockets [ˌstʌf wʌnz 'pɒkɪts]	sich die Taschen vollstopfen, sich eine goldene Nase verdienen
to exploit [ɪk'splɔɪt]	ausbeuten
to pocket ['pɒkɪt]	einstecken, einstreichen, einsacken
partly ['pɑːtli]	teilweise
quantity ['kwɒntəti]	Menge
charge [tʃɑːdʒ]	Preis, Gebühr
ingredient [ɪn'griːdiənt]	Bestandteil
circumstances ['sɜːkəmstənsɪz]	Umstände

page 101

to assess [ə'ses]	einschätzen
attitude ['ætɪtjuːd]	Einstellung, Haltung
consideration [kənˌsɪdə'reɪʃn]	Erwägung, Überlegung
counter-argument [ˌkaʊtər 'ɑːgjumənt]	Gegenargument

ethical ['eθɪkl]	ethisch, (moralisch) verantwortlich
thesis ['θi:sɪz]	These
in advance [ɪn əd'vɑ:ns]	im Voraus
prohibited [prə'hɪbɪtɪd]	verboten
union ['ju:niən]	Gewerkschaft
vote [vəʊt]	Stimme
certification mark [ˌsɜ:tɪfɪ'keɪʃn mɑ:k]	Gütesiegel
trademark ['treɪd mɑ:k]	Markenzeichen
to **certify** ['sɜ:tɪfaɪ]	bescheinigen, beglaubigen
standard ['stændəd]	Norm
forced labour [ˌfɔ:st 'leɪbə]	Zwangsarbeit
independent [ˌɪndɪ'pendənt]	unabhängig
collective(ly) [kə'lektɪv]	gemeinsam, kollektiv
to **negotiate** [nɪ'gəʊʃieɪt]	verhandeln, aushandeln
working conditions [ˌwɜ:kɪŋ kən'dɪʃnz]	Arbeitsbedingungen
equitable ['ekwɪtəbl]	gerecht
equal ['i:kwəl]	gleich
to **establish** [ɪ'stæblɪʃ]	einrichten, herstellen
to **avoid** [ə'vɔɪd]	vermeiden, verhindern
injury ['ɪndʒəri]	Verletzung
to **aim** [eɪm]	darauf abzielen
to **cover** ['kʌvə]	*(Kosten)* decken
premium ['pri:miəm]	Prämie
partially ['pɑ:ʃəli]	teilweise, zum Teil
to **allow for sth** [ə'laʊ fə]	etw vorsehen
practices ['præktɪsɪz]	Verfahren
trader ['treɪdə]	Händler/in

page 102

sweat [swet]	Schweiß
sweatshop ['swetʃɒp]	*Betrieb mit ausbeuterischen Arbeitsbedingungen*
24/7 [twenti ˌfɔ: 'sevn]	rund um die Uhr
bargain ['bɑ:gɪn]	gutes Geschäft, Schnäppchen
improvement [ɪm'pru:vmənt]	Verbesserung
multinational [ˌmʌlti'næʃnəl]	Multi, Großkonzern
naive [naɪ'i:v]	naiv
truth [tru:θ]	Wahrheit
tax revenue ['tæks revənju:]	Steuereinnahmen
chemicals ['kemɪklz]	Chemikalien
to **feed** [fi:d]	ernähren
stuff [stʌf]	Sachen
to **be well off** [bi ˌwel 'ɒf]	gut dran sein
dignified ['dɪgnɪfaɪd]	würdevoll, würdig
campaigner [kæm'peɪnə]	Aktivist/in
to **rob sb of sth** [rɒb]	jdn einer Sache berauben
childhood ['tʃaɪldhʊd]	Kindheit
coal miner ['kəʊlmaɪnə]	Kohlebergarbeiter/in
prostitute ['prɒstɪtju:t]	Prostituierte/r
carpet ['kɑ:pɪt]	Teppich
to **turn a blind eye** [tɜ:n ə ˌblaɪnd 'aɪ]	wegsehen
exploitation [ˌeksplɔɪ'teɪʃn]	Ausbeutung
slavery ['sleɪvəri]	Sklaverei

page 103

editor ['edɪtə]	Herausgeber/in, Redakteur/in
self-respect [ˌself rɪ'spekt]	Selbstachtung
agreement [ə'gri:mənt]	Abkommen
subsistence farming [səb'sɪstəns fɑ:mɪŋ]	Subsitenzwirtschaft
to **pick** [pɪk]	sammeln, suchen, lesen
rubbish tip ['rʌbɪʃ tɪp]	Müllkippe
supply of money [səˌplaɪ əv 'mʌni]	Geldmenge
to **ignore** [ɪg'nɔ:]	hinwegsehen über, ignorieren

page 104

lyrics ['lɪrɪks]	Liedtext
reference ['refərəns]	Erwähnung, Verweis
bunch [bʌntʃ]	(Bananen-)Staude
to **stack** [stæk]	stapeln
to **lift** [lɪft]	heben, hochheben
ripe [raɪp]	reif
to **hide** [haɪd]	verbergen, verstecken
deadly ['dedli]	tödlich
tarantula [tə'ræntʃələ]	Tarantel
to **originate** [ə'rɪdʒɪneɪt]	entstehen, seinen Ursprung haben
root [ru:t]	Wurzel
to **enslave** [ɪn'sleɪv]	versklaven
abolition [ˌæbə'lɪʃn]	Abschaffung
to **achieve** [ə'tʃi:v]	erlangen
insight ['ɪnsaɪt]	Einblick
to **record** [rɪ'kɔ:d]	aufnehmen
carnival ['kɑ:nɪvl]	Karneval
satirical [sə'tɪrɪkl]	satirisch
affairs [ə'feəz]	Angelegenheiten
overseer ['əʊvəsɪə]	Vorarbeiter/in
poisonous ['pɔɪzənəs]	giftig
spider ['spaɪdə]	Spinne

page 105

common(ly) ['kɒmən]	häufig, verbreitet
tropical ['trɒpɪkl]	tropisch
leaf, leaves [li:f, li:vz]	Blatt, Blätter
plate [pleɪt]	Teller
to **wrap** [ræp]	einwickeln
commercial [kə'mɜ:ʃl]	kommerziell
colonist ['kɒlənɪst]	Siedler/in
steamship ['sti:mʃɪp]	Dampfschiff
railroad ['reɪlrəʊd]	Eisenbahn
to **distribute** [dɪ'strɪbju:t]	versenden
whereas [ˌweər'æz]	während
carton ['kɑ:tn]	Kiste, Karton
to **weigh** [weɪ]	wiegen
density ['densəti]	Dichte
toxic ['tɒksɪk]	giftig
pest [pest]	Schädling
weed [wi:d]	Unkraut
processing ['prəʊsesɪŋ]	Verarbeitung

page 106

to **reassure** [ˌri:ə'ʃʊə]	beruhigen
packet ['pækɪt]	Packung
organic [ɔ:'gænɪk]	Bio-
bean [bi:n]	Bohne

trolley ['trɒli] — Einkaufswagen
to emit [ɪ'mɪt] — emittieren, ausstoßen
refrigerated [rɪ'frɪdʒəreɪtɪd] — gekühlt, Kühl-
to spew [spju:] — spucken, speien
fumes [fju:mz] — Abgase
underage [ˌʌndər'eɪdʒ] — minderjährig
strawberry ['strɔ:bəri] — Erdbeere

SECRETARIAL ACTIVITIES

FILE A

page 108

secretarial [ˌsekrə'teəriəl] — Sekretariats-, Büro-
celebrity [sə'lebrəti] — Prominente/r
convention [kən'venʃn] — Tagung, Konferenz
passionate(ly) ['pæʃənət] — leidenschaftlich
charity ['tʃærəti] — Kampagne, Aktion (für wohltätige Zwecke)
fee [fi:] — Honorar

page 109

to **forward** ['fɔ:wəd] — weiterleiten
double room [ˌdʌbl 'ru:m] — Doppelzimmer
nearby ['nɪəbaɪ] — in der Nähe
to **pick sb up** [ˌpɪk 'ʌp] — jdn abholen
speech [spi:tʃ] — Rede, Vortrag
to **donate** [dəʊ'neɪt] — spenden
invitation [ˌɪnvɪ'teɪʃn] — Einladung
on sb's behalf [ɒn bɪ'hɑ:f] — in jds Namen
to **be delighted to do sth** [bi dɪ'laɪtɪd tə du:] — etw gern tun
to **entitle** [ɪn'taɪtl] — betiteln
mission ['mɪʃn] — Auftrag, Mission
mission statement ['mɪʃn steɪtmənt] — Leitbild
as regards [əz rɪ'gɑ:dz] — hinsichtlich, bezüglich
to **point out** [ˌpɔɪnt 'aʊt] — darauf hinweisen
vegetarian [ˌvedʒə'teəriən] — Vegetarier
payment ['peɪmənt] — Zahlung
appearance [ə'pɪərəns] — Auftritt
donation [dəʊ'neɪʃn] — Spende
terms [tɜ:mz] — Bedingungen, Konditionen

page 110

salutation [ˌsælju'teɪʃn] — *(Brief:)* Anrede
body ['bɒdi] — *(Brief:)* Haupttext
complimentary close [ˌkɒmplɪˌmentri 'kləʊz] — *(Brief:)* Schlussformel
recipient [rɪ'sɪpiənt] — Empfänger/in
to **take the initiative** [ˌteɪk ði ɪ'nɪʃətɪv] — die Initiative ergreifen
regards [rɪ'gɑ:dz] — Grüße
cheers [tʃɪəz] — tschüs, danke
Must rush [:ˌmʌst 'rʌʃ] — Ich muss weg. *(Brief:)* In Eile
capital letter [ˌkæpɪtl 'letə] — Großbuchstabe
text message ['tekst mesɪdʒ] — SMS

page 111

bold [bəʊld] — fett (gedruckt)
exclamation mark [eksklə'meɪʃn mɑ:k] — Ausrufezeichen
to **sign off** [ˌsaɪn 'ɒf] — *(Brief:)* beenden, unterschreiben

page 112

directions [də'rekʃnz] — Wegbeschreibung
assistance [ə'sɪstəns] — Hilfe

page 113

castle ['kɑ:sl] — Schloss, Burg
the more the merrier [ðə ˌmɔ: ðə 'meriə] — je mehr, desto fröhlicher

FILE B

page 114

voicemail ['vɔɪsmeɪl] — Anrufbeantworter
to **be available** [bi ə'veɪləbl] — *(Telefon:)* zu sprechen sein
to **be unavailable** [bi ˌʌnə'veɪləbl] — *(Telefon:)* nicht zu sprechen sein
to **leave a message** [ˌli:v ə 'mesɪdʒ] — *(Telefon:)* eine Nachricht hinterlassen
to **hold the line** [həʊld ðə 'laɪn] — *(Telefon:)* am Apparat bleiben
to **take a message** [ˌteɪk ə 'mesɪdʒ] — *(Telefon:)* etw ausrichten
to **catch** [kætʃ] — verstehen, mitkriegen
You're breaking up [:jɔ: ˌbreɪkɪŋ 'ʌp] — *(Telefon:)* Das Netz geht weg.

page 115

office hours ['ɒfɪs aʊəz] — Bürozeiten, Arbeitszeit
to **get back to sb** [ˌget 'bæk tə] — sich bei jdm melden, jdn zurückrufen
speaker ['spi:kə] — Redner/in
unofficial [ˌʌnə'fɪʃl] — inoffiziell

page 116

upper-case [ˌʌpə 'keɪs] — großgeschrieben
lower-case [ˌləʊə 'keɪs] — kleingeschrieben
to **react to sth** [ri'ækt tə] — auf etw reagieren
marvellous ['mɑ:vələs] — großartig
to **apologize** [ə'pɒlədʒaɪz] — sich entschuldigen

page 117

to **act sth out** [ˌækt 'aʊt] — etw (vor-, durch)spielen

FILE C

page 118

appointment [ə'pɔɪntmənt] — Termin
sunglasses ['sʌnglɑ:sɪz] — Sonnenbrille

page 120

to **rest** [rest] — sich ausruhen
out of action [ˌaʊt əv 'ækʃn] — lahmgelegt
TV station [ˌti: 'vi: steɪʃn] — Fernsehsender
to **get in touch with sb** [ˌget ɪn 'tʌtʃ wɪð] — sich mit jdm in Verbindung setzen
to **be up and about** [bi 'ʌp ənd ə'baʊt] — auf den Beinen sein

availability [ə,veɪlə'bɪləti] Verfügbarkeit
to **decline** [dɪ'klaɪn] ablehnen

page 121

chat show ['tʃæt ʃəʊ] Talkshow
to **arrange** [ə'reɪndʒ] *(Termin)* ausmachen
charity ['tʃærəti] Hilfsorganisation, guter Zweck

Father ['fɑ:ðə] Pater, Pfarrer
to **autograph** ['ɔ:təgrɑ:f] signieren
to **auction** ['ɔ:kʃn] versteigern
photo shoot ['fəʊtəʊ ʃu:t] Fotoaufnahmen
boycott ['bɔɪkɒt] Boykott
fur [fɜ:] Pelz
statue ['stætʃu:] Statue
Christ [kraɪst] Christus

FILE D

page 122

travel arrangements ['trævl əreɪndʒmənts] Reisevorbereitungen
booking ['bʊkɪŋ] Buchung, Reservierung
gatehouse ['geɪthaʊs] Torhaus
a shame [ə 'ʃeɪm] schade

page 123

underground ['ʌndəgraʊnd] U-Bahn
the Tube [ðə tju:b] *die Londoner U-Bahn*
minicab ['mɪnikæb] Funktaxi
coach [kəʊtʃ] Bus
coach service ['kəʊtʃ sɜ:vɪs] Busverbindung
train service ['treɪn sɜ:vɪs] Zugverbindung
complicated ['kɒmplɪkeɪtɪd] kompliziert
study ['stʌdi] Arbeitszimmer

page 124

departure [dɪ'pɑ:tʃə] Abfahrt, Abflug
carrier ['kæriə] Fluggesellschaft
to **depart** [dɪ'pɑ:t] abfahren, abfliegen
duration [dju'reɪʃn] Dauer
connecting flight [kə,nektɪŋ 'flaɪt] Anschlussflug
luggage ['lʌgɪdʒ] Gepäck
shopping bag ['ʃɒpɪŋ bæg] Einkaufstasche

page 125

interchange ['ɪntətʃeɪndʒ] Übergang, Umsteigen
entrance ['entrəns] Eingang

FILE E

page 126

reservation [,rezə'veɪʃn] Reservierung
unplugged [,ʌn'plʌgd] ohne Strom, *(Musik:)* akustisch

search [sɜ:tʃ] Suche
to **select** [sɪ'lekt] auswählen
to **type in** [,taɪp 'ɪn] eingeben
grading ['greɪdɪŋ] Einstufung
board [bɔ:d] Verpflegung

guide price ['gaɪd praɪs] Richtpreis
to **widen** ['waɪdn] verbreitern, erweitern
to **search** [sɜ:tʃ] durchsuchen, suchen

page 127

self-catering [,self 'keɪtərɪŋ] Selbstversorgung, für Selbstversorger
half board [,hɑ:f 'bɔ:d] Halbpension
full board [,fʊl 'bɔ:d] Vollpension
entertainment [,entə'teɪnmənt] Unterhaltung(selektronik)
bread roll [,bred 'rəʊl] Brötchen
jam [dʒæm] Marmelade
cereal ['sɪəriəl] Getreideflocken
porridge ['pɒrɪdʒ] Haferbrei
bacon ['beɪkən] Speck
single room [,sɪŋgl 'ru:m] Einzelzimmer
en suite [,ɒ 'swi:t] mit eigenem Bad
shower ['ʃaʊə] Dusche
bathtub ['bɑ:θtʌb] Badewanne
furnished ['fɜ:nɪʃt] möbliert, ausgestattet
flat [flæt] Wohnung
cleaner ['kli:nə] Reinigungskraft
amenities [ə'mi:nətiz] Annehmlichkeiten
spa [spɑ:] Wellnessbereich
surcharge ['sɜ:tʃɑ:dʒ] Aufpreis
rate [reɪt] (Zimmer-)Preis
booking fee ['bʊkɪŋ fi:] Buchungsgebühr
deposit [dɪ'pɒzɪt] Anzahlung
to **secure (sth)** [sɪ'kjuə] (sich etw) sichern

page 128

agent ['eɪdʒənt] Mitarbeiter/in
booked up [,bʊkt 'ʌp] ausgebucht
to **hire sth** ['haɪə] etw mieten
confirmation [,kɒnfə'meɪʃn] Bestätigung

page 129

cancellation [,kænsə'leɪʃn] Stornierung, Absage
follow-up ['fɒləʊ ʌp] Anschluss-
security number [sɪ'kjʊərəti nʌmbə] Sicherheitsnummer

page 130

dancer ['dɑ:nsə] Tänzer/in
microwave ['maɪkrəweɪv] Mikrowelle
refrigerator [rɪ'frɪdʒəreɪtə] Kühlschrank

FILE F

page 131

due to ['dju: tə] aufgrund
to **land** [lænd] landen
delay [dɪ'leɪ] Verspätung
in case [ɪn 'keɪs] für den Fall, dass
to **spoil** [spɔɪl] verderben
agenda [ə'dʒendə] Terminplan, -kalender

page 133

native speaker [,neɪtɪv 'spi:kə] Muttersprachler/in
impolite [,ɪmpə'laɪt] unhöflich

COMMERCIAL CORRESPONDENCE

FILE 1

page 134

letterhead ['letəhed]	Briefkopf
reference ['refərəns]	Zeichen, Referenz
special marking [ˌspeʃl 'mɑːkɪŋ]	Vermerk, Kennzeichnung
attention (Attn.) [ə'tenʃn]	zu Händen
subject line ['sʌbdʒɪkt laɪn]	Betreffzeile
to arrange [ə'reɪndʒ]	vereinbaren
to enclose [ɪn'kləʊz]	beifügen, beilegen
signature ['sɪgnətʃə]	Unterschrift
enclosure(s) (Enc, Encs) [ɪn'kləʊʒə]	Anlage(n)

page 135

postal address [ˌpəʊstl ə'dres]	Postadresse
to misunderstand [ˌmɪsʌndə'stænd]	falsch verstehen
confidential [ˌkɒnfɪ'denʃl]	vertraulich
air mail ['eə meɪl]	Luftpost
registered (letter) ['redʒɪstəd]	Einschreiben
recorded delivery [rɪˌkɔːdɪd dɪ'lɪvəri]	Einschreiben mit Rückschein
envelope ['envələʊp]	Briefumschlag
usage ['juːsɪdʒ]	Gebrauch, Gepflogenheit
punctuation [ˌpʌŋktʃu'eɪʃn]	Interpunktion

page 136

postcode ['pəʊstkəʊd]	Postleitzahl
signatory ['sɪgnətri]	Unterzeichnete/r
equivalent [ɪ'kwɪvələnt]	Entsprechung, Übersetzung

page 138

mixed up [ˌmɪkst 'ʌp]	durcheinander

page 139

to dictate [dɪk'teɪt]	diktieren
catalogue ['kætəlɒg]	Katalog
accountant [ə'kaʊntənt]	Buchhalter/in
invoice ['ɪnvɔɪs]	Rechnung
dated ['deɪtɪd]	*(Datum:)* vom
above-mentioned [ə'bʌv 'menʃnd]	oben genannt
overdue [ˌəʊvə'djuː]	überfällig
perfume ['pɜːfjuːm]	Parfüm
reaction [ri'ækʃn]	Reaktion
photocopy ['fəʊtəʊkɒpi]	Fotokopie

FILE 2

page 140

wear [weə]	Bekleidung
accessory [ək'sesəri]	Accessoire
importer [ɪm'pɔːtə]	Importeur
wholesaler ['həʊlseɪlə]	Großhändler
reasonable ['riːznəbl]	vernünftig, angemessen
to grant [grɑːnt]	gewähren, einräumen
terms of delivery [ˌtɜːmz əv dɪ'lɪvəri]	Lieferbedingungen
terms of payment [ˌtɜːmz əf 'peɪmənt]	Zahlungsbedingungen
delivery period [dɪ'lɪvəri pɪəriəd]	Lieferzeit

page 141

to cover ['kʌvə]	abdecken, *(Thema)* behandeln
quotation [kwəʊ'teɪʃn]	Preisangebot

page 142

to request sth [rɪ'kwest]	etw anfordern, erbitten
considerable [kən'sɪdərəbl]	erheblich, beträchtlich

page 143

costume jewellery ['kɒstjuːm dʒuːəlri]	Modeschmuck
well-established [ˌwel ɪ'stæblɪʃt]	gut eingeführt, etabliert

page 144

requirements [rɪ'kwaɪəmənts]	Bedarf
favourable ['feɪvərəbl]	günstig
comprehensive [ˌkɒmprɪ'hensɪv]	umfassend
destination [ˌdestɪ'neɪʃn]	Bestimmungsort
to call on sb ['kɔːl ɒn]	jdn besuchen
substantial [səb'stænʃl]	beträchtlich, erheblich

page 146

to go down well (with sb) [gəʊ ˌdaʊn 'wel]	(bei jdm) gut ankommen
to call by [ˌkɔːl 'baɪ]	vorbeikommen
to place an order [ˌpleɪs ən 'ɔːdə]	einen Auftrag erteilen, eine Bestellung aufgeben
terms and conditions [ˌtɜːmz ənd kən'dɪʃnz]	Konditionen, (Allgemeine) Geschäftsbedingungen
to source sth [sɔːs]	etw beziehen
to assure [ə'ʃʊə]	versichern, zusichern

FILE 3

page 147

trial order ['traɪəl ɔːdə]	Probebestellung, Probeauftrag

page 148

to quote sth [kwəʊt]	nennen, angeben
in writing [ɪn 'raɪtɪŋ]	schriftlich, in Schriftform
distributor [dɪ'strɪbjətə]	Großhändler
receipt of order [rɪˌsiːt əv 'ɔːdə]	Auftragseingang, Auftragserhalt
initial order [ɪˌnɪʃl 'ɔːdə]	Erstbestellung, Erstauftrag
net [net]	netto
open account [ˌəʊpən ə'kaʊnt]	offenes Zahlungsziel
Incoterm ['ɪnkəʊtɜːm]	Internationale Handelsklausel

page 149

reference ['refərəns]	Bezug
to **submit** [səb'mɪt]	*(Angebot)* unterbreiten
lipstick ['lɪpstɪk]	Lippenstift
unit ['ju:nɪt]	Einheit, Stück

page 150

in the meantime [ɪn ðə 'mi:ntaɪm]	in der Zwischenzeit
while stocks last [waɪl ˌstɒks 'lɑ:st]	solange der Vorrat reicht
letter of credit (L/C) [ˌletər əv 'kredɪt]	Akkreditiv
bank transfer ['bæŋk trænsfɜ:]	Überweisung
preferential terms [prefəˌrenʃl 'tɜ:mz]	Sonderkonditionen, bevorzugte (Zahlungs-) Bedingungen

page 152

trade discount ['treɪd dɪskaʊnt]	Handelsrabatt
quantity discount ['kwɒntəti dɪskaʊnt]	Mengenrabatt

FILE 4

page 154

acknowledgement [ək'nɒlɪdʒmənt]	Auftragsbestätigung
unit price [ˌju:nɪt 'praɪs]	Stückpreis
total ['təʊtl]	Gesamtbetrag, Summe
total price [ˌtəʊtl 'praɪs]	Gesamtpreis
packing ['pækɪŋ]	Verpackung, Versandverpackung
completion [kəm'pli:ʃn]	Fertigstellung
account (a/c) [ə'kaʊnt]	Konto
confirmation of order [kɒnfəˌmeɪʃn əv 'ɔ:də]	Auftragsbestätigung
advice of dispatch [ədˌvaɪs əv dɪ'spætʃ]	Versandanzeige, Versandmitteilung

page 155

subtotal ['sʌbtəʊtl]	Zwischensumme
value added tax (VAT) [ˌvælju: 'ædɪd tæks]	Mehrwertsteuer, Umsatzsteuer
sturdy ['stɜ:di]	stabil, fest
receipt of invoice [rɪˌsi:t əv 'ɪnvɔɪs]	Rechnungseingang, -erhalt

page 156

to **pack** [pæk]	verpacken
lightweight ['laɪtweɪt]	leicht
currency sign ['kʌrənsi saɪn]	Währungssymbol
film [fɪlm]	Folie
tape [teɪp]	Band, Klebeband
to **decorate** ['dekəreɪt]	dekorieren, verzieren
self-adhesive [ˌself əd'hi:sɪv]	selbstklebend
to **stick** [stɪk]	kleben
roll [rəʊl]	Rolle
minimum order quantity [ˌmɪnɪməm 'ɔ:də kwɒntəti]	Mindestbestellmenge
with order [wɪð 'ɔ:də]	bei Auftragserteilung

to **qualify for sth** ['kwɒlɪfaɪ fə]	zu etw berechtigt sein

page 157

cash discount ['kæʃ dɪskaʊnt]	Skonto

page 158

to **trust** [trʌst]	vertrauen, hoffen

page 159

bulky goods [ˌbʌlki 'gʊdz]	Sperrgüter, Massengüter
coal [kəʊl]	Kohle
perishable ['perɪʃəbl]	verderblich
multimodal transport [ˌmʌltiməʊdl 'trænspɔ:t]	kombinierte Beförderung, multimodaler Transport

page 160

at the latest [ət ðə 'leɪtɪst]	spätestens
due [dju:]	fällig
to **transfer** ['trænsfɜ:]	überweisen
to **complete an order** [kəmˌpli:t ən 'ɔ:də]	einen Auftrag fertigstellen, ausführen
to **draw sb's attention to sth** [ˌdrɔ: sʌmbədiz ə'tenʃn tə]	jdn auf etw aufmerksam machen
high-resolution [ˌhaɪ reʒə'lu:ʃn]	hochauflösend

page 161

rejection [rɪ'dʒekʃn]	Ablehnung

page 162

to **execute** ['eksɪkju:t]	ausführen

FILE 5

page 165

reminder [rɪ'maɪndə]	Mahnung
consignment [kən'saɪnmənt]	Lieferung, Sendung
dispatch [dɪ'spætʃ]	Versand
ready for dispatch [ˌredi fə dɪ'spætʃ]	versandbereit, versandfertig
to **remit** [rɪ'mɪt]	überweisen

page 166

commercial invoice [kəˌmɜ:ʃl 'ɪnvɔɪs]	Handelsrechnung

page 167

matte [mæt]	matt
shipment ['ʃɪpmənt]	Versand
seaworthy ['si:wɜ:ði]	seetüchtig

page 168

abbreviation [əˌbri:vi'eɪʃn]	Abkürzung
francs [fræŋks]	(Schweizer) Franken
to **deduct** [dɪ'dʌkt]	abziehen

page 170

regular customer [ˌregjələ 'kʌstəmə]	Stammkunde/-in, Bestandskunde
warehouse ['weəhaʊs]	Lager
to **overlook** [ˌəʊvə'lʊk]	übersehen

page 171

unreliable [ˌʌnrɪ'laɪəbl]	unzuverlässig
trusted ['trʌstɪd]	zuverlässig
unpaid [ˌʌn'peɪd]	nicht bezahlt
forceful ['fɔ:sfl]	deutlich, eindringlich
final demand [ˌfaɪnl dɪ'mɑ:nd]	letzte Mahnung
deadline ['dedlaɪn]	Frist
non-payment [ˌnɒn 'peɪmənt]	Nichtzahlung
senior executive [ˌsi:niər ɪg'zekjətɪv]	leitende/r Angestellte/r
to **escape one's notice** [ɪˌskeɪp wʌnz 'nəʊtɪs]	entgehen, übersehen
to **note** [nəʊt]	feststellen
whatever the case may be [wɒtevə ðə ˌkeɪs meɪ 'bi]	wie dem auch sei, in jedem Fall
without delay [wɪðaʊt dɪ'leɪ]	unverzüglich
to **disregard sth** [ˌdɪsrɪ'gɑ:d]	etw als gegenstandslos betrachten

page 172

remittance [rɪ'mɪtns]	Überweisung
to **take steps** [ˌteɪk 'steps]	Schritte einleiten
to **recover sth** [rɪ'kʌvə]	etw sicherstellen, beschaffen
owing ['əʊɪŋ]	fällig, ausstehend
prompt [prɒmpt]	umgehend
to **settle** ['setl]	regeln, erledigen

page 173

to **provide for sth** [prə'vaɪd fə]	etw vorsehen
with regard to [wɪð rɪ'gɑ:d tə]	bezüglich
to **insist** [ɪn'sɪst]	darauf bestehen
to **fail to do sth** [ˌfeɪl tə 'du:]	versäumen, etw zu tun
to **discontinue sth** [ˌdɪskən'tɪnju:]	etw einstellen, abbrechen

FILE 6

page 175

dissatisfied [dɪs'sætɪsfaɪd]	unzufrieden
freight [freɪt]	Fracht
air freight ['eə freɪt]	Luftfracht

page 176

to **unpack** [ˌʌn'pæk]	auspacken
freight forwarder ['freɪt fɔ:wədə]	Spediteur
in transit [ɪn 'trænzɪt]	beim Transport
to **mix sth up** [ˌmɪks 'ʌp]	etw durcheinander-bringen, etw verwechseln
right away [ˌraɪt ə'weɪ]	sofort
to **rush sth** [rʌʃ]	etw auf dem schnellsten Weg hinbringen
gesture ['dʒestʃə]	Geste
inconvenience [ˌɪnkən'vi:niəns]	Unannehmlichkeiten

page 177

to **threaten** ['θretn]	drohen
to **cancel** ['kænsl]	stornieren

page 178

to **ensure** [ɪn'ʃʊə]	sicherstellen, dafür sorgen
to **be obliged to do sth** [bi ə'blaɪdʒd tə]	sich genötigt sehen, etw zu tun

page 179

to **examine** [ɪg'zæmɪn]	untersuchen
sleeve [sli:v]	Ärmel
neck [nek]	Hals, Halsausschnitt
narrow ['nærəʊ]	eng, schmal
discrepancy [dɪs'krepənsi]	Diskrepanz
to **appreciate sth** [ə'pri:ʃieɪt]	für etw Verständnis haben

page 180

sleeveless ['sli:vləs]	ärmellos
fashionable ['fæʃnəbl]	in Mode

page 181

to **regret** [rɪ'gret]	bedauern
rough handling [ˌrʌf 'hændlɪŋ]	unsachgemäße Behandlung/Handhabung
wardrobe ['wɔ:drəʊb]	Kleiderschrank
discoloured [ˌdɪs'kʌləd]	verfärbt
to **be up to sth** [bi 'ʌp tə]	einer Sache entsprechen
to **obtain** [əb'teɪn]	etw erhalten, etw beziehen
by return [baɪ rɪ'tɜ:n]	postwendend
reduction [rɪ'dʌkʃn]	Nachlass, Reduzierung

FILE 7

page 185

hospitality [ˌhɒspɪ'tæləti]	Hotel- und Gaststättengewerbe
recruitment [rɪ'kru:tmənt]	Personalbeschaffung
entry level ['entri levl]	Einstiegsniveau
desirable [dɪ'zaɪərəbl]	wünschenswert
promotion prospects [prə'məʊʃn prɒspekts]	Beförderungsaussichten, Aufstiegschancen
environment [ɪn'vaɪrənmənt]	Umfeld, Umgebung
to **review** [rɪ'vju:]	bewerten, prüfen
uniform ['ju:nɪfɔ:m]	Uniform
command [kə'mɑ:nd]	Beherrschung
appearance [ə'pɪərəns]	Erscheinung(sbild), Aufreten, Aussehen
passion ['pæʃn]	Leidenschaft
customer care ['kʌstəmə keə]	Kundendienst

page 186

résumé (AE) ['rezjumeɪ]	Lebenslauf
font [fɒnt]	Schrift, Zeichensatz
to **tailor** ['teɪlə]	individuell anpassen
profile ['prəʊfaɪl]	Porträt, Profil
basic knowledge [ˌbeɪsɪk 'nɒlɪdʒ]	Grundkenntnisse

primary school ['praɪməri sku:l]	Grundschule
referee [ˌrefə'ri:]	Referenzgeber/in

page 187

ambition [æm'bɪʃn]	Ehrgeiz, Bestreben
higher education entrance qualifications [ˌhaɪə edʒuˌkeɪʃn 'entrəns kwɒlɪfɪkeɪʃnz]	Fachhochschulreife
selective secondary school [sɪˌlektɪv 'sekəndri sku:l]	Realschule
certificate [sə'tɪfɪkət]	Zeugnis, Bescheinigung
extra-curricular [ˌekstrə kə'rɪkjulə]	außerschulisch
ballroom dancing ['bɔ:lru:m dɑ:nsɪŋ]	Gesellschaftstanz
date of birth [ˌdeɪt əv 'bɜ:θ]	Geburtsdatum
marital status [ˌmærɪtl 'steɪtəs]	Familienstand
nationality [ˌnæʃə'næləti]	Staatsangehörigkeit

page 188

driving licence ['draɪvɪŋ laɪsns]	Führerschein
school leaving certificate [ˌsku:l li:vɪŋ sə'tɪfɪkət]	Schulabgangszeugnis
Red Cross [ˌred 'krɒs]	Rotes Kreuz
grammar school ['græmə sku:l]	Gymnasium
university entrance qualifications [ju:nɪˌvɜ:səti 'entrəns kwɒlɪfɪkeɪʃnz]	Abitur, Hochschulreife
car licence ['kɑ: laɪsns]	Führerschein Klasse 3
vocational school (AE) [vəʊˌkeɪʃənl 'sku:l]	Berufsschule, Berufskolleg, Gewerbliche Schule

page 189

vacancy ['veɪkənsi]	freie/offene Stelle
post [pəʊst]	Stelle
to entitle sb to sth [ɪn'taɪtl]	jdn zu etw berechtigen

page 190

animator ['ænɪmeɪtə]	Animateur/in
requirements [rɪ'kwaɪəmənts]	Anforderungen
to act [ækt]	schauspielern
minimum age [ˌmɪnɪməm 'eɪdʒ]	Mindestalter
board and lodging [ˌbɔ:d ənd 'lɒdʒɪŋ]	Kost und Logis
adult education college [ˌædʌlt edʒu'keɪʃn kɒlɪdʒ]	Volkshochschule
suited to/for sth ['su:tɪd]	für etw geeignet

page 191

to enable sb to do sth [ɪ'neɪbl tə du:]	jdm etw ermöglichen

page 192

to recharge [ˌri:'tʃɑ:dʒ]	aufladen
battery ['bætəri]	Akku
to perform sth [pə'fɔ:m]	etw aufführen
to judge [dʒʌdʒ]	beurteilen
to swap [swɒp]	tauschen

FILE 8

page 193

glossary ['glɒsəri]	Glossar
term [tɜ:m]	Begriff
ownership ['əʊnəʃɪp]	Besitzverhältnisse
capitalization [ˌkæpɪtəlaɪ'zeɪʃn]	Kapitalisierung
stock market ['stɒk mɑ:kɪt]	Börse
numerous ['nju:mərəs]	zahlreich
barrier ['bæriə]	Grenze, Schranke
essential [ɪ'senʃl]	unabdingbar, unbedingt wichtig
obligation [ˌɒblɪ'geɪʃn]	Pflicht, Verpflichtung
customs duty [ˌkʌstəmz 'dju:ti]	Zollgebühr(en)
documentation [ˌdɒkjumen'teɪʃn]	Papiere
loading ['ləʊdɪŋ]	Verladung
unloading [ˌʌn'ləʊdɪŋ]	Entladung
to revise [rɪ'vaɪz]	überarbeiten
to keep up with sth [ˌki:p 'ʌp wɪð]	mit etw Schritt halten
revision [rɪ'vɪʒn]	Überarbeitung, Neubearbeitung
mode of transport [ˌməʊd əf 'trænspɔ:t]	Transportart
inland ['ɪnlænd]	Binnen-
waterway ['wɔ:təweɪ]	Wasserstraße
carrier ['kæriə]	Frachtführer

page 194

to hand sth over [ˌhænd 'əʊvə]	etw übergeben
carriage ['kærɪdʒ]	Beförderung, Transport
main carriage [ˌmeɪn 'kærɪdʒ]	Hauptlauf
to insure [ɪn'ʃʊə]	versichern
import duty ['ɪmpɔ:t dju:ti]	Einfuhrzoll
port of shipment [ˌpɔ:t əf 'ʃɪpmənt]	Verladehafen
port of destination [ˌpɔ:t əv destɪ'neɪʃn]	Bestimmungshafen

page 195

pre-carriage [ˌpri: 'kærɪdʒ]	Vorlauf
post-carriage [ˌpəʊst 'kærɪdʒ]	Nachlauf
contract of carriage [ˌkɒntrækt əv 'kærɪdʒ]	Beförderungsvertrag
export clearance ['ekspɔ:t klɪərəns]	(Erledigung der) Ausfuhrformalitäten

page 196

to **issue** ['ɪʃuː]	ausstellen
document of title [ˌdɒkjumənt əf 'taɪtl]	Traditionspapier
apparent [ə'pærənt]	augenscheinlich
order ['ɔːdə]	Zustand
foul [faʊl]	faul
to **accompany** [ə'kʌmpəni]	begleiten

page 197

haulage company ['hɔːlɪdʒ kʌmpəni]	(Straßen-)Spedition
holder ['həʊldə]	Inhaber/in
policy ['pɒləsi]	Versicherungspolice
to **cover sth** ['kʌvə]	etw versichern
restriction [rɪ'strɪkʃn]	Beschränkung, Einschränkung
on approval [ɒn ə'pruːvl]	zur Ansicht
customs (authority) ['kʌstəmz ɔːθɒrəti]	Zoll(behörde)

page 199

payee [ˌpeɪ'iː]	Zahlungsempfänger/in
in favour of sb/sth [ɪn 'feɪvər əv]	zugunsten von jdm/etw
guarantee [ˌgærən'tiː]	Garantie
irrevocable [ɪ'revəkəbl]	unwiderruflich
to **stipulate** ['stɪpjuleɪt]	festlegen

page 200

to **present** [prɪ'zent]	*(Dokumente)* vorlegen

A–Z word list

Dieses Wörterverzeichnis enthält alle Wörter in **Focus on Business 4th Edition** in alphabetischer Reihenfolge. Nicht aufgeführt sind die Wörter aus der *Basic word list* sowie internationale Wörter wie *hotel*, *e-mail* usw.
Wörter, die in den Hörverständnisübungen vorkommen, sind mit einem *T*, und Wörter, die in den *Partner Files*, mit einem *F* hinter der Seitenzahl gekennzeichnet.

24/7 *102* rund um die Uhr

A

abbreviation *201* Abkürzung
abolition *104* Abschaffung
about, to **be ~ to do sth** *44* im Begriff sein, etw zu tun; etw tun wollen/werden
above-mentiond *139* oben genannt
abroad, from ~ *40T* aus dem Ausland
access *16* Zugriff, Zugang
accessible *84F* erreichbar, zugänglich
accessories *54* Zubehör
accessory *140* Accessoire
accidentally *18* unabsichtlich
accommodation *13* Unterkunft
to **accompany** *196* begleiten
according to *12* gemäß, nach, zufolge
to **account for sth** *74* etw ausmachen
account (a/c) *154* Konto; **bank ~** *34* Bankkonto, Girokonto; **open ~** *148* offenes Zahlungsziel
account executive *61* Kontakter/in, Berater/in
account services *61* Kontakt
accountancy *31* Buchhaltung, Rechnungswesen
accountant *139* Buchhalter/in
accounting *88* Buchhaltung; **cost ~** *24* Kalkulation, Kostenrechnung
accounts *6* Buchhaltung(sabteilung)
accounts assistant *8* Buchhaltungsassistent/in
accounts manager *8* Leiter/in der Buchhaltung
accurate(ly) *73* genau
to **achieve** *26* erzielen; *104* erlangen
acknowledgement *154* Auftragsbestätigung
to **act** *64* handeln; 190 schauspielern; **~ sth out** *117* etw (vor-, durch)spielen
action *64* Handlung, Aktion, Maßnahme(n); **out of ~** *120T* lahmgelegt; to **put sth into ~** *76* etw in die Tat umsetzen
to **adapt (to sth)** *91* sich anpassen (an etw)
adapter *53* Passstück, Adapter
addition, in ~ *39* außerdem
to **address sth** *71* sich mit etw befassen
address, postal ~ *135* Postadresse
adequate *29* angemessen
administrative *7* Verwaltungs-
to **admit** *57T* zugeben
adult *16* Erwachsene/r
adult education college *190* Volkshochschule
advance, in ~ *101* im Voraus
advantage *7* Vorteil
to **advertise (sth)** *37* (für etw) Werbung machen; **~ a job** *40* eine Stelle ausschreiben; **~ sth** *31* etw anbieten
advertising *27* Werbung
advertising agency *61* Werbeagentur
advertising campaign *61* Werbekampagne
advertising space *61* Werbefläche(n), Werbezeit(en), Anzeigenraum
advertisment *27* Anzeige, Annonce
advice *17* Rat, Ratschlag/Ratschläge; to **give sb (a piece of) ~** *30* jdm etw raten, jdm einen Ratschlag erteilen
advice of dispatch *154* Versandanzeige, Versandmitteilung
to **advise** *17* raten
advisor *26* Berater/in
advocate *82* Befürworter
affairs *104* Angelegenheiten
to **affect sb/sth** *81* sich auf jdn/etw auswirken
to **afford sth** *11* sich etw leisten
affordable *77* preiswert
afield, far ~ *55T* weit weg
age, for ~s *45* eine Ewigkeit; **legal ~** *99* gesetzliches Mindestalter; **minimum ~** *190* Mindestalter
agency *61* Agentur
agenda *131T* Terminplan, -kalender
agent *128* Mitarbeiter/in
agent *50* Vertreter, Vertretung
agreement *103* Abkommen
agriculture *75* Landwirtschaft
to **aim** *101* darauf abzielen
aimed at sb *67* an jdn gerichtet, für jdn
air freight *175* Luftfracht
air mail *135* Luftpost
aircraft *79* Flugzeug(e)
all, at ~ *29* überhaupt
to **allow for sth** *101* etw vorsehen
along with *62* zusammen mit
alongside *69* neben, entlang
alternative *69* Alternative
altogether *55T* insgesamt
ambition *187* Ehrgeiz, Bestreben
amenities *127* Annehmlichkeiten
among *62* (mitten) in
amount *41* Menge, Betrag
animator *190* Animateur/in
annual(ly) *99* jährlich
to **answer the phone** *6* ans Telefon gehen
anxious(ly) *92* besorgt, beunruhigt, ängstlich
anyway *54T* wie dem auch sei
apart from *24* außer, abgesehen von
to **apologize** *116* sich entschuldigen
apology *54* Entschuldigung
apostrophe *20* Apostroph
apparent *196* augenscheinlich
to **appeal to sb** *61* für jdn attraktiv sein, jdn ansprechen
to **appear** *56* auftauchen, erscheinen; 74 scheinen
appearance *109* Auftritt; 185 Erscheinung(sbild), Aufreten, Aussehen
appliance *51* Gerät, Haushaltsgerät
applicant *12* Bewerber/in
application *40* Bewerbung; *62* Anwendung
application management *91* Anwendungsentwicklung
to **apply for sth** *34* etw beantragen; 40 sich für/auf etw bewerben; **~ to sth** *26* für etw gelten

appointment *118* Termin
to **appreciate** *95* schätzen, zu schätzen wissen; *179* für etw Verständnis haben
apprenticeship *13* Lehre, Ausbildung
to **approach sb** *95* auf jdn zugehen, jdn ansprechen
appropriate *10* passend, angemessen
approval, on ~ *197* zur Ansicht
to **approve of sth** *64* etw gut finden
approximately *41* ungefähr, zirka
architecture *69* Architektur
archive *6* Archiv
area *26* Gegend; *31* Gebiet, Bereich, Feld
to **arouse** *64* wecken, erregen
to **arrange** *121* (Termin) ausmachen; *134* vereinbaren
arrangements *29* Vorkehrungen, Maßnahmen
arrival *16* Ankunft
as good as new *26* (so gut) wie neu
as regards *109* hinsichtlich, bezüglich
aspect *58* Aspekt, Seite
to **assemble** *97* montieren, zusammenbauen
to **assess** *101* einschätzen
asset *81* Vorteil, etwas Gutes
assets, fixed ~ *26* Sachanlagen, Sachwerte
assistance *112* Hilfe
assistant *20* Assistent/in
to **associate** *57T* verbinden, assoziieren
to **assure** *146T* versichern, zusichern
at all *29* überhaupt
at last *37* endlich
at the latest *160* spätestens
athlete *57T* Sportler/in
athletics *57T* Sport, Leichtathletik
atmosphere *74* Atmosphäre
to **attach** *31* *(E-Mail:)* anhängen; 53 anschließen, anbringen
attendance *82* Zuschauerzahl
attention *64* Aufmerksamkeit; **~ (Attn.)** *134* zu Händen; to **draw sb's ~ to sth** *160* jdn auf etw aufmerksam machen; to **pay ~** *67* aufmerksam sein
attitude *101* Einstellung, Haltung
to **attract** *81* anziehen, anlocken; **~ sb's attention** *64* jds Aufmerksamkeit wecken/fesseln
attraction *96* Anziehungspunkt
attractive *95* attraktiv
to **auction** *121* versteigern
audience *62* Publikum; **target ~** *62* Zielpublikum, Zielgruppe
author *82* Verfasser/in, Autor/in
authority *76* Behörde
to **autograph** *121* signieren
availability *120* Verfügbarkeit
available *39* verfügbar, erhältlich; to **be ~** *114* *(Telefon:)* zu sprechen sein
to **average sth** *69* etw durchschnittlich erreichen
average *71* Durchschnitt
aviation *71* Luftfahrt
to **avoid** *17* vermeiden; *101* verhindern
aware, to be ~ of sth *81* etw wissen, sich einer Sache bewusst sein
awareness *57* Bewusstsein
awesome *75T* fantastisch
awful *21* furchtbar

B

to **back sth up** *29* *(Daten)* sichern
back-breaking *51* äußerst anstrengend
background *38* Herkunft; *39* Hintergrund
to **backpack** *44* mit dem Rucksack reisen
backpacker *12* Rucksacktourist/in
bacon *127* Speck
bacteria *72* Bakterien
to **bake** *59T* backen
to **balance** *49F* ausgleichen, ins Gleichgewicht bringen; *71* im Gleichgewicht halten
ballroom dancing *187* Gesellschaftstanz
to **ban sb** *35* jdn sperren
bank account *34* Bankkonto, Girokonto
bank transfer *150* Überweisung
bankrupt, to go ~ *37* Pleite gehen
bankruptcy *43* Konkurs, Pleite
bar *40T* Stange, Hebel
bar chart *38* Balkendiagramm, Säulendiagramm
barely *99* kaum
bargain *102* gutes Geschäft, Schnäppchen
barrier *193* Grenze, Schranke
based, to be ~ on sth *52* auf etw basieren
basic knowledge *186* Grundkenntnisse
basics *26* grundsätzliche Dinge
bathtub *127* Badewanne
battery *192T* Akku
bean *106* Bohne
to **bear sth** *41* etw tragen
bear *59T* Bär
to **beat** *75T* schlagen
to **beg the question** *99* die Frage aufwerfen
behalf, on sb's ~ *109* in jds Namen
behind the scenes *6* hinter den Kulissen
to **belong to sb** *38* jdm gehören
belt *69* Gürtel
beneficial to *83* nützlich, gewinnbringend für
to **benefit** *81* nützen, Nutzen bringen
benefit *64* Nutzen, Vorteil
benefits *94F* Zusatzleistungen, Vergünstigungen
beyond, to go way ~ sth *91* weit über etw hinausgehen
bill *29* Rechnung
billboard *61* Reklametafel, Plakatwand
billion *41* Milliarde
biofuel *69* Biokraftstoff
bird's nest *82* Vogelnest
to **blame sb** *21* jdm die Schuld geben
blind, to turn a ~ eye *102* wegsehen
block of flats *55T* Mietshaus, Wohnblock
bloody *75T* verdammt
blouse *40F* Bluse
board *126* Verpflegung; **full ~** *127* Vollpension; **half ~** *127* Halbpension
board and lodging *190* Kost und Logis
board game *44* Brettspiel
body *110* *(Brief:)* Haupttext
bold *111* fett (gedruckt)
booked up *128* ausgebucht
booking *122* Buchung, Reservierung
booking fee *127* Buchungsgebühr
bookshop *36* Buchhandlung
to **boost** *81* stärken, Auftrieb geben
border *99* (Landes-)Grenze
bored *18* gelangweilt
boring *62* langweilig
to **borrow sth from sb** *25* sich etw von jdm leihen
boss *10* Chef/in
bottom, at the ~ *92* (ganz) unten
bottom-up *49F* von unten nach oben
to **bow** *46* sich verbeugen
boycott *121* Boykott
bracket *14* Klammer
brain *88* Gehirn
to **brainstorm** *59T* Ideen sammeln
to **brainwash sb** *57T* jdn einer Gehirnwäsche unterziehen
branch *55T* Filiale, Niederlassung
brand *41* Marke

bread roll *127* Brötchen
to **break** *78* brechen; ~ **down** *51* kaputtgehen; **You're ~ing up.** *114* *(Telefon:)* Das Netz geht weg.
break *15* Pause; to **take a ~** *15* eine Pause machen
breeze *69* Wind
to **brew** *61* sich zusammenbrauen, gären
bricklayer *55T* Maurer/in
brief *61* Dossier, Anweisungen; *67* Auftrag; **product ~** *58* Produktbeschreibung
brief(ly) *74* kurz
briefcase *25* Aktenkoffer
briefing *39* Informationen
Briton *37* Brite/Britin
broad(ly) *61* breit
brochure *61* Prospekt
broken *19* kaputt
budget *67* Budget, Haushalt, Etat
budget deficit *82* Haushaltsdefizit
building contractor *55* Bauunternehmer/in, Bauunternehmen
bulky goods *159* Sperrgüter, Massengüter
to **bully** *21* mobben, tyrannisieren
bunch *104* (Bananen-)Staude; **a ~ of** *89T* eine Menge
to **burn** *59T* anbrennen; ~ **down** *41* abbrennen
business, core ~ *51* Kerngeschäft; to **close a ~** *34* ein Geschäft aufgeben; to **go into ~** *26* sich selbständig machen; to **put sb out of ~** *29* jdn in den Bankrott treiben; to **set up a ~** *37* ein Unternehmen gründen
business card *19* Visitenkarte
business idea *26* Geschäftsidee
business licence *37* Gewerbeschein, Gewerbeerlaubnis
business plan *26* Geschäftsplan
business start-up *26* Unternehmensgründung
business studies *78* Betriebswirtschaft(slehre)
busy, to keep ~ *16* sich beschäftigen
button *75T* Knopf, Taste
to **buy sth up** *51* etw aufkaufen
buyer *62* Einkäufer/in
by mistake *21* irrtümlich
by return *181* postwendend
by-product *71* Neben-, Abfallprodukt

C

cable channel *62* Kabelsender
to **calculate** *37* ausrechnen, berechnen, kalkulieren
calculation *82* Berechnung
to **call sb** *16* jdn anreden; **~ by** *146T* vorbeikommen; **~ on sb** *144* jdn besuchen
camel *14* Kamel
campaigner *102* Aktivist/in
can *30* Dose
canal *69* Kanal
to **cancel** *177* stornieren
cancellation *129* Stornierung, Absage
canteen *55T* Kantine
capable *75* fähig
capacity *72* Fassungsvermögen, Zuladung
capita, per ~ *86* pro Kopf
capital *36* Hauptstadt; **in ~s** *52* in Großbuchstaben
capital letter *110* Großbuchstabe
capitalization *193* Kapitalisierung
caption *46* Bildunterschrift
car boot sale *31* Trödel, Flohmarkt
car hire *27* Autovermietung
car licence *188* Führerschein Klasse 3
car park *40T* Parkplatz
carbon (dioxide) *68* Kohlenstoff, Kohlendioxid
carbon-neutral *69* CO2-neutral
to **care about sb/sth** *57* sich um jdn/etw kümmern, am Herzen liegen; to **not ~** *79* egal sein
career *15* Karriere, Laufbahn
careers advisor *34* Berufsberater/in
cargo *71* Fracht
carnival *104* Karneval
carpet *102* Teppich
carriage *194* Beförderung, Transport; **contract of ~** *195* Beförderungsvertrag; **main ~** *194* Hauptlauf; **post-~** *195* Nachlauf; **pre-~** *195* Vorlauf
carrier *124* Fluggesellschaft; *193* Frachtführer
to **carry on** *47* weitermachen; **~ sth out** *58* etw durchführen
carton *105* Kiste, Karton
case *31* Fall; **in ~** *131* für den Fall, dass; **in ~ of fire** *76* im Brandfall; **whatever the ~ may be** *171* wie dem auch sei, in jedem Fall; **lower-~** *116* kleingeschrieben; **upper-~** *116* großgeschrieben
cash *12* Bargeld; *41* Geld, liquide Mittel
cash discount *157* Skonto
cash flow *37* Einnahmen, Geldzufluss
cash register *9* Registrierkasse
cashier *55* Kassierer/in
castle *113* Schloss, Burg
casual *16* leger
casual work *11* Gelegenheitsarbeit(en)
catalogue *139* Katalog
to **catch** *114* verstehen, mitkriegen
catch 22 *78* Dilemma, ausweglose Situation
category *68* Kategorie
cause and effect *93* Ursache und Wirkung
celebrity *108* Prominente/r
century *39* Jahrhundert
cereal *127* Getreideflocken
certificate *187* Zeugnis, Bescheinigung
certification mark *101* Gütesiegel
to **certify** *101* bescheinigen, beglaubigen
chair *21* Stuhl
chairman *41* Vorsitzende/r
challenge *77T* Herausforderung, (schwierige) Aufgabe
challenging *95* (heraus)fordernd, schwierig
Chamber of Commerce *76* Handelskammer
championship *81* Meisterschaft
chances are *95* sehr wahrscheinlich
channel *62* Sender; **cable ~** *62* Kabelsender; **the English C~** *37* der Ärmelkanal
chaos *62* Chaos
character *12* Charakter
to **charge** *26* *(Preis etc.)* verlangen
charge *100* Preis, Gebühr; **parking ~** *77* Parkgebühr
charity *108* Kampagne, Aktion (für wohltätige Zwecke); *121* Hilfsorganisation, guter Zweck
charity shop *31* *Laden einer Wohltätigkeitsorganisation*
chart *52* Tabelle; **bar ~** *38* Balkendiagramm, Säulendiagramm; **organization ~** *18* Organigramm; **pie ~** *38* Tortendiagramm
chassis *75* Fahrgestell
chat show *121* Talkshow
chauffeur-driven *27* mit Chauffeur
to **check sb/sth out** *65T* sich jdn/etw ansehen
cheers *110* tschüs, danke
chefing *44* Tätigkeiten als Koch/Köchin
chemicals *102* Chemikalien
chicken *55T* Huhn
Chief Executive Officer (CEO) *50* Vorstandsvorsitzende/r
child labor *(AE)* *99* Kinderarbeit
childhood *102* Kindheit
Christ *121F* Christus
cigarette *84F* Zigarette
circle *42* Kreis
circumstances *100* Umstände

citizen *39* Bürger/in
city council *76* Stadtverwaltung
to **claim** *74* fordern; 83 behaupten
classmate *72* Klassenkamerad/in
clause *56* Nebensatz, Satzteil
cleaner *127* Reinigungskraft
cleaning supplies *26* Reinigungsmittel
to **clear sth up** *80* etw klären
clearance, export ~ *195* (Erledigung der) Ausfuhrformalitäten
clearly *40T* deutlich
clerk *89* Angestellte/r
clever *18* intelligent, klug; *61* geschickt
client *63* Kunde/Kundin
client base *92* Kundenstamm
climate *71* Klima
climate change *71* Klimawandel
to **clock in/out** *47* die Uhr stechen
to **close sth down** *87* etw *(Fabrik etc.)* schließen; ~ **a business** *34* ein Geschäft aufgeben
close *43* eng; 52 nahe, in der Nähe; **complimentary ~** *110* *(Brief:)* Schlussformel
cloth *99* Stoff
clothing, item of ~ *40F* Kleidungsstück
coach *123* Bus
coach service *123* Busverbindung
coal *159* Kohle
coal miner *102* Kohlebergarbeiter/in
coastal *74* Küsten-
coffee break *8* Kaffeepause
to **coincide with sth** *82* mit etw zusammenfallen
colleague *12* Kollege/-in
collective(ly) *101* gemeinsam, kollektiv
college *6* Berufsschule, Berufsfachschule
colonist *105* Siedler/in
column *26* Kolumne
to **combine** *49* verbinden, kombinieren
to **come up with sth** *59* sich etw einfallen lassen, sich etw ausdenken
comfortable *16* bequem
comical *64* komisch, lustig
command *185* Beherrschung
comment *6* Kommentar
to **comment on sth** *70* etw kommentieren
commerce *66* Handel; **Chamber of C~** *76* Handelskammer
commercial *62* Werbespot; 105 kommerziell
commercial course *36* kaufmännische Ausbildung
commercial invoice *166* Handelsrechnung
commission *84F* Kommission
to **commit oneself to sth** *26* sich auf etw einlassen, sich auf etw festlegen
committee *81* Komitee, Ausschuss
common(ly) *105* häufig, verbreitet; to **have sth in ~** *62* etw gemeinsam haben
community *78* Gemeinde, Gemeinschaft
company *7* Unternehmen, Gesellschaft, Firma; **limited liability ~ (LLC)** *(US) 42* Gesellschaft mit beschränkter Haftung (GmbH); **parent ~** *50* Muttergesellschaft; **private limited ~ (Ltd)** *(UK) 41* Gesellschaft mit beschränkter Haftung (GmbH); **proprietary limited ~ (Pty Ltd)** *(Aus, NZ) 42* Gesellschaft mit beschränkter Haftung (GmbH); **public limited ~ (plc)** *(UK) 41* Aktiengesellschaft (AG)
to **compare** *48* vergleichen
comparison *96* Steigerung (von Adjektiven)
to **compete** *84* (in Wettbewerben) antreten
competition *67* Wettbewerb
competitive *91* *(Preis:)* günstig
competitor *51* Konkurrent/in
to **complain** *21* sich beschweren
complaint *7* Reklamation, Beschwerde
to **complete an order** *160* einen Auftrag fertigstellen, ausführen
completion *154* Fertigstellung
complicated *123* kompliziert
complimentary close *110* *(Brief:)* Schlussformel
component *62* Bestandteil, Komponente
comprehensive *144* umfassend
computing *29* Informatik
conceived, to be ~ for sb *58* für jdn gedacht sein
to **concentrate** *17* sich konzentrieren
concept *58* Idee, Konzept
concern *56* Konzern; *71* Befürchtung, Bedenken, Sorge
to **concern sb** *32* jdm Sorgen machen
concerned *49* betroffen, beteiligt
concerned *84F* besorgt, beunruhigt
concerning *7* betreffend
concert *45* Konzert
conclusion *74* Fazit, Schluss
concrete *77T* Beton
condition *52* Bedingung; *96* Zustand
conditions, terms and ~ *146T* Konditionen, (Allgemeine) Geschäftsbedingungen
confidential *135* vertraulich
to **confirm** *60* bestätigen
confirmation *128* Bestätigung
confirmation of order *154* Auftragsbestätigung
conflict *49* Streit(igkeiten), Konflikt
congestion *77* Stau(s)
to **congratulate sb on sth** *60* jdn für etw beglückwünschen
congratulations (on sth) *16* herzlichen Glückwunsch (zu etw)
to **connect** *53* anschließen, verbinden
connecting flight *124* Anschlussflug
connection *53* Verbindung, Anschluss
conscience *78* Gewissen
consequence *79* Folge, Konsequenz
conservation *69* Einsparung, Sparen
conservative *16* konservativ
to **conserve** *70* sparen, einsparen
to **consider sth** *54T* etw berücksichtigen; *78* etw in Betracht ziehen; ~ **sth sth** *75T* etw für etw halten
considerable *142* erheblich, beträchtlich
considerably *69* erheblich, beträchtlich
consideration *101* Erwägung, Überlegung
considered, to be ~ sth *62* als etw gelten
consignment *165* Lieferung, Sendung
to **consist of sth** *79* aus etw bestehen
constant *62* konstant, gleichbleibend
construction *70* Bau
construction material *69* Baumaterial, Baustoff
consumer *59T* Verbraucher/in
consumption *69* Verbrauch, Konsum
to **contact sb** *6* sich mit jdn in Verbindung setzen
to **contain** *7* enthalten
contented *51* zufrieden
context *75* Zusammenhang
contract *67* Vertrag, *hier:* Auftrag
contract of carriage *195* Beförderungsvertrag
contractor, building ~ *55* Bauunternehmer/in, Bauunternehmen

to **contrast** *70* einander gegenüberstellen
contrast, in ~ *41* im Gegensatz (dazu)
to **contribute** *70* beitragen; 98 einen/seinen/ihren Beitrag leisten
contribution *72* Beitrag
contributor *12* Verfasser/in (eines Beitrags)
control *51* Steuerung
convenient *54T* passend, praktisch, angenehm
convention *108* Tagung, Konferenz
conventional *71* herkömmlich, konventionell
conversation *16* Gespräch; to **strike up a ~** *77T* eine Unterhaltung beginnen
to **convert** *37* umbauen, umwandeln
converter *72* Wandler
to **convince** *81* überzeugen
to **coordinate** *61* koordinieren
copy, to **write ~** *61* texten, Werbetexte verfassen
copy editor *62* Redakteur/in
copywriter *63* Werbetexter/in
core business *51* Kerngeschäft
corner *95* Ecke
corporate *55T* Unternehmens-, Geschäfts-
corporation *89T* Konzern
corporation (Corp./Inc.) *(US)* *42* Aktiengesellschaft (AG)
correspondence, written ~ *95* Schriftverkehr
cost accounting *24* Kalkulation, Kostenrechnung
costume jewellery *143* Modeschmuck
cotton *98* Baumwolle
countable *30* zählbar
counter-argument *101* Gegenargument
to **cover** *69* bedecken; *101* *(Kosten)* decken; *141* abdecken, *(Thema)* behandeln; ~ **sth** *197* etw versichern
cover flap *79* Umschlagklappe
cover letter *40* Anschreiben, Begleitschreiben
to **crash** *19* abstürzen
crazy *59* verrückt
cream *51* Rahm
creation *77* Schaffung
to **create** *18* schaffen, kreieren, *(Eindruck)* hinterlassen
creative (department) *61* Kreation
creativity *61* Kreativität
credit *55T* Kredit; **letter of ~ (L/C)** *150* Akkreditiv
credit card *20* Kreditkarte
crisis *80* Krise
critical *77T* kritisch
critically *71* äußerst
to **criticize** *22* kritisieren
crocodile *14* Krokodil
crop *98* Pflanzen (auf einem Feld), Ernte
cross *80* Kreuz
to **cross** *99* überqueren
crowd, to **stand out from the ~** *11* aus der Menge herausstechen
crowded *47* überfüllt, vollgestopft
crowding *77* Übervölkerung
culture *36* Kultur
cup *19* Tasse
currency *80* Währung
currency sign *156* Währungssymbol
current *39* aktuell
currently *9* derzeit, zur Zeit
custom *47* Brauch, Sitte
customer, regular ~ *170* Stammkunde/-in, Bestandskunde
customer care *185* Kundendienst
customer satisfaction *62* Kundenzufriedenheit
customer service *6* Kundendienst, Kundenbetreuung
customs (authority) *197* Zoll(behörde)
customs duty *193* Zollgebühr(en)
to **cut** *71* senken; ~ **costs** *94* Kosten senken; ~ **down on sth** *56* etw kürzen, einsparen; ~ **off the phone** *43* das Telefon abstellen
cutlery *40F* Besteck
CV (= curriculum vitae) *(BE)* *11* Lebenslauf
cycling *69* Fahrradfahren

D

damage *41* Schaden
to **damage** *68* schaden, (be)schädigen
damaging *83* schädlich
dancer *130* Tänzer/in
data *29* Daten
data entry *89* Dateneingabe
data storage *92* Datenspeicherung, Speicherplatz
date of birth *187* Geburtsdatum
dated *139* *(Datum:)* vom
day shift *40* Tagschicht
dead *85* tot
deadline *171* Frist
deadly *104* tödlich
to **deal with sth** *7* etw erledigen, etw bearbeiten; 21 mit etw umgehen; ~ **with sb/sth** *67* es mit jdm/etw zu tun haben
deal *55T* Geschäft
dealer *53* Händler
debt *81* Schuld(en)
decent *94* anständig, ordentlich
decision, to **take a ~** *42* eine Entscheidung fällen
to **decline** *120* ablehnen
to **decorate** *61* einrichten, gestalten; 156T dekorieren, verzieren
to **decrease** *80* zurückgehen, abnehmen
decrease *39* Abnahme, Rückgang
to **deduct** *168* abziehen
deficit *81* Verlust, Defizit; **budget ~** *82* Haushaltsdefizit
to **defend** *21* verteidigen
to **define** *58* definieren, festlegen
to **defy sth** *81* sich über etw hinwegsetzen
delay *131* Verspätung
delayed *23* verspätet
delighted, to **be ~** *31* sich freuen; to **be ~ to do sth** *109* etw gern tun
delightful(ly) *37* herrlich
to **deliver** *47* liefern
delivery *30* Lieferung; **recorded ~** *135* Einschreiben mit Rückschein; **terms of ~** *140* Lieferbedingungen
delivery period *140* Lieferzeit
demand *56* Nachfrage; *69* Bedarf; **final ~** *171* letzte Mahnung
to **demolish** *82* abreißen
to **demonstrate** *46* vorführen, zeigen
density *105* Dichte; **high-~** *69* dicht bevölkert
to **depart** *124* abfahren, abfliegen
department *6* Abteilung; **head of ~** *19* Abteilungsleiter/in
department store *61* Warenhaus
departure *124* Abfahrt, Abflug
to **depend on sth** *78* von etw abhängig sein
dependent on *77* abhängig von
deposit *37* Kaution; *127* Anzahlung
desalination plant *70* Entsalzungsanlage
to **deserve sth** *94F* etw verdienen
design *53* Konstruktion
to **design** *26* gestalten; *67* entwerfen; *71* konstruieren
desirable *185* wünschenswert
desire (for sb/sth) *64* Verlangen, Wunsch (nach jdm/etw)
desperate(ly) *37* verzweifelt, unbedingt
despite *96* trotz
destination *77T* Reiseziel; *144* Bestimmungsort; **port of ~** *194* Bestimmungshafen
to **destroy** *78* zerstören
destruction *77* Zerstörung

to **detail** *26 (Auto:)* gründlich waschen, reinigen
determination *11* Entschlossenheit
to **determine** *58* ermitteln, bestimmen
developer *69* Entwickler/in
developing country *86* Entwicklungsland
device *51* Gerät, Apparat
diagram *39* Grafik, Diagramm
to **dictate** *139* diktieren
dignified *102* würdevoll, würdig
diligent(ly) *99* gewissenhaft, fleißig
dining room *40T* Speisesaal
directions *112* Wegbeschreibung
director *42* Vorstandsmitglied
disadvantage *7* Nachteil
to **disagree with sb** *48* anderer Meinung als jd sein, jdm nicht zustimmen
to **disappear** *56* verschwinden
disappointed (with sb/sth) *66* enttäuscht (von jdm/etw)
disapproval *66* Missbilligung
discharge *72* Ablassen
discoloured *181* verfärbt
to **discontinue sth** *173* etw einstellen, abbrechen
discount *22* Rabatt, Nachlass; **cash ~** *157* Skonto; **quantity ~** *152* Mengenrabatt
discounted *99* billig, Billig-
to **discover** *77T* entdecken
discrepancy *179* Diskrepanz
disgusting *61* ekelhaft
to **dislike** *50* nicht mögen
disorganized *16* chaotisch
to **dispatch** *21* versenden
dispatch *165* Versand; **ready for ~** *165* versandbereit, versandfertig; **advice of ~** *154* Versandanzeige, Versandmitteilung
to **displace** *84F* verdrängen, vertreiben
to **display** *58* ausstellen, präsentieren
display *97* Bildschirm, Display; to **be on ~** *61* ausgestellt sein/werden, zu sehen sein
dispute *21* Streit, Disput
to **disregard sth** *171* etw als gegenstandslos betrachten
dissatisfied *175* unzufrieden
distance *55T* Entfernung
distant *43* entfernt, fern, entlegen
to **distribute** *58* vertreiben; *95* verteilen; *105* versenden
distribution *86* Verteilung
distributor *148* Großhändler
district *82* Bezirk, Bereich, Viertel
to **disturb** *45* stören
to **diversify** *51* verbreitern, auffächern, diversifizieren
diversity *79* Verteilung
diving *37* Tauchen
diving instructor *37* Tauchlehrer/in
division *47* Trennung
to **do: This will have to do.** *67* Das muss reichen.
dockworker *99* Hafenarbeiter
document of title *196* Traditionspapier
documentation *193* Papiere
dolphin *14* Delphin
domestically *93* im Inland
dominance *80* Vorherrschaft, Dominanz
dominant *86* vorherrschend
to **donate** *109* spenden
donation *109* Spende
to **double** *59T* sich verdoppeln
double room *109* Doppelzimmer
dozen *62* Dutzend
dramatic(ally) *80* dramatisch
to **drape** *69* einhüllen, verhüllen
to **draw sth up** *26* etw erstellen
drawback *75T* Nachteil, Schattenseite
dress *43* Kleid; *95* Kleiderordnung, Kleidung
to **dress up** *95* sich elegant kleiden
to **dress the part** *17* sich der Rolle entsprechend kleiden
to **drive sth** *89T* etw ankurbeln
driving licence *188* Führerschein
drop *69* Tropfen
drug *85* Droge; 87 Medikament, Arzneimittel
to **dry up** *74* austrocknen
duchess *58* Herzogin
due *160* fällig
due to *131* aufgrund
duration *124* Dauer
duty, customs ~ *193* Zollgebühr(en); **import ~** *194* Einfuhrzoll

E

early shift *40* Frühschicht
to **earmark sth for sth** *84* etw für etw vorsehen
earnings *98* Einnahmen
earth *71* Erde
ease *73* Leichtigkeit, Einfachheit
easy-going *56* angenehm, locker
eco-friendly *70* umweltfreundlich
ecological *72* ökologisch, Umwelt-
economic *77* wirtschaftlich
economic growth *82* Wirtschaftswachstum
economic sector *86* Wirtschaftssektor
economy *81* Wirtschaft
eco-warrior *78* Öko-Aktivist/in
editor *103* Herausgeber/in, Redakteur/in
educated *96* (gut) ausgebildet
education *59* Schulbildung
effect *74* Auswirkung
effective *62* wirkungsvoll, effektiv
effectiveness *62* Wirksamkeit, Effektivität
efficiency *48* Effizienz
effort *95* Bemühen, Bemühungen
either *72* jede/r/s (von beiden)
the elderly *74* die Alten
electrician *41* Elektriker/in
electricity *69* Strom, Elektrizität
to **eliminate** *71* unterbinden, eliminieren
to **email** *31* mailen
embarrassing *21* peinlich
to **emigrate** *39* auswandern
emigration *39* Auswanderung
emirate *69* Emirat
emission *69* Emission
to **emit** *106* emittieren, ausstoßen
emotional *78* Gefühls-, gefühlsmäßig
empire *41* Reich
to **employ** *52* beschäftigen, anstellen
employable *82* anwendbar, praktisch einsetzbar
employee *6* Angestellte/r, Beschäftigte/r
employee records *8* Personalakte
employer *6* Arbeitgeber/in
employment *44* Anstellung, Beschäftigung, Arbeit
to **empty** *71* leeren, löschen
to **enable sb to do sth** *191* jdm etw ermöglichen
to **enclose** *134* beifügen, beilegen
enclosure(s) (Enc, Encs) *134* Anlage(n)
to **encourage** *64* fördern
end, at sb's ~ *95* bei jdm; **in the ~** *21* schließlich, letztendlich; **to make ~s meet** *11* über die Runden kommen
to **end up with sth** *81* am Ende mit etw dastehen
endangered *71* bedroht
ending *54* Schluss, Ende
energy *16* Energie
energy requirements *69* Energiebedarf, -verbrauch
energy source *68* Energiequelle
engaging *64* fesselnd
engine *71* Motor, Maschine
enjoyable *10* angenehm, schön
enormous *88* gewaltig, enorm
to **enquire about sth** *62* sich nach etw erkundigen, fragen
enquiry *37* Anfrage
to **enslave** *104* versklaven

en suite *127* mit eigenem Bad
to **ensure** *178* sicherstellen, dafür sorgen
to **enter** *85* betreten, einreisen; ~ **sth** *21* etw eingeben
entertainment *127* Unterhaltung(selektronik)
enthusiasm *26* Begeisterung, Enthusiasmus
entire *70* gesamte/r/s
entirely *69* völlig, ausschließlich
to **entitle** *109* betiteln; ~ **sb to sth** *189* jdn zu etw berechtigen
entrance *125T* Eingang
entrepreneur *96* Unternehmer/in
entry level *185* Einstiegsniveau
entry visa *85* Einreisevisum
envelope *135* Briefumschlag
environment *57* Umwelt; *185* Umfeld, Umgebung
environmental *70* Umwelt-
environmental friendliness *74* Umweltfreundlichkeit
environmentalist *75T* Umweltschützer/in
environmentally friendly *43* umweltfreundlich
to **envisage** *69* vorhaben
equal *101* gleich
equally *55T* gleichermaßen
equipment *26* Geräte, Ausstattung
equitable *101* gerecht
equivalent *136* Entsprechung, Übersetzung
to **escape one's notice** *171* entgehen, übersehen
essential *193* unabdingbar, unbedingt wichtig
to **establish** *101* einrichten, herstellen
to **estimate** *39* schätzen
ethical *101* ethisch, (moralisch) verantwortlich
evacuation, fire ~ point *40F* Sammestelle/-punkt bei Feueralarm
evenly *49F* ausgeglichen, gleichmäßig
eventually *74* letztendlich, schließlich
ever since *35* seitdem
evidence *82* Nachweis(e), Beweis(e)
to **examine** *179* untersuchen
executive, senior ~ *171* leitende/r Angestellte/r
exception *57T* Ausnahme
exceptional *90* außergewöhnlich
excerpt *53* Auszug, Auschnitt
exchange *27* Austausch, Tausch
to **exchange** *46* austauschen
excited about sth *58* von etw begeistert
excitement *44* Aufregung, Spannung
exclamation mark *111* Ausrufezeichen
excuse *58* Ausrede
to **execute** *162* ausführen
exhibition *45* Ausstellung
to **exist** *62* es geben, existeren
exotic *11* exotisch
to **expand** *51* ausweiten
expansion *96* Expansion
expatriot *37 jd, der im Ausland lebt*
expenses *26* Kosten, Auslagen
experience *12* Erlebnis
experience *6* Erfahrung
expert *49* Fachmann, Experte/-in
explanation *54* Erläuterung, Erklärung
explicit(ly) *63* ausdrücklich, wörtlich
to **exploit** *100* ausbeuten
exploitation *102* Ausbeutung
to **export** *50* exportieren, ausführen
export clearance *195* (Erledigung der) Ausfuhrformalitäten
export sales director *47* Vertriebsleiter/in Export
to **express** *16* ausdrücken, zum Ausdruck bringen
exporter *69* Exporteur
extension *55T* Anbau
extensive *72* ausgedehnt, beträchtlich
external *91* extern
extra training *21* Fortbildung
extra-curricular *187* außerschulisch
extraordinarily *36* außergewöhnlich
eye, to **turn a blind ~** *102* wegsehen

F

fabric *69* Gewebe, Stoff, Tuch
to **face sth** *22* vor etw stehen; **Let's ~ it.** *78* Seien wir ehrlich.
face-to-face *44* persönlich
facilities *56* Anlage(n); *84* Einrichtungen; **production ~** *51* Produktionsstätte(n), Werk(e)
factory *33* Fabrik
to **fade** *76* nachlassen, schwächer werden
to **fail** *33 (Unternehmen:)* Pleite gehen; 41 es nicht schaffen, scheitern; ~ **to do sth** *173* versäumen, etw zu tun
fall *82* Rückgang
to **fall off sth** *23* von etw herunterfallen
to **fall ill** *37* erkranken, krank werden
to **fall in love with sb/sth** *77T* sich in jdn/etw verlieben
to **familiarize oneself with sth** *58* sich mit etw vertraut machen
far afield *55T* weit weg
faraway *11* weit entfernt, fern, entlegen
fare *11* Fahrpreis
farming *77T* Landwirtschaft
farmland *74* Ackerland
fashion *31* Mode
fashionable *180* in Mode
fashionista *98* Modefan, Modefreak
Father *121* Pater, Pfarrer
fault, sb's ~ *21* jds Schuld
favour, in ~ of sb/sth *199* zugunsten von jdm/etw; to **be in ~ of sth** *79* für etw sein
favourable *144* günstig
fear *56* Angst
to **fear** *41* fürchten, befürchten
to **feature** *61* vorkommen, eine Rolle spielen; ~ **sth** *71* etw zum Gegenstand haben
featuring *64 (Film:)* mit
federal *99* Bundes-
fee *29* Gebühr; *108* Honorar; **booking ~** *127* Buchungsgebühr
to **feed** *102* ernähren
female *59* weiblich, Frau
fiercely *79* äußerst, heftig
figure *26* Zahl
to **figure out** *59* herausfinden
to **file** *66* einreichen
to **fill in** *16* ausfüllen
film *156T* Folie
fin *71* Flosse
final demand *171* letzte Mahnung
to **finance** *42* finanzieren
finance services *88* Finanzdienstleitungen
financial *6* Finanz-, finanziell
to **find out** *21* (es) herausfinden, (es) erfahren
to **find your way around** *17* sich zurechtfinden
findings *70* Ergebnisse
fine *76* Geldstrafe
to **fire sb** *22* jdn (fristlos) entlassen, jdn feuern
fire, in case of ~ *76* im Brandfall
fire alarm *40T* Feueralarm
fire evacuation point *40F* Sammestelle/-punkt bei Feueralarm
fire exit *40F* Notausgang
firm *17* Firma
first aid *13* Erste Hilfe
first name *16* Vorname

first-rate *52* erstklassig
fish fingers *55T* Fischstäbchen
fisherman *37* Fischer
fishing, to **go** ~ *45* angeln/fischen gehen
to **fit in** *16* sich anpassen, sich einfügen
fixed *49* fest
fixed assets *26* Sachanlagen, Sachwerte
flash, in a ~ *37* im Nu
flat *127* Wohnung; **block of** ~s *55T* Mietshaus, Wohnblock
flexibility *92* Flexibilität
flight *23* Flug
flight attendant *80* Flugbegleiter/in
flowchart *99* Flussdiagramm
fluent(ly) *96 (Sprache:)* fließend
to **focus on sth** *67* sich auf etw konzentrieren
folks *6* Leute
to **follow** *22* folgen
follow-up *129* Anschluss-
font *186* Schrift, Zeichensatz
food chain *92* Nahrungskette
foolish *84F* töricht, dumm, unklug
for ages *45* eine Ewigkeit
for free *32* umsonst
to **force** *51* zwingen
forced labour *101* Zwangsarbeit
forceful *171* deutlich, eindringlich
foreign *12* Auslands-, ausländisch, fremd
foreign language *15* Fremdsprache
to **form** *41* bilden
form letter *6* Formbrief, Serienbrief
formal *16* formell, förmlich
former *82* ehemalige/r/s
fortunate *98* glücklich, vom Glück begünstigt
to **forward** *109* weiterleiten
foul *196* faul
to **found** *50* gründen
founder *51* Gründer/in
francs *168* (Schweizer) Franken
free, for ~ *32* umsonst
freelance *94* selbständig, freiberuflich
freelancer *92* Freiberufler/in
freight *175* Fracht
freight forwarder *176* Spediteur
frequency *14* Häufigkeit
fresh *55T* frisch
friend, to **make** ~s *10* Freunde finden, Freundschaft(en) schließen
friendliness *47* Freundlichkeit
frozen foods *55T* Tiefkühlkost
fuel *26* Treibstoff; 68 Brennstoff, Kraftstoff
fuel cell *71* Brennstoffzelle
to **fulfil** *92* erfüllen
full board *127* Vollpension
full-page *61* ganzseitig
full-time *11* Vollzeit-
fully automated *69* vollautomatisch
fumes *106* Abgase
fun, to **be** ~ *13* Spaß machen
to **function** *53* funktionieren
to **fund** *41* finanzieren
funds *84F* Gelder
fur *121* Pelz
furious *21* wütend
furnished *127* möbliert, ausgestattet
furthest from sth *47* am weitesten von etw entfernt

G

to **gain** *82* erwerben, gewinnen, sammeln; 87 erlangen
gap *7* Lücke, Zwischenraum
gap year *11 das Jahr zwischen Schulabgang und Studienbeginn*
garage *26* Autowerkstatt; *50T* Garage
garment *98* Kleidungsstück
gatehouse *122* Torhaus
gear *35* Ausrüstung
geek *91* Nerd, Freak
general, in ~ *39* im Allgemeinen
to **generate** *43* erzeugen
gently *80* sanft
geographic *79* geographisch
gesture *176* Geste
to **get along with sb** *11* mit jdm zurechtkommen
to **get around** *78* sich fortbewegen, herumkommen
to **get back to sb** *115T* sich bei jdm melden, jdn zurückrufen
to **get in touch with sb** *120T* sich mit jdm in Verbindung setzen
to **get into trouble** *29* in Schwierigkeiten geraten, sich Ärger einhandeln
to **get married** *44* heiraten
to **get sb down** *21* jdn bedrücken, jdn deprimieren
to **get sb down for sth** *40T* jdn für etw vorsehen
to **get sb involved in sth** *64* jdn an etw beteiligen, jdn in etw einbeziehen
to **get started** *26* loslegen
to **get sth across** *80F* etw klarmachen, etw vermitteln
to **get to know sb** *54T* jdn kennenlernen
ghost town *82* Geisterstadt
to **give sb (a piece of) advice** *30* jdm etw raten, jdm einen Ratschlag erteilen
glamorous *61* glanzvoll
glasses *57* Brille
global warming *74* Erderwärmung
glossary *193* Glossar
to **glow** *60* leuchten
to **go ahead** *67* anfangen, loslegen
to **go down well (with sb)** *146T* (bei jdm) gut ankommen
to **go places** *11* herumkommen
to **go public** *56* an die Börse gehen
to **go way beyond sth** *91* weit über etw hinausgehen
to **go wrong** *31* einen Fehler machen
goal *23 (Fußball etc.:)* Tor; *51* Ziel
goods *27* Güter, Ware(n)
gorgeous *75T* (wunder)schön, prächtig
government *55T* Regierung, öffentliche Verwaltung
to **grab** *67* packen, greifen
grade *72* Note
grading *126* Einstufung
grammar school *188* Gymnasium
grandparents *31* Großeltern
to **grant** *140* gewähren, einräumen
grapes *14* Trauben
graphic artist *62* Grafiker/in
grateful *89T* dankbar
greenhouse gas *71* Treibhausgas(e)
to **greet** *45* begrüßen
grievance procedure *21* Beschwerdeverfahren
grocery store *58* Lebensmittelgeschäft
Gross Domestic Product (GDP) *82* Bruttoinlandsprodukt (BIP)
group *41* Konzern
to **grow** *70* etw anbauen; ~ **up** *17* erwachsen werden
growth *82* Wachstum; **economic** ~ *82* Wirtschaftswachstum
guarantee *199* Garantie
guest house *85* Pension
guest of honour *47* Ehrengast
guide price *126* Richtpreis
guilty *78* schuldig
guitar *25* Gitarre
gulf *69 (Meer:)* Golf
gym *50T* Fitnessklub
gymnastics *84* Turnen

H

habit *59* Gewohnheit
hairdresser *55* Friseur/in
half board *127* Halbpension
to **hand sth in** *21* etw einreichen
to **hand sth over** *194* etw übergeben
to **handle sth** *6* etw bearbeiten; *29* etw erledigen; *29* mit etw umgehen, etw bewältigen; *76* mit etw hantieren, etw anfassen

handling, rough ~ *181* unsachgemäße Behandlung/Handhabung
handmade *31* handgemacht
hanger *98* Kleiderbügel
to **happen** *31* passieren
happiness *48* Glück, Zufriedenheit
happy, to **be ~ to do sth** *50T* etw gern tun
harassment *21* Schikane, Mobbing
hard, to **give sb a ~ time** *21* jdm das Leben schwer machen; to **have a ~ time** *64* es schwer haben, schwerfallen
hardware store *53* Eisenwarenhandlung, Baumarkt
hard-working *18* fleißig
harmful *69* schädlich
to **harness** *71* nutzen
to **harvest** *98* ernten
to **hate** *9* hassen, überhaupt nicht mögen
haul, long-~ flight *78* Langstreckenflug; **short-~ flight** *80F* Kurzstreckenflug
haulage company *197* (Straßen-)Spedition
hazard *72* Gefahr
to **head** *99* (in Richtung von etw) gehen, fahren
head *42* Leiter/in, Chef/in
head of department *19* Abteilungsleiter/in
head office *50* Zentrale
headache *23* Kopfschmerzen
heading *52* Überschrift
headphones *65T* Kopfhörer
headquarters *50* Zentrale
health and safety *40T* Arbeitsschutz
health insurance *56* Krankenversicherung
health-conscious *62* gesundheitsbewusst
heart *59* Herz
heat *69* Hitze
to **heat** *51* erhitzen
heatwave *74* Hitzewelle
hectare *69* Hektar
heel *44* *(Schuh:)* Absatz
helmet *35* Helm
helpful *44* hilfsbereit
helpfulness *47* Hilfsbereitschaft
to **hesitate** *40F* zögern
to **hide** *104* verbergen, verstecken
high street *10* Hauptgeschäftsstraße
high-density *69* dicht bevölkert
higher education entrance qualifications *187* Fachhochschulreife
high-resolution *160* hochauflösend
high-skill *87* hochqualifiziert
to **hire sb** *67* jdn engagieren, beauftragen, einstellen; **~ sth** *128* etw mieten
history *81* (die) Geschichte
to **hold** *66* gelten; 82 *(Veranstaltung etc.)* abhalten; **~ the line** *114* *(Telefon:)* am Apparat bleiben
holder *197* Inhaber/in
holiday-maker *77T* Urlauber/in
homework *26* Hausaufgaben
honest *6* ehrlich
horrible *13* schrecklich, fürchterlich
horse racing *36* Pferderennen
hose *53* Schlauch; **water intake ~** *53* Wasserzulaufschlauch
hospital *55T* Krankenhaus
hospitality *185* Hotel- und Gaststättengewerbe
host *47* Gastgeber
to **host sth** *81* etw ausrichten
hotel maid *40* Zimmermädchen
hourly wage *91* Stundenlohn
household *51* Haushalt, Haushalts-
housekeeping *44* Hauswirtschaft
housing *51* Wohnungen, Wohnraum, Unterkunft
however *26* allerdings, jedoch
huge *73* gewaltig, riesig
hull *71* (Schiffs-)Rumpf
human *49F* menschlich
Human Resources (HR) *40F* Personalabteilung; **~ Manager** *40F* Personalleiter/in
hunger *99* Hunger
hurry, to **be in a ~** *6* es eilig haben
hydrogen *71* Wasserstoff
hygienic *55T* hygienisch

I

to **identify with sb/sth** *49F* sich mit jdm/etw identifizieren
idle, to **lay ~** *37* *(Boot:)* (ungenutzt) im Hafen liegen
to **ignore** *103* hinwegsehen über, ignorieren
ill, to **fall ~** *37* erkranken, krank werden
illegal *29* verboten, illegal
illness *56* Krankheit
to **imagine sth** *40* sich etw vorstellen
imagination *11* Phantasie
to **immigrate** *39* einwandern
immigration *39* Einwanderung
immigration officer *85* Grenzbeamte/r
impact *78* Auswirkung, Folge, Einfluss; to **make an ~** *62* einen Eindruck hinterlassen
to **implement** *74* einführen, umsetzen
impolite *133* unhöflich
to **import** *43* importieren, einführen
import duty *194* Einfuhrzoll
importance *47* Bedeutung, Wichtigkeit
importer *140* Importeur
impossible *78* unmöglich
to **impress** *17* beeindrucken
impression *16* Eindruck; to **give the ~ that ...** *95* den Eindruck erwecken, dass ...
improvement *102* Verbesserung
incentive *76* Anreiz
to **include** *26* einbeziehen; *41* umfassen; *53* beifügen
included *44* inbegriffen, enthalten
income *50* Einkommen
incompetent *21* inkompetent
inconvenience *176* Unannehmlichkeiten
Incoterm *148* Internationale Handelsklausel
to **increase** *29* erhöhen; *51* steigern
increase *39* Zunahme, Steigerung
increasingly *74* zunehmend
indeed *87* in der Tat
independence *87* Unabhängigkeit
independent *101* unabhängig
individual *17* individuell
individuality *16* Individualität
induction *19* Einführung
to **industrialize** *87* industrialisieren
industry *62* Branche; 86 Industrie
inevitably *82* zwangsläufig
inexpensive *71* preisgünstig
to **influence** *74* beeinflussen
influence *57* Einfluss
informal *26* informell, zwanglos, locker
infrastructure *70* Infrastruktur
ingredient *100* Bestandteil
initial order *148* Erstbestellung, Erstauftrag
initiative *11* Eigeninitiative, Initiative; to **take the ~** *110* die Initiative ergreifen
injury *101* Verletzung
inland *193* Binnen-
innovative *71* innovativ
insight *104* Einblick
insignificant *82* unbedeutend
to **insist** *173* darauf bestehen
inspiration *72* Anregung
to **inspire** *61* anregen
installation guide *53* Aufbauanleitung
instance, for ~ *21* zum Beispiel
instead of *12* anstatt
instruction *45* Anweisung, Anleitung; *76* Aufforderung
instructor *11* Lehrer/in

insurance *51* Versicherung; **health ~** *56* Krankenversicherung; **medical ~** *51* Krankenversicherung
to **insure** *194* versichern
intake *72* Zufuhr, Aufnahme; **water ~ hose** *53* Wasserzulaufschlauch
intangible *82* immateriell
integral part *78* fester Bestandteil
to **integrate** *78* integrieren
integrated circuit *97* integrierter Schaltkreis, Mikrochip
to **intend** *12* beabsichtigen
interchange *125* Übergang, Umsteigen
internal *91* intern
to **interpret** *80* dolmetschen
interview *6* Vorstellungsgespräch
to **interview** *95* ein Vorstellungsgespräch führen
interviewer *18 Person, die ein Vorstellungsgespräch führt*
to **invent** *56* erfinden
inventor *41* Erfinder
investigation *58* Forschung, Ermittlung(en)
to **invest** *42* investieren
investment *41* Einlage; *55T* Geldanlage; 87 Investitionen
invitation *109* Einladung
invoice *139* Rechnung; **commercial ~** *166* Handelsrechnung; **receipt of ~** *155* Rechnungseingang, -erhalt
to **involve** *7* mit sich bringen, einbeziehen, beinhalten
involved, to **get sb ~ in sth** *64* jdn an etw beteiligen, jdn in etw einbeziehen
irregular *14* unregelmäßig
irrevocable *199* unwiderruflich
issue *70* Frage, Streitpunkt, Problem
to **issue** *196* ausstellen
italics, in ~ *7* kursiv
item *31* Artikel; 57 Gegenstand
item of clothing *40F* Kleidungsstück

J

jam *127* Marmelade
jewellery *31* Schmuck; **costume ~** *143* Modeschmuck
job, to **learn on the ~** *17* lernen am Arbeitsplatz
job advertisment *6* Stellenanzeige
job interview *44* Vorstellungsgespräch
job title *16* Berufsbezeichnung
job training *77* Berufsausbildung
to **judge** *192* beurteilen

K

kangaroo *14* Känguru
keen *35* begeistert
to **keep up with sth** *22* sich über etw auf dem Laufenden halten; *193* mit etw Schritt halten
to **keep busy** *16* sich beschäftigen
keyboard *9* Tastatur
to **kid: Just kidding.** *75T* Kleiner Scherz.
kite *71* Drachen
knowledge, basic ~ *186* Grundkenntnisse

L

label *59* Etikett
to **label** *46* beschriften, etikettieren
labour *39* Arbeit, Arbeitskraft; **child ~** *99* Kinderarbeit
labour intensive *90* arbeitsintensiv
labour market *39* Arbeitsmarkt
labour-saving *51* arbeitssparend
labourer *99* Arbeiter/in
lack *77* Mangel
to **land** *131* landen
landline *47* Festnetztelefon
last, at ~ *37* endlich
to **last** *26* halten; 44 dauern; **while stocks ~** *150* solange der Vorrat reicht
late shift *40* Spätschicht
lately *45* in letzter Zeit
latest *7* neueste/r/s; **at the ~** *160* spätestens
to **launch sth** *67* etw auf den Markt bringen
launch, product ~ *58* Produkteinführung
law *81* Gesetz; to **pass a ~** *92* ein Gesetz verabschieden
law enforcement *84F* Strafverfolgung
law firm *10* Anwaltskanzlei
law of nature *81* Naturgesetz
to **lay sb off** *91* jdn entlassen, jdm betriebsbedingt kündigen
to **lay idle** *37 (Boot:)* (ungenutzt) im Hafen liegen
to **laze about** *45* faulenzen, herumfaulenzen
lazy *16* nachlässig, faul
leaf, leaves *105* Blatt, Blätter
leaflet *22* Faltblatt
leaflet *61* Faltblatt, Informationsblatt
to **learn on the job** *17* lernen am Arbeitsplatz
leather *32* Leder
to **leave a message** *114 (Telefon:)* eine Nachricht hinterlassen
to **leave port** *71* auslaufen

legal age *99* gesetzliches Mindestalter
leisure *47* Freizeit
to **lend sb sth** *19* jdm etw leihen
length *79* Länge, Dauer
lesson *35* Lektion
letter of credit (L/C) *150* Akkreditiv
letterhead *134* Briefkopf
level *39* Niveau; 76 (Öl-, Wasser-) Stand; 78 Ebene; **sea ~** *74* Meeresspiegel
to **level out** *80* sich einpendeln
liability *41* Haftung; *81* Belastung
to **liberate** *51* befreien
library *36* Bibliothek
licence, business ~ *37* Gewerbeschein, Gewerbeerlaubnis; **car ~** *188* Führerschein Klasse 3; **driving ~** *188* Führerschein
life expectancy *51* Lebenserwartung
lifestyle *69* Lebensweise, Lebensführung
to **lift** *104* heben, hochheben
lift, to **give sb a ~** *24* jdn (mit dem Auto) mitnehmen
to **light up** *60* aufleuchten
lighting *95* Beleuchtung, Licht
lightweight *156* leicht
likely *80* wahrscheinlich; to **be ~ to do sth** *12* etw wahrscheinlich tun werden
to **limit** *63* beschränken
limit *55T* Grenze; **The sky's the ~.** *55T* Nach oben sind keine Grenzen gesetzt.
limited *41* begrenzt, beschränkt; **private ~ company (Ltd)** *(UK) 41* Gesellschaft mit beschränkter Haftung (GmbH); **proprietary ~ company (Pty Ltd)** *(Aus, NZ) 42* Gesellschaft mit beschränkter Haftung (GmbH); **public ~ company (plc)** *(UK) 41* Aktiengesellschaft (AG)
limited liability company (LLC) *(US) 42* Gesellschaft mit beschränkter Haftung (GmbH)
limited partnership *51* Kommanditgesellschaft (KG)
to **linger** *98* im Raum stehen
to **link** *56* verbinden
lipstick *149* Lippenstift
litre *30* Liter
live-in job *44 Arbeitsstelle mit Kost und Logis*
load *21* Ladung
to **load** *99* verladen, laden
loading *193* Verladung
loads of *78* eine Menge
loan *37* Darlehen, Kredit
local *36* örtlich, ortsansässig, lokal

the locals *77T* die Einheimischen
located, to **be ~ in ...** *50* in ... ansässig sein, seinen/ihren Sitz in ... haben; *77* in ... liegen
location *50* Standort
lodging, board and ~ *190* Kost und Logis
long-haul flight *78* Langstreckenflug
longing(ly) *61* sehnsüchtig
long-term *52* langfristig
to **look forward to sth** *10* sich auf etw freuen
looks *75T* (gutes) Aussehen
lorry *21* Lastwagen, Lkw
loss *42* Verlust
lotus blossom *88* Lotosblüte
love, to **fall in ~ with sb/sth** *77T* sich in jdn/etw verlieben
to **lower** *74* senken
lower-case *116* kleingeschrieben
low-paid *12* Niedriglohn-
low-wage country *51* Niedriglohnland
loyal *51* treu, loyal
luck, Good ~! *16* Viel Glück!
luckily *29* glücklicherweise
luggage *124* Gepäck
luxury *12* Luxus
lyrics *104* Liedtext

M

machine *27* Maschine; *48* Gerät,
magic *64* Zauberei, Magie
magically *81* wie durch Zauberhand
mail order *41* Versandhandel
main carriage *194* Hauptlauf
mainland *77T* Festland
mainly *45* hauptsächlich
to **maintain** *90* behalten, beibehalten; *99* (nach wie vor) behaupten; ~ **sth** *82* etw unterhalten, instandhalten
major *41* groß, bedeutend
majority, vast ~ *73* (bei weitem) größter Teil, Löwenanteil
to **make sth up** *94* etw ausmachen, bilden
to **make sense** *16* sinnvoll/logisch sein
to **make sure** *16* sicherstellen, sich vergewissern
to **make way for sth** *82* für etw Platz machen
male *59* männlich, Mann
management *21* Geschäftsführung
managing director *19* Geschäftsführer/in
mangrove *69* Mangrove
man-made *74* von Menschen verursacht
to **manufacture** *51* herstellen, fertigen
manufacture *87* Herstellung, Fertigung
manufacturer *50* Hersteller
marine *72* Meeres-
marital status *187* Familienstand
maritime *71* Schifffahrts-
mark *21* Zeichen, Kreuz
to **mark** *40T* kennzeichnen
marked(ly) *80* deutlich, merklich
to **market** *58* vermarkten
market *26* Markt
market research *27* Marktforschung
marketplace *31* Marktplatz
marking, special ~ *134* Vermerk, Kennzeichnung
married, to **get ~** *44* heiraten
marvellous *116* großartig
mask *55T* Maske
mass *77T* Masse
massive *99* riesig
match *81* Spiel, Partie
to **match sth** *12* etw zuordnen, zu etw passen
material *90* materiell
matte *167* matt
matter *54* Angelegenheit, Sache
to **maximize** *75T* maximieren
mayor *76* Bürgermeister/in
meaning *80F* Sinn, Bedeutung
means *66* Mittel; ~ **of travel** *69* Fortbewegungsart/-mittel
meantime, in the ~ *150* in der Zwischenzeit
meanwhile *47* in der Zwischenzeit
measure *70* Maßnahme; *74* Maß; to **take ~s** *70* Maßnahmen ergreifen
meat *55T* Fleisch
mechanic *55* Mechaniker/in
media *61* Medien
medic *90* Arzt/Ärztin
medical insurance *51* Krankenversicherung
medicine *75* Medizin
medium-sized *55T* mittelgroß, mittelständisch
to **meet (sth)** *91 (Bedarf, Norm etc.)* erfüllen, befriedigen, entsprechen
meeting *16* Besprechung, Sitzung
to **melt** *78* schmelzen
member of parliament (MP) *36* Parlamentsabgeordnete/r
member state *39* Mitgliedsstaat
to **mention** *45* erwähnen
merchandise *83* Handelsware, hier: Fanartikel, Lizenzartikel
mermaid *61* Meerjungfrau
merry: the more the merrier *113* je mehr, desto fröhlicher
message, to **leave a ~** *114 (Telefon:)* eine Nachricht hinterlassen; to **take a ~** *114 (Telefon:)* etw ausrichten
method *62* Methode, Art (und Weise)
microwave *130* Mikrowelle
migration *39* Migration; *87* Abwanderung, Verlagerung
mileage *75* Spritverbrauch
miles per gallon (mpg) *75* Meilen pro Gallone
miles per hour (mph) *75* Meilen pro Stunde
military *31* Militär(-)
to **mind** *50T* etwas dagegen haben
mind you *77T* allerdings
mind-numbing *89* stumpfsinnig, todlangweilig
to **mine** *97* abbauen, fördern
mine *97* Bergwerk, Mine
minerals *97* Mineralien, Bodenschätze
minicab *123* Funktaxi
to **minimize** *51* auf ein Minimum beschränken, minimieren
minimum age *190* Mindestalter
minimum order quantity *156T* Mindestbestellmenge
minimum wage *99* Mindestlohn
minor *92* klein, unbedeutend
minority *81* Minderheit
mirror *69* Spiegel
misery, to **make sb's life a ~** *21* jdm das Leben schwer machen, jdm das Leben zur Hölle machen
to **miss** *17* versäumen, verpassen
missing *15* vermisst; to **be ~** *40T* fehlen
mission *109* Auftrag, Mission
mission statement *109* Leitbild
mistake, by ~ *21* irrtümlich
to **misunderstand** *135* falsch verstehen
to **mix sth up** *176* etw durcheinanderbringen, etw verwechseln
mixed *35* gemischt
mixed up *138* durcheinander
mixture *11* Mischung
mobile *26* mobil
mobile phone *9* Mobiltelefon, Handy
mode *75* Modus, Art
mode of transport *193* Transportart
model *64* Modell
to **model sth on sth** *69* etw einer Sache zum Vorbild nehmen, etw einer Sache nachbilden
monetary *72* finanziell, Geld-
money, spending ~ *11* Taschengeld; **supply of ~** *103* Geldmenge

money pit *82* Kostenfalle, Millionengrab
monthly *99* monatlich
most notably *87* vor allem
to **motivate** *94* motivieren
motorway *55T* Autobahn
mountaineering *43* Bergsteigen
mouse *19* Maus
move *39* Bewegung
multimodal transport *159* kombinierte Beförderung, multimodaler Transport
multinational *102* Multi, Großkonzern
multiple *99* vielfach
Must rush. *110* Ich muss weg. *(Brief:)* In Eile
myth *62* Mythos, Märchen, Legende
mythology *64* Mythologie

N

naive *102* naiv
name tag *76* Namensschild
narrow *179* eng, schmal
nation *68* Staat, Nation
nationality *187* Staatsangehörigkeit
native *77* Einheimische/r, einheimisch
native speaker *133* Muttersprachler/in
natural disaster *74* Naturkatastrophe
nearby *109* in der Nähe
neck *179* Hals, Halsausschnitt
to **negate** *78* aufheben
negative *9* verneinend
to **negotiate** *101* verhandeln, aushandeln
nervous *16* nervös
nest, bird's ~ *82* Vogelnest
net *148* netto
network *29* Netzwerk
nevertheless *95* nichtsdestotrotz, dennoch
noisy *55T* laut
non-payment *171* Nichtzahlung
not yet *6* noch nicht
notably, most ~ *87* vor allem
to **note** *171* feststellen
notepad *19* Notizblock
notes *16* Notizen; **to take ~** *16* sich Notizen machen
notice *7* Hinweis, Bekanntmachung; **at short ~** *54T* kurzfristig; to **escape one's ~** *171* entgehen, übersehen
novelty *58* Neuheit
now and then *8* ab und zu
nowadays *50T* heutzutage
numerous *193* zahlreich

O

to **object to sth** *79* etwas gegen etw haben
obligation *193* Pflicht, Verpflichtung
obliged, to **be ~ to do sth** *178* sich genötigt sehen, etw zu tun
obscene *81* unverschämt
to **obtain** *181* etw erhalten, etw beziehen
occasionally *8* gelegentlich
ocean *72* Ozean, Weltmeer
off, I'm ~ to bed. *6* Ich gehe dann mal ins Bett; to **be well ~** *102* gut dran sein
office hours *115T* Bürozeiten, Arbeitszeit
official *21* offiziell
off-shore *88* Auslands-
Olympic *81* olympisch
Olympics *81* Olympische Spiele
open account *148* offenes Zahlungsziel
opera *45* Oper
to **operate** *79* (geschäftlich) tätig sein
operation *87* Betrieb
opinion, in your ~ *7* deiner/Ihrer Meinung nach
opposite *18* engegengesetzt, gegensätzlich
optimism *88* Zuversicht, Optimismus
order *196* Zustand; **with ~** *156T* bei Auftragserteilung; **confirmation of ~** *154* Auftragsbestätigung; **in ~ to** *26* um ... zu; **initial ~** *148* Erstbestellung, Erstauftrag; **minimum ~ quantity** *156T* Mindestbestellmenge; **receipt of ~** *148* Auftragseingang, Auftragserhalt; **trial ~** *147* Probebestellung, Probeauftrag; to **complete an ~** *160* einen Auftrag fertigstellen, ausführen; to **place an ~** *146T* einen Auftrag erteilen, eine Bestellung aufgeben
ordinary *74* normal
organic *106* Bio-
organization chart *18* Organigramm
to **organize** *7* organisieren
organizer *81* Organisator/in
original(ly) *31* ursprünglich
to **originate** *104* entstehen, seinen Ursprung haben
orphanage *78* Waisenhaus
out of action *120T* lahmgelegt
out of stock *53* nicht vorrätig, nicht lieferbar
to **outsource** *89T* (Arbeit) auslagern
outsourcing *51* Auslagern
oven *59T* Ofen, Herd
overall *80* gesamt
overdue *139* überfällig
overhead locker *80F* Gepäckfach (über den Sitzen)
to **overlook** *170* übersehen
overnight *79* über Nacht
overpriced *77* überteuert
overseas *92* Auslands-
overseer *104* Vorarbeiter/in
to **overtake** *75* überholen
overtime, to do ~ *48* Überstunden machen
owing *172* fällig, ausstehend
own, on one's ~ *49* allein
owner *26* Besitzer/in, Inhaber/in
ownership *193* Besitzverhältnisse

P

to **pack** *156* verpacken
package *29* Paket
packaging *58* Verpackung
packet *106* Packung
packing *154* Verpackung, Versandverpackung
paint *26* Farbe, Lack
to **paint sth up** *37* etw (neu) anmalen, streichen
palm *69* Palme
paperwork *6* Unterlagen; *37* Formalitäten, Büroarbeit
paradise *37* Paradies
parallel bars *84* Barren
parent company *50* Muttergesellschaft
to **park** *20* parken
parking charge *77* Parkgebühr
parking space *20* Parkplatz
parliament *36* Parlament; **member of ~ (MP)** *36* Parlaments-abgeordnete/r
partially *101* teilweise, zum Teil
participant *84F* Teilnehmer/in
partly *100* teilweise
partnership, limited ~ *51* Kommanditgesellschaft (KG)
to **pass** *16* vorübergehen; *75* vorbeifahren, überholen; **~ sth on** *99* etw weitergeben, -leiten; **~ sth out** *95* etw verteilen; **~ a law** *92* ein Gesetz verabschieden
passenger *47* Fahrgast, Passagier
passion *185* Leidenschaft
passionate(ly) *108* leidenschaftlich
passport *85* Reisepass
patient *96* geduldig
pattern *74* Muster, Verhalten
to **pay sth off** *81* etw abbezahlen
to **pay attention** *67* aufmerksam sein
pay *44* Bezahlung, Lohn
payee *199* Zahlungsempfänger/in

payment *109* Zahlung; **terms of ~** *140* Zahlungsbedingungen
peace *65T* Frieden
pedestrian *69* Fußgänger/in
pen *19* Stift
pension *85* Rente
pension scheme *51* betriebliche Altersversorgung, Rentenversicherung
pensioner *85* Rentner/in
per capita *86* pro Kopf
percentage *72* Anteil, Prozentsatz
to **perform** *27* ausführen, durchführen; 192 aufführen
performance *75T* Leistung
perfume *139* Parfüm
perishable *159* verderblich
permanent *44* *(Stelle:)* unbefristet
permission *38* Erlaubnis, Genehmigung
personnel *6* Personal
personnel assistant *8* Personalassistent/in
personnel manager *8* Personalchef/in
perspective *94F* Perspektive
pest *105* Schädling
pesticide *98* Schädlingsbekämpfungsmittel
petrol *75* Benzin
pharmaceutical *87* Pharma-
pharmaceuticals *87* Arzneimittel
photo shoot *121* Fotoaufnahmen
photocopier *10* Fotokopierer
photocopy *139* Fotokopie
to **photocopy** *6* fotokopieren
to **photograph** *14* fotografieren
physical *22* körperlich
to **pick** *14* pflücken; *103* sammeln, suchen, lesen; ~ **sth** *95* sich etw aussuchen; ~ **sb up** *109* jdn abholen
to **picture** *58* abbilden; ~ **sb** *75T* sich jdn vorstellen
pie chart *38* Tortendiagramm
pill *51* Pille
pillar *62* Säule
place, to go ~s *11* herumkommen
to **place** *80F* legen; ~ **an order** *146T* einen Auftrag erteilen, eine Bestellung aufgeben
placement, work ~ *6* Praktikum
planning *11* Planung
to **plant** *41* pflanzen, anpflanzen
plant *51* Werk, Betrieb, Anlage; *72* Pflanze
plantation *69* Anpflanzung, Plantage
plate *105* Teller
playable *66* abspielbar
pleased, to be ~ to do sth *55T* etw gern tun
pleasure *49* Vergnügen
to **pocket** *100* einstecken, einstreichen, einsacken
point, What's the ~? *21* Welchen Sinn soll das haben?
to **point out** *109* darauf hinweisen
poisonous *104* giftig
polar ice cap *78* Polkappe
policy *66* Politik, Vorgehensweise, Regelung; *197* Versicherungspolice
polish *26* Politur
polite *54* höflich
politeness *47* Höflichkeit
politics *43* Politik
to **pollute** *68* verschmutzen
pollution *77* Verschmutzung
pommel horse *84* Seitpferd
popularity *72* Beliebtheit
population *39* Bevölkerung
porridge *127* Haferbrei
port *71* Hafen; to **leave ~** *71* auslaufen
port of destination *194* Bestimmungshafen
port of shipment *194* Verladehafen
position *44* Posten, Stellung, Stelle
possession *97* Besitz, Besitztum
post *189* Stelle
postal address *135* Postadresse
post-carriage *195* Nachlauf
postcode *136* Postleitzahl
poster *61* Plakat
potential *12* potentiell, künftig
to **pour in** *37* *(Aufträge etc.)* (in großer Zahl) eingehen
poverty *87* Armut
to **power** *75T* antreiben
power plant *70* Kraftwerk
practical *78* praktisch
practices *101* Verfahren
pre-carriage *195* Vorlauf
to **predict** *74* voraussagen, vorhersagen; *92* vorhersehen, abschätzen
preference *40* Vorliebe
preferential terms *150* Sonderkonditionen, bevorzugte (Zahlungs-) Bedingungen
premises *37* Geschäftsräume
premium *101* Prämie
preparation *12* Vorbereitung; 58 Zubereitung
to **prepare sth** *48* etw erstellen
prepared, to **be ~ to do sth** *42* bereit sein, etw zu tun
present *8* Gegenwart; *75* gegenwärtig, aktuell; **at ~** *9* gegenwärtig
to **present** *38* vorstellen, präsentieren; *200* *(Dokumente)* vorlegen
to **preserve** *72* schützen, bewahren
president *50* Präsident/in
to **press** *46* drücken
pressure *51* Druck
prestigious *81* renommiert, angesehen
pretty *37* ziemlich
previous *22* vorige/r/s, vorherige/r/s
price *31* Preis; **guide ~** *126* Richtpreis; to **set a ~** *58* einen Preis festlegen/festsetzen
pricing *60* Preisgestaltung
primarily *59T* hauptsächlich, vorrangig
primary *77T* Haupt-, primär, hauptsächlich
primary school *186* Grundschule
principle *66* Prinzip, Grundsatz
print *61* Druck
to **print** *26* drucken
printed *7* gedruckt
priority, top ~ *94F* oberste Priorität
private *22* privat, eigene/r/s; **in ~** *21* unter vier Augen
private limited company (Ltd) *(UK)* *41* Gesellschaft mit beschränkter Haftung (GmbH)
process *58* Verfahren, Ablauf, Prozess
processing *105* Verarbeitung
to **produce** *52* produzieren, herstellen, fertigen
product *27* Produkt, Erzeugnis; **by-~** *71* Neben-, Abfallprodukt
product brief *58* Produktbeschreibung
Product Development (PD) *58* Produktentwicklung
product launch *58* Produkteinführung
production facilities *51* Produktionsstätte(n), Werk(e)
productive *60* produktiv
productivity *94F* Produktivität
profession *77T* Beruf
professional *16* professionell
profile *186* Porträt, Profil
to **profit** *83* profitieren
profit *31* Gewinn
profit margin *50* Gewinnspanne
prohibited *101* verboten
project *36* Projekt
to **project** *88* prognostizieren, vorhersagen
projection *80* Prognose
to **promote sth** *58* etw bewerben
promotion prospects *185* Beförderungsaussichten, Aufstiegschancen
prompt *68* Stichwort; *172* umgehend
proper(ly) *16* richtig
property *41* Eigentum
proportion *80* Anteil
to **propose** *61* vorschlagen; ~ **a toast** *47* einen Toast ausbringen

proprietary limited company (Pty Ltd) *(Aus, NZ)* *42* Gesellschaft mit beschränkter Haftung (GmbH)
proprietor *53* Inhaber/in
propulsion *72* Antrieb
prosperity *77* Wohlstand
prostitute *102* Prostituierte/r
to **prove** *21* beweisen
to **provide** *56* zur Verfügung stellen, anbieten; *69* bieten; ~ **for sth** *173* etw vorsehen
provider *50* Anbieter
public(ly) *48* öffentlich; to **go** ~ *56* an die Börse gehen
the public *7* die Öffentlichkeit
public limited company (plc) *(UK)* *41* Aktiengesellschaft (AG)
public sector *91* öffentliche Hand, öffentlicher Dienst
public transport *48* öffentliche Verkehrsmittel
publicly owned *51* börsennotiert
pumpkin *59T* Kürbis
punctual(ly) *46* pünktlich
punctuality *48* Pünktlichkeit
punctuation *135* Interpunktion
to **purchase** *62* kaufen
purchase *7* Kauf
purchasing *6* Einkauf, Beschaffung
purchasing assistant *8* Einkaufsassistent/in
purchasing manager *8* Einkaufsleiter/in
purchasing power *89T* Kaufkraft
pure *50* rein
to **purify** *70* klären
purpose *59* Zweck
to **push** *40T* stoßen, drücken
to **put** *21* *hier:* formulieren, sagen
to **put up with sth** *21* sich etw gefallen lassen
to **put sb out of business** *29* jdn in den Bankrott treiben
to **put sth into action** *76* etw in die Tat umsetzen

Q

qualifications, higher education entrance ~ *187* Fachhochschulreife; **university entrance** ~ *188* Abitur, Hochschulreife
qualified *26* ausgebildet, mit Abschluss
to **qualify** *37* einen/seinen/ihren Abschluss machen; *156* zu etw berechtigt sein
quality *32* Qualität
quantity *100* Menge; **minimum order** ~ *156T* Mindestbestellmenge
quantity discount *152* Mengenrabatt
quarter *51* Quartal
query *6* Anfrage; 54T Frage
question mark *59* Fragezeichen
questionnaire *48* Fragebogen
to **queue** *46* sich anstellen, anstehen
to **quit** *95* kündigen
quotation *92* Zitat; *141* Preisangebot
to **quote sth** *148* nennen, angeben

R

rabbit *41* Kaninchen
race car *75* Rennwagen
racetrack *81* Rennbahn
racing *75T* Rennen, Renn-
racist *77T* rassistisch
rack *98* Kleiderstange; *99* Regal
radio station *55T* Radiosender
rail *71* Bahn
railroad *105* Eisenbahn
railway *77T* Eisenbahn
rainforest *78* Regenwald
rainy *80F* regnerisch
to **raise sth** *47* etw erheben, hochheben
range (of products) *51* Sortiment, Angebot, Palette
to **rank** *77* einstufen
ranking *77* Einstufung, Bewertung
rapid(ly) *69* schnell, rasch
rare(ly) *6* selten
rate *78* Tempo; 127 (Zimmer-)Preis
raw material *69* Rohstoff(e)
to **react to sth** *116* auf etw reagieren
reaction *139* Reaktion
ready for dispatch *165* versandbereit, versandfertig
realistic *59T* realistisch
to **realize sth** *31* etw erkennen, wissen
reason *11* Grund; *48* Motiv, Beweggrund
reasonable *140* vernünftig, angemessen
to **reassure** *106* beruhigen
receipt *45* Quittung, Beleg
receipt of invoice *155* Rechnungseingang, -erhalt
receipt of order *148* Auftragseingang, Auftragserhalt
to **receive** *31* erhalten
reception *44* Rezeption, Empfang
recession *88* Rezession
to **recharge** *192T* aufladen
recipient *110* Empfänger/in
to **recognize** *57* erkennen, wiedererkennen
to **record** *104* aufnehmen
record label *41* Plattenfirma
recorded delivery *135* Einschreiben mit Rückschein
records *6* Daten, Akten, Unterlagen; **employee** ~ *8* Personalakte
to **recover** *56* sich erholen; ~ **sth** *172* etw sicherstellen, beschaffen
recovery *82* Erholung
recruitment *185* Personalbeschaffung
Red Cross *12* Rotes Kreuz
to **reduce** *29* senken, reduzieren
reduction *181* Nachlass, Reduzierung
to **refer to sth** *54* in etw nachschlagen; *80* auf etw verweisen, sich auf etw beziehen
referee *186* Referenzgeber/in
reference *104* Erwähnung, Verweis; *134* Zeichen, Referenz; *149* Bezug
refrigerated *106* gekühlt, Kühl-
refrigerator *130* Kühlschrank
refund *35* (Kosten-)Erstattung
to **refuse** *37* sich weigern, ablehnen
to **regard: as regards** *109* hinsichtlich, bezüglich
regard, with ~ to *173* bezüglich
regardless *79* ungeachtet
regards *110* Grüße
regional *55T* regional
to **register with sth** *36* sich bei etw anmelden
registered (letter) *135* Einschreiben
to **regret** *181* bedauern
regular, on a ~ basis *49* regelmäßig
regular customer *170* Stammkunde/-in
regulations *40T* Vorschriften, Bestimmungen
rejection *161* Ablehnung
to **relate to sth** *95* sich auf etw beziehen
relationship *49F* Beziehung
relative *73* relativ
relaxed *50T* locker
to **release** *68* freisetzen
reliable *44* zuverlässig
to **rely on sth** *77* auf etw angewiesen sein
to **remain** *80* bleiben
remarkably *71* erstaunlich
to **remind sb** *76* jdn (an etw) erinnern
reminder *165* Mahnung
to **remit** *165* überweisen
remittance *172* Überweisung
remote *65T* Fern-

to **remove** *62 (Kleidung:)* ausziehen; ~ **sth** *78* etw entfernen
renewable *68* erneuerbar
repair *26* Reparatur
to **repair** *26* reparieren
to **replace** *7* ersetzen, austauschen
reply *14* Antwort
to **report sb/sth** *96* jdn/etw melden
representative *8* Vertreter/in
reputation *67* Ruf
request *53* Anfrage, Wunsch, Bitte
to **request sth** *142* etw anfordern, erbitten
to **require** *29* erfordern, benötigen; 70 verlangen
requirements *144* Bedarf; *190* Anforderungen
to **research** *26* untersuchen, recherchieren, erforschen; ~ **sth** *17* Nachforschungen über etw anstellen, etw recherchieren
research *26* Nachforschungen, Recherche; to **do** ~ *50* recherchieren, Nachforschungen anstellen
Research and Development (R&D) *58* Forschung(s-) und Entwicklung(sabteilung)
reservation *126* Reservierung
reservations *79* Bedenken
reserved, All rights ~. *53* Alle Rechte vorbehalten.
to **resettle** *74* umsiedeln
resident *69* Bewohner/in, Einwohner/in
resignation *21* Kündigung
resolution, high-~ *160* hochauflösend
to **resolve** *78* lösen, auflösen
resource *76* Ressource, Rohstoff
to **respect** *25* respektieren
responsibility *16* Aufgabenbereich, Zuständigkeit; *41* Verantwortung, Haftung; to **take** ~ *49F* Verantwortung übernehmen/tragen
responsible *58* verantwortlich, zuständig
to **rest** *120T* sich ausruhen
restoration *26* Restaurierung, Aufarbeitung
restriction *197* Beschränkung, Einschränkung
résumé *(AE) 186* Lebenslauf
retail *6* Einzelhandel
retailer *82* Einzelhändler/in
retirement *92* Ruhestand
to **return sth** *33* etw zurückgeben
return, by ~ *181* postwendend
return flight *13* Hin- und Rückflug
to **reveal** *71* enthüllen
revenue *69* Einnahmen; **tax** ~ *102* Steuereinnahmen
to **review** *185* bewerten, prüfen
to **revise** *193* überarbeiten
revision *193* Überarbeitung, Neubearbeitung
to **rewrite** *20* neu schreiben, umformulieren
to **ride sth** *14* auf etw reiten
right, All ~s reserved. *53* Alle Rechte vorbehalten; ~ **to work** *51* Recht auf Arbeit
right away *176* sofort
rigid *71* starr
to **ring** *44* anrufen; *47* klingeln, läuten
ripe *104* reif
rise *89* Aufstieg, Anstieg
to **rise** *74* steigen; *87* aufsteigen, aufstreben; ~ **by** *39* ansteigen um
roaring success *37* ein voller Erfolg
to **rob sb of sth** *102* jdn einer Sache berauben
rocket *75* Rakete
to **role-play** *44* mit verteilten Rollen spielen
roll *156T* Rolle
roll-on roll-off vessel *72* Fähre, RoRo-Schiff
room attendant *40* Raumpfleger/in
root *104* Wurzel
rough handling *181* unsachgemäße Behandlung/Handhabung
roughly *84* ungefähr
round-the-world trip *13* Weltreise
route *17* Weg, Strecke, Route
routine *94* Tagesablauf, Routine
rubbish *77* Müll
rubbish tip *103* Müllkippe
rudimentary *37* bruchstückhaft
to **run sth** *38* etw führen, etw betreiben; ~ **out** *68* versiegen, sich erschöpfen; ~ **out of sth** *14* kein ... mehr haben
rupee *89T* Rupie
rural *88* ländlich, bäuerlich
to **rush sth** *176* etw auf dem schnellsten Weg hinbringen; **Must rush.** *110* Ich muss weg. *(Brief:)* In Eile

S

to **sack sb** *94* jdn entlassen, rausschmeißen
to **sacrifice** *72* opfern
safety, health and ~ *40T* Arbeitsschutz
to **sail out to sea** *45* aufs Meer hinausfahren
salary *19* Gehalt, Lohn
sale *31* Verkauf
sales *8* Verkauf, Vertrieb; *51* Verkaufsumsatz
sales assistant *8* Verkäufer/in
sales director *56* Verkaufsleiter/in
sales representative *24* (Handels-) Vertreter/in
salutation *110 (Brief:)* Anrede
sample *59T* Muster, Probe
satirical *104* satirisch
to **save** *11* sparen; 78 retten
say *78* zum Beispiel
scale *74* Umfang
scared, to be ~ *11* Angst haben
scene, behind the ~s *6* hinter den Kulissen
schedule *58* Terminkalender; *92* Terminplan
to **schedule** *58 (Termin)* ansetzen
school, grammar ~ *188* Gymnasium; **primary** ~ *186* Grundschule; **secondary** ~ *59* weiterführende Schule, Hauptschule; **selective secondary** ~ *187* Realschule; **vocational** ~ *(AE) 188* Berufsschule, Berufskolleg, Gewerbliche Schule
school leaving certificate *188* Schulabgangszeugnis
school-leaver *11* Schulabgänger/in
scientist *78* (Natur-)Wissenschaftler/in
score *49* Ergebnis, Punkte(stand)
to **score** *23 (Tor)* schießen, erzielen
scratch *27* Kratzer
scratched *26* zerkratzt, verkratzt
screen *65T* Bildschirm
sea, to sail out to ~ *45* aufs Meer hinausfahren
sea level *74* Meeresspiegel
to **search** *126* durchsuchen, suchen
search *126* Suche
search engine *50T* Suchmaschine
seasonal *44* Saison-
to **seat (1000)** *82* Platz für (1000) Menschen bieten
seat *26* Sitz; *45* Platz
seat heating *65T* Sitzheizung
seatbelt *80F* Sicherheitsgurt
seaworthy *167* seetüchtig
secondary *77T* sekundär, Folge-
secondary school *59* weiterführende Schule, Hauptschule
second-hand *26* gebraucht
secretarial *108* Sekretariats-, Büro-
secretary *20* Sekretär/in
section *39* Abschnitt; *134* Abteilung
sector, economic ~ *86* Wirtschaftssektor; **public** ~ *91* öffentliche Hand, öffentlicher Dienst

to **secure (sth)** *127* (sich etw) sichern
security number *129* Sicherheitsnummer
security service *60* Wachdienst
seductive(ly) *62* verführerisch
to **seek** *26* suchen
to **seem** *83* scheinen
to **select** *126* auswählen
selective secondary school *187* Realschule
self-adhesive *156T* selbstklebend
self-catering *127* Selbstversorgung, für Selbstversorger
self-confident *11* selbstbewusst, selbstsicher
self-respect *103* Selbstachtung
seller *35* Verkäufer
semi-conductor *97* Halbleiter
senior executive *171* leitende/r Angestellte/r
sense, to **make** ~ *16* sinnvoll/logisch sein
sensible *40F* vernünftig, (Schuhe:) bequem, robust
to **separate** *26* trennen
separate *49* getrennt
serious *43* ernstzunehmend
to **serve** *72* dienen; ~ **sb** *8* jdn bedienen
service *27* Dienstleistung; **coach** ~ *123* Busverbindung; **train** ~ *123* Zugverbindung
to **set sth up** *37* etw einrichten
to **set up a business** *37* ein Unternehmen gründen
to **settle** *172* regeln, erledigen; ~ **down** *39* sich niederlassen
sewing machine *98* Nähmaschine
sex *59* Geschlecht
sexual *22* sexuell
shade *69* Schatten
to **shake hands** *46* sich die Hand geben, die Hände schütteln
a shame *122* schade
Shame on you. *57T* Schäm dich!
shamrock *59* Kleeblatt
shape *55T* Form
shaped *58* geformt, Form-
to **share** *41* teilen
share *41* Aktie; 58 Anteil
shareholder *41* Aktionär/in; *51* Teilhaber/in, Gesellschafter/in
sharp(ly) *80* steil
shift *40* Schicht; **day** ~ *40* Tagschicht; **early** ~ *40* Frühschicht; **late** ~ *40* Spätschicht
to **shine** *26* glänzen
to **ship** *58* versenden
shipment *167* Versand; **port of** ~ *194* Verladehafen
shipping *71* Schiffstransport, Schifffahrt, Schiffs-
shipping container *71* Versandcontainer
shocked *21* schockiert
to **shoot** *62 (Film:)* drehen, Aufnahmen machen
shopping bag *124* Einkaufstasche
shopping mall *62* Einkaufszentrum, -passage
short notice, at ~ *54T* kurzfristig
shortage *74* Mangel, Knappheit
short-haul flight *80F* Kurzstreckenflug
shot *62 (Film:)* Einstellung, Aufnahme
show *26* Ausstellung
shower *127* Dusche
to **shrink** *39* schrumpfen
shy *11* schüchtern
sick, to **be** ~ *65T* sich übergeben (müssen); **the** ~ *74* die Kranken
side, to **take sb's** ~ *21* für jdn Partei ergreifen
to **sign off** *111 (Brief:)* beenden, unterschreiben
to **sign sb up** *41* jdn unter Vertrag nehmen
signatory *136* Unterzeichnete/r
signature *134* Unterschrift
significant *74* bedeutend, erheblich
to **signify** *72* bedeuten, bezeichnen
similar *7* ähnlich
similarity *70* Ähnlichkeit
single room *127* Einzelzimmer
ski slope *81* Skipiste
skiing *78* Skilaufen
skiing instructor *13* Skilehrer/in
skill *11* Fähigkeit, Fertigkeit; **high-**~ *87* hochqualifiziert
ski-resort area *78* Skigebiet
skirt *44* Rock
sky *55T* Himmel; **The ~'s the limit.** *55T* Nach oben sind keine Grenzen gesetzt.
slack *16* flau, untätig
slave *94F* Sklave
slavery *102* Sklaverei
sleep *16* Schlaf
sleeve *179* Ärmel
sleeveless *180* ärmellos
slight(ly) *80* leicht
small business *26* Kleinbetrieb; Kleinunternehmen
smart *44 (Kleidung:)* elegant, schick
snow *78* Schnee
soap *26* Seife
sociable *44* gesellig
social *51* gesellschaftlich; to **meet ~ly** *48* sich privat treffen
social event *48* geselliges Treffen
social package *56* Sozialleistungen
society *41* Gesellschaft
solar collector *69* Sonnenkollektor
solar panel *71* Solarmodul
solar power *43* Solarenergie, Solarstrom
solar-powered *70* solarbetrieben
sold out *83* ausverkauft
sole trader *41* Einzelunternehmer/in
solidarity tax *84F* Solidaritätszuschlag
solution *31* Lösung
to **solve** *54T* lösen
to **sort sth** *68* etw einsortieren, einordnen
source *53* Quelle
to **source sth** *146T* etw beziehen
spa *127* Wellnessbereich
to **spare** *55T* erübrigen
speaker *115T* Redner/in
special marking *134* Vermerk, Kennzeichnung
speciality *87* Spezialität, Spezialgebiet
specific *55T* speziell, spezifisch
speech *109* Rede, Vortrag
speech bubble *36* Sprechblase
speed *75* Geschwindigkeit
spending money *11* Taschengeld
to **spew** *106* spucken, speien
spider *104* Spinne
spirituality *87* Spiritualität
to **spoil** *131T* verderben
sporting event *81* Sportereignis, -veranstaltung
to **spray** *98* sprühen
spray painter *26* Lackierer/in
spreadsheet *31* Tabellenkalkulationsdatei
squalid *99* ärmlich, menschenunwürdig
square *59T* quadratisch
to **stack** *104* stapeln
stadium *81* Stadion
staff *7* Personal, Belegschaft
stage *70* Abschnitt, Etappe, Stadium, Schritt
to **stand in for sb** *37* jdn vertreten, jds Platz einnehmen
to **stand out from the crowd** *11* aus der Menge herausstechen
standard *101* Norm
standpoint *58* Standpunkt
star *59* Stern
to **start** *24* (Auto:) anspringen
start-up, business ~ *26* Unternehmensgründung
state *84* Staat, Land; **member** ~ *39* Mitgliedsstaat
statement *22* Aussage
state-of-the-art *70* auf dem neuesten Stand der Technik
statue *121F* Statue

steadily *56* stetig, kontinuierlich
to **steal** *20* stehlen
steamship *105* Dampfschiff
steel *50* Stahl
stem *59T* Stengel, Stiel
step *48* Schritt; to **take ~s** *172* Schritte einleiten
to **step** *78* betreten
stereo system *57* Stereoanlage
to **stick** *156T* kleben; **~ together** *21* zusammenhalten
sticker *59* Aufkleber
still room *40F* Teeküche
to **stipulate** *199* festlegen
stock *6* Ware(n); *31* (Waren-) Bestand; **in ~** *33* vorrätig, auf Lager; **out of ~** *53* nicht vorrätig, nicht lieferbar; **while ~s last** *150* solange der Vorrat reicht
stock exchange *41* Börse
stock market *193* Börse
to **store** *26* lagern; *71* speichern
store *6* Geschäft, Laden
straight *48* sofort, gleich
strategist *62* Stratege/-in
to **strategize** *62* (die strategisch besten Lösungen) finden
strategy *58* Strategie
strawberry *106* Erdbeere
strength *44* Stärke
strict *47* streng
to **strike up a conversation** *77T* eine Unterhaltung beginnen
structure *31* Struktur
to **structure** *54* strukturieren
student *6* Schüler/in, Berufsschüler/in
study *82* Untersuchung, Studie; 123 Arbeitszimmer
stuff *102* Sachen
to **stuff one's pockets** *100* sich die Taschen vollstopfen, sich eine goldene Nase verdienen
stupid *16* albern, dumm
sturdy *155* stabil, fest
style *17* Stil
subject line *134* Betreffzeile
to **submit** *149 (Angebot)* unterbreiten
subsidiary *50* Tochtergesellschaft
subsistence farming *103* Subsitenzwirtschaft
substance *85* Substanz
substandard *87* minderwertig
substantial *144* beträchtlich, erheblich
substitute *29* Ersatz(-)
subtotal *155* Zwischensumme
to **succeed** *17* Erfolg haben
success *26* Erfolg; **a roaring ~** *37* ein voller Erfolg
to **suffer** *94F* leiden; **~ from sth** *56* an etw leiden; **~ sth** *88* etw erleiden
to **suggest** *17* vorschlagen; *74* hinweisen auf, hindeuten auf
suggestion *54T* Vorschlag
suit *91* Anzug, Hosenanzug, Kostüm, *hier:* Anzugträger
suitable *17* geeignet, passend
suite, en ~ *127* mit eigenem Bad
suited to/for sth *190* für etw geeignet
sum *38* Summe, Betrag
to **summarize** *59* zusammenfassen
summary *32* Zusammenfassung
sun roof *65T* Schiebedach
sunglasses *118* Sonnenbrille
sunlight *69* Sonnenlight
supervisor *21* Vorgesetzte/r
supervisory *44* Aufsichts-, leitend, vorgesetzt
to **supplement** *69* ergänzen
supplier *31* Lieferant, Zulieferer
supplies *26* Verbrauchsgüter; *78* Vorrat, Vorräte
to **supply** *53* liefern, anbieten; **~ sb** *55T* jdn beliefern
supply *53 (Strom, Wasser etc.:)* Anschluss, Versorgung
supply chain *99* Lieferkette
supply of money *103* Geldmenge
support *19* Unterstützung, Kundendienst
to **support** *74* untermauern; *94F* unterstützen
supposed, to be ~ to do sth *75* etw tun sollen
to **suppress** *78* verdrängen, unterdrücken
surcharge *127* Aufpreis
sure, to make ~ *16* sicherstellen, sich vergewissern
surname *20* Nachnahme
surprising *6* erstaunlich
to **surround** *99* umgeben
surrounding area *55T* Umgebung
survey *57* Umfrage
to **survey sb** *57* jdn befragen
to **survive** *88* überleben
sustainable *69* nachhaltig
to **swap** *192* tauschen
sweat *102* Schweiß
sweatshop *102 Betrieb mit ausbeuterischen Arbeitsbedingungen*
synchronized swimming *84* Synchronschwimmen

T

to **tackle sth** *71* etw angehen, etw in Angriff nehmen
to **tailor** *186* individuell anpassen
to **take sth down** *22* etw aufnehmen
to **take sth in** *16* etw aufnehmen
to **take off** *37* abheben, losgehen
to **take sb on** *67* jdn annehmen, übernehmen
to **take part in sth** *19* an etw teilnehmen
to **take place** *95* stattfinden
talk *19* Vortrag, Rede
talks *56* Gespräche, Verhandlungen
tan *78* Sonnenbräune
tape *156T* Band, Klebeband
tarantula *104* Tarantel
target audience *62* Zielpublikum, -gruppe
target group *58* Zielgruppe
taste *57* Geschmack
tax *84F* Steuer, Abgabe; **value added ~ (VAT)** *155* Mehrwertsteuer, Umsatzsteuer
tax revenue *102* Steuereinnahmen
taxpayer *81* Steuerzahler/in
to **teach oneself sth** *25* sich etw beibringen
technical *75* technisch
technically speaking *41* genau genommen, fachsprachlich
technician *24* Techniker/in
technology *22* Technik, Technologie
teenage *37* im Teenageralter
temporary *82* vorübergehend, befristet
tempting *94* verlockend
tennis court *81* Tennisplatz
term *193* Begriff; **in ~s of** *72* was ... angeht; **in the long ~** *84F* langfristig, auf lange Sicht
terms *109* Bedingungen, Konditionen; **preferential ~** *150* Sonderkonditionen, bevorzugte (Zahlungs-) Bedingungen
terms and conditions *146T* Konditionen, (Allgemeine) Geschäftsbedingungen
terms of delivery *140* Lieferbedingungen
terms of payment *140* Zahlungsbedingungen
text message *110* SMS
textile *99* Textil-
textiles *87* Textilien
theatre *44* Theater
thesis *101* These
thief, thieves *20* Dieb, Diebe
thorough(ly) *26* gründlich
though *21* allerdings, aber, jedoch
to **threaten** *177* drohen
throughout *69* überall, in ganz
to **throw** *99* werfen
ticket *11* Fahrkarte, (Flug-)Ticket
tidy *95* aufgeräumt, ordentlich
time, at all ~s *76* ständig; **in ~** *37* rechtzeitig; **on ~** *17* pünktlich; to **give sb a hard ~** *21* jdm das Leben schwer machen; to **have a hard ~** *64* es schwer haben, schwerfallen;

to **take ~ off** *11* sich frei nehmen; **~ flew** *37* die Zeit verging wie im Flug
time-consuming *51* zeitraubend
timetable *47* Fahrplan
tiny *69* winzig
tip *45* Trinkgeld
tired *6* müde
tiring *56* anstrengend
title, document of ~ *196* Traditionspapier
toast, to **propose a ~** *47* einen Toast ausbringen
toilet *19* Toilette
ton *71* Tonne
tone, to **set the ~** *70* den Ton/Takt vorgeben
tool *27* Werkzeug
toothpaste *57T* Zahncreme
top, at the ~ table *47* am Kopfende des Tisches
top priority *94F* oberste Priorität
top-down system *49F* hierarchisches System
topic *47* Thema
torn *26* zerschlissen
total *154* Gesamtbetrag, Summe
total *27* Gesamt-
total price *154* Gesamtpreis
to **touch** *65T* berühren, anfassen
touch, to **get in ~ with sb** *120T* sich mit jdm in Verbindung setzen
touch control module *97* Touchscreen-Steuermodul
tour *19* Rundgang
tourism *77* Tourismus
tournament *80* Turnier
toxic *105* giftig
trade *71* Handel, Handelsverkehr
trade discount *152* Handelsrabatt
trademark *101* Markenzeichen
trader *101* Händler/in; **sole ~** *41* Einzelunternehmer/in
to **train sb** *20* jdn schulen, jdn ausbilden
train service *123* Zugverbindung
trainers *32* Turnschuhe
training *11* Ausbildung; **extra ~** *21* Fortbildung
to **transfer** *160* überweisen
transfer, bank ~ *150* Überweisung
to **transform** *99* verwandeln
transit *69* Beförderung, Transport; **in ~** *176* beim Transport
translation *10* Übersetzung
to **transport** *71* befördern, transportieren
transport, mode of ~ *193* Transportart; **multimodal ~** *159* kombinierte Beförderung, multimodaler Transport; **public ~** *48* öffentliche Verkehrsmittel
transportation *75* Beförderung, Transport(wesen)
travel arrangements *122* Reisevorbereitungen
travel time *17* Fahrzeit
to **treat** *7* behandeln
treatment *21* Behandlung
trekking *43* Wandern
trial order *147* Probebestellung, Probeauftrag
trial run *16* Probelauf
trillion *71* Billion
to **triple** *80* sich verdreifachen
trolley *106* Einkaufswagen
tropical *105* tropisch
trouble, to **get into ~** *29* in Schwierigkeiten geraten, sich Ärger einhandeln
trousers *40F* Hose
to **trust** *158* vertrauen, hoffen
trusted *171* zuverlässig
truth *102* Wahrheit
try, to **give sth a ~** *37* etw ausprobieren
tube *30* Tube; **the T~** *123 die Londoner U-Bahn*
tune *78* Song, Lied
turbine *69* Turbine
turbulence *80F* Turbulenzen
to **turn sth into sth** *67* etw zu etw machen
to **turn sth over to sb/sth** *96* etw an jdn/etw übergeben
to **turn to** *40* (Seite) aufschlagen
to **turn to sb** *66* sich an jdn wenden
to **turn out** *82* sich herausstellen
to **turn out great** *59T* sehr gut gelingen
to **turn sth down** *67* etw ablehnen
turnover *26* Umsatz *(UK)*
turns, to **take ~** *54* sich abwechseln; to **take it in ~** *44* sich abwechseln
TV station *120T* Fernsehsender
twinkle *62* Zwinkern
to **type in** *126* eingeben
typical *61* typisch

U

unable *79* nicht in der Lage, unfähig
unavailable, to **be ~** *114 (Telefon:)* nicht zu sprechen sein
uncountable *30* unzählbar
underage *106* minderjährig
to **underestimate** *81* unterschätzen
underground *123* U-Bahn
underlined *18* unterstrichen
to **undertake** *84* unternehmen, in Angriff nehmen
underwater *37* unter Wasser, Unterwasser-
underwear *62* Unterwäsche
unemployment *37* Arbeitslosigkeit
unexpected(ly) *80* unerwartet
unfair *94F* unfair
unfriendliness *47* Unfreundlichkeit
uniform *59T* einheitlich, Einheits-; *185* Uniform
union *101* Gewerkschaft
Unique Selling Point/Proposition (USP) *58* Alleinstellungsmerkmal
uniqueness *73* Einzigartigkeit
unit *149* Einheit, Stück
unit price *154* Stückpreis
university entrance qualifications *188* Abitur, Hochschulreife
unknown *41* unbekannt
unlike *51* anders als, im Gegensatz zu
unlimited *41* unbegrenzt, unbeschränkt
to **unload** *99* entladen
unloading *193* Entladung
unofficial *115T* inoffiziell
unoriginal *62* herkömmlich, unoriginell
to **unpack** *176* auspacken
unpaid *171* nicht bezahlt
unplugged *126* ohne Strom, *(Musik:)* akustisch
unreliable *171* unzuverlässig
unthinkable *89T* undenkbar
unwanted *22* unerwünscht
unwilling to do sth *67* nicht bereit, etw zu tun
unwise *94F* unklug
unwittingly *51* ohne es zu ahnen
up, to **be ~ to sth** *181* einer Sache entsprechen; **It's ~ to you.** *21* Die Entscheidung liegt bei dir; to **be ~ and about** *120T* auf den Beinen sein
to **update** *6* auf den neusten Stand bringen, aktualisieren
upper-case *116* großgeschrieben
upright *59T* aufrecht
urban *69* städtisch, Stadt-
urgent *54* dringend, eilig
usage *135* Gebrauch, Gepflogenheit

V

vacancy *189* freie/offene Stelle
vacation *94* Urlaub
vacuum cleaner *28* Staubsauger
valid *85* gültig
valuable *76* wertvoll
value *27* Wert; **good ~ for money** *57* preiswert
value added tax (VAT) *155* Mehrwertsteuer, Umsatzsteuer

valve *53* Ventil
van *26* Transporter, Kleinbus; *55T* Lieferwagen
vapour *71* Dampf
variety *71* Vielzahl, Vielfalt
various *63* unterschiedlich
to **vary** *40T* variieren, unterschiedlich sein
vast majority *73* (bei weitem) größter Teil, Löwenanteil
vegetarian *109* Vegetarier
vehicle *26* Fahrzeug
venture *37* Vorhaben, Unternehmen, Wagnis, Gründung
venue *83* Veranstaltungsort, -stätte
versatility *73* Vielseitigkeit
vessel *71* Schiff; **roll-on roll-off ~** *72* Fähre, RoRo-Schiff
victim *21* Opfer
view *7* Ansicht
viewpoint *79* Standpunkt, Blickwinkel
vintage car *27* Oldtimer
vintage clothes *31* edle/klassische Second-Hand-Kleidung
virgin *41* Jungfrau
virus *72* Virus
visa, entry ~ *85* Einreisevisum
to **visualize** *93* bildlich darstellen, visualisieren
vocabulary *80F* Wortschatz
vocational school *(AE) 188* Berufsschule, Berufskolleg, Gewerbliche Schule
vocational training college *(BE) 36* Berufsschule, Berufskolleg, Gewerbliche Schule
voicemail *114* Anrufbeantworter
volume *76* Volumen, Menge
voluntary *12* freiwillig
volunteer *40* Freiwillige/r, ehrenamtlich Tätige/r
vote *101* Stimme

W

wage *39* Lohn, Gehalt; **hourly ~** *91* Stundenlohn; wage, **minimum ~** *99* Mindestlohn; **low-~ country** *51* Niedriglohnland
Wait a minute. *6* Moment mal!
waiting *44* Kellnern
wallpaper *60* Tapete
wardrobe *181* Kleiderschrank
warehouse *170* Lager
warming, global ~ *74* Erderwärmung
washing machine *51* Waschmaschine
to **waste** *76* verschwenden, vergeuden
waste *69* Müll, Abfall
wastewater *70* Abwasser
water buffalo *89T* Wasserbüffel
water polo *84* Wasserbal
water sports *14* Wassersportarten
waterway *193* Wasserstraße
wave energy *71* Wellenenergie
wax *26* Wachs
way, to **find your ~ around** *17* sich zurechtfinden; to **make ~ for sth** *82* füw etw Platz machen
weak *37* schwach, schlecht
weakness *44* Schwäche
wealthy *12* wohlhabend, reich
weapon *71* Waffe
wear *140* Bekleidung
wedding *27* Hochzeit
weed *105* Unkraut
to **weigh** *105* wiegen
welfare *84F* Wohl
Well done! *16* Gut gemacht!
well-being *74* Wohlbefinden
well-established *143* gut eingeführt, etabliert
whale *78* Wal
wheel *75T* Rad
wheelchair *84* Rollstuhl
whenever *47* immer, wenn; jedesmal, wenn
whereas *105* während
wherever *47* überall, wo
whichever *66* wer/was (auch immer), egal welche/r/s
while stocks last *150* solange der Vorrat reicht
whilst *78* während
whirlwind *62* Wirbelwind, Trubel
wholesaler *140* Großhändler
whopping *82* gewaltig, saftig
wide *31* groß, weit
to **widen** *126* verbreitern, erweitern
wife *89T* (Ehe-)Frau
wildlife *84F* Tiere (in freier Wildbahn)
willing *31* bereit, willens
win *75T* Sieg
windy *80F* windig
winner *89* Gewinner/in
wish *31* Wunsch
with order *156T* bei Auftragserteilung
without delay *171* unverzüglich
to **wonder** *31* sich fragen
wool *50* Wolle
work, right to ~ *51* Recht auf Arbeit
work experience *6* Praktikum
work of art *61* Kunstwerk
work placement *6* Praktikum
work routine *18* Arbeitsablauf
worker *16* Arbeiter/in
working conditions *101* Arbeitsbedingungen
working hours *40F* Arbeitszeiten
workplace *16* Arbeitsplatz
world cup *81* Weltpokal
world marketplace *88* Weltmarkt
world's cargo *71* weltweites Frachtaufkommen, Welthandel
worth *31* Wert
wrap *59* Folie
to **wrap** *105* einwickeln
to **write sth out** *45* etw ausstellen
to **write copy** *61* texten, Werbetexte verfassen
writing, in ~ *148* schriftlich, in Schriftform
written correspondence *95* Schriftverkehr
wrong, to **go ~** *31* einen Fehler machen

Y

yet, not ~ *6* noch nicht
youth *11* Jugend
youth centre *36* Jugendzentrum
youth hostel *11* Jugendherberge

Irregular verbs

be	was/were	been	*sein*
beat	beat	beaten	*schlagen, besiegen*
become	became	become	*werden*
begin	began	begun	*anfangen, beginnen*
bend	bent	bent	*(sich) beugen*
blow	blew	blown	*wehen, blasen, ziehen*
break	broke	broken	*brechen*
breed	bred	bred	*sich vermehren, sich ausbreiten*
bring	brought	brought	*(mit)bringen*
build	built	built	*bauen*
burn	burnt/burned	burnt/burned	*(ver)brennen*
buy	bought	bought	*kaufen*
catch	caught	caught	*fangen, fassen, erreichen*
choose	chose	chosen	*(aus)wählen*
come	came	come	*kommen*
cost	cost	cost	*kosten*
cross-breed	cross-bred	cross-bred	*kreuzen*
cut	cut	cut	*schneiden*
deal	dealt	dealt	*versetzen, verteilen*
dig	dug	dug	*graben*
do	did	done	*tun, machen*
draw	drew	drawn	*zeichnen*
dream	dreamt/dreamed	dreamt/dreamed	*träumen*
drink	drank	drunk	*trinken*
drive	drove	driven	*fahren*
eat	ate	eaten	*essen*
fall	fell	fallen	*fallen*
feed	fed	fed	*füttern, ernähren*
feel	felt	felt	*(sich) fühlen, empfinden*
fight	fought	fought	*kämpfen*
find	found	found	*finden*
fit	fit/fitted	fit/fitted	*passen, entsprechen, anbringen*
fly	flew	flown	*fliegen*
forbid	forbade	forbidden	*verbieten*
forget	forgot	forgotten	*vergessen*
get	got	got (*AE* gotten)	*bekommen*
give	gave	given	*geben*
go	went	gone	*gehen, fahren*
grow	grew	grown	*wachsen*
hang	hung	hung	*hängen*
have	had	had	*haben*
hear	heard	heard	*hören*
hide	hid	hidden	*(sich) verstecken*
hit	hit	hit	*schlagen*
hold	held	held	*halten, festhalten*
hurt	hurt	hurt	*verletzen*
keep	kept	kept	*behalten*
know	knew	known	*kennen, wissen*
lay	laid	laid	*legen*
lead	led	led	*führen*
lean	leant/leaned	leant/leaned	*sich lehnen, sich beugen*
learn	learnt/learned	learnt/learned	*lernen*
leave	left	left	*abfahren, verlassen, weggehen*
let	let	let	*lassen*
lie	lay	lain	*liegen*
light	lit	lit	*anzünden, beleuchten*
lose	lost	lost	*verlieren*
make	made	made	*machen*
mean	meant	meant	*meinen, bedeuten*
meet	met	met	*treffen*
overcome	overcame	overcome	*überwinden, überwältigen*
override	overrode	overridden	*sich hinwegsetzen über*
panic	panicked	panicked	*in Panik geraten*
pay	paid	paid	*bezahlen*
put	put	put	*setzen, stellen, legen*
quit	quit/quitted	quit/quitted	*verlassen, aufhören*
read	read	read	*lesen*
repay	repaid	repaid	*zurückzahlen*
rewrite	rewrote	rewritten	*umschreiben*
ride	rode	ridden	*reiten, fahren*
ring	rang	rung	*anrufen, läuten*
rise	rose	risen	*(an)steigen*
run	ran	run	*laufen, rennen*
say	said	said	*sagen*
see	saw	seen	*sehen*
seek	sought	sought	*suchen*
sell	sold	sold	*verkaufen*
send	sent	sent	*senden, schicken*
set	set	set	*setzen, stellen*
shake	shook	shaken	*schütteln*
shine	shone	shone	*scheinen, glänzen*
show	showed	shown	*zeigen*
shrink	shrank	shrunk	*schrumpfen, zurückgehen*
shut	shut	shut	*schließen*
sing	sang	sung	*singen*
sink	sank	sunk	*sinken*
sit	sat	sat	*sitzen*
sleep	slept	slept	*schlafen*
slide	slid	slid	*(ab)rutschen, (ab) sacken*
smell	smelt/smelled	smelt/smelled	*riechen*
speak	spoke	spoken	*sprechen*

spell	spelt/ spelled	spelt/ spelled	*buchstabieren*
spend	spent	spent	*ausgeben, verbringen*
spread	spread	spread	*(sich) verbreiten*
stand	stood	stood	*stehen*
steal	stole	stolen	*stehlen*
swim	swam	swum	*schwimmen*
take	took	taken	*nehmen*
teach	taught	taught	*unterrichten, beibringen*
tell	told	told	*sagen, erzählen*
think	thought	thought	*denken*
throw	threw	thrown	*werfen*
under-stand	under-stood	under-stood	*verstehen*
wake	woke	woken	*aufwachen, aufwecken*
wear	wore	worn	*tragen*
win	won	won	*gewinnen*
write	wrote	written	*schreiben*

Quellenverzeichnis

Cover: Alamy RM/Ben Cooper

S. 6/1/istockphoto/avdeev007, S. 6/2/Alamy/G. Robinson, S. 11/Oxana Rödel (2), S. 12/1/Alamy/Dan Vincent, S. 12/2/Alamy/travelis environment, S. 12/3/Alamy/P. Cole, S. 13/ODI, S. 14/istock/Holger Mette, S. 19/ODI, S. 20/ODI, S. 21/Fotofinder/vario images, S. 23/1-6/ODI, S. 26/Alamy/allOver photography, S. 29/1/Alamy/Image Source, S. 29/2/shutterstock/Ibynek Jirousek, S. 31/Hintergrund/shutterstock/mysontuna, S. 31/1/Getty/Sharon Dominick, S. 31/2/istock/Maartje van Caspel, S. 32/ODI, S. 34/shutterstock, S. 35/1/Fotofinder/vario images, S. 35/2/ODI, S. 36/1/istock, S. 36/2/shutterstock/Goodluz, S. 36/3/shutterstock/SFC, S. 37/Alamy/i love images/active, S. 40/shutterstock/EDHAR, S. 41/1/shutterstock/J van der Wolf, S. 41/2/Alamy/Chuck Franklin, S. 41/3/Alamy/Kurt Brady, S. 41/4/Corbis/Gregor Schuster, S. 41/5/Picture-Alliance/EPA/Justin Lane, S. 41/6/Alamy/Carlo Bollo, S. 42/1/shutterstock/auremar, S. 42/2/shutterstock/wavebreakmedia ltd, S. 42/3/CorbisRF/moodboard (WV), S. 43/1/shutterstock/Istvan Csak, S. 43/2/shutterstock/iofoto, S. 43/3/Istockphoto/Juanmonino, S. 46/1/Alamy/format4, S. 46/2/Alamy/Dinodia Photos/RF Photos of India, S. 46/3/Istock/btrenkel, S. 46/4/Istock/DouglasFrees, S. 46/5/Alamy/Payless Images, Inc., S. 46/6/Alamy/Fredrikke Wetherilt, S. 46/7/shutterstock/Josh Resnick, S. 46/8/Istock, S. 47/1/Alamy/R_R, S. 47/2/Alamy/View Stock China, S. 49/Shutterstock/EDHAR, S. 50/Alamy/SiliconValleyStock, S. 51/1/Fotofinder/TV-yesterday, S. 51/2/Fotofinder/transit/Thomas Haertrich, S. 53/shutterstock/Kurhan, S. 55/1/Alamy/H. Mark Weidman Photography, S. 55/2/ shutterstock/Dmitry Kalinovsky, S. 55/3/shutterstock/Monkey Business Images, S. 55/4/Alamy/Radius Images, S. 55/5/shutterstock/dean bertoncelj, S. 55/6/Alamy/Jeff Greenberg, S. 57/1/Alamy/Yuri Arcurs, S. 57/2/Alamy/Form Advertising/Shoosh, S. 57/3/Alamy/Montgomery Martin, S. 58/1/Alamy/Huntstock, S. 58/2/Alamy/image100 BusinessH, S. 58/3/shutterstock/paulaphoto, S. 58/4/shutterstock/Kary1974, S. 59/shutterstock/Dmitriy Shironosov, S. 59/ODI, S. 60/shutterstock/Sideways Design, S. 61/1/Alamy/Chris Batson, 61/2/Alamy/Wavebreak Media ltd, S. 63/Shutterstock/scusi0-9, S. 64/Alamy/Wavebreak Media ltd (WV S. 61), S. 65/1/Fotofinder/Joker, S. 65/2/shutterstock/aopsan, S. 65/3/Fotofinder/Caro/Westermann, S. 66/shutterstock/Lorelyn Medina, S. 66/2/Alamy/Purestock/SuperStock, S. 68/1/shutterstock/visdia, S. 68/2/shutterstock/afotoshop, S. 68/3/PictureAlliance/M. Rahmanian, S. 68/4/PictureAlliance/Horst Ossinger, S. 68/5/PictureAlliance/J. Hayward, S. 68/6/PictureAlliance/Wildlife/D.Harms, S. 69/1/PictureAlliance/Balkis Press, S. 69/2/Picture-Alliance/Balkis Press, S. 72/PictureAlliance/moodboard/James Lauritz, S. 76/ODI, S. 77/1/Alamy/M. Willis, S. 77/2/Alamy/Russ Nolan, S. 77/3/Alamy/Alvey & Towers Picture Library, S. 77/4/Shutterstock/Zanna Karelina, S. 77/5/Alamy/FLPA/Peter Reynolds, S. 77/7/Alamy/vario images/Ulrich Baumgarten, S. 77/8/Alamy/joeysworld.com, S. 77/9/Alamy/incamerastock/ICP, S. 78/shutterstock/JetKat, S. 80/ Fotofinder/J. Eckel, S. 81/Alamy/Ria Novosti, S. 82/Alamy/Lou Linwei, S. 83/Shutterstock/M. Godbehear, S. 84/1/shutterstock/Zorana Djokic, S. 84/2/shutterstock/Pete Saloutos, S. 84/3/PictureAlliance/Camera4, S. 84/4/shutterstock/ Schmid Christophe, S. 84/5/shutterstock/tankist276, S. 84/6/Picture-Alliance/dpa/Revierfoto, S. 87/1/shutterstock/AjayBhaskar, S. 87/2/Corbis/David H. Wells, S. 88/1/Alamy/Marco Cristofori, S. 88/2/Alamy/Fredrik Renander, S. 89/1/shutterstock/SnowWhiteimages, S. 89/2/Alamy/David Gee, S. 90/1/AKG images, S. 90/2/shutterstock/Worldpics, S. 90/3/shutterstock/michaeljung, S. 90/4/shutterstock/Amy Dunn, S. 91/1/shutterstock/Angela Waye, S. 91/2/shutterstock/Sergei Butorin, S. 92/shutterstock/Monkey Business Images, S. 94/Alamy/LutzPape, S. 95/ODI, S. 97/mitte/shutterstock/H.Buchholz, S. 97/1-7/shutterstock, S. 98/1/Fotofinder/Caro/Kaiser, S. 98/2/Shutterstock/Lisovskaya Natalia, S. 98/3/Shutterstock/A. Chernookaya, S. 98/4/Shutterstock/Ksenia Palimski, S. 98/5/Shutterstock/art&design, S. 98/8/Shutterstock/Karkas, S. 100/Fotofinder/Visum/Panos Pictures, S. 103/Fotofinder/David McIntyre /Black Star/imagetrust, S. 104/1/AKG images, S. 104/2/Corbis/Hulton-Deutsch Collection, S. 105/1/Corbis/Gary Braasch, S. 105/2/Corbis/John Coletti, S. 106/ODI, 112/1/Fotofinder/T.Krueger, S. 112/2/shutterstock/HLPhoto, S. 113/shutterstock/P. Kosminder, S. 115/shutterstock/Claire VD, S. 120/PictureAlliance/Martin Gerten, S. 121/1/shutterstock/M. Wismiewska, S. 121/2/stutterstock/S_L, S. 122/1/Fotofinder/Buck/mediacolors, S. 122/2/Fotofinder/BildagenturHuber, S. 123/1/shutterstock/OlgaElnur,123/2/shutterstock/P.Matthew, S. 124/Fotofinder/Weisflog, S. 125/shutterstock, S. 126/shutterstock, S. 137/ODI, S. 138/Shutterstock/Nuzza, S. 139/1/shutterstock/viktor1, S. 139/2/ shutterstock/Olinchuk, S. 139/3/shutterstock/inhabitant, S. 140/shutterstock, S. 141/1/ shutterstock/Sam Dcruz, S. 141/2/PictureAlliance/Achim Scheidemann,

S. 145/1/shutterstock/photo25th, S. 145/2/shutterstock/raresirimiee, S. 153/1/shutterstock/Diana Rich, S. 153/shutterstock/Lauren Jane, S. 155/shutterstock/Claudio Zaccherini, S. 158/CV-Archiv, S. 159/1/shutterstock/ultimathule, S. 159/2/shutterstock/R. Asento, S. 159/3/shutterstock/s_oleg, S. 159/4/shutterstock/egd, S. 159/5/PictureAlliance/Tschanz-Hofmann, S. 160/istockphoto/gerenme, S. 163/shutterstock/gordana Sermek, S. 164/ODI, S. 168/shutterstock, S. 169/shutterstock/Irina Rogova, S. 170/shutterstock/D.Shironosov, S. 175/ODI, S. 178/shutterstock/Luxe, S. 182/1/shutterstock/trekandshoot, S. 182/2/shutterstock/Anna Lurge, S. 183/shutterstock/Neftali, S. 186/1/shutterstock, S. 186/2–4/Best Western Monkbar Hotel, York, S. 192/1/Corbis/Ocean, S. 191/2/Alamy/Kathy deWitt, S. 200/shutterstock, S. 212/shutterstock/Edyta Pawlowska.

Mit freundlicher Unterstützung folgender Unternehmen:
S. 57/1/Nike Deutschland, S. 57/2/Adidas, S. 57/3/Diesel Deutschland GmbH, S. 57/4/Fossil GmbH, S. 57/5/Elmex GABA GmbH, S. 57/6/Nivea Beiersdorf AG, S. 71/SkySails GmbH, S. 72/Reederei Wallenius-Wilhelmsen, S. 75/Porsche AG (2), S. 101/1/Soil Association Certification, Bristol, S. 101/2/Fairtrade Deutschland, S. 101/3/Red Tractor Assurance, London, S. 101/4 Europäische Kommission, Brüssel, S. 101/5/Rainforest Alliance, NY, S. 154/Soyang Europe GmbH

Texte:
S. 104/VG Musik, S. 99/Huffington Post, S. 101/Fairtrade

Nicht alle Copyright-Inhaber konnten ermittelt werden; deren Urheberrechte werden hiermit vorsorglich und ausdrücklich anerkannt.

CANADA & UNITED STATES OF AMERICA

Abbreviations CANADA:

NB = New Brunswick
P.E.I. = Prince Edward Island

Abbreviations UNITED STATES:

CT = Connecticut
DE = Delaware
NH = New Hampshire
NJ = New Jersey
MA = Massachusetts
MD = Maryland
PA = Pennsylvania
RI = Rhode Island
VT = Vermont